Entrepreneurial Marketing

REAL STORIES AND SURVIVAL STRATEGIES

Bruce Buskirk
Pepperdine University

Molly Lavik
Founder, Mentorography™

Australia · Canada · Mexico · Singapore · Spain · United Kingdom · United States

Entrepreneurial Marketing: Real Stories and Survival Strategies
Bruce Buskirk and Molly Lavik

VP/Editorial Director:
Jack Calhoun

VP/Editor-in-Chief:
Michael Roche

Acquisitions Editor:
Steve Hazelwood

Developmental Editor:
Taney Wilkins

Marketing Manager:
Nicole Moore

Production Editor:
Robert Dreas

Manufacturing Coordinator:
Diane Lohman

Compositor:
Argosy Publishing

Printer:
Globus Printing
Minster, Ohio

Design Project Manager:
Stacy Jenkins Shirley

Cover and Internal Designer:
Grannan Graphic Design

Cover Photography Credits:
Top row, left to right:
  Paul Orfalea
  Alice Williams

  Christos M. Cotsakos, Ph.D.
  Jamie Tanaka

Top row, fourth photo furthest on the right:
  Anita Roddick OBE
  © Brian Moody

Bottom row, left to right:
  Dirk Gates
  Courtesy of the Graziadio
  School of Business and
  Management
  at Pepperdine University

  Nicolas G. Hayek
  Courtesy of
  The Swatch Group Ltd.

  Guy Kawasaki
  Photo by Bryn Colton

  Ken Park
  © 2003 Michael Nagle

COPYRIGHT © 2004
by South-Western, a division of Thomson Learning. Thomson Learning™ is a trademark used herein under license.

Printed in the United States of America
1 2 3 4 5 06 05 04 03

For more information contact South-Western, 5191 Natorp Boulevard, Mason, Ohio 45040.
Or you can visit our Internet site at:
http://www.swlearning.com

ALL RIGHTS RESERVED.
No part of this work covered by the copyright hereon may be reproduced or used in any form or by any means—graphic, electronic, or mechanical, including photocopying, recording, taping, Web distribution or information storage and retrieval systems—without the written permission of the publisher.

For permission to use material from this text or product, contact us by
Tel (800) 730-2214
Fax (800) 730-2215
http://www.thomsonrights.com

Library of Congress Control Number: 2002116030

ISBN: 0-324-15863-7

*This book is dedicated to my father, Richard H. Buskirk,
a great textbook writer, and to Sherry my lifelong friend.*

– **Bruce Buskirk**

*I dedicate this book to my husband,
Hans Lavik, for making my dreams come true.*

– **Molly Lavik**

BRIEF CONTENTS

Preface	xv
Acknowledgments	xxv
Introduction	xxviii
Mini Module on Assessing Market Opportunity	xxxvi
About the Authors	xlii

STRATEGY MENTOR MODULE | **Formulating Killer Strategies for Your Business** — 1

Christos M. Cotsakos, Ph.D.
Former Chairman and CEO, E*TRADE Financial

FINANCING MENTOR MODULE | **Marketing's Role in Raising Finances for Your New Venture** — 27

Guy Kawasaki
Founder and CEO, Garage Technology Ventures, Inc.

BRANDING MENTOR MODULE | **Branding That Works** — 65

Leonard Armato
Founder, Management Plus Enterprises and
Commissioner, AVP Pro Beach Volleyball Tour

VIRAL MARKETING MENTOR MODULE | **Crafting a Viral Marketing Phenomenon** — 89

Anita Roddick OBE
Non-Executive Director and Founder, The Body Shop

CRM MENTOR MODULE	Creating a Company Culture That Fosters Effective Customer Relationship Management (CRM)	115

Paul Orfalea
Founder, Kinko's, Inc.

DISTRIBUTION MENTOR MODULE	Devising Distribution-Dominating Tactics	143

Ken Park
Founder and President, BBM. HyperCD

NEW PRODUCTS MENTOR MODULE	Savvy Strategies for Marketing New Products	169

Dirk Gates
Founder, Xircom—An Intel Company

PUBLIC RELATIONS MENTOR MODULE	The Art of Budget-Boosting Public Relations	197

Nicolas G. Hayek
Chairman of the Board, The Swatch Group Ltd.

Conclusion	229
Appendix	239
Index	241

CONTENTS

Preface xv

Acknowledgments xxv

Introduction xxviii

Mini Module on
  Assessing Market Opportunity xxxvi

About the Authors xlii

STRATEGY MENTOR MODULE
Formulating Killer Strategies for Your Business
Christos M. Cotsakos, Ph.D.
Former Chairman and CEO, E*TRADE Financial 1

In the Beginning 2
    Putting It on the Line 3
    Heroes 3
    Enlisting in the Army 4
    In the Army 4
    Dream Wounds 4
    Lessons Learned in Vietnam 5
    Getting into College 5
Career Background 6
    Early Days for Christos at E*TRADE 8
Strategies to Ensure Long-term Profitability at E*TRADE 9
Dramatic Changes at E*TRADE 10
    Do It with Humor and a Big Bang Approach 11

About-Face 12
    ~~Change Agent?~~ No Way!
    He Plays His Own Game, Not Someone Else's 12
    Creating Heroes 13
Guiding Principles 14
A Great Leader 14
    Christos' Right Hand 14
The Storyteller 15
    Permission to Fail 16
Should You Put It on the Line? 17
    An Alternative to Putting It All on the Line 17
Consumers Want Great Service
    but Prefer Self-Service to Poor Service 18
    Product Highlight 18
Historic Perspective of the Financial Industry 19
The Vision 21
The Growth Path 22
In Good Company 22
Swarms 23
Build Killer Strategies 23
Endnotes 25

FINANCING MENTOR MODULE
Marketing's Role in Raising Finances for Your New Venture
Guy Kawasaki
Founder and CEO,
Garage Technology Ventures, Inc.   **27**

In the Beginning 29
Guy Shines Up Apple 30
    Guy's Hindsights 32
How Garage Got Started 32
    A Venture Capitalist 32
Stock Market Downturn 35
The Angel Alternative 35
Persevering through Tough Times 36
Garage Opens New Doors
    in Effort to Adapt in Post Dot-Com World 37
How a Marketing Master Markets 38

"Warning: Do Not Pass Go!" or Do Not Seek
    Venture Capital Financing Unless You Are Qualified! 39
        Guy Has Good Karma 40
The Entrepreneurial Marketing Campaign Backbone 41
Evangelize Your Venture 41
        Market Definition 42
        Value Proposition 44
        Elevator Pitch 45
        Executive Summary 49
        Corporate Overview Presentation 55
        That Was Then This is Now 56
        Things to Keep in Mind 56
Key Question—Should Our Firm Seek Venture Capital? 57
Endnotes 61

BRANDING MENTOR MODULE
Branding That Works
Leonard Armato
Founder, Management Plus Enterprises and Commissioner, AVP Pro Beach Volleyball Tour   65

Who Is Leonard Armato? 66
Leonard's Background 67
        Where Does His Drive Emanate From? 67
        Superstar Agent 68
        Shaq as a Global Icon 69
        The World of New Media Convergence 70
        The Entertainment Arena 70
The Digital Media Campus 71
    The Demise of the First Iteration
        of the Digital Media Campus 71
        Market Downturn 71
Recognizing Market Opportunity 72
        Grassroots Activities Matter 73
The Origins of the Term *Branding* 75
Leonard's Competitive Side 76
Carpe Diem! 76
Branding on a Shoestring—AVP Applies MCS™ 77
The Brand Advantage 79
        Understanding the Essence of Brand Advantages 79

Star Power 80
Integrated Marketing Communications 80
    Origins of IMC 81
Developing Brand Resilience 82
Positive Mental Attitude 83
Brand Ambassadorship 83
Brand Identity Guide (Enforce the Brand Identity Guidelines) 85
The Final Brand Element—Evaluation 85
Endnotes 87

VIRAL MARKETING MENTOR MODULE

Crafting a Viral Marketing Phenomenon
Anita Roddick OBE
Non-Executive Director and Founder, The Body Shop — 89

Anita's Entrepreneurial Spirit 92
An Entrepreneur Born Out Of Necessity 92
An Evolving Product Offering 93
Anita Adopts a Socially Responsible Company Culture 93
Storytelling 93
Staying True to Her Beliefs 94
The Trade Principle 94
Bringing in Customers 95
Principles before Profit 96
Dispelling the Beauty Myth 96
Take It Personally 98
Genesis of Viral Marketing Phenomenon at The Body Shop 99
The Viral Marketing Message 100
Staying in the Loop 100
The People on the Front Line 101
Leadership Counts 101
The Beauty Myth 103
Ethics Matters 103
Solving Other People's Problems Solves Your Own 106
Igniting Customer Demand 106
The Magic Ingredient 109
    Word-of-Mouth Occurrence 109
Endnotes 111

CRM MENTOR MODULE
Creating a Company Culture That Fosters Effective Customer Relationship Management (CRM)
Paul Orfalea
Founder, Kinko's, Inc.   115

Paul's Early Years 116
Hiding a Secret 117
The Impact of a Caring Mother and Father 117
    The Impact of the Mundane 118
    It's What You Save that Counts 118
    News Junkie 118
    College Days 118
    On the Brink of Brilliance 119
Kinko's Is Born 119
    The Early Days of Kinko's 121
    Kinko's Expands 121
    Paul's Role at Kinko's 121
Game Plan for Expansion of Kinko's 122
    Prominent Partnerships 122
    "The Company Picnic" 123
The Kinko's Philosophy 123
    Obsessed with Quality 125
    Turning a Negative Into a Positive 125
Kinko's Takes a Capital Investment 127
Moving On 127
Brief Analysis of the Kinko's Business Market Space 129
Partners, Not Franchisees 129
Slow, Continuous Growth 130
    Empowering Others 132
    The Balancing Act 132
Let Innovation Reign 134
Customer Satisfaction 136
Market Research 136
Taking a Proactive Posture 137
Lifelong Learners 139
Endnotes 140

DISTRIBUTION MENTOR MODULE

Devising Distribution-Dominating Tactics
Ken Park
Founder and President, BBM. HyperCD — 143

In the Beginning 144
Ken Empowers Direct Customer Distribution 148
Ten Minutes to Go 150
Under Ken's Watch 152
Virtual Marketing Arenas 153
The Business of Small Businesses 154
Distribution-Dominance Solar System Model 156
    Elaboration on the Distribution-Dominance
    Solar System Model 157
    Hold Business Relationships Sacred 158
Ken Park's Gamble 158
The Internet's Impact on Distribution 159
    Customer Usage Profiles 160
    Sales Revenues 160
    Customer Feedback Loops 160
    Word-of-Mouth Occurrences 161
Connected Constituencies 161
Traditional Channels 161
Partnering with Key Influencers 162
    Byproduct of the MLS HyperCD 163
Utilize Virtual Marketing Arenas 163
Endnotes 167

NEW PRODUCTS MENTOR MODULE

Savvy Strategies for Marketing New Products
Dirk Gates
Founder, Xircom—An Intel Company — 169

In the Beginning 170
Xircom's Vision 172
    The Naming Process of Xircom 172
Making a Very Small Business Seem Larger 174
The Right Venture Capitalists 175

Mentors to Dirk 175
Implementing Key Strategies 176
Innovative New Products 177
    Highlights of Xircom's Product Innovations
      from 1997 to 2001 178
    A Serious Issue 179
    New Phase of Career 180
The History of New Product Marketing 181
Recognizing Market Opportunity 181
Vision 183
Distinctive Logo Marks 184
Market Research for the Entrepreneur 184
    History of Market Research 185
    Tips for Gathering Market Research 185
Dirk's New Product Philosophy 186
"All-Star" Board 187
Tear Down the Walls 187
Inspiring Operational Excellence 188
Devising New Product Strategies 190
    New Product Launch Event Plan 191
Fulfilling Customer Needs 192
Endnotes 194

PUBLIC RELATIONS MENTOR MODULE

The Art of Budget-Boosting Public Relations

Nicolas G. Hayek
Chairman of the Board,
The Swatch Group Ltd.   **197**

In the Beginning 199
    An Entrepreneur Is Born 199
Early Career 200
    The Swiss Economic Miracle 203
The Backdrop on the Birth of Swatch 203
    Creating an Emotional Attachment to Your Watch 204
The Product Pyramid 204
Public Relations Activities to Impact the Bottom Line 206
Nicolas Today 206
Recent History of Swiss Watchmaking 208

Low-Cost Quality Watch	211
Celebrity Spokespeople	213
24/7/365	215
Storytelling	216
Secrets to Nicolas' Success	219
What Is a Watch?	220
Endnotes	222

Conclusion 229

So What Does It All Mean?	229
Overarching Mentor Insights	229
Customer Focus	231
Management Team	232
Storytelling	232
Innovation	233
Ethics	234
Luck	235
Updates on Featured Entrepreneurial Marketers	235
Christos M. Cotsakos, Ph.D.	235
Guy Kawasaki	235
Leonard Armato	235
Anita Roddick OBE	236
Paul Orfalea	236
Ken Park	236
Dirk Gates	236
Nicolas G. Hayek	237
Future Predictions for Entrepreneurial Marketing	237
Up, Up and Away!	237
Endnotes	238

Appendix 1:
Let's Talk Business Network, Inc 239

Endnotes	240

Index 241

PREFACE

We promised ourselves that, if we were ever fortunate enough to be at the head of a classroom, we would be enthralling and entertaining. We would not give our students any excuse to yawn. This is a promise we've tried to keep while writing *Entrepreneurial Marketing: Real Stories and Survival Strategies*.

To make the subject matter come alive, we tell the true stories of some of the most brilliant entrepreneurial marketers of our time. We will share with you their insights, driving philosophies, and secrets of success. We will show you how they devised survival strategies to overcome insurmountable odds. We will divulge to you the entrepreneurial marketing techniques that have catapulted these leaders to unprecedented success.

Our working definition of entrepreneurial marketing is:

> The process by which brave souls initiate the buying and selling of products and/or services directed at launching a new business venture or developing an extension of an existing enterprise.[1]

One must be a risk taker of sorts to engage in entrepreneurial marketing because the processes required to successfully market a new venture or extension of an existing enterprise are always disruptive to the status quo. Entrepreneurial marketers are change agents of the highest caliber. They take existing marketing processes and disrupt them before ultimately transforming them into new ways of doing business.

We've been fortunate to be able to view new frontiers through these marketers' eyes. We've been able to live and learn vicariously from their amazing experiences and we're excited to be able to offer you the same fascinating adventure.

We utilize the near-perfect vision of hindsight to explore the lives and business practices of eight entrepreneurial marketers who have been savvy enough to overcome the obstacles involved in establishing a sound business. These entrepreneurial marketers have persevered by devising exceptional survival strategies. Our goal is to impart the wisdom behind the development and implementation of these survival strategies.

Mentorographers Lavik and Buskirk

---

[1] Definition of entrepreneurial marketing developed by Molly Lavik, June 1, 2002.

Writing Style

Entrepreneurial Marketing: Real Stories and Survival Strategies utilizes the popularity of the biography back-story to entice readers to gain firsthand knowledge of successful techniques for marketing new ventures or expanding existing enterprises. Mentorography™,[2] is the word Molly Lavik coined to describe this style of writing. Mentorographies are biographies on the driving philosophies of founders that impart valuable insights to entrepreneurial marketers. Mentorographies also provide a practical analysis of the entrepreneurial marketer's craft. The mentorographies in this book are captivating and inspirational ways to learn from others. This book is organized by mentorographies and is divided into Mentor Modules. Each Mentor Module focuses on the business concepts that constitute entrepreneurial marketing and the connecting insights that support the Entrepreneurial Marketing Domain.[3]

The Entrepreneurial Marketing Domain

The study of entrepreneurial marketing sits at a crossroad between the entrepreneurship discipline and the marketing discipline. The intersection of these two disciplines is known as the Entrepreneurial Marketing Domain.

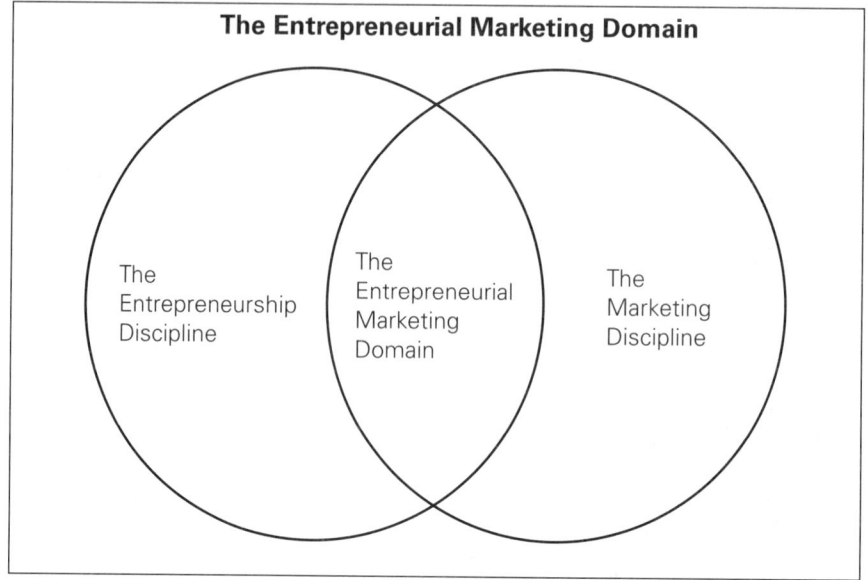

Organizational Structure

This Preface describes the writing style and structure of *Entrepreneurial Marketing: Real Stories and Survival Strategies*. In the Introduction we examine some of the underlying concepts and guiding principles that have

---

[2] Mentorography is coined by Molly Lavik, June 12, 2002.

[3] The Entrepreneurial Marketing Domain is coined by Molly Lavik and Bruce Buskirk, June 5, 2002.

an impact on entrepreneurial marketing. A Mini Module dedicated to the concept of assessing market opportunity follows. Next, we have eight sections, featuring the real stories of pioneers of this domain, called Mentor Modules. The Mentor Modules delve into the business concepts that constitute entrepreneurial marketing.

Mentor Modules at a Glance

1. Strategy Mentor Module

Christos M. Cotsakos, Ph.D.,
Former Chairman & CEO,
E*TRADE Financial

3. Branding Mentor Module

Leonard Armato, Founder,
Management Plus Enterprises and
Commissioner, AVP Pro Beach Volleyball Tour

2. Financing Mentor Module

Guy Kawasaki, Founder & CEO,
Garage Technology Ventures, Inc.

4. Viral Marketing Mentor Module

Anita Roddick OBE
(Order of the British Empire)
Non-Executive Director and Founder,
The Body Shop

(continues)

5. CRM Mentor Module

Paul Orfalea, Founder,
Kinko's, Inc.

7. New Products Mentor Module

Dirk Gates, Founder,
Xircom—An Intel Company

6. Distribution Mentor Module

Ken Park, Founder & CEO,
BBM. HyperCD

8. Public Relations Mentor Module

Nicolas G. Hayek,
Chairman of the Board,
The Swatch Group Ltd.

Each Mentor Module is divided into two parts. Mentorography Part I chronicles the development of the Mentor's driving philosophies relevant to entrepreneurial marketing. Mentorography Part II features an analysis of the craft of each profiled entrepreneurial marketer. The entrepreneurs featured in this book were selected specifically because they provide valuable insights into entrepreneurial marketing.

From researching each profiled business leader, we have ascertained ten main guiding principles per module and dubbed them "Mentor Insights." Mentor Insights are the 60-second concise summary of the main guiding principles that support the module topics and provide a road map for success for each business concept. These entrepreneurial marketing mottos can serve as readily identifiable guiding principles that you can apply to your business ventures. The Mentor Insights are meant to serve as a practical application for the business concepts covered in this book. In Part I and Part II, a summary list appears featuring the ten Mentor Insights specific to each module's topic on:

- Strategy
- Financing
- Branding
- Viral Marketing
- CRM (Customer Relationship Management)
- Distribution
- New Products
- Public Relations

As Part I unfolds, the Mentor Insights mark the beginning of a discussion on life experiences that led the entrepreneurial marketer to formulate certain driving philosophies. In Part II, the same Mentor Insights mark the beginning of discussions on an analysis of the featured Mentor's craft. A Mentor Insight pointer symbol

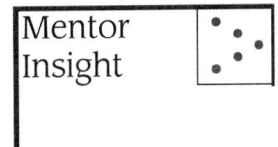

appears usually in the left margin along with the specific Mentor Insight to alert you when a particular Mentor Insight is about to be covered. We encourage you to ponder these insights and to develop some of your own.

Preface   xix

We also have included some additional learning tools:

- Soliloquy: The Soliloquy is where the featured Mentor discloses in first person their inner thoughts.
- Mentor Milestones: Mentor Milestones are a timeline of the major accomplishments of the featured Mentor.
- Mentor Methods: The book features business approaches and processes from the profiled Mentor's work as well as graphs, diagrams and conceptual analogies that we have created or adapted to further elaborate and explain each Mentor's entrepreneurial marketing craft. These Mentor Methods conceptually symbolize the processes behind the discussed entrepreneurial marketing concepts.
- List of Helpful Hints: Helpful Hints are a to do list of suggested tips and techniques to provide a mini instruction guide for accomplishing an underlying theme of one of the business concepts featured in each Mentor Module.
- Historical Perspectives: Concise Historical Perspectives are featured throughout the book.
- Specially Selected Excerpts: We have hand-picked Specially Selected Excerpts from the Mentor's marketing plans, web sites, press releases and corporate mission statements to share with you primarily in Part II of the modules.
- Rhetorical Questions in Callout Bubbles: Some of the modules feature Rhetorical Questions set off in Callout Bubbles that are designed to give you questions to consider before pursuing a certain business practice or process in entrepreneurial marketing.
- Definitions of Entrepreneurial Marketing terms: These terms are accompanied by definitions that are easy to understand.
- Mentorography Questions: Mentorography Questions appear at the end of each module and give the reader an opportunity to apply what they have learned in real-world, practical scenarios.
- *Entrepreneurial Marketing: Real Stories and Survival Strategies* web site: Check out **http://buskirklavik.swlearning.com** for updates and links to additional information on the featured Mentors and their ventures.

The benefit behind providing these learning tools in each Mentorography is that readers are able to have a "virtual mentoring experience" without an in-person encounter with the business leaders we have profiled.

Throughout this book we have strived to simplify the Mentorographies. We have done this by providing these learning tools. We recognize that there are further elaborations on these concepts and theories; however, we have strived to distill these concepts in recognition that one of the entrepreneurial marketer's biggest enemies is time. We hope this book is useful in allowing you to skim when necessary. We also hope that you will utilize this text as an outlined and simplified handbook for entrepreneurial marketing.

We have some special notes about this book. We've alternated the use of the words "his" and "her" and "he" and "she" for a smoother reading style for the sentences that contain these pronouns. We did want to underscore that by choosing this alternating style we in no way imply a gender bias in an entrepreneurial marketer in any situation. We have taken painstaking care to ensure the accuracy of the information on the upcoming pages. We apologize in advance if any inaccuracies have occurred. We will have a section on the web site that accompanies this book dedicated to posting any inaccuracies, clarifications and updates when necessary at: http://buskirklavik.swlearning.com.

Entrepreneurial Marketing: Real Stories and Survival Strategies concludes with a summary of the Overarching Mentor Insights, an update on the Mentors profiled, and a prediction about where entrepreneurial marketing may be headed.

Writing Roles

We decided to partner on writing this book because of the unique perspectives we each represent. Bruce Buskirk is a veteran academic who has recently started several entrepreneurial ventures. Molly Lavik is a serial entrepreneur who has recently stepped into academia as an adjunct professor. This meant that we had two distinct viewpoints similar in style to the type of differing opinions that legendary movie critics Siskel & Ebert had.

Despite our differing viewpoints, this book was written with a collaborative spirit. We jointly conducted most of the interviews with the entrepreneurs featured in this book. Molly Lavik did the majority of the background research for the interviews and wrote the first draft of the book. Bruce Buskirk then did a thorough re-write adding in academic and differing marketing perspectives. We then had a lively debate over the information that would be included in the final draft. After reaching a consensus, each module was sent to the person who we wrote about for accuracy and additional insights. Through this process, we feel we've been able to capture the entrepreneurial marketing insights of these business leaders.

Conceptual Model of Entrepreneurial Marketing

We have developed the Entrepreneurial Marketing Wheel to give you a conceptual model of entrepreneurial marketing. This model also reflects the overall organization of how this book is structured. We advocate the use of this conceptual model of entrepreneurial marketing because it illustrates the nonlinear and interactive nature of this evolving domain. We encourage you to use the Entrepreneurial Marketing Wheel as a guide to understanding not only the business concepts and insights covered here, but also the relationship of these items in the context of your own venture.

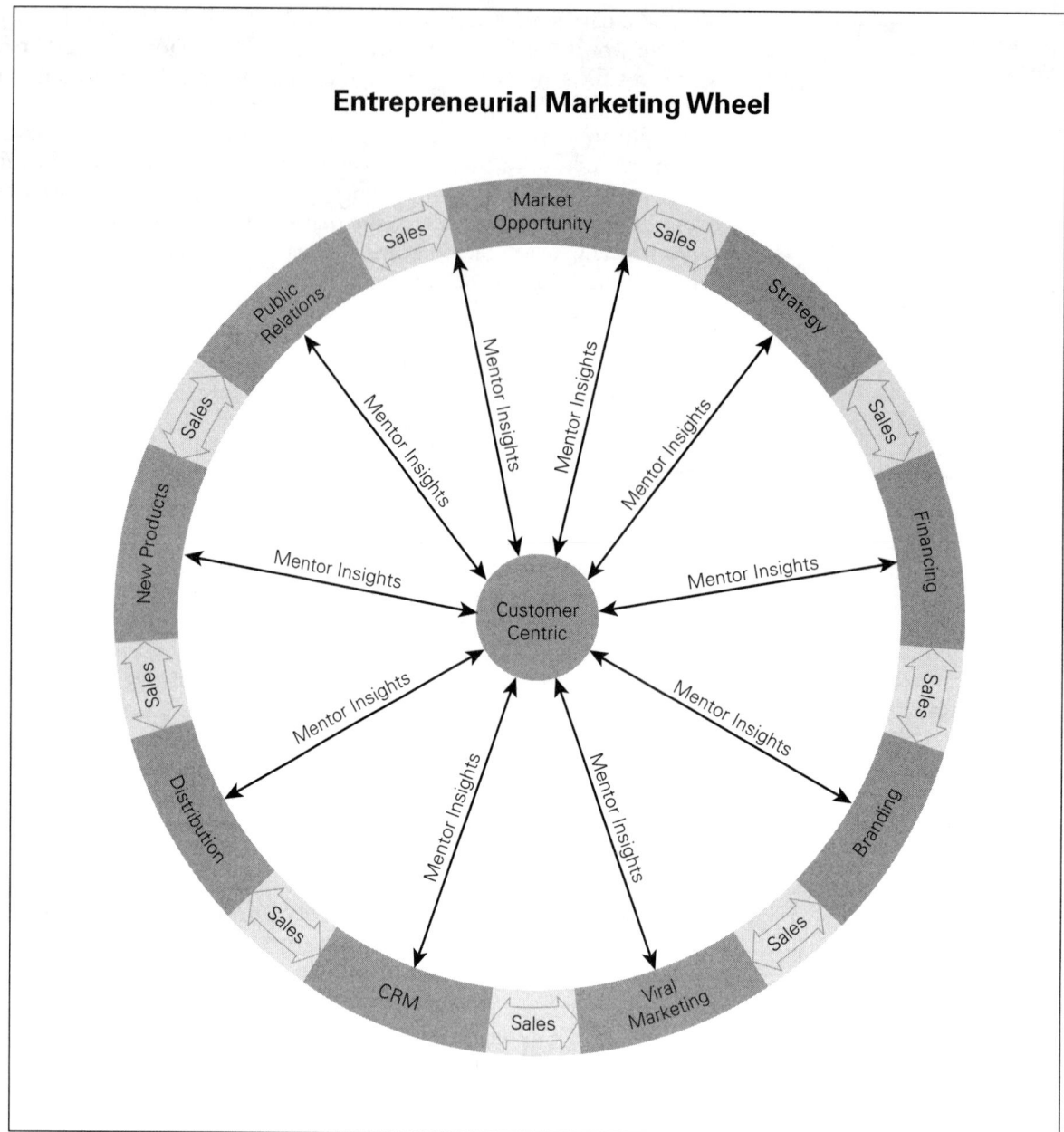

We have put together answers to frequently asked questions to explain the wheel analogy.

Frequently Asked Questions
Regarding the Entrepreneurial Marketing Wheel

What Is the Entrepreneurial Marketing Wheel?

The Entrepreneurial Marketing Wheel represents the interaction of business concepts that make up the Entrepreneurial Marketing Domain. The Entrepreneurial Marketing Domain is populated by those brave souls who initiate the buying and selling of products and/or services directed at launching a new business venture or developing an extension of an existing enterprise.[4]

Why a Wheel Shape?

Since the business concepts that form entrepreneurial marketing are not linear in nature and are highly interactive, it is necessary to represent these concepts in a format that demonstrates this nature. We have used an analogy of a wheel to conceptualize the Entrepreneurial Marketing Domain.

The business concepts (market opportunity, financing, strategy, branding, viral marketing, CRM, distribution, new products, and public relations) can be thought of as the rim that holds a wheel together. These business concepts can be represented in a cyclical design because the entrepreneurial marketer must continuously evaluate and implement or re-implement these concepts. It is dangerous to deal with each of these concepts one at a time in a sequential order, since each requires continuous attention and refinement.

Customer-centric focus is at the hub of the wheel. The concept of being customer centric supports, connects, and holds together the other business concepts. An entrepreneurial marketer should make sure that each business concept is centered around the customer. Losing a direct connection with one's customers' needs, even for a short time, can cause the best-intentioned entrepreneur to "spin her wheels." The spokes of the wheel connect the business concepts to the Customer Centric hub. The spokes of this wheel are svelte yet strong in design just as this book's Mentor Insights are designed to be. The entrepreneurial marketing business concept's correlating Mentor Insights are represented by the spokes of the wheel because of their similarity in design.

Sales are represented as the inter-connecting elements of the business concepts in the rim of the wheel. A strong wheel rim provides a powerful foundation to propel a new venture or expanded enterprise in the direction of a sustainable and profitable business model.

What Does the Entrepreneurial Marketing Wheel Have to Do with This Book?

The Entrepreneurial Marketing Wheel reflects the overarching organization of this book. Rather than chapter numbers, business concept headings accompanied by the words Mentor Module are emphasized. This further reflects the structure of the wheel, reemphasizing that the sections of this book should not be read or taken in a linear fashion. Flipping back and forth between modules serves as a better structural model for the entrepreneurial marketer. There is no "Customer Centric Mentor Module," since customer-centric concepts are core to each section and are dispersed

(continues)

---

[4] Definition of entrepreneurial marketing developed by Molly Lavik, June 1, 2002.

throughout each module. Since customer centricity is at the heart of entrepreneurial marketing, we felt that it was more important to emphasize this concept continuously than to break it out separately. The Mentor Insights (spokes of the wheel) connect the business concepts to the customer-centric focus of entrepreneurial marketing. Sales is also not broken out into a separate section nor referred to as a business concept. Sales are the connecting factor for your venture. There is no aspect of entrepreneurial marketing that does not call for sales. Whether you are crafting marketing strategies to help raise financing for your new venture or launching your new product at a trade show, you must incorporate a healthy dose of sales into the process. If you are one of those people (and you know who you are) who want to go into marketing and not sales, we suggest you find a new focus outside of entrepreneurial marketing activities.

A further elaboration on the entrepreneurial marketer's role in sales is important. Entrepreneurial marketers often have to put together a persuasive sales pitch to convince an existing enterprise to expand or create a new venture. The entrepreneurial marketer is responsible for selling a new venture business concept to would be investors by devising compelling marketing strategies. The entrepreneurial marketer needs to solicit buy-in for a new brand campaign from key stakeholders in order for a new or improved brand to be approved. Customer relationship management systems are not inexpensive and often require the entrepreneurial marketer to solicit and forge strategic partnerships to offset the expense. Distribution systems require a savvy salesperson to seal the deal. New products need resources to pay for necessary research and development activities as well as to launch these new products into the marketplace. The entrepreneurial marketer is instrumental in soliciting these funds. Public relations activities do have a price tag associated with them although it's considerably less than what it costs to advertise. The entrepreneurial marketer is needed to convince others to allocate the resources necessary to produce effective public relations campaigns. As you will see from reading the mentorographies in this book, sales or a component of the sales process is a key aspect of each profiled entrepreneurial marketer's road to success.

Is There Anything Else We Should Know about the Entrepreneurial Marketing Wheel?

Yes. The Entrepreneurial Marketing Domain is evolving and dynamic. This book's particular view of entrepreneurial marketing won't be found in some of the well-established theories about marketing. We are attempting to share some of the most recent insights of entrepreneurial marketing. Each day brings new insights from the pioneering people who are practicing in this domain, and through these entrepreneurial-spirited individuals, the newest techniques will continue to emerge. For on-going updates on those enhancements, we invite you to visit **http://buskirklavik.swlearning.com**.

We recommend that you refer back to the Entrepreneurial Marketing Wheel on p. xxii of the Preface while reading each section of this book as a continuous reminder of the concepts to consider for marketing a new venture or an expanded enterprise.

Thank you for your interest in entrepreneurial marketing. We hope you enjoy the journey on the following pages as you read about some of the most successful and resourceful entrepreneurial marketers of our time.

ACKNOWLEDGMENTS

The publishing of *Entrepreneurial Marketing: Real Stories and Survival Strategies* is made possible by the inspiration, coaching and assistance of many people. We would like to acknowledge everyone for helping us make this book possible. We are extremely grateful for your help with this book. We are also extremely grateful to you for helping us get all the entrepreneurial marketing concepts down on paper so that we can share these real-world learning insights with everyone.

Bruce Buskirk would like to thank his colleagues David Ralph, Morgan Miles, Gerald Hills, Ed Popper, Tom O'Malia, Bill Gardiner, John Rehfeld, Frieda Gehlen and Scott Fletcher for their help and insights. Of course this book would not be possible without the input of Molly Lavik and the assistance of her husband, Hans, who both nurtured this project every step of the way. Bruce gives special thanks to his wife Sherry for her understanding and support during the past two years, and the tolerance and assistance of his children: Brian, Bob and Katie.

Molly Lavik would like to thank her MBA students at Pepperdine University's Graziadio School of Business and Management who helped her pioneer the creation of the curriculum of the course "Marketing New Ventures." She would like to thank these students as well as the students of her other entrepreneurial-related courses for giving her feedback on the classroom testing of many of the concepts that appear in this book. She would also like to thank her colleagues at the Graziadio School's Malibu campus for giving her on-going feedback and encouragement through the many days and nights of writing the book. Molly Lavik also extends a major thank you to Bruce Buskirk and James Goodrich for encouraging and supporting her for bringing progressive approaches to real-world education into the classroom. She extends a heartfelt thank you to her teaching colleagues at the Graziadio School's Malibu campus: Kathryn Fitzgerald, Charla Griffy-Brown, Dave McMahon, Margaret Elizabeth Phillips, and Honorio Todino. She gives a special thank you to Shawn Church for helping her develop the Entrepreneurial Start-up Strategy and Business Plan Writing curriculum at the Graziadio School as well as allowing her to do classroom testing with the students and coaching her on financial modeling concepts not to mention reminding her to not to lose the entrepreneurial spirit.

A special thank you is given for their words of encouragement and support to the faculty at the Graziadio School's Culver City center, including Charles W. Fojtik, Velios Kodomichalos, and W. Scott Sherman. Molly Lavik extends appreciation and acknowledgment to the new Dean of the Graziadio School, Linda Livingstone, for supporting and encouraging the faculty to publish scholarly academic work that has a real-world business application. She would also like to thank the administration at the Graziadio School for their help. A special thank you is extended to Scott Fletcher for helping us get the first draft in order and encouraging us to persevere through the writing process and thank you to his colleague Frieda L. Gehlen. Molly extends a thank you to Gordon Brooks who never grew tired of listening, Doris Jones who was always there for us and Michele Valdovinos for her continuous words of encouragement. Molly also gives a special thanks to Michael Sims. She especially thanks Jason Bender and Tim Pavell. Molly extends many words of appreciation to Kathleen Gardner, her Mentor, for setting the ultimate example in publishing. She also thanks her former student, Christian F. Munz, for being there when she really needed him to help with the German translation. Additionally, she thanks Morgan Miles, Jimmy Hill, and Tom O'Malia, Director Emeritus, Lloyd Greif Center for Entrepreneurial Studies, University of Southern California. She would also like to thank her friends who encouraged her and listened when she needed to talk about the writing process: Megan Cariola, Brooks Ferguson, John DeGolyer, Beth Moeller, Debbie Menin, Joanie Kotick, Chris Pohl, and Richard and May Darnielle as well as thank her fellow entrepreneurial friends on the Entrepreneurial Roundtable: Elisabeth Flack, Colleen Edwards, Kristina Schultz, and Stacy Robin Meranus. Thank you goes out to Mitchell Schlimer from Let's Talk Business Network, Inc. for his help. She also thanks her family for their warm words of encouragement: Hans Lavik and Bandit, Karen and Arne Lavik, Eric, Lori, Erica, Lars and Salty, Nils, Randi, and Bjorn Lavik, Arthur and Nancy Wachs, and Chris, Kathy and Lindsey Wachs. And she wishes to thank Richard H. Buskirk for providing a textbook legacy to follow as well as her co-author Bruce Buskirk for being there around the clock through thick and thin to make this book come to life and his family for their support and understanding during the process.

We would like to jointly thank the following people.

We gratefully thank and acknowledge the important contributions of the Mentors we profiled to this book: Christos M. Cotsakos, Ph.D., Guy Kawasaki, Leonard Armato, Anita Roddick OBE, Paul Orfalea, Ken Park, Dirk Gates and Nicolas G. Hayek. We thank them for letting us bring the stories of their lives to the pages of this book. We would also like to thank and gratefully acknowledge the profiled Mentors' co-workers for their continuous support: Brigitte VanBaelen, Jared Arnold, Raul Avila, Melissa Freidman, Linda Walker, Tony Lee, Helen Cocker, Karen Bishop, Bill Eyres, Tania Thompson, Yvonne Durell, Susan Flook, Lois Mitchell, Maggie Thill, Tanaya Cook, Tom Bannon, Béatrice Howald, Massimo Ballola, Katy Jolidon, and Sandra Obergsell. We would also like to thank the photographers for the remarkable photographs they took that are featured in this book. These photographers include: Michael Nagle, Jon Fox, Jinette Park, Alice Williams, Jamie Tanaka, Bryn Colton, and Brian Moody. We would like to thank and applaud the team at South-Western, a division of Thomson Learning for their unswerving commitment and support of this book: Jack Calhoun, Steven Hazelwood, Taney Wilkins, Pamela Person, Nicole Moore, Linda Ellis, Jenny Fruechtenicht, Christina Loehrke, Bob Dreas, and Stacy Shirley.

We would also like to extend a major thank you to the team at Argosy Publishing: Karen Cheng, Sally Boylan, and Laura Proietti.

We extend a major thank you to Malcolm Gladwell for granting permission for us to adapt excerpts of some of his landmark work in the book. Additionally, we thank the companies, organizations, authors, and/or their publishers who gave us permission to reprint and/or adapt their remarkable work: John Hatfield, Adrian Murdoch, Dr. Dirk Lehrach, Jay Humphlett, Peter A. Arturi, Lynn Luczkowski, Francine Della Catena, Denise C. Petratos, Irene Valverde, David Seitz, Greg Bibb, Cathy Nolan, Amy Keller, Dave Deal, Agnes Fisher, Michelle Johnson, Matthew Budman, Trey Fitz-Gerald, Brett Crosby, Norman Goldstein, Matthew Gerry, Daphne Ben-Ari, and Joe R. Howry.

We extend a major thank you to the faculty who participated through South-Western in the academic review of this book for their honest and candid feedback that we cherished and attempted to always incorporate, including: Michael V. Laric, University of Baltimore; Thomas M. Tworoger, Nova Southeastern University; Ken Fairweather, LeTourneau University; Morgan P. Miles, Georgia Southern University; Mary Lou Lockerby, College of DuPage; and Patricia E. Kriska, Southern Methodist University.

We apologize in advance for any major contributors to this book that we neglected to mention. Please check out **http://buskirklavik.swlearning.com** for updates on additional acknowledgments.

INTRODUCTION

Chasing an Insight

Chasing that remarkable idea or insight that is going to transform your new venture into a masterpiece can be an elusive endeavor. This introduction is designed to give you some background and context to entrepreneurial marketing techniques so that you can take full advantage of the insights in the Mentor Modules that follow. We begin this introduction by outlining the characteristics that we have found in an entrepreneurial marketer's mindset. Next we discuss the significance of being categorized as a small business to an entrepreneurial marketer. We also provide a brief historical perspective of small businesses. We felt some discussion dedicated to the topic of small businesses was appropriate because many entrepreneurial marketers are committed to helping new ventures start from often humble beginnings. The eight entrepreneurial marketers profiled in this book mostly started their ventures as small businesses or operate today in the marketplace as successful small businesses. The introduction concludes with a timeline of selected significant events in the development of entrepreneurial marketing that led to the present interpretation of the body of knowledge that we refer to as the Entrepreneurial Marketing Domain. Historical perspectives are a frequent theme of this book and can be utilized to gain an understanding of what has transpired in the past so that you can apply this knowledge toward devising successful strategies for the future.

The Mindset of the Entrepreneurial Marketer

What type of mind does a person who is successful in marketing a new venture possess? Are there certain characteristics that make up the successful entrepreneurial marketer's mindset? This book will provide answers to these questions.

We found common characteristics in the Mentors we profiled. These common characteristics included having:

- **Vision**—Able to create and communicate an easily understandable mission for what the new venture does in order to successfully launch a new business. This is accomplished while inspiring others to join you in your new enterprise.

- **Creativity**—Ability to inject imagination and uniqueness into the new business venture. It takes skill and ingenuity to create a new venture equipped with strategies to outsmart the competition.

- **Focus**—Able to maintain the vision of the company with unwavering diligence. It's very easy to get sidetracked especially if you find it necessary to evolve the original vision. Ironically, we have encountered many successful entrepreneurial marketers who get bored easily. How then were they able to maintain their focus? We will explore this in future modules.

- **Passion**—Desiring to succeed under your own steam on a business venture. In the upcoming chapters we will explore the passionate natures of successful entrepreneurial marketers and attempt to analyze where such passion emanates from and how it is sustained even in the face of insurmountable challenges.

- **Drive**—Possessing intrinsic energy to accomplish the business goal even in the face of adversity. This book will catalog the remarkable drive of successful entrepreneurial marketers while exploring some of the insecurities they overcame.

- **Perseverance**—Able to keep going even when faced with seemingly insurmountable obstacles.

- **Opportunistic Nature**—Sees the possibilities even before they exist. Can take advantage of an upcoming trend or unite unrelated processes to create a unique business venture. Each entrepreneurial marketer we profile is an opportunist who was able to take advantage of an opportunity often before others even knew an opportunity existed.

- **Problem Solving Ability**—Thrives on coming up with solutions to complex challenges. This book will describe some major challenges and explain how the entrepreneurial marketer was able to develop strategies to overcome these situations.

- **Self-discipline**—Able to be organized and regimented in pursuit of a successful business venture. This characteristic allows the entrepreneurial marketer to walk the fine line between being creative and inventive while still accomplishing thousands of daily processes in order for the venture to prosper.

- **Frugality**—Knows how to stretch every cent so that expenditures are as low as possible. We have recently seen the antithesis of this characteristic with the rise and fall of the dot-com industry. Companies that were spending entire advertising budgets on one Super Bowl ad or having million-dollar parties or outrageously extravagant offices now have one thing in common—bankruptcy.

- **Empathy**—Able to put yourself in another's shoes and therefore able to show sensitivity and understanding of what others are communicating in the start-up environment. Empathy may be the one characteristic the entrepreneurial marketer can utilize to sustain the new venture through a start-up scenario where many of your staff may be underpaid.

- **Social Responsibility**—Ethics, caring and humanitarianism are characteristics that are commonly found in today's entrepreneurial marketer. At perhaps no other time in our history has social responsibility been more needed. We have gone to great lengths to identify entrepreneurial marketers who potentially give back to the world more than they ever receive. We will share with you through these examples the processes to create a socially responsible organization.

- **Spirituality**—We have found that the successful entrepreneurial marketer has often devoted time to spirituality development. Meditation and positive affirmations are two common examples of this found in our study. We refer to the term spirituality not in a religious context but instead pertaining to what fulfills one's soul.

- **Good Timing**—Able to identify a market opportunity and know when it's the optimum time to launch a new venture or expansion of an existing enterprise. We will chronicle the timing of decisions of successful entrepreneurial marketers and shed light on how they knew when to make their entrepreneurial marketing moves.

- **Luck**—Can a person be predisposed to be lucky? Is luck a human behavior or a karmic universal predisposition? We will explore what, if any, insights lead to a lucky entrepreneurial marketer.

How Can One Analyze an Entrepreneurial Marketer's Mindset?

We have suggested that there are similar frameworks in the mindsets of successful entrepreneurial marketers, but there are many entrepreneurial people in the business arena who possess the above list of characteristics yet still fail. There are several reasons for this. The first is time. The journey to entrepreneurial marketing success is paved with failures. Successful entrepreneurial marketers persevere. They outlast their challenges. Second, one can possess all these characteristics yet still fall short of their goals. For example, if your timing is good, there may be someone else who has even better timing. Third, one can simply be the victim of bad luck. While many subscribe to the theory that entrepreneurial marketers make their own luck, experience has shown too many outstanding people fall victim to the unforeseen. Their only power over these misfortunes is to survive, and try again. Fourth, some of these characteristics contradict one another. If you are visionary you may be focused at first, but later become passionate about a new vision and split your focus. In the end, a successful entrepreneurial marketer must have the discipline and the intuition to focus on the objective. There is no instruction manual or road map. You can learn from those who have tried and triumphed previously; and you can certainly benefit from studying what land mines derailed your predecessors. For these reasons we advocate mentoring as an outstanding technique for entrepreneurial marketers.

As mentioned previously, we feature in each Mentor Module ten major guiding principles we call Mentor Insights. We encourage you to adopt these Mentor Insights. They offer access to the knowledge needed to predispose your new venture or expanded enterprise toward success. The Mentor Insights provide a method for harnessing the promise of a good idea.

Small Businesses

Entrepreneurial marketers have been known to transform adversity into opportunity by forming new small businesses or spinning off parts of larger businesses. Understanding the opportunities afforded to small businesses is a worthwhile pursuit for an entrepreneurial marketer.

U.S. Small Business Administration

The SBA (Small Business Administration) is part of the United States government's Department of Commerce and defines a small business as "A business smaller than a given size as measured by its employment, business receipts, or business assets."[1] We recommend you visit the SBA web site at **http://www.sba.gov** to familiarize yourself with the Small Business Act (Public Law 85-536, as amended). The SBA web site will also offer you insights regarding the criteria for receiving a small business classification. This criteria varies from industry to industry.

Understanding if your venture qualifies as a small business is helpful because there is assistance that the United States government provides to small businesses. The following excerpt from the Small Business Act section (b) (1 clarifies the type of assistance that the United States government and associated agencies provide to small businesses.

" . . . (b) (1 It is the declared policy of the Congress that the Federal Government, through the Small Business Administration, acting in cooperation with the Department of Commerce and other relevant State and Federal agencies, should aid and assist small businesses, as defined under this Act, to increase their ability to compete in international markets by—

(A) enhancing their ability to export;

(B) facilitating technology transfers;

(C) enhancing their ability to compete effectively and efficiently against imports;

(D) increasing the access of small businesses to long-term capital for the purchase of new plant and equipment used in the production of goods and services involved in international trade;

(E) disseminating information concerning State, Federal, and private programs and initiatives to enhance the ability of small businesses to compete in international markets; and

(F) ensuring that the interests of small businesses are adequately represented in bilateral and multilateral trade negotiations."[2]

---

[1] SBA (U.S. Small Business Administration), "Glossary of Terms," http://www.sba.gov/8abd/indexglossary.html, accessed January 15, 2003.

[2] Public Law 85-536, 85th Cong., 2d sess. (18 July 1958), *Small Business Act*, U.S. Code, Vol. 7, Title 15—Commerce and Trade, Sec. (b) (1. (2000).

As an entrepreneurial marketer, you have the responsibility to identify and seek government assistance associated with the small business classification. The first phase of a small business's development has traditionally meant that an entrepreneurial marketer has few if any staff members to assist with the marketing activities and a small to non-existent operating budget for financing the development of marketing strategies and campaigns. That is why it's critical that you find assistance as a small business from other sources such as government agencies. The period of time when a new venture debuts as a small business is a time that the entrepreneurial marketer's resourcefulness is put to the test.

History of Small Businesses

Throughout much of history, the majority of businesses have been small. Before the industrial revolution, there were few reasons for a business to be large. Materials from mine operations and trading goods transported on ships were about the largest scale of operations. The largest organizations of the pre-industrialized world tended to be governments, because governments needed to be large to gain economic superiority during war. Transportation traditionally has been a barrier to reaching extended markets, and communication tied to transportation limited the coordination of a geographically disperse organization.

The industrial revolution gave an advantage to large-scale centralized production. Populations migrated toward these centers of production. Transportation and communication were slow to address the needs of these large production centers, but their eventual development helped the burgeoning large companies substantially. Transportation and communication has progressed to the point today that few firms feel restricted by a lack of efficient inexpensive transportation or communication.

One economist of the 1930s worried that large corporations would stifle competition and innovation—that capitalism would fail as corporations became larger and larger and prevented needed changes before entrepreneurial marketers were able to bring them to market. We now know these fears to be unfounded. We can now see large corporations self-destructing under the weight of their dis-economies of scale, or being destroyed by smaller businesses better able to serve the niche markets that make up the "mass market" that had been the source of the large firms' existence. Advances in transportation and communication served to make the large corporation possible, but they also give great economies to the small business.

The widespread global adoption of the Internet, networked communications and wireless channels has also benefited the small business owner. Small businesses can now reach far-flung markets via low-cost communication channels and deliver their products via improved international carriers and channels. Large companies no longer have an advantage over small businesses in marketing communications. No longer are small companies at a disadvantage, because small companies can use the Internet affordably to have the same presence in the market space. Entrepreneurial marketers are able to develop and implement successful marketing strategies, even at a small business that may be resource challenged, by using innovations like the Internet. These types of innovations enable entrepreneurial marketers at even the smallest of businesses to "chase-down" their prolific ideas and insights so that they may be implemented.

Selected Significant Events in Entrepreneurial Marketing

We can further understand the entrepreneurial marketer mindset, at a small to large sized business, by looking at some of the historic events and trends that shaped the evolution of entrepreneurial marketing.

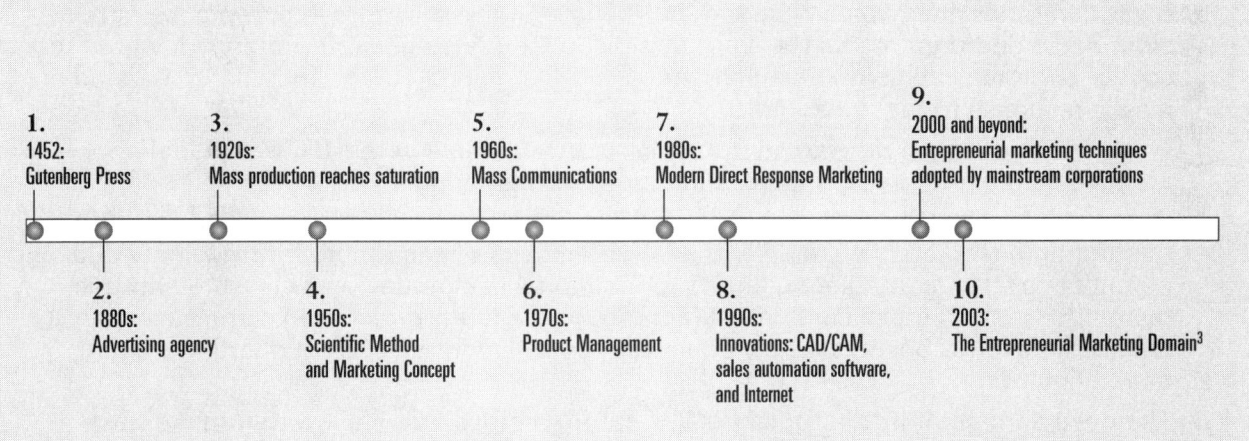

1. 1452: Gutenberg Press
2. 1880s: Advertising agency
3. 1920s: Mass production reaches saturation
4. 1950s: Scientific Method and Marketing Concept
5. 1960s: Mass Communications
6. 1970s: Product Management
7. 1980s: Modern Direct Response Marketing
8. 1990s: Innovations: CAD/CAM, sales automation software, and Internet
9. 2000 and beyond: Entrepreneurial marketing techniques adopted by mainstream corporations
10. 2003: The Entrepreneurial Marketing Domain[3]

Elaboration on Significant Events in Entrepreneurial Marketing

1. Gutenberg Press—Peter F. Drucker in *Management Challenges for the 21st Century* states, "Printing's greatest impact, however, was on the core of pre-Gutenberg Europe: the church. Printing made the Protestant Reformation possible."[4] The Gutenberg press was adopted by many and allowed for the rapid and broad distribution of Luther's list of grievances. Craftsmen would employ broadsheets for the next few centuries as a means of promoting their goods and crafts; however, without large-scale production, the power of print was underutilized.

2. Advertising agencies developed as an offshoot of newspapers giving the 15% industry standard discounts to advertisers that produced and brought in their own advertisements instead of relying upon the advertising service normally provided by the newspaper. This was the first step in moving promotion and advertising away from production and sales activities within a company and advertising agency.

(continues)

---

[3] The Entrepreneurial Marketing Domain is coined by Molly Lavik and Bruce Buskirk, June 5, 2002.

[4] Peter F. Drucker, *Management Challenges for the 21st Century*, (HarperBusiness, a division of HarperCollins Publishers, Inc., New York, 1999), p. 105.

3. In the late 1920s, industrial inventories started to increase. The traditional method of lowering inventory was to lower price; however, at this point many markets had become saturated, and price reductions failed to lower inventories. Overseas dumping was attempted, but led only to trade tariff wars. Market saturation is one way to account for the great worldwide depression of the thirties. Power in the business world shifted at this point from those with the ability to produce goods to those who had the ability to market those goods.

4. The Marketing Concept targeted customers' needs as the source for the development of new products, along with all other aspects of marketing. Marketers attempted to apply the Scientific Method to the area of social research in marketing. The Scientific Method brought social research techniques of psychology, sociology, and social anthropology and combined them with advances in statistics to create the field of consumer behavior and advanced marketing research that was needed to drive the Marketing Concept. These techniques became the basis for an increasing number of marketing campaigns.

5. Mass communications blossomed in the 1960s with the widespread acceptance of television. Radio and print media were not diminished, but also grew. Technology lowered the cost of communication in almost all areas, and the market consistently demonstrated an elastic response to the lower prices.

6. Product management, having started at Procter & Gamble in the 1960s, is widely adopted as the preferred organizational form for marketing.

7. Direct response marketing was made possible by advances in computer technology. For the first time marketers were able to analyze millions of customers for their individual potential, tailor their marketing efforts to individual customers, and measure and track the response from those customers. More importantly for direct marketers' success, they could show a positive return on investment (ROI) in the current quarter to upper management.

8. The development of the laptop and sales automation software allowed firms to push the technology developed in direct marketing to field salespeople. Salespeople became more efficient in reaching their target market, and were able to better tailor their marketing efforts because they had better information about their customers. CAD/CAM (Computer Aided Design/Computer Aided Marketing) systems further allowed for efficient and timely tailoring of products when needed. The plethora of goods and services whose marketing efforts seek our attention has expanded to the point where media are saturated. Media price increases did not discourage growth and demand for advertising space. People increasingly are avoiding and/or ignoring marketing communications because they have reached the limits of their daily ability to take in marketing messages. Consumers have turned to the Internet as a means of obtaining desired market information as needed. Cost effectiveness of mass advertising has begun to fall. The Internet yielded a gold-rush mentality that led to the demise of many entrepreneurial marketers. Still, there are survivors.

9. Corporations are currently shifting from a reliance on mass advertising and mass distribution to more cost-effective means of promotion and distribution. This feat is accomplished through developing entrepreneurial-spirited people as company team members. The innovative corporate culture that emerged during the dot-com boom of the late 1990s didn't disappear with the bust of the dot-com industry. Instead, mainstream corporations adopted it. This evolution in culture gives corporations an infusion of creative and visionary people. Entrepreneurial marketing is now the corporate standard.

(continues)

10. The collective body of evolving knowledge at the intersection of the entrepreneurship discipline and the marketing discipline is distilled into a concise, uniformly understandable body of knowledge that is identified as the Entrepreneurial Marketing Domain. Recognizing this working body of knowledge leads to business pioneers having the opportunity to create profitable ventures in today's depressed economic environment.

We encourage you to consider the historic perspective of entrepreneurial marketing and the evolution of this domain as you read this book and chase your own ideas and insights.

MINI MODULE ON ASSESSING MARKET OPPORTUNITY

BY MOLLY LAVIK

Discovery of market opportunity launches entrepreneurial marketer.

As I look out onto the horizon I sense a market opportunity in the management of new and established businesses. This new market opportunity has to do with a subtle shift in the role and importance of the marketing function within an organization. Today's management structure places great importance on the financial and operational processes of businesses. In the not so distant future, I predict a world where the entrepreneurial marketing function will take center stage. I predict a world in which the entrepreneurial marketer will be the driving force behind a new venture really "taking off" with a sustainable business model. The day is dawning when the entrepreneurial marketer, and the ingenuity and expertise this type of person possesses, will be indispensable to an organization.

Have I accurately assessed the market opportunity for the future role of entrepreneurial marketers? Only time will tell. I believe that gauging market opportunity is a skill that can be developed. I've dedicated this Mini Module to sharing with you some ideas on how to strengthen your ability to assess market opportunity so that you can make your new venture soar.

Lifting Off:
Identifying Emerging Market Trends

New ventures develop often when emerging trends in the marketplace create new niches. Recognizing these trends and understanding their implications is perhaps the hardest part of being a successful entrepreneurial marketer. You can learn how to recognize emerging trends. Here are some things you can do to enhance your trend-emergence recognition skills.

Recognizing Emerging Trends

1. Follow the Futurist: Faith Popcorn and Alvin Toffler are two futurists whose predictions and recognition of emerging trends have been

closely followed. Futurists' predictions are often based on exhaustive research.

2. Stay Abreast of Current Events: Following the media's coverage of current events is one of the best ways to recognize the shift in people's behaviors as well as public opinions.

3. Look for New Painkillers: Stay on constant alert for items that are causing people pain. The greater the pain, the more money someone will pay for a painkiller.

4. Dream: As children we were discouraged from daydreaming in class. However, taking time out during the day to let your mind wander through possibilities and scenarios is a way to discover an emerging trend. Practice dreaming by letting your imagination go and allowing the mind to form free associations.

5. Be a Voracious Reader: The greater variety of books and literature you read, the more likely you are to come across some material that may give you the insight to predict a new trend. Entrepreneurial marketers are often known for their voracious appetite for reading.

6. Sit in on Panels: Trade shows and networking events are two places where you can readily find panel discussions. Panel topics tend to be fresh and free flowing. Often there are fragments of new ideas shared during these lively discussions. The more of these types of events you attend, the greater your chances are of finding an emerging trend.

7. Stay in Tune with Children: Children are fortunate that they aren't shackled by the same cultural blinders and selective perception as adults. Spending time with young children can sometimes be enlightening when you are trying to recognize new trends.

8. Watch TV: New programming in television, especially networks like HBO, can expose you to evolving behaviors of your potential customers.

9. Follow the Music: Listen to the lyrics of new songs. Musicians often sing about trends before the rest of us realize they are emerging. Changes in the style of newly released music can be an indication of a new trend.

10. Don't Just Laugh at the Jokes: Follow the jokes and the meaning behind the jokes that comedians perform. The characteristics of popular satire sometimes provide insight into public opinion before a trend actually emerges.

11. Follow Fashion: New fashion lines can sometimes be an indication of an emerging trend or the resurgence of a previous trend.

12. The Mood of the Nation: A shift in the emotions and moods of a country can be a precursor to the emergence of a new trend.

13. Meditate: Give your mind a break from the constant chatter and dialogue of your inner voice. When you clear your mind, a revelation for an emerging trend may just "bubble up" to your consciousness.

14. Travel to the Ends of the Earth: There is no substitute for traveling as a great way for getting introduced to emerging trends. Trends can start in a different part of the globe and move to other regions.

15. Review Old Trends: The old saying "history repeats itself" may be a cliché but it is also true. Be nostalgic. You just may rediscover something.

16. Rely on Intuition: Some refer to this as "trusting your gut reaction." Sometimes a new trend can be spotted not because of anything concrete but because of a feeling you have about an opportunity.

17. Be in Touch with Students' Areas of Research: Students are engaged in the pursuit of knowledge on a wide variety of topics. Understanding which topics are of utmost interest to students can point to a new trend.

There are countless books, articles, symposiums, and a variety of other outlets for learning more about market trends. In this book we expose you to people who have been successful with repeatedly identifying new trends. We encourage you to keep your antenna finely tuned toward the emergence of new trends.

Gaining Altitude: Assessing Market Opportunity

How can you ultimately learn to effectively access market opportunity? How did Levi Strauss know that the most lucrative "gold" in the hills was in the rivets of jeans and not the mountainside? How does one accurately predict that people will want to purchase, for a profit, a product or service? The truth is no one can always predict accurately; there is no crystal ball. You can study those who have done it and learn from them. You can learn when to factor market opportunity assessment into the start-up process. Having studied successful entrepreneurial marketers for many years, I have identified certain actions that may help you to succeed in assessing market opportunity.

Helpful Hints for Assessing Market Opportunity

- Be on the lookout for emerging trends
- Conduct extensive research to confirm the existence of a market
- Stay focused
- Allot time (before you do other work) to determine if there is a market
- Be open and flexible about your market opportunity findings
- Continuously assess the sustained existence of the market opportunity
- Don't confuse a market opportunity with a passing fad
- Trust your intuition as a tool for assessing market opportunity

- Conduct as much of the market opportunity assessment as possible yourself
- Make sure the market opportunity you discover is large enough to sustain your new venture or expanded enterprise
- Have the courage to recognize when a market opportunity is not there
- Think outside the box

When to Access Market Opportunity

A good slogan to remember when accessing market opportunity is: "Do Not Pass GO Until . . ." This means that the entrepreneurial marketer should not enter seriously into any venture until she has thoroughly researched the market opportunity. Otherwise, she risks discovering the business model is not sustainable too late to do anything about it—a painful and often financially devastating discovery. Here are questions to answer before accessing market opportunity:

Is there a customer for this product or service? Is there someone who will buy the product or service you're considering selling? You can't effectively answer this question until you have personally spoken to the potential customer and ascertained that this person will buy your product. You need to know as much about this customer as the customer knows about himself: What are the demographics of this customer? What influences his buying behavior? What factors could lead to this customer changing his mind about buying the product or services? What will be the impact of a crisis during an emerging trend?

What will it cost to make a sale to this customer? If there is a common pitfall for entrepreneurial marketers, it's greatly underestimating the cost to acquire and repeatedly sell to a customer. The entrepreneurial marketer must account for every last penny it will take to make the sale. Commonly missed expenses include: staff time, travel and related expenses, overhead for office, payroll taxes, social security employer matching expenses, unemployment payroll related expenses, marketing expenses, and the overall amount of time it takes to make a sale.

Is my timing right for this market opportunity? You will have a brief window of opportunity to launch your new venture or expansion of an existing enterprise. Misjudging your timing is often the difference between success and failure with assessing market opportunity. If you are too early, you have the right product or service but your market is not ready for it yet. If you are too late, giant competitors may have acquired a loyal following, blocking new entries to the market.

Can I sell this product or service for a profit? Even if you have an existing customer, and have accurately estimated what it will cost you to acquire that customer, you might not have a sustainable business model until revenues outweigh the expenses. If you cannot reach this point without the aid of a venture capitalist, then we suggest not entering the business. That's because if you enlist the aid of a VC, their assistance comes not only with an investment but also with strings attached. Historically, new businesses that are venture funded are asked to greatly accelerate their growth rate. This causes the new entity to make cash and resource expenditures at a pace that doesn't always allow for the new business to grow through incremental profits. The new venture becomes highly leveraged financially. All it takes then is one bad turn in the economy to make the new business fail. You need to find the incremental steps you can take to get to profitability. This is not easy. Again, there is no road map, but remember that patience is needed to reach profitability. Be open and flexible and recognize that along the way to profitability you might stumble on to a product or service that is in higher demand than the original concept.

When Do I Give Up On My Product Or Service?

In the characteristics of an entrepreneurial marketer perseverance was listed. There is a point, however, where you need to "pull the plug" and refocus your energies. You know you have reached this point when:

- You have run out of resources and can't further leverage any of the methods suggested in this book
- The customers who said they would buy your product during your research phase are no longer interested
- You can't effectively market to your customer
- It costs you more than you make to sell your product or service

During market opportunity assessment, there are times when the entrepreneurial marketer needs to "hit the brakes" and stop. Not stopping fast enough can lead to a failed business and/or bankruptcy. There are also times when an entrepreneurial marketer should "step on the accelerator" and drive on to new market opportunity territories. Knowing when to stop and go in your new venture market opportunity assessment isn't easy.

To help you decide when to move forward with and when to forego an opportunity, please see the Stop and Go Signs for Assessing Market Opportunity Matrix.

It's common for an entrepreneurial marketer to get caught up in what seems like a great idea or business concept. This matrix is a concise, easy to reference and somewhat simplistic way to make decisions on judging market opportunity. This matrix suggests four major causes for a new venture to not find a profitable market opportunity. Recognizing when you are on the verge of going through a Stop Sign without braking is critical. You can refer back to these stop signs in this matrix as constant reminders of when to turn your market opportunity strategy in another direction. If you encounter any of the four Go Signs when you are assessing market opportunity, don't take time out to pat yourself on the back. This is because if you look over your shoulder you may see someone else realizing what you have discovered. Keep "driving on" if you are encountering all Go Signs.

Stop and Go Signs for Assessing Market Opportunity Matrix

No Customers for the Product	Customers' Purchase Motivations Unknown	Unprofitable Sales of the Product	Resources Running Out
STOP	STOP	STOP	STOP
Trends Indicate Emerging Market Opportunity	Timing Right to Attract Customers for the Product	Total Costs for Selling the Product Known	Sales to Customers Yield Sustainable Profitable Results
GO	GO	GO	GO

Soaring Ahead: Successfully Assessing Market Opportunity Existence

It may take a few heart-felt failures, but if you practice and follow the suggestions offered in this Mini Module, you can increase your chances of successfully assessing market opportunity. Remember, your goal is to successfully assess market opportunity repeatedly through the life of your business. You should also have the courage to recognize when your concept does not merit potential market opportunity. There is often as much to be saved by realizing a market does not exist as there is to be gained by finding that one does. As an entrepreneurial marketer, you can play a significant role in helping your new venture "soar to greater heights" by knowing how to assess market opportunity.

ABOUT THE AUTHORS

Bruce Buskirk holds a B.S. degree in marketing from the University of Southern California, a M.S. degree in marketing from Louisiana State University, and a Ph.D. in marketing from Michigan State University. His areas of interest include entrepreneurship, high-tech marketing, and international marketing among many other areas. Bruce developed his interest and vocation in entrepreneurship from his father, the late Richard H. Buskirk, who for many years directed the Entrepreneurship Program at the University of Southern California. He has authored three textbooks: *Retailing* and *Selling* with McGraw Hill Book Co. (both co-authored with his father) and *Readings and Cases in Direct Marketing* with the National Textbook Company. Recently he has been president of the Southern California Chapter of the American Marketing Association, and chair of the Department of Marketing, Economics, and Quantitative Methods at the Graziadio School of Business and Management at Pepperdine University. He is an active consultant and expert witness. He currently lives in Newport Beach, California, with his wife, Sherry, three children and two dogs.

Molly Lavik received her bachelor's degree in Mass Communications from Purdue University and a Master of Science degree in Technology Management from Pepperdine University's Graziadio School of Business and Management. Molly pioneered the creation of the Marketing New Ventures MBA course curriculum at Pepperdine University's Graziadio School where she is an adjunct professor teaching marketing and entrepreneurship related courses. She is a self-professed serial entrepreneur who creates business ventures centered around helping founders achieve their entrepreneurial dreams. Her most recent venture, Mentorography™, develops educational solutions that utilize real-life lessons of leaders to provide powerful learning options. Visit **http://www.mentorography.com** for more information. Molly resides in Redondo Beach, California, with her husband, Hans, and cat, Bandit.

STRATEGY MENTOR MODULE

Formulating Killer Strategies for Your Business

CHRISTOS M. COTSAKOS, PH.D.,
Former Chairman and CEO, E*TRADE Financial

Mentorography Part I

What does it take to formulate killer strategies for your start-up? Christos M. Cotsakos, former chairman and CEO of E*TRADE Financial knows. E*TRADE brings together a personalized and fully integrated financial services solution that includes investing, banking, lending, planning, and advice. Delivered in a multi–touch point platform, the products, services, content, and information at E*TRADE Financial are available to customer households through E*TRADE Financial Centers, Zones, ATMs, and branded Web sites throughout the world. Securities products and services are offered by E*TRADE Securities LLC (member NASD/SIPC), bank products and services are offered by E*TRADE Bank (member FDIC), mortgages are offered by E*TRADE Mortgage Corp., and E*TRADE Financial Advisor is a service of E*TRADE Advisory Services, Inc., an investment adviser registered with the SEC. In 2001, E*TRADE's revenues were $1.3 billion with four million active customer accounts whose assets/deposits totaled $53 billion. E*TRADE Bank is the 11th largest insured U.S. Savings Bank, with the second largest ATM Network. E*TRADE has 3,500 associates in 12 countries. E*TRADE is an emerging company that has managed to be profitable during some very challenging times. Today, the company is recognized as a global leader and innovator in the personal financial services industry.

A study of the recent leader of E*TRADE, Dr. Christos Cotsakos, provides valuable Mentor Insights into the key underpinnings you need to formulate killer strategies for your start-up. In this module we will explore the Mentor Insights that Christos and the E*TRADE leadership team utilized in formulating these strategies.

Mentor Insights

- Feature storytelling
- Practice continuous obsolescence
- Fail fast and often
- Utilize innovation and imagination
- Surround yourself with the best people
- Be willing to put everything on the line for what you believe in
- Play your game, not someone else's
- Diversify your portfolio
- Direct resources toward brand and technology
- Instill credibility with the customer

In the Beginning

Let's begin by exploring the early years of Christos' life so that we can shed light on the origins of his tactical and strategic brilliance. This is the story of Christos M. Cotsakos and the entrepreneurial mindset of a great leader.

Christos is the fourth of five children born to Greek immigrant parents. Children of Greek descent are born into a heritage of storytellers. Christos will draw upon this heritage to feature storytelling in E*TRADE's marketing campaigns and business practices.

His dad was a short-order cook in the days when short-order cooks were both cook and bottle-washer. Christos credits his feelings about obsolescence to his father's strong feelings about not having anyone in his family go into the restaurant business.

This had a profound impact on Christos. He realized that there was a time for ending business processes. Christos' dad had a sixth-grade education but offset his lack of education by being well read. Christos credits his father, a gambler, for his street smarts. His father provided an early role model for what would become Christos' risk-loving personality. This risk-taking personality would eventually empower Christos to fail fast and often, and to inspire others to do likewise.

Mentor Insights

Feature storytelling

Practice continuous obsolescence

Fail fast and often

Christos M. Cotsakos Milestones

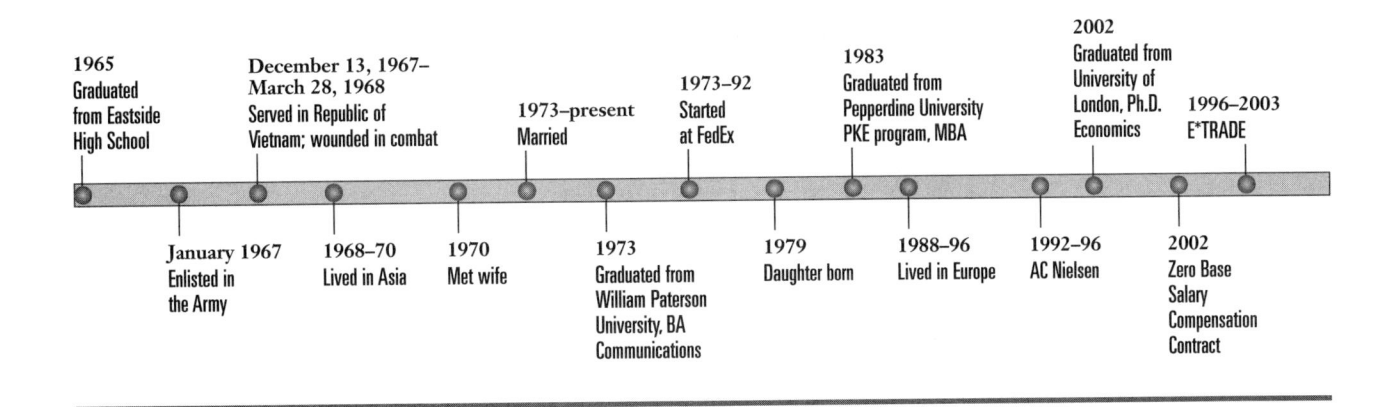

1965 Graduated from Eastside High School

January 1967 Enlisted in the Army

December 13, 1967–March 28, 1968 Served in Republic of Vietnam; wounded in combat

1968–70 Lived in Asia

1970 Met wife

1973–present Married

1973 Graduated from William Paterson University, BA Communications

1973–92 Started at FedEx

1979 Daughter born

1983 Graduated from Pepperdine University PKE program, MBA

1988–96 Lived in Europe

1992–96 AC Nielsen

2002 Graduated from University of London, Ph.D. Economics

2002 Zero Base Salary Compensation Contract

1996–2003 E*TRADE

Putting It on the Line

Growing up in blue-collar New Jersey, Christos learned at an early age the importance of a high risk leading to a high reward. Christos' family had little money to spare. When Christos was born, he was colicky and required an extended hospital stay. To raise the $800 needed to pay the hospital bill, Christos' father played a series of card games around town, winning $900—more than he had won before or has since. He paid the $800 bill and gave the extra $100 to Christos' mother.

Restlessness characterized Christos' childhood. Nothing seemed to hold his attention. He was a disruptive student. Restlessness even impacted his sleeping habits; he never slept more than four or five hours a night. In high school, Christos failed Spanish and was sent to summer school, where his teacher made him a special offer: If Christos didn't disrupt the classroom, the teacher would pass him even though he hadn't learned Spanish.

Life wasn't easy. Christos worked at night in an assortment of jobs, and was always cooking up ideas. He recalls one fondly: He saw an advertisement in a comic book for greeting-card sales. The company sends you, in advance, the greeting cards to sell with the understanding that, once you sell them, you will send in the money. You kept 25¢ for every box of cards sold. Christos set up a neighborhood distribution network with his friends to extend his sales capability, while sharing the profits based on performance. Christos learned early about the power of teamwork, distribution networks, and incentives.

Christos attended Eastside High School in Paterson, New Jersey. He acted up, cut classes, asked a lot of questions, and eventually learned what it is like to be thrown out of class—he almost failed to graduate.

Heroes

Christos found his mentors and heroes in biographical TV movies, and wherever leadership and strategy were exhibited. One hero was General George Patton, as were other military leaders. Christos was also fascinated by Alfred Hitchcock movies, particularly their storytelling nature. Christos' heroes also included his father, his sergeant in Vietnam, his local parish priest, the dean who helped him get into business school, and

Formulating Killer Strategies for Your Business **Module 1**

Frederick W. Smith, Chairman and CEO of FedEx. Christos would learn from what Fred did as well as from what he did not do.

Enlisting in the Army

Christos had always admired the discipline, patriotism, ceremony, parades, and comradeship of the military and recalls his fondness for the values of the military (duty, honor, country, family, community). He decided to enlist when the United States became involved in the Vietnam War. His goal was to fly jets for the Air Force. Christos recalls his enlistment:

> In those days you would go to the post office to join the military. All the military recruiters were located in a row. My goal was to join the Air Force so that I could fly jets. I walked into the post office and met with the Air Force recruiter and he asked me three questions:
>
> Do you have a college degree? Do you have a high school degree? Do you have any references? I answered, "No," "Barely," and "No." That's how I found out I couldn't fly jets—because I didn't have a college degree.
>
> I went to the Navy recruiter next. The Navy, I thought, has those aircraft carriers so if I can't fly a jet for the Air Force, maybe I can fly a jet for the Navy. So I went to enlist in the Navy. I had the exact same experience with the Navy recruiter.
>
> I went to the Marines recruiter next, but he wasn't there. He was literally out to lunch.
>
> At the end of the post office hallway stood the Army recruiter, waving to me to "come on down." By this time, I had realized jets were out but I thought maybe I could convince the recruiter to let me fly helicopters. I told him I wanted to fly helicopters but I didn't have a college education. The Army recruiter said, "Sure, you can fly helicopters for us."
>
> And that is how I ended up enlisting in the Army and subsequently going to Vietnam.[1]
>
> – Christos M. Cotsakos

In the Army

Originally Christos thought he was going to school to learn to fly helicopters. This was not the case. Christos was placed in the signal corps with the 82nd Airborne division as a cryptographer. He found encryption fascinating and began taking classes in that subject. In December of 1967, Christos went into combat as a rifleman with the 101st Airborne division in Vietnam. Christos was transferred into the 101st Airborne because of the great need in Vietnam. A large percentage of his unit was wounded or killed during Christos' time in daily combat.

Dream Wounds

Mentor Insight
Utilize innovation and imagination

Christos realized that visualizing his dream wound proved how far your imagination can take you if you let it. In later years he would expand his recognition of the power of imagination to include innovation. Christos and his friend were wounded at about the same time in the Ashau Valley, when Christos had been in combat for 106 days. No one would ever know for sure if they were wounded by enemy or friendly fire.

> *While in the dregs of fighting in combat in Vietnam, a friend and I talked about what we would do if we were shot. We agreed if we were mortally wounded or before we were captured that we would kill each other rather than live that way. We also discussed what our "dream wounds" would be. That is what type of wound—if we had to be wounded—the wound would be. For my friend, the dream wound was being shot in the fleshy part of the midsection. He thought this was a good place to be shot: safe and you would have an OK scar. However, I thought this would not be my dream wound because if the bullet went in it could bounce around and hit a vital organ. For me the dream wound would be the upper thigh because a bullet could enter the thigh, an area that had a lot of fleshiness and would cause the least damage. The primary dream, however, was to not get shot or captured and to survive with your team.[2]*
>
> – Christos M. Cotsakos

Remarkably, both Christos and his friend received their dream wounds. Christos was awarded the Bronze Star with V for Valor, the Army Commendation Medal with V for Valor, the Purple Heart for wounds received in combat, the Air Medal, the Combat Infantryman's Badge, and Parachute Wings as well as other ribbons and citations. In Vietnam, he was promoted to sergeant and led an infantry fire team and squad with the 101st Airborne Division. He was discharged honorably in January 1970.

Lessons Learned in Vietnam

Christos' philosophy about the importance of who is around you in the foxhole was the origin of his understanding of the need to formulate a strong leadership team. The lessons that Christos learned in Vietnam are:

- Skill level is important.
- Never leave your wounded or your dead.
- Be zealous about life.
- People are family but that isn't necessarily the same as loyalty and trust.
- Act fast and smart—everything can be gone in a moment.
- Don't do anything halfway.
- People and personalization are critical to getting things done.
- Be prepared to die for what you believe in: physically, spiritually, or economically.

Getting into College

Entering college was no ordinary event for Christos.

Mentor Insight
Surround yourself with the best people

> *What matters most is who you have in the foxhole with you when they yell . . . incoming![3]*
>
> – Christos M. Cotsakos

Mentor Insight
Be willing to put everything on the line for what you believe in

> As a decorated veteran and an infantry squad leader from the Republic of Vietnam, I didn't have the grades or typical background out of high school to qualify for going to college. I eventually was accepted to college in part through a favor from my brother. My brother worked on the campaign for the mayor of Paterson, New Jersey, and asked the mayor if he could help me get into a state school. The mayor set up an interview for me with an associate admissions dean [at William Paterson University] who reviewed transcripts. However, the Mayor made it clear that this would not necessarily get me accepted. The meeting with the associate admissions dean lasted for four hours. The dean decided to take a chance on me based solely on the stories I told him and what I had learned in life; however, he made it clear to me that if there were any problems, I was out.[4]
>
> – Christos M. Cotsakos

Mentor Insight

Play your game, not someone else's

Christos' unorthodox method for getting accepted to college would leave an indelible mark on his psyche and reinforce the importance of changing the game to accomplish your goals.

Years later Christos would remember the admission's opportunity that was extended to him by William Paterson University when he and his wife would make a substantial donation to the University.

> It's a young program that's really aimed at middle-class America . . . Here's an opportunity to benefit a lot of individuals that are just like me, with working class parents.[5]
>
> – Christos M. Cotsakos

Career Background

After joining the company in 1973, Christos worked at Federal Express for 18 years and eventually became part of the senior leadership team. Christos was restless at FedEx and, although he loved the company and admired the chairman, he wanted to strike out and follow his own dream. Christos wanted to understand consumer behavior and media better. He believed this combination would be a mega force shaping tomorrow's business. Christos was being recruited by several companies; he decided to join AC Nielsen, a Dun & Bradstreet company. At AC Nielsen, Christos shared the position of CEO with a colleague who was also chairman of the company and, therefore, had one more "stripe" than Christos. Christos says he will "never" work in a similar situation. Four years after Christos joined the company, the last straw came when Christos' co-CEO expanded the executive offices despite Christos' opposition. Christos had been telecommuting from Europe and he and his partner didn't agree over where he was to be located. While his co-CEO was fixated on building out the corporate office (one of many issues they clashed on), Christos had been focused on ways to transform the company and position it for the future.

Christos chose to take a break for a while. Tami accurately predicted the break wouldn't last very long. Two weeks later, Christos was being recruited for several positions.

One executive search firm introduced Christos to Bill Porter, the founder of E*TRADE. Christos recalls that initially he wasn't really interested; he was looking to run something bigger. When Christos told some of his friends that he was talking to Bill Porter about an opportunity with E*TRADE, his friends told him he must be crazy.

The first meeting Christos had with Bill Porter was a breakfast where they exchanged ideas about the industry. Christos discovered that he and Bill had "double vision"—different but complementary views on how to build this business. Breakfast ran to several hours.

Meanwhile another recruiter had called Christos to assure him that he would be in touch shortly to formalize an agreement on an offer with another company.

At Bill Porter's suggestion, Christos met some of the employees of E*TRADE. As Christos recalls, "Bill was very insightful, and meeting with the associates got me in the foxhole with them." Christos looked at the company's front- and back-office operations and reviewed their business model and marketing plans. He liked a lot of what he saw about the company: The team was young, energetic, and made up of some very good people.

Christos then met several board members—"smart businessmen, good chemistry," he thought. The other recruiter called again and Christos said that he would call back shortly.

That week, Bill Porter asked Christos to run E*TRADE and told him he could run the company the way he wanted to run the company. Christos called the other recruiter and told him, "A funny thing happened on the way to a start-up." The recruiter responded, "Are you crazy?"

Christos was not crazy. He was simply playing his game and not someone else's while putting everything on the line (his credibility and career) for what he now believed in—E*TRADE.

Christos and Bill focused their discussions on how to build E*TRADE into a trusted brand and new-age company. Christos started working for E*TRADE immediately. Christos recalls that Bill was a serial entrepreneur and an excellent founder. Christos' first priority was to raise additional capital for the company in order to solidify its balance sheet and net capital before it went public.

Mentor Insights

Play your game, not someone else's

Be willing to put everything on the line for what you believe in

Early Days for Christos at E*TRADE

In those early days at E*TRADE, when the stock went below its cash value, the company could easily have been purchased by someone else. Christos recalls the company being "circled by vultures"—investors and companies that were potentially interested in purchasing E*TRADE. Christos believes that had E*TRADE been purchased in the very early days it would have become part of someone else's culture, which would have killed the Esprit de Coeur and eventually the business.

> *When I started at E*TRADE I quickly realized we only had several days in which to raise $10 million. Never in my life had so many people said no so quickly, so many times. I finally got some others to put in a couple million dollars by telling them I would put in almost $1 million of my own money. On the last day that I had left to raise the money, I met with SoftBank. I got the meeting with a senior executive by calling him up and saying he needed to have breakfast with me because I had an investment opportunity that he couldn't pass up and time was critical! At the end of our breakfast I asked him if he had the authority to commit $10 million on the spot. He said nobody had ever asked him that before, we shook hands, no paperwork, and the deal was done. That is when I relearned that life is about trust, integrity, and honor.*
>
> *We cut the deal, which included going public at an estimated price of $12 to $14 a share. At the time, we believed E*TRADE's shares would price on or about the midpoint. The market turned cold, and our stock ended up being priced at $10.50 for the IPO. I had to go back to SoftBank and say, "I know this is below your recent investment, but look: If in six months you don't feel you are getting your money's worth, I will personally return the investment with interest."*
>
> *This was another lesson about trust and building a long-term business relationship.*
>
> *Eventually SoftBank and I would do another private transaction, this time for $400 million. I also added a caveat that the stock could once again drop below the purchase price but if SoftBank believed in our business model, they should hang in there with us. The stock did take a hit below SoftBank's initial investment and Softbank, because they believed in E*TRADE's leadership and vision, was once again good to its word. We have since formed a great working relationship based on mutual trust and respect.*[6]
>
> – Christos M. Cotsakos

During the height of the bull market, E*TRADE would eventually attain a market capitalization of $13 billion, with the stock splitting twice. Today it's one of a handful of survivors that run a profitable business during one of the worst market downturns in history.

Christos went to work with his team at E*TRADE to build the brand and rebuild its technology platform. He worked on a totally redesigned strategy that would require millions of investment dollars in marketing and technology in order to reposition the company. The new strategy included a planned strategic moratorium on profitability to invest in building and fortifying the brand and reinvesting in the technology infrastructure. At the same time the company enhanced its product offering, expanded globally, and diversified its revenue streams by making strategic inroads in the banking industry. He was not sure he would have the support of all his board members because the cost and the risk were high. Christos was so convinced this was the only way for E*TRADE to survive that if he could not rally the board behind Destination E*TRADE, he told the board he knew he would have to resign. The calculated risk paid off brilliantly for the company.

Strategies to Ensure Long-term Profitability at E*TRADE

> **Mentor Insights**
>
> Diversify your portfolio
>
> Practice continuous obsolescence

Destination E*TRADE was introduced as a new platform at E*TRADE. Initially, the launch of Destination E*TRADE was rocky at best. Christos saw the trends shaping the industry and wanted to stay ahead of the curve; he wanted the vision to be simple in concept but sweeping and revolutionary in practice. Destination E*TRADE marked the beginning of E*TRADE diversifying its products.

Christos was able to re-establish the company's profitability by obsolescing business processes every 90 days. The concept of obsolescence is elaborated further in Part II. He was relentless about what he would accept in work performance at E*TRADE. For example, he implemented a performance leadership program at E*TRADE where the bottom-performing 10 percent of associates were helped to find jobs that better suited them inside or outside of E*TRADE. By implementing this program among others, Christos was able to successfully avoid mass layoffs during the more challenging times.

> *I don't believe in mass layoffs except as a last resort. If it ever came down to me being in that position I would first take a salary cut, then if needed my executive team would take a salary cut. If that still wasn't enough, the staff would take a salary cut. By having a program that continuously helps the lowest 10 percent of staff who are not performing find work elsewhere in conjunction with other performance leadership programs, we have been able to avoid mass layoffs. I have taken zero salary twice in six years.[7]*
>
> *– Christos M. Cotsakos*

Christos passionately claims (usually while accentuated by pounding his fist rhythmically on the table) that you have to be relentless in your pursuit of what you believe in. You have to treat people with respect and dignity. But you also must be honest and up-front with everyone about their performance and fit. You must act quickly but compassionately. Every business competes in a tough and very complex environment. No company, big or small, young or old, is safe if you are inefficient.

> **Mentor Insight**
> Utilize innovation and imagination

At E*TRADE, innovation is inbred, from its technologically advanced product line to its frequent calculated risks. Those who aren't innovators don't last or belong at E*TRADE. Under Christos' leadership, E*TRADE morphed four or five times into different business focuses as an important strategy to stay ahead of the game.

Dramatic Changes at E*TRADE

> **Mentor Insights**
> Diversify your portfolio
>
> Direct resources toward brand and technology

E*TRADE changed dramatically over the years of Christos' leadership. Christos established a multichannel strategy. He diversified the portfolio of products at E*TRADE. A recent innovation is Personalized Digital Financial Media (ETFN=E*TRADE Financial Network), which is the dynamic delivery of interactive, streaming, multimedia financial content and tools. Today, less than one third of E*TRADE's business is online trading. When Christos started in 1996, E*TRADE had fewer than 50,000 active accounts; at the time of his departure in January of 2003 the company had more than 4 million active accounts. The company now has the second largest ATM network, with more than 11,000 E*TRADE ATMs—each of which carries the E*TRADE logo in all its periwinkle-and-green splendor. E*TRADE has a multi–touch point strategy that includes a state-of-the-art online media center in New York City that provides original E*TRADE Financial–branded and third-party financial news and content through dynamic, streaming video and audio, giving E*TRADE an important real-time connection to the markets and the news makers in investing and personal finance. The company has four additional financial centers in Boston, Beverly Hills, Denver, and San Francisco. These financial centers feature sophisticated, high-tech, trading floors for active traders where E*TRADE customers and visitors can access their accounts, work one-on-one with a licensed Relationship Specialist, and gain access to E*TRADE Financial–branded content and financial news programming. The company also has 43 E*TRADE Financial Zones located inside Target stores. And the exciting news about these Zones and ATMs is that E*TRADE can create 15 Zones or install hundreds of ATMs for the price of one traditional bank branch. The Zones leverage a partnership company's distribution network at minimal cost and the ATMs were a cost-effective acquisition that further leveraged E*TRADE's multi–touch point strategy. The additional research and development, touch point resources, and costs were minimized. Cost minimization is an important behavior that is consistently a strategy at E*TRADE. The multi–touch point strategy bolstered shareholder value at E*TRADE and increased the value proposition for the customer. The firm also offers a suite of comprehensive financial investment services.

To help build this robust and diverse product line, E*TRADE has acquired 13 companies for $3 billion. To help assimilate the acquisitions, E*TRADE has an associates team that goes in, listens, looks, explains, and integrates the E*TRADE experience. Christos admitted that it was never easy to integrate acquisitions. Within 120 days, E*TRADE re-brands the acquired company's guiding principles, CARE values (CARE stands for Customer Experience, Accountability, Responsibility, E*nnovation), products, and services. Christos explains the process:

> *The integration is critical. It starts at the negotiating table and it never ends. It is a constant process of bringing out the best in everybody and incorporating it in our combined cultures. Only the best people, processes, and products survive.[8]*
>
> *– Christos M. Cotsakos*

> **Mentor Insight**
>
> Direct resources toward brand and technology

> **Mentor Insight**
>
> Be willing to put everything on the line for what you believe in

Do It with Humor and a Big Bang Approach

Christos pioneered the use of irreverent humor in marketing an investment firm. Memorable campaigns, coupled with a coordinated marketing strategy and a big bang advertising budget, catapulted the E*TRADE brand into being one of the most recognized brands in the world. Christos and his team had accomplished this unprecedented feat in five years while most companies take 30 years to achieve comparable results.

E*TRADE has spent an enormous amount of money building the E*TRADE brand. The E*TRADE board was unsure when Christos initially told them he needed to spend more than 50 percent of expenses on marketing. He told the board he did not know if he could stay if the company did not take advantage of this once-in-a-generation opportunity. The marketing expenditure was the key to the future success of the brand and the overall survivability of the company. As time went on, Christos, during his leadership at E*TRADE, was able to significantly reduce his marketing expenditures once he had instilled the company's trust and credibility in consumers. Initially, he spent a very large amount on advertising, including buying the half-time Super Bowl sponsorship for three consecutive years.

> *The grandest marketing event of all time is the Super Bowl. We have made unique and controversial advertisements for the Super Bowl such as when we used the chimp. E*TRADE is a young company with intellectual honesty that reaches consumers through humor, which is the best way to communicate. One of the most successful advertisements was the chimp ad, especially when we brought the chimp back a second time showing the dot-com implosion. The chimp returns riding a horse through an empty and desolate Dot.comville and at the end sheds a tear spoofing the well-known pollution commercial from the seventies that highlighted an Indian chief's sadness over damage to our environment. This was a poignant ad that once again resonated with the consumer. It was one of our best in a series of provocative ads.[9]*
>
> *– Christos M. Cotsakos*

The following are snapshots from the memorable E*TRADE advertisements that featured the chimp.

©E*TRADE Securities, Inc. Images courtesy of E*TRADE Financial

About-Face

After Christos had done such a fine job in quickly building a household brand name in E*TRADE, he planned to change the brand name. With E*TRADE's diversified portfolio of products, the name E*TRADE no longer truly encompassed the breadth of the company offerings. After all, as of 2001 online trading represented less than one third of products currently offered at E*TRADE. So how is the name going to change? The answer is organically, in much the same way that Federal Express changed to FedEx. The new name is going to evolve from E*TRADE to — ?. The tactics to accomplish this strategy are well under way at E*TRADE. That is, in fact, part of the reason why Christos moved E*TRADE from being traded on the NASDAQ under the symbol EGRP to the New York Stock Exchange under the symbol of ET.

Mentor Insight
Play your game, not someone else's

~~Change Agent?~~ No Way!
He Plays His Own Game, Not Someone Else's

Christos and his leadership team did a lot to make the E*TRADE associates (he does not use the term employees) feel like family and to give them an exciting, challenging performance-based corporate culture to work in. The cubicles are spacious and have a high-tech, high-energy feel to them. The cubicles go a long way toward making the corporate culture horizontally rather than hierarchically structured—Christos' cubicle was no different from anyone else's. There are cappuccino and beverage bars situated throughout the offices. The company cafeteria has a wide variety of menu

> *I'm not, and have never been, a change agent. Instead, I change the rules of engagement. I set new standards. Change agents reengineer the existing structure; I use different rules. It's like the analogy of the bear chasing the alligator. To survive you need to play your own game on your own turf in your own way. You need to play your game and not someone else's.*[10]
>
> *– Christos M. Cotsakos*

items. Christos rarely wears anything other than jeans and he definitely never wears socks or a tie—not even for the ceremony that was held when he took his company from NASDAQ to the NYSE. In fact, Christos and his executives may all be absolutely brilliant and high-flying performers, but they are also all very down to earth and easy to talk with. They are everyday people.

Creating Heroes

At E*TRADE there is a leadership awards process. It's a recognition program that works without getting anyone's sign-off. Anyone at the company can elect someone else via e-mail for a "Bodacious" type award. No witnesses are needed. Christos remembers that when he was in Vietnam there had to be two witnesses to a good deed or for bravery for someone to be qualified for an award. Christos feels that because of this rule many heroic soldiers in Vietnam didn't get decorated. Not so for an E*TRADE Star award. E*TRADE has had as many as 600 Star awards in one month. E*TRADE also has the "Leadership at the Edge" program, which rewards business leaders for exceptional performance and risk taking. The winners receive stock options for themselves as well as stock options and cash awards to give to associates who have helped to make them successful and cash awards to be distributed to charities of their choice.

Associate recognition programs like those offered at E*TRADE recognize and encourage great work performance. E*TRADE's programs, which salute the best, perpetuate Christos' philosophy about surrounding yourself with the best people.

By maintaining a horizontal organization and a positive atmosphere that encourages innovation and imagination, Christos had developed a culture where it is permissible to fail. In fact, Christos evangelized failing often and, above all, failing fast so that you can move on to the next possibility, which may be the winning solution. And Christos himself admits to having had some big failures, including a major system outage during the IPO roadshow as well as a computer glitch that lasted for three successive days and could have shut down the entire system.

In fact Christos has rules of engagement for a crisis:

Tell it fast

Tell it accurately

Tell it all

Swarm

Fix it

Mentor Insights
Surround yourself with the best people
Fail fast and often

Guiding Principles

E*TRADE's strategic matrix is given to every associate. It is a one-page graphic that easily explains what was Christos' vision and direction for the company. The dictum is, if what you are working on does not fit this strategic matrix, "don't do it." E*TRADE's mission statement is also simple: E*TRADE Financial empowers customers to make better-informed, value-added financial decisions. (Love all customers . . . deliver a quality earnings stream . . . do it the E*TRADE Financial way.) At the core of the company's guiding principles are six simple precepts: 1) Living our CARE (Customer experience, Accountability, Responsibility, E*nnovation) Values; 2) Complying with our Code of Professional Conduct (Mentor Method 1.1); 3) Practicing Good Corporate Governance; 4) Empowering and educating customers; 5) Delivering performance leadership; and 6) Creating and unlocking shareowner and stakeholder value.

Mentor Method 1.1

CAT 9 Requirements[11]

Customers	Associates	Time
Service	Spirituality	Security
Simplicity	Sharing	Speed
Savings	Shareowner and Stakeholder Value	Scalability

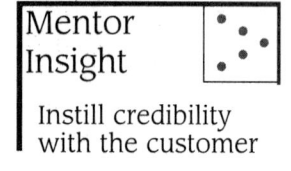

Mentor Insight

Instill credibility with the customer

Christos' and E*TRADE's relentless focus on all customers (internal and external), as illustrated by the CARE values and CAT 9 Requirements, instilled credibility and trust with all of E*TRADE's customers. E*TRADE also has a very strict code of conduct for all associates.

A Great Leader

What does it take to get others to follow your vision at every twist and turn? Christos M. Cotsakos embodies the characteristics of a great leader. He seeks to continuously improve himself. He received an MBA from Pepperdine University's President and Key Executive program as well as a Ph.D. in Economics from the University of London. He spends time working and learning from different groups of people in the private, public, educational, and political sector. Christos believes that to be good at your job, you have to be eclectic in your life and an expert in your profession. Christos has received numerous recognitions and awards from industry and educational institutions. He believes that you have to stay globally connected 24 hours a day, 7 days a week, 365 days a year.

Christos' Right Hand

This chapter would not be complete without mention of Brigitte VanBaelen, Chief Community Development Officer and Corporate Secretary and member of the officer team of E*TRADE. Christos repeatedly states that Brigitte is the glue that keeps his and the leadership team's ideas together. He first met her a decade ago at AC Nielsen. She had come in as a temp to help with the reception desk. Before long, Brigitte was taking on work from six different people. She is fluent in five languages and has a command of two others. As part of her corporate officer responsibility, Brigitte makes herself available seven days a week to accommodate the busy schedule of the leadership team and board of directors. Brigitte is one of those rare individuals you would want to have in the foxhole with you when someone yells, "incoming." Brigitte is just one member of the eclectic and talented E*TRADE leadership team. She has had an unconventional career path; she is a self-starter, self-motivated, self-directed, and performance driven. In other words, like Christos, she is an E*TRADEr.

Mentorography Part II

In this half of the chapter, we will analyze the Mentor Insights of Christos M. Cotsakos that exemplify the key guiding principles you need to formulate your own killer strategies. The Mentor Insights we will continue to expand on are:

Mentor Insights

- Feature storytelling
- Fail fast and often
- Be willing to put everything on the line for what you believe in
- Play your game, not someone else's
- Instill credibility with the customer
- Utilize innovation and imagination
- Direct resources toward brand and technology
- Diversify your portfolio
- Practice continuous obsolescence
- Surround yourself with the best people

The Storyteller

Mentor Insight: Feature storytelling

As a Greek descendant, Christos is part of a culture steeped in a rich storytelling heritage. Christos has translated his love of storytelling into his business processes by making well-told stories the centerpiece of his marketing. For example, E*TRADE advertisements first poked fun at brokers, then bankers, and now mutual fund managers. E*TRADE's advertising agencies, along with the E*TRADE team, created ads that attacked the status quo and showed customers how they could take more control and be more self-directed. Christos and his leadership team had always given consumers credit for being smart, believing that if you respect who they

> *The advertisements all had to have a single voice, a clear message delivered with a sense of humor . . . always being at the edge, but never being over the top. Good advertising respects the consumer, resonates with their changing lifestyles, and establishes a valuable and trusted connection between the company and the customer.[12]*
>
> – Christos M. Cotsakos

are the consumer will get the message. There are four major messages or story lines in E*TRADE's advertising:

1. Boot your broker (or banker or mutual fund manager). This tongue-in-cheek approach of poking fun at the broker was designed to break through the noise and clutter of other advertisements.
2. Someday we will all invest this way. This story is about building the online investing category.
3. E*TRADE is the number one place to invest online.
4. It's your money.

Permission to Fail

Christos had created a corporate culture that not only gave permission to try something and fail but that encouraged and rewarded this type of behavior. In business cultures outside America, failure is often met with disgrace. In entrepreneurial-spirited ventures such as E*TRADE, taking risks that could lead to failure is encouraged. Christos' only caveat is to fail quickly and do not extend the experience any longer than is necessary.

An entrepreneurial marketer often doesn't have the budget or resources to create campaigns that will cut through the clutter into consumers' selective perceptions. Creating advertisements that are cutting-edge and risky takes guts and can meet with great results. Cases in point are the award-winning chimpanzee advertisements that E*TRADE used as their Super Bowl television spots. Risky advertisements can flop, too: One E*TRADE advertisement with a military dictator in the story line never even aired because of the negative social implications of the message. Were the advertising agency and E*TRADE team let go because of this expensive mistake? Absolutely not! In fact, the E*TRADE creative team and advertising agency are intact today, still taking risks and pushing the envelope on advertising campaign development.

E*TRADE would most likely not be enjoying the success it does today without the risk-taking attitude that was developed under Christos' leadership. So what does it take to develop marketing-minded individuals who are risk-taking and can follow Christos' motto to fail fast and often? The following ideas may help to create a risk-taking culture for developing strategies for your entrepreneurial venture.

Helpful Hints for Fostering Fearlessness of Failure in Marketers

- Update your mission statement and vision to include language that encourages risk-taking behavior.
- Have a marketing reward and award program for risk-taking people.
- Promote and/or increase the salary of someone who took a risk and failed and communicate to your staff that he was promoted because he took a risk.

Mentor Insight

Fail fast and often

- Submit press releases to the media on company stories about the failures of your marketing campaigns and how you are proud of people who keep trying and taking risks.
- Engage in open communication regarding the permissibility of failing on risk-taking strategic planning ideas.
- Conduct company brainstorming sessions where cutting-edge ideas are encouraged.
- Create a company wall of fame where failed strategies, advertising, and marketing campaigns are proudly displayed.
- Utilize humor.
- Continuously solicit ideas from your team, stakeholders, and customers on how you can continue to foster risk-taking strategic ideas and marketing campaigns.

Should You Put It on the Line?

> **Mentor Insight**
> Be willing to put everything on the line for what you believe in

Christos M. Cotsakos, Ph.D. was able to propel E*TRADE to unprecedented success by putting everything on the line—including considering leaving the company—for the principles and ideas he believed in. While this technique worked well for Christos, we do advise some caution. Entrepreneurs by their very nature are passionate people. Enthusiasm and passion often play a role when you are crafting killer strategies. Many successful entrepreneurs like Christos repeatedly put it on the line for what they believe. But these people also have a great sense of when to play this card and when not to. Do not bluff. You need to realize that when you put it all on the line there is a possibility that you may be walking away empty-handed. You shouldn't put it all on the line unless you are comfortable with the worst possible scenario. If you were the highest-ranking person at your company with a long-term track record of success like Christos, your chances of success when putting it on the line would have been certainly higher. Learning when to put it on the line and when to bite your tongue is an art that often isn't fully developed in an entrepreneur until she's played a couple of losing hands. There is no doubt, however, that at times you will need this technique to keep your entrepreneurial venture afloat during the darker days. You will certainly have those days, rest assured.

An Alternative to Putting It All on the Line

> **Mentor Insight**
> Play your game, not someone else's

A less risky alternative to putting it all on the line is to play your own game, at which Christos is also a master. Christos established his own game in the financial services industry by not playing the game of the established brick-and-mortar financial services firms. E*TRADE's game is being played online. When you redefine the game you are playing, not only can you define your rules but you can also create a level playing field for your entrepreneurial venture. You can be a master of your own game if you ask yourself these questions when you are trying to create strategies for your venture that will blow your competition out of the water.

1. Is this company going to survive?
2. Can I come up with a solution to this problem by introducing a new way of doing something?
3. What strategies can I develop to position the venture to beat the competition if I change the rules of engagement?

Consumers Want Great Service but Prefer Self-Service to Poor Service

> **Mentor Insight**
> Instill credibility with the customer

> **Mentor Insights**
> Play your game, not someone else's
>
> Utilize innovation and imagination

Whether you are playing your own game or someone else's in business you need to pay close attention to customer service. No entrepreneurial marketing business strategy is complete if it does not offer customer satisfaction. You can increase customer satisfaction by finding ways to improve your credibility with the customer. Good customer service is one of the best ways to do this. Many large companies today are struggling with finding ways to offer good customer service. The rise of the customer relationship management (CRM) industry is one of the byproducts of this struggle. At E*TRADE, Christos recognized early on that the size and scope of his business practices did not always allow the highest quality of customer service during peak usage periods. Christos once again changed the rules of engagement to create financial service products that allowed the customer online access to self-service instead of the remote possibility of poor service. Christos did this by introducing an innovative online investment product.

Product Highlight

A simulation of E*TRADE's online investing product is truly amazing. It allows you to automate your financial well-being in record time. For example, if you have an E*TRADE online account, you can receive messages that alert you the minute your investing goals are off course. This is called a Goal Tracker Alert. Through a chat function, alternative solutions are offered that you can instantly perform to get your investments back in line with your goals. You can also plan trips, buy and sell products, and receive customized advertisements of your choice. You can even become eligible to win exciting prizes. The system is very efficient and super fast.

E*TRADE's online investment product is a milestone in offering personal service to the customer. Not too many years ago, consumers asked a store clerk for each desired item and gas station attendants always filled tanks. The shift to self-service has its roots in a fundamental set of forces. The steady progress of technology joined with innovation to produce an abrupt change in the delivery mode of services and service-dependent products.

Whether it's self-service or administered, good customer service is critical for any venture, since it affects customer satisfaction. Many people view customer satisfaction as a direct function of dollars spent per customer on customer service (see Mentor Method 1.2). This is dangerous thinking because satisfying customers depends on listening to their needs and wishes and exceeding them. It's not about allocating large amounts of resources to build massive organizational structures to service customers. Additionally, it is crucial to recognize the impact of customer dissatisfaction. Many customers discontinue their relationship with a firm because they find one they like better, but those who leave because they are dissatisfied tend to give negative word-of-mouth testimonials for years.

Mentor Method 1.2

Misconception of the Relationship between Customer Service Efforts and Customer Satisfaction[13]

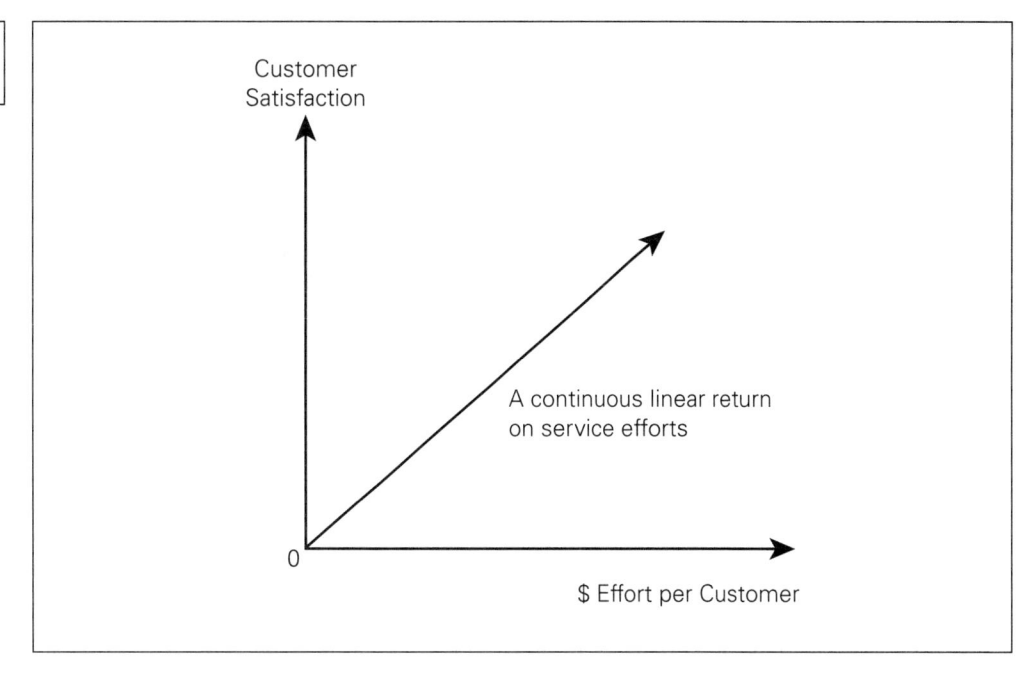

Customer Satisfaction vs. $ Effort per Customer — A continuous linear return on service efforts.

In Mentor Method 1.3 on page 20, one can see the premise "People want great service but prefer self-service to poor service." Great service comprises many components. Some of the major components include anticipating customer needs, providing easy-to-access and efficient communication feedback methods, training and empowering service providers, and exceeding customer expectations. The *S* shape of the customer satisfaction curve gets many firms in trouble. When the firm has a difficult period, and each department is cut by 10 percent, customers may respond with a long-term decline greater than 10 percent.

E*TRADE has continuously instilled credibility with its customer base by offering online investment products and other products that return the power base to the customer. At E*TRADE the customer is in the driver's seat. The financial services customer didn't use to wield this type of power. In fact, years ago, great service for financial service customers was reserved to only the very wealthy. There are some significant lessons to be learned from exploring the historical perspective of the financial industry.

Historic Perspective of the Financial Industry

One can better understand just how significant the financial services offered at E*TRADE are by examining the historic perspective of the financial industry. Banking practices became highly regulated during, and

Mentor Method 1.3

People Prefer Self-Service to Poor Service[14]

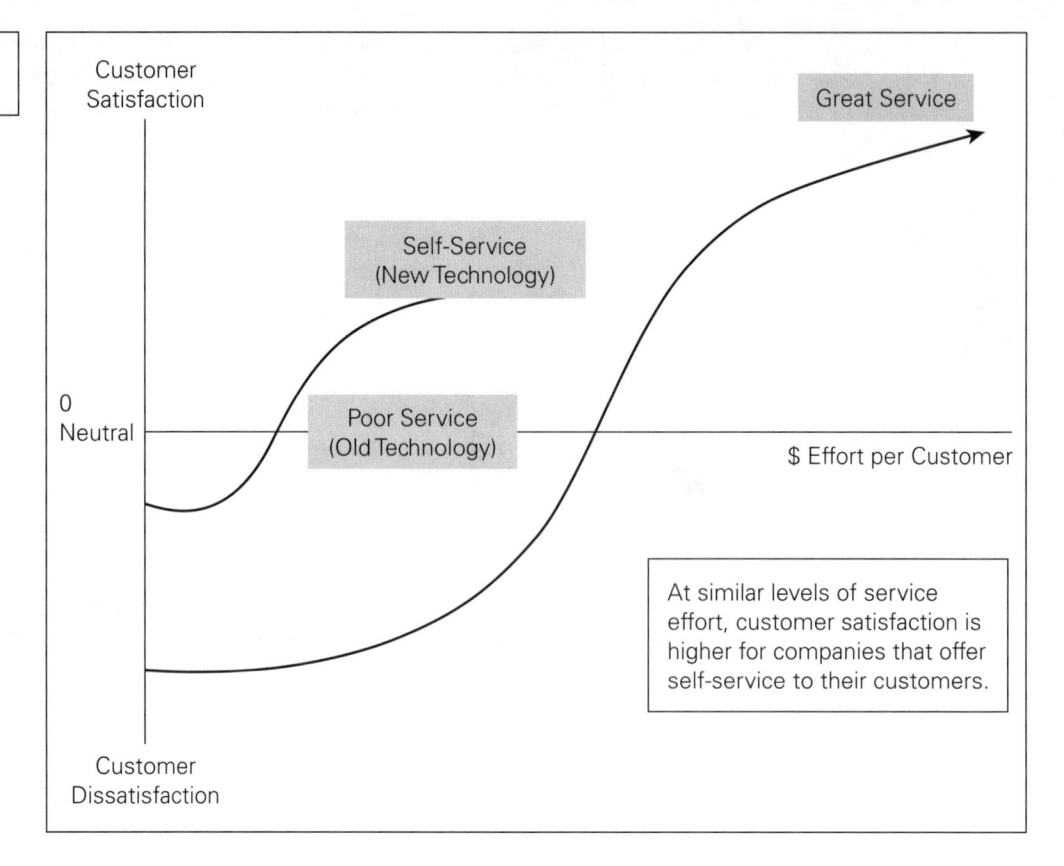

Graph: Customer Satisfaction vs. $ Effort per Customer
- Self-Service (New Technology) curve rises steeply to "Great Service"
- Poor Service (Old Technology) curve remains in Customer Dissatisfaction region
- 0 Neutral axis

At similar levels of service effort, customer satisfaction is higher for companies that offer self-service to their customers.

---

following, the depression of the 'Thirties. Each American town had a First National Bank of wherever that followed the rules and regulations flowing from depression era legislation. Market segmentation was not much of an issue as product offerings were legislated. Bankers attempted to make money primarily through loans and investments, and only secondly did they turn to attracting deposits via superior service. Great service was reserved for those with a great deal of money. Stockbrokers were for the wealthy.

Banks and stockbrokers became competitors during the 'Eighties and 'Nineties, but each profession retained its core strength in traditional services. While both professions realize that their customers want one-stop shopping for all of their financial services, neither has been flexible enough to deliver the global product demanded in the marketplace.

While the traditional "brick and mortar" banking systems have been slow to innovate their business practices, E*TRADE and a handful of other financial services businesses have been reinventing the financial services industry with products like the aforementioned automated online investment product.

What is the major difference between traditional banks and E*TRADE that allows E*TRADE to revolutionize the financial services industry? E*TRADE is willing to expend a significant amount of resources on the technology needed to make changes. In addition, E*TRADE is directing an equally significant amount of resources to raise awareness of the E*TRADE brand.

Mentor Insight

Direct resources toward brand and technology

> **Mentor Insight**
>
> Diversify your portfolio

The Vision

Christos envisioned himself in a sprint, relay, and marathon . . . simultaneously building a one-stop, self-directed financial services platform for the global mainstream consumer that includes securities, banking, mortgages, credit cards, and lines of credit. His plans were to leverage that consumer trust into related businesses, starting with insurance and foreign exchange and on to any business where transaction ease and secure money exchange are important. E*TRADE has a long-term strategy that includes a diversified portfolio of product offerings. Christos was a proponent of minimal bricks and maximum clicks seeing a synergy between the two.

E*TRADE entered the marketplace with a brilliant strategy, as a high-tech, low-cost, fast, self-service stock brokerage for wealthy innovators who were frustrated with their brokers and commissions. E*TRADE used cutting humor to belittle brokers and offered revenge for the disgruntled investor. Like most entry strategies, this was a highly targeted rifle shot at a segment of great profitability. E*TRADE's quick rise to the top of the financial services charts can be directly correlated to the imagination that went into the development of its brand strategy with marketing tactics such as the "Boot Your Broker" advertising campaign. E*TRADE was soaring to the top of the financial services chart based not only on its imaginative marketing campaigns but also on its innovative product lines. The marketing tactics were also targeted initially at an audience that was most likely to be influenced by E*TRADE's message. (See Mentor Method 1.4.) This segment tended to be highly populated by innovators. Innovators are more likely to switch to something new and promising. In entrepreneurial marketing practices as well as when you are formulating key strategies for your business, it's important to remember to segment your marketing to targeted audiences. Mentor Method 1.4 provides an illustration of E*TRADE's target being one subsegment of the financial service market represented as Target Segment A/Financial Service B.

> **Mentor Insight**
>
> Utilize innovation and imagination

Mentor Method 1.4

Typical Financial Services Firms Use Single Segment Concentration[15]

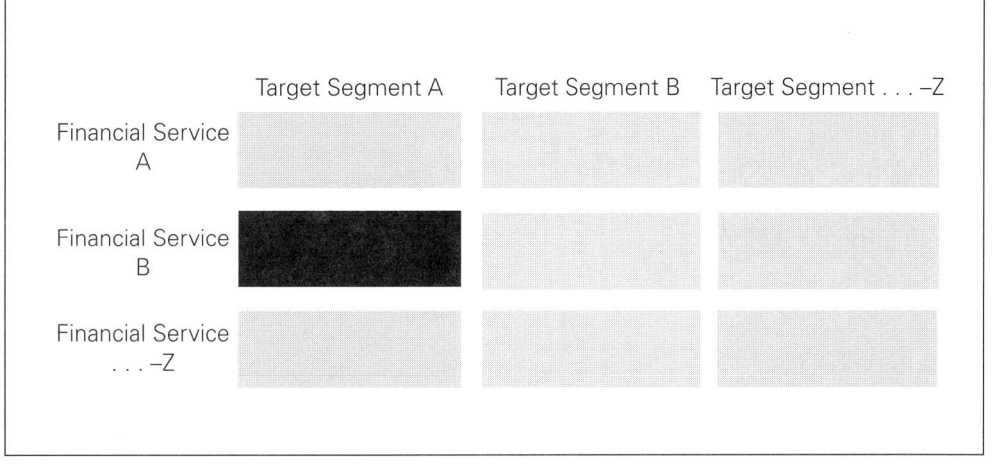

	Target Segment A	Target Segment B	Target Segment . . . –Z
Financial Service A			
Financial Service B	■		
Financial Service . . . –Z			

DEFINING THE BUSINESS: THE STARTING POINT OF STRATEGIC PLANNING by Abell, Derik F., ©1980. Adapted by permission of Pearson Education, Inc., Upper Saddle River, NJ.

Mentor Insight

Diversify your portfolio

The Growth Path

Once E*TRADE was established in stock brokering, Christos quickly moved to expand the product offering to the same customer base. With a much fuller line of financial services, E*TRADE then addressed expanding its customer base. Mentor Method 1.5 shows theoretically the different market segments that E*TRADE is now poised to expand into.

Mentor Method 1.5

E*TRADE Utilizes Market Specialization by Providing a Full Line of Financial Services to a Single Segment[16]

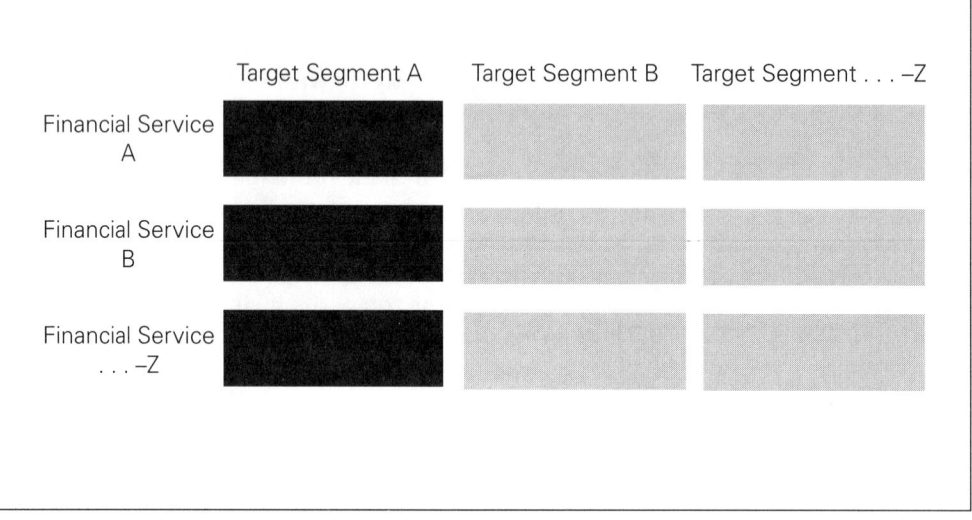

	Target Segment A	Target Segment B	Target Segment . . . –Z
Financial Service A	■	□	□
Financial Service B	■	□	□
Financial Service . . . –Z	■	□	□

DEFINING THE BUSINESS: THE STARTING POINT OF STRATEGIC PLANNING by Abell, Derik F., ©1980. Adapted by permission of Pearson Education, Inc., Upper Saddle River, NJ.

In Good Company

Mentor Insight

Practice continuous obsolescence

An entrepreneurial venture can't expand into new markets successfully unless it has a strong leadership team. Whether you are formulating killer strategies, developing top-notch marketing campaigns, or trying to bootstrap your entrepreneurial venture, knowing when to say good-bye to underperforming members of your team is key to survival. At E*TRADE, the bottom 10 percent of performers are regularly helped to find employment elsewhere. By doing this, E*TRADE has avoided any mass layoffs. Christos calls this practicing obsolescence. As an entrepreneur you have so many priorities and crises competing for your limited time that it can be easy to turn a blind eye to a slacker. If, however, you are serious about formulating the best strategies in the business you need a team to implement these strategies, and it's much harder to assemble a great team than it is to formulate your ideas. Don't postpone dealing with work performance issues. You will save time in the long run by dealing with issues as they arise and if necessary inviting those who are not adding to the team to find other work opportunities.

Entrepreneurial Marketing

> **Mentor Insight**
>
> Surround yourself with the best people

Christos had repeatedly managed to attract outstanding staff to E*TRADE. His marketing department was no exception. Christos had surrounded himself with some of the best and brightest individuals in the marketing industry.

Swarms

With so many talented people around, E*TRADE is using a tactic ideal for formulating great strategies when there is a crisis or a challenge. This technique is known as a swarm.

> *I do not attend most meetings. Instead I have a system called swarms or swarm meetings. The rules of engagement of a swarm are that the most competent people around who can solve a problem are invited to an approximately 20-minute meeting. The concept behind a swarm is to find a person to help and to help fast. I don't care for traditional meetings where everyone is politically correct and you go over yesterday's news. It's not about historical information, not at the end of the day. It's where you're going, not where you've been, that's critically important.*
>
> *When I first started having swarms it was hard on people because they would be in the middle of something and then they were called into a sudden swarm. It took a while before the swarm process was woven into the corporate culture. Now it is highly sought after at E*TRADE to be included in a swarm meeting. If you are called, it means you are valuable; you are an expert in an area. You're trusted, you're someone who knows how to get things done and done right.*[17]
>
> – Christos M. Cotsakos

Build Killer Strategies

Christos' success in formulating killer strategies can be distilled into a number of key factors:

1. A clear, actionable corporate vision
2. A lack of fear of failure in leaping into new segments and services. Fail fast and often
3. Failing fast, often, and not dwelling upon retribution for failures
4. Leadership through hard work and long hours
5. Development of a corporate culture of excellence in line with the mission of the company
6. Dogged personal attention to the details of marketing
7. The best people
8. Be willing to put everything on the line for what you believe in
9. Innovation and imagination

10. Diverse portfolio (multi-channel)
11. Continuous obsolescence
12. Laughing at yourself—laugh at the status quo
13. Spending large sums on brand and technology
14. Credibility
15. Changing the rules of engagement
16. Empowered consumers
17. Featuring storytelling in your business practices

Mentorography Conclusion

Christos developed the backbone for developing courageous strategies through the challenges of growing up in a working-class neighborhood and through serving in the Vietnam War. By working in a variety of companies throughout the world he learned how to fine-tune these strategies and motivate others to join forces with him in implementing the tactics to make these strategies successful. Christos is an outstanding case study of what it takes to formulate killer strategies. He gives us the following Mentor Insights behind formulating killer strategies:

Mentor Insights

- Feature storytelling
- Fail fast and often
- Be willing to put everything on the line for what you believe in
- Play your game, not someone else's
- Instill credibility with the customer
- Utilize innovation and imagination
- Direct resources toward brand and technology
- Diversify your portfolio
- Practice continuous obsolescence
- Surround yourself with the best people

Mentorography Questions

1. Give an example of a situation in business in which you could play your own game, not someone else's.
2. How can a firm plan for the effects of technology on its corporate strategy?
3. Why invest in brand equity when you plan to change the nature of the meaning of the brand?
4. How risky is a strategy of rapid change?
5. What are the characteristics of the person you would want in the foxhole with you when you hear someone yell "incoming!"?

Endnotes

[1] Christos M. Cotsakos interview conducted by Bruce Buskirk and Molly Lavik, October 5, 2001.

[2] Ibid.

[3] Christos M. Cotsakos, *It's Your Money. The E*TRADE Step-by-Step Guide to Online Investing*, (HarperBusiness, An Imprint of HarperCollins Publishers, New York, 2000), p. 1.

[4] Christos M. Cotsakos interview conducted by Bruce Buskirk and Molly Lavik, October 5, 2001.

[5] Reprinted with permission of The Associated Press.

[6] Christos M. Cotsakos interview conducted by Bruce Buskirk and Molly Lavik, October 5, 2001.

[7] Ibid.

[8] Ibid.

[9] Ibid.

[10] Ibid.

[11] Courtesy of Christos M. Cotsakos, Chairman and CEO, E*TRADE Financial, October 5, 2001.

[12] Christos M. Cotsakos interview conducted by Bruce Buskirk and Molly Lavik, October 5, 2001.

[13] Developed by Bruce Buskirk, March 2002.

[14] Ibid.

[15] DEFINING THE BUSINESS: THE STARTING POINT OF STRATEGIC PLANNING by Abell, Derik F., © 1980. Adapted by permission of Pearson Education, Inc., Upper Saddle River, NJ., Derik F. Abell, *Defining the Business: The Starting Point of Strategic Planning*, (Prentice Hall, Englewood Cliffs, N.J., 1980), pp. 192–196.

[16] Ibid.

[17] Christos M. Cotsakos interview conducted by Bruce Buskirk and Molly Lavik, October 5, 2001.

FINANCING MENTOR MODULE

Marketing's Role in Raising Finances for Your New Venture

GUY KAWASAKI
Founder and CEO,
Garage Technology Ventures, Inc.

Mentorography Part I

> **Mentor Insight**
> Give permission to believe

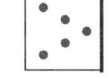

Financing plays an essential role in entrepreneurial marketing because entrepreneurial marketers, by our definition, need to drive the process of securing financing for their new venture or expanded enterprise. Specifically, the entrepreneurial marketer must ignite financers' interest by authoring the venture's positioning in the marketplace. Positioning elements include the market definition, value proposition, elevator pitch, executive summary, and company overview presentation. This list of materials forms the backbone of the entrepreneurial marketing campaign. The role of the entrepreneurial marketing campaign is to give potential investors a compelling argument to finance the venture. The marketing materials persuade the financer by giving the financer permission to believe that profitable returns are possible. Many books are dedicated to new venture financing; we have provided you with a crash course. We recommend augmenting this understanding of marketing's role in raising financing with relevant readings and seminars dedicated to capturing the interest and resources of financers. For a list of possible seminars, we encourage you to visit the web site of the subject matter of this Mentor Module: **http://www.garage.com**.

This Mentor Module focuses on a master at defining marketing's role in financing, Guy Kawasaki. Guy Kawasaki is perhaps best known as the man who popularized the term *evangelism* in the technology industry.

Entrepreneurs typically define an evangelist as someone who enthusiastically advocates, with the express intention of driving sales, the reasons why you can't exist without a certain product or service.[1]

In this module you will learn how Guy Kawasaki, a famous former employee of Apple Computer, evangelized Apple's products via emotional appeals that persuaded customers to buy and cherish Apple products. Guy may not have been the first, or highest ranking, evangelist at Apple, but he is credited with developing a fiercely loyal following of Macintosh owners. Guy's legendary evangelism skills provide us with a Mentor Insight into having passion for your venture. Guy is presently focusing his passion on new ventures by helping entrepreneurs acquire venture capital. "An unabashed self-promoter, both his admirers and detractors liken him to a latter day P.T. Barnum."[2] Guy is also the author of seven books including the following national bestsellers:

> **Mentor Insight**
> Have passion for your venture

- *Selling the Dream: How to Promote Your Product, Company, or Ideas—and Make a Difference—Using Everyday Evangelism*[3]

- *How to Drive Your Competition Crazy: Creating Disruption for Fun and Profit*[4]

- *Rules for Revolutionaries: The Capitalist Manifesto for Creating and Marketing New Products and Services*[5]

Today Guy helps fellow entrepreneurs develop their business vision. In 1998, Guy founded what is now known as Garage Technology Ventures, a company dedicated to raising seed capital for technology start-ups by providing the services of an innovative investment bank.

We can glean valuable Mentor Insights on marketing's role in financing for new ventures by chronicling Guy Kawasaki's life.

The Mentor Insights explored in this section are:

Mentor Insights

- Give permission to believe
- Have passion for your venture
- Focus on customers
- Stay focused
- Incorporate proprietary technology
- Choose your investors wisely
- Develop a strong management team
- Seek angel investors
- Bootstrap your business
- Seek venture capital financing when qualified

Guy Kawasaki Milestones

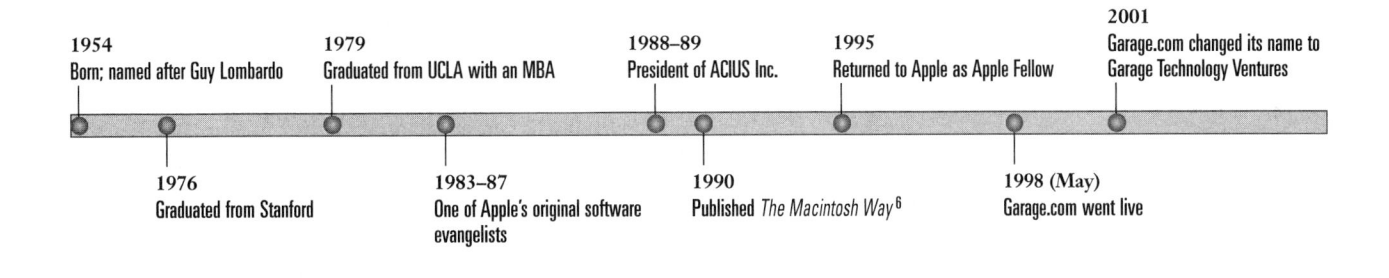

- **1954** — Born; named after Guy Lombardo
- **1976** — Graduated from Stanford
- **1979** — Graduated from UCLA with an MBA
- **1983–87** — One of Apple's original software evangelists
- **1988–89** — President of ACIUS Inc.
- **1990** — Published *The Macintosh Way* [6]
- **1995** — Returned to Apple as Apple Fellow
- **1998 (May)** — Garage.com went live
- **2001** — Garage.com changed its name to Garage Technology Ventures

In the Beginning

Guy Kawasaki grew up in Honolulu. He has fond memories of his youth.

> *I was raised in a middle class family in Hawaii. My father was a fireman, then he was a real estate broker and then he was a state senator. And my mother was at home all the way. I had a very pleasant childhood. I'm not trying to work through any problems with my entrepreneurship or anything. I've had just a good life.*[7]
>
> – Guy Kawasaki

There were three people in Guy's high school days who had a big influence on him. One was his English teacher in high school, who Guy feels would be "laughing in heaven because he would have predicted that I would be a writer." There were also two high school football coaches who had a major influence on him.

After high school, Guy attended Stanford and received a bachelor's degree in Psychology. When he entered the UCLA MBA program he went to work at a jewelry manufacturing company where he counted diamonds. After graduation, he accepted a sales and marketing job at the same company.

Then two events took place that would forever alter Guy's destiny. The first, his purchase of the Apple II, was a life altering experience because it marked the beginning of his love for computers. From the first moment he touched the Apple II he loved word processing and databases.

The second event occurred when a college classmate and good friend from Stanford, Mike Boich, was recruited to work for Apple Computer as Apple's first software evangelist. Mike arranged for Guy to interview with Steve Jobs and the Macintosh marketing manager of Apple at the time, Mike Murray. Guy wasn't right for that particular job but it didn't matter to him. He knew from that point forward that his future was meant to be in personal computers.

Guy was eventually hired as director of marketing for Eduware Software. Eduware was acquired shortly thereafter by Peachtree Software out of Atlanta. Guy didn't have an interest in moving to Atlanta but the luck that seems to be present in his career surfaced just at that critical moment in time with a call from Mike Boich telling him of another job opening at Apple. With his tenacious and indomitable spirit in tow, Guy returned to Apple for a second chance at obtaining his dream job. This time Guy was hired on as a software evangelist responsible for meeting with software developers and inspiring them to write Macintosh products. Guy's days at Apple as a software evangelist are immortalized in Apple legend.

"Kawasaki joined Apple in 1983, and he would prove critical to the success of the Macintosh. Young, dynamic, and boyishly handsome, Kawasaki was a smooth talker and natural-born salesman."[8]

> Working with the Macintosh division was just truly an amazing experience because we were going to change the world. We had this new computer, it was so different, so innovative, so revolutionary. It was just a great time. I can't tell you how exciting it was. It was just the coolest thing in the world! Macintosh was smoking hot! Everybody wanted to see it. Everybody was curious about it. It doesn't get much better than that.[9]
>
> – Guy Kawasaki

Guy Shines Up Apple

> . . . [The developers] were artists who we gave software to write programs they dreamed about.[10]
>
> – Guy Kawasaki

". . . [Guy had] landed a job at Apple Computers as software evangelist where he became part of the team that developed the Apple Macintosh. Though neither the first nor the last person to hold this position, probably no one did more in the late 1980s and early [19]90s to convince companies to use the Mac. He was unstoppable. His column in *MacUser* was unmissable: he developed into one of the most entertaining acts on the management speaker circuit and wrote some of the seven books he has to his name . . ."[11]

Guy is held in the highest esteem among the early Mac software developers because he preached to Mac users the revolutionary impact their work was having on society. These Mac users called the Microsoft alternative software, "Windoze."

> Back then you knew that Microsoft was the enemy so we were trying to do them in. I don't know that they were trying to do us in but we were trying to do them in. It's good in a revolution to have a good enemy. You must have an enemy. You have to focus. It's funny though that Microsoft now makes very, very good Macintosh software; I even use a lot of Macintosh software from Microsoft.[12]
>
> – Guy Kawasaki

Entrepreneurial Marketing

In the late 1980s, Guy departed Apple briefly to put his own entrepreneurial ideas to work for him when he started ACIUS, a 4th dimension relational database business. Next he wrote his first of seven business book blockbusters, *The Macintosh Way: The Art of Guerilla Management*, and launched his career as a sought-after consultant. His entrepreneurial spirit really began to soar after that when he started his second new venture that he called Fog City Software named after a San Francisco summer day. Fog City Software developed e-mail clients and e-mail list servers. Guy's return to Apple in June of 1995 came with the prestigious title and distinction of "Apple Fellow."

> *Most Apple fellows and every Apple Fellow before and after me were recruited for technical reasons in engineering and research. I had a marketing fellowship. My job was to make sure that the Macintosh cult was happy with Apple. So that is what I did. I was an evangelist when I was an Apple Fellow. I would speak to user groups just to keep the cult happy.[13]*
>
> – Guy Kawasaki

Guy has a reputation for having charisma and no small ego. "'I am a warrior and a warrior needs a war.' Kawasaki said in a press statement shortly after returning to Apple. 'My war is to bring cool Macintosh software to fruition, create the finest developer program in the industry, and kick Microsoft's butt—in this order.'"[14] Guy's enthusiasm for the Mac computer was infectious. His enthusiasm and passion for the product would prove an important element in the battle to keep Mac stalwarts from losing hope. Guy's evangelistic approach also gave Mac loyalists the inspired words—the "gospel"—that allowed them to believe the seemingly impossible: that the floundering line of Apple products could survive the onslaught of the proliferation of the PC. It was during these troubled times at Apple that Guy's unique blend of enthusiasm and comedic temperament endeared him to a growing universe of Mac advocates.

"One of his first ideas upon returning was to start an Internet newsletter called 'EvangeList.' Therein, he posted anything and everything positive he could find about the Macintosh, such as the tidbit that Macs were being used by everyone from climbers on Mount Everest to Coptic monks in the Sahara. 'EvangeList' proved wildly popular, surging from a thousand Internet subscribers to about fifty thousand in 1997."[15]

The creation of "EvangeList" instilled in Guy the importance of giving your customers something positive to hang on to and believe in, especially during challenging times.

Guy demonstrated the importance of customer focus. Guy's almost fanatical approach to the loyal Mac customers sustained Apple through some very bleak times. Customer focus is one of Guy Kawasaki's career trademarks. Guy recognizes that he is more focused than most, but he credits 90 percent of this to just liking what you do.

Mentor Insights

Have passion for your venture

Give permission to believe

Mentor Insight

Focus on the customer

Guy's Hindsights

Like Guy himself, Guy's hindsights are informative, entertaining, and inspiring. Guy is a popular public speaker for everything from conferences to graduations. In a 1994 high school graduation speech, he implored graduates to remember these ten things:

"10 Live off your parents as long as possible.

 9 Pursue joy, not happiness.

 8 Challenge the known and embrace the unknown.

 7 Learn to speak a foreign language, play a musical instrument, and play non-contact sports.

 6 Continue to learn.

 5 Learn to like yourself or change yourself until you can like yourself.

 4 Don't get married too soon.

 3 Play to win and win to play.

 2 Obey the absolutes.

 1 Enjoy your family and friends before they are gone."[16]

How Garage Got Started

"Mr. Kawasaki, [in 1998 at the age of] 44, ha[d] taken a leave of absence from Apple Computer to concentrate on Garage.com, an Internet-based company that . . . [would] match high-technology entrepreneurs with private investors and take stakes of its own in promising ventures. The name alludes to the fabled beginnings of many high-technology giants in their founders' garages."[17] © 1998 by The New York Times Co. Reprinted by permission. [17, 18]

> I want to help the next Apple get started...[18]
>
> – Guy Kawasaki

A Venture Capitalist

Venture capitalists are usually associated groups of investors, but they can also be a single investor. They are sophisticated investors seeking companies with the potential to go public or merge or, on rare occasions, companies in which to take a long-term equity position. Venture capitalists are as interested in getting out of the investment as they are in investing—often more so. They need to see how they get all their money back, in multiple fold, before investing. Venture capitalists can provide coaching. Sometimes they are referred to as "vulture capitalists" for their ability to gain more equity in the firm than the start-up team is comfortable with, and for their actions to build market value quickly, take gains quickly, and leave quickly with little concern for the long-term health of the venture.[19]

Guy has become a venture capitalist and he is applying the same dedication to this new role as he has to his previous positions.

> *At Apple my job was to convince people to write Macintosh versions of their software. In a sense, I am now an evangelist for any technology: I evangeli[z]e venture capitalists to entrepreneurs and I evangeli[z]e entrepreneurs to venture capitalists. I have just broadened what I do.[20]*
>
> *– Guy Kawasaki*

Mentor Insight
Stay focused

Guy's focus is evident in all his actions. An ability to stay focused is critical to marketing's role in raising finances for your venture. Developing the marketing package required for financing will consume everything you have to offer. It's your responsibility as the entrepreneurial marketer to effectively develop the materials: market definition value proposition, elevator pitch, executive summary, and company overview presentation. You must stay focused on the goal of expertly developing these marketing materials to have an opportunity to raise resources and finances for the new venture or expanded enterprise.

Mentor Insight
Incorporate proprietary technology

Garage's emphasis on incorporating proprietary technology is valuable because it (the theme of Guy's planned investments at Garage) is a way to create barriers to entry against competitors and create a strong competitive advantage in the marketplace.

"THE idea for the venture grew out of a failed pitch that Mr. Kawasaki and Richard Karlgaard, the new publisher of *Forbes*, made to Craig Johnson, a well-connected Silicon Valley technology lawyer, over lunch in September 1997. The two men wanted to create an Internet site that would offer inside information on doing business in major metropolitan areas. When they asked Mr. Johnson to represent them and become a partner, he wasn't wowed. But, Mr. Kawasaki recalled, "[H]e said, 'I see a pony in this pile of manure,'" and came up with the idea for Garage.com on the spot. Today, the three men are founding partners with large stakes."[21]

© 1998 by The New York Times Co. Reprinted by permission.

Guy recalls how he raised the finances for Garage.

> *The first round was for true believers. John Dean, then the CEO of Silicon Valley Bank, "got it" immediately and led the first round. Shortly thereafter, we raised money from a venture capital firm called Advanced Technology Ventures. Honestly, the partner, Jos Henkens, did it mostly because we were friends and because he thought that it was a good investment for helping to make ATV more visible—as opposed for purely financial returns. Frank Quattrone, then at DMG, was also an early believer.*
>
> *When the period of irrational exuberance happened, we were able to raise money from top-tier VCs like Mayfield, Sequoia, 3i, Draper Fisher Jurvetson, and Highland Capital. With them came other investors like E*TRADE, Goldman Sachs, and Credit Suisse First Boston. All in all, we raised about $44 million.[22]*
>
> *– Guy Kawasaki*

Marketing's Role in Raising Finances for Your New Venture **Module 2**

> **Mentor Insight**
>
> Choose your investors wisely

The financers Guy worked with at Garage were some of the top financers in the technology sector. We've provided a list of some of these financers. Choose your investors wisely. You will be working very closely with your investors and if they don't share the same philosophy and approach to your business, you may be in for some turbulence. Additionally, you want investors who will provide more than just cash. Seek investors who can provide strategic guidance, mentorship, and customer leads and will help the venture get through the inevitable crisis. We will explore in greater depth in the second half of this module why the right financers are crucial.

Guy Kawasaki's Investors:
A List of Investment Banks and Venture Capitalists

>   Silicon Valley Bank
>   Advanced Technology Ventures (ATV)
>   DMG
>   Mayfield
>   Sequoia
>   3i
>   Draper Fisher Jurvetson
>   Highland Capital
>   E*TRADE Financial
>   Goldman Sachs
>   Credit Suisse First Boston (CSFB)

> **Mentor Insight**
>
> Develop a strong management team

Guy's founding partners and investors are great examples of the tenet, develop a strong management team, central to creating marketing for raising finances. By putting together a highly skilled as well as high-profile group of founders and investors, Guy created the foundation of a top-notch management team. Typically "management team" refers to the hands-on managers running a company and not the investors and board members. In an early-stage enterprise, however, investors and board members may play a more hands-on role in the formation of the venture. For this reason we use the phrase "management team" to refer to not only the team of managers doing the daily work but also to the investors and board members.

In addition, Guy's notoriety and popularity made him a magnet for attracting great players onto his team. An entrepreneurial marketing campaign is greatly bolstered by having a credible and well-recognized management team. As we will elaborate in the second half of this module, the content of the entrepreneurial marketing campaign excites financers as well as the management team. In other words, it's not just how you say it but also what you have to say and who you have to say it to that counts with financers.

"The least replicable element their company has, Mr. Kawasaki's partners say, is Mr. Kawasaki. 'For this to be a success, you need a magnet, someone who is well known in the entrepreneurial community, and Guy is a perfect fit there,' said Jos Henkens, a member of Garage's . . . board and a general partner of Advanced Technology Ventures, which manage[d] $300 million in venture capital [in 1998.]"[23]

© 1998 by The New York Times Co. Reprinted by permission.

Stock Market Downturn

Since April 2000, a stock market correction has turned the venture capital industry upside down. "Investments in new companies in the Bay Area fell 27% in the fourth quarter of . . . [2000] according to a Money Tree survey by . . . [PricewaterhouseCoopers/Thomson Venture Economics/National Venture Capital Association MoneyTree™ Survey.[24]] Fewer individual investors are willing to risk their own lucre on new companies. This is forcing young companies to delay their IPOs, thereby slamming the gate on the main avenue that allows venture capitalists to make money. Young entrepreneurs have been hit worst. Seed funding [dropped significantly] . . ."[25]

This downward spiral "has called Kawasaki's own business model and profitability into question."[26] According to critics, Garage's deal flow has been reduced to a trickle. The company's reputation and profitability rely on revenue from the profitable bootcamps for Startups[27] (conferences offered to train management teams of startups) and investment banking fees.[28] Though Guy is coy about how much Garage earns from them, Garage recently hosted eight two-day bootcamps for would-be entrepreneurs, each of which was attended by approximately 500 budding CEOs who paid . . . [$700[29]]–$1,200 each to learn how to launch a technology company.[30] Corporate sponsors add to the profitability of these events. Revenue from these events and investment banking fees allows Garage to persevere through tough economic times.

The Angel Alternative

Angels are early investors who aren't necessarily members of the financial services industry and whose money develops the business plan or venture before you seek major funding. Angels tend to be people who believe either in the venture team or in the social value of the business concept. Often they are as much help in their promotion of the venture as in their funding.[31]

Guy himself may have ultimately become a hybrid between venture capitalist and investment banker but when he wrote *Selling the Dream: How to Promote Your Product, Company, or Ideas—and Make a Difference—Using Everyday Evangelism* in 1991, he endorsed the importance of seeking angel investors. This is a building block of evangelism, as described in *Selling the Dream*.

Mentor Insight

Seek angel investors

Angels

Angels are the second building block of evangelism. They are people who share your vision and provide wings, *such as emotional support, expert advice, and sometimes money—as a mother bird uses her wing to shelter her young. (By contrast, traditional investors and venture capitalists provide* weights *through their aggressive demands and desires for quick financial returns.)*[32]

– Guy Kawasaki

Persevering through Tough Times

Guy sums up 2001 in this way: "'Only true believers in entrepreneurship started companies, they had lower valuations, only people with technology could get funded. It was a great year.' And as for Garage . . . ? 'We are going to be extremely tight-fisted [frugal] and conservative, and when the sun starts shining again we will be there, with Ray-Bans and suntan lotion on.'"[33]

> **Mentor Insight**
>
> Bootstrap your business

The conservative approach that Guy describes adopting for Garage is known as bootstrapping your business. Bootstrapping is about being frugal in your business processes as well as funding your venture from your operating revenues. Guy may have raised $44 million in investment capital, but it's the bootcamp seminar series and investment banking fees that are providing self-financing to help Garage through the tough times. In an interview about his most recent book, *Rules for Revolutionaries: The Capitalist Manifesto for Creating and Marketing New Products and Services*, an interesting dialogue took place regarding misplaced priorities.

[Interviewer:] "I wanted to ask about a couple of specific examples that you talk about in the book, like giving your employees lousy furniture and putting them in a small space. Does that actually happen at Garage . . . ?

[Guy Kawasaki:] That's meant to be kind of tongue-in-cheek, but in my career, I've noticed that the companies that have the nicest buildings and the most beautiful, matched, highly developed chairs are always the ones that go out of business. I'm not saying it's causation—it's correlation. It means the company either has too much money or has too much ego tied up in the "Come-to-my-palace" mentality. If there is a single telling factor about the riskiness of a company, it is a certain type of chair."[34]

The reason this quote is valuable to an entrepreneurial marketer is because it's your job to make sure that the new venture has its spending priorities straight. Spending money on impressive office furniture, for example, is not going to help a new venture have the needed reserve funds for when a crisis or important opportunity presents itself. Bootstrapping is a way to conserve spending resources for a new venture.

We will explore bootstrapping your business in greater detail in the second half of this module.

Guy has suggestions for enduring tough times that can be summed up as "Kawasaki's Top 10 for start-ups."[35]

"Kawasaki's Top 10 for start-ups

1. Tides also go out. The assumption has been that they come in and stay high. The bubble is a lousy metaphor for the Internet economy. The tide may go out, but the ocean is still there.
2. Excel is more important than PowerPoint. The hard part is delivering the numbers. There was a time when entrepreneurs figured they could raise $250,000 per presentation slide—20 slides equals $5 m[illion.]
3. Name-brand investors do not ensure the success of the company. Many companies have failed because of arrogance. In Silicon Valley, it is difficult to find a venture capitalist who invested in B2B [Business to Business] or B2C [Business to Consumer.]
4. Invest in companies, not sectors. The on-line dog food sector was huge. The fiber-optic sector got cold. Anything could get funded.
5. The right order is to make the product then to launch it.
6. Companies are processes, not events.
7. It is better to be better than bigger.
8. Matches light forest fires, not atom bombs. There was the assumption that you raise $50 m[illion] not $5 m[illion] as most of that would go on a Superbowl ad.
9. Too much money is worse than too little. You end up flying on Concorde and worrying about matching furniture. It makes lazy companies.
10. The leading cause of failure is death. When you run out of money you are dead. Keep your cash balance high and your burn rate low. Until you die, you haven't failed."[36]

Reprinted with permission of Up Magazine.

Garage Opens New Doors in Effort to Adapt in Post Dot-Com World

Guy Kawasaki quietly operated beneath a shroud of anonymity for several months after withdrawing its initial public offering late in 2000. In the fall of 2001, the firm resurfaced as Garage Technology Ventures and the company is now redefining itself in a post dot-com world.[37]

"Formerly known as Garage.com, the small investment bank has recently started making a number of changes to its business model in order to stay afloat in a difficult market that has already forced many of its competitors . . . to close up shop for good."[38]

". . . Like most of its peers before it, Garage has attempted to diversify its business model more than once. The company has been operating as a placement agent [a company that locates financing for a business venture] for a few years . . ."[39]

Garage's new business model is not just placing deals but also directly investing in those deals.[40]

"Through partnerships with 3i Group PLC, an international venture capital firm with $11 billion under management, and the California Public Employees Retirement System (CalPERS), [which provides retirement and health benefit services to more than 1.3 million members and nearly 2,500 employers,[41]] Garage is . . . raising two separate funds."[42]

Garage would go on to raise these two separate funds. The capital from these two funds is used today for seed money to assist Garage's private placement clients with developing their ventures so they are of interest to additional investment sources.[43]

"... The funds are expected to be invested over several years and will back somewhere between 25 and 40 companies in the enterprise software, Internet infrastructure and ... communication sectors."[44]

> *We are now a hybrid of a VC [venture capital] and [an] I-bank [investment bank]. We can write checks or syndicate a deal. In the long term, this will help us make money...*[45]
>
> – Guy Kawasaki

Reprinted and adapted with permission from *Private Equity Week*, October 22, 2001. © 2001 Thomson Financial. All Rights Reserved.[37, 38, 39, 42, 44, 45]

How a Marketing Master Markets

Garage adopted not only a strategy to persevere through the tough times but also some strong marketing techniques that set it apart from the competition.

Using events such as the Bootcamp for Startups conference series is a marketing technique that generates profit for Garage while simultaneously spreading awareness of Garage to the company's key constituents. Event marketing is an ideal way for Garage to "strut its stuff" to target customers. Because Garage doesn't allocate many resources to the marketing function, the company is able to use resources to attract and retain top-level managers as well as keep money in the bank to get through the current downturn in the economy. An example of Garage's event marketing can be seen in this excerpt from the company's web site.

> *We depend on three methods: PR generating stories, speaking at events, and running our own conferences. What's more important is what we use very sparingly: advertising. If you see an ad or hear a radio spot, it's almost always for an event. We don't pay for "branding" per se. We "brand" through all our other activities.*[46]
>
> – Guy Kawasaki

> "Early-stage technology companies face a broad spectrum of challenges, especially in today's turbulent market. From setting up your company, incorporating, and protecting your intellectual property, to raising capital, negotiating the best deal, and securing the right investors, today's startup can't afford to make mistakes.
>
> Startup Strategies 2002 is a one-day conference presented by Brobeck, a leading international law firm specializing in private equity and emerging growth companies, and Garage Technology Ventures, an innovative venture capital investment bank serving technology companies and

(continues)

Entrepreneurial Marketing

investors. Brobeck and Garage have extensive experience helping high technology startups build strong companies. Join executives from both firms, as well as local experts, as they share their experience, insight, and advice with entrepreneurs.

This intensive, high-energy event delivers tactical advice in areas including: fundraising, venture capital terminology, and deal structure; critical elements to successfully structure your company; negotiating a successful deal with investors; positioning, market definition, and value proposition statements; and creating a compelling elevator pitch, executive summary, and company overview presentation.

The conference closes with a dynamic 3-keynote finale delivered by Guy Kawasaki, CEO of Garage Technology Ventures, former Mac evangelist, and author of seven books including *Rules for Revolutionaries, How to Drive Your Competition Crazy, Selling the Dream,* and *The Macintosh Way*.

Whether you're starting your first company or your fifth, you'll benefit from our up-to-the-minute information about startup and fundraising trends and practices. Don't miss this opportunity to meet, network with, and learn from local and Silicon Valley startup experts and entrepreneurs. Check out the agenda, learn about our speakers, and register to attend today. For questions, email info@startupstrategies2002.com."[47]

We're not sure that there is any finer example than Garage of a company that is using marketing to help with financing their firm. When Guy has these events he presides as the keynote speaker and invites his current and potential financers to participate on panels and lead sections of the series. Through these events, Guy has created a way to endear himself with his customer base while simultaneously raising awareness of his company to his targeted audiences.

"Warning: Do Not Pass Go!" or Do Not Seek Venture Capital Financing Unless You Are Qualified!

> **Mentor Insight**
> Seek venture capital financing when qualified

Entrepreneurial marketers leave one of Garage's seminars armed with the criteria and knowledge they need to know if they even qualify to seek venture capital dollars. It is essential that when an entrepreneurial marketer is expected to develop marketing materials to go after VC financing, he has the insight to know when the attempt is futile. Venture capitalists don't fund all start-ups. They fund only start-ups that meet a strict list of criteria. See The Ten Qualifying Criteria for Obtaining Venture Capital Financing, in Part II of this module.

Guy Has Good Karma

And why wouldn't he? He produces these great start-up seminar series that help those that desperately need his advice. He also lives by a strict karmic code.

"Guy Kawasaki's Karmic Code . . .

1. Ignore people's current status in life. Some people only take care of people who are already successful and ignore anyone at a level beneath them. That's narrow-minded thinking because you never know when the little people will get lucky.

2. Help people whose help you don't need. Don't just do things because you think you'll get something out of it . . .

3. Focus on the little and analog things. Send handwritten thank-you notes. Buy baby gifts. Those simple acts of kindness are repaid by the bucketfuls.

4. Never think of the world as a zero-sum game. Don't think that someone else's good luck will take luck away from you. There is infinite good luck in the world.

5. Pay back society . . . When you pay back, it comes back to you."[48]

Reprinted by permission of FORBES ASAP Magazine © 2002 Forbes Inc.

Guy's Predictions About the Venture Capital World

After a very tough time during 2001 and 2002, the market will return. This market will be very different because of an emphasis on profitability and pay-as-you-go investing.

I also believe that raising venture capital will become such a complex process that entrepreneurs are going to need an "industry" to help in the process.[49]

– Guy Kawasaki

Mentorography Part II

In the second half of this module we will use Guy Kawasaki and Garage Technology Ventures as role models to analyze marketing's role in attracting financing. We will impart the wisdom behind Guy's Mentor Insights while continuing the crash course on marketing's role in attracting financing. The Mentor Insights we are exploring are:

Mentor Insights

- Give permission to believe
- Have passion for your venture
- Focus on customers
- Stay focused
- Incorporate proprietary technology
- Develop a strong management team
- Choose your investors wisely
- Seek angel investors
- Bootstrap your business
- Seek venture capital financing when qualified

The Entrepreneurial Marketing Campaign Backbone

Mentor Insight
Give permission to believe

Let's begin by discussing the start-up strategy seminars produced by Guy Kawasaki. These seminars give entrepreneurial marketers the formal knowledge that they need to put together marketing materials to attract financing. These start-up strategy sessions also coach entrepreneurial marketers on what materials to incorporate to give their targeted financers permission to believe their venture will yield a profitable investment. Let's examine the master of marketing materials to gain wisdom on what one can include in one's marketing materials to give investors permission to believe in the product or service.

Evangelize Your Venture

Mentor Insight
Have passion for your venture

The Entrepreneurial Marketing Campaign starts and ends with you. The vast bulk of entrepreneurs start their businesses out of a love for the science or art in which they are engaged, or in an attempt to make a difference in the world. Seldom is the motivation riches, power, or status.

Having a huge amount of passion for your venture is essential in marketing's quest to raise finances for your new venture. Guy Kawasaki started Garage Technology Ventures first and foremost for the following reason.

> *I wanted to help the next generation of entrepreneurs create great technology companies. I also wanted to make a lot of money, but the money was just one result of fulfilling our mission of helping people build great technology companies.*[50]
>
> – Guy Kawasaki

Marketing's Role in Raising Finances for Your New Venture **Module 2**

Never forget that you play an integral role in communicating a passionate and persuasive message with the entrepreneurial marketing campaign. The potential investors who are on the receiving end of your pitches are also evaluating you. While you're presenting, these prospects have questions running through their heads that include:

> Is my investment in good hands with this team?
>
> How will these founders behave during a crisis?
>
> Will I enjoy working with these people during the rough times?
>
> Are they trustworthy?
>
> Do they have the perseverance to make it?
>
> Do I want to take the risk on these people?

This is where you must make sure that a substantial amount of passion and enthusiasm is present in every step of the pitch. You can't anticipate financing from investors if the entrepreneurs and their marketing campaign do not display heartfelt passion for the new venture.

You are the defining element behind the marketing materials that traditionally make up the entrepreneurial marketing campaign backbone. A thorough understanding of these materials is essential for you as an entrepreneurial marketer to be successful in positioning the venture. The entrepreneurial marketing campaign materials traditionally are:

- Market definition
- Value proposition
- Elevator pitch
- Executive summary
- Corporate overview presentation

Market Definition

Your market definition shows what products and services your venture is engaged in and also shows, by naming targeted segments, that you understand whom you are selling those products and services to. Most importantly, the market definition communicates the major problem your venture is solving.[51]

Garage's Market Definition. "Garage Technology Ventures is *the* leading venture capital investment bank *for* premier high-technology startups seeking value-added investors *who* fear failure due to the inefficient fundraising process."[52]

The three questions your market definition should answer are:

1. What are your products or services?
2. Who are you selling your products or services to?
3. What is the major problem the venture is solving?

These questions are clearly and concisely answered by Garage's market definition. Garage has also done a respectable job of precisely identifying its targeted segments. The following six steps are the tactics that Guy suggests you consider when preparing your market definition. These tactics are discussed in the Perfecting Your Positioning Workshop in Garage's Startup Strategies seminars.[53]

Step 1: Who do you help? Specifically, who are your constituents, users, and primary and secondary customers? Define the type of constituents you have. In Garage's case, the constituents are premier high-technology companies and investors. Start broad and narrow your focus until you achieve a clear and sharp market focus. This is a crucial first step, because focusing on your customers—the right customers—can make the difference between a successful and an unsuccessful new venture. When you provide a sharp and clear identification of your target customers, it can highlight a proven track record. Too often entrepreneurs get caught up in multiple venture ideas and lose their focus on customers of their original concept. There is no substitute for a track record with customers to capture the interest of an investor. Prospective investors consistently write checks for founders with a track record of customers.

Mentor Insight
Focus on customers

> *Pigs will floss before this maxim changes: The best way to drive your competition crazy is to make your customers happy. To make your customers happy, you have to focus on them. And if you always focus on your customers, you may never need to fire a shot at your competition, and you don't need to read the rest of this book.*[54]
>
> – Guy Kawasaki

Step 2: What is your burning problem? This is where you put in plain English what your constituents' "pain" is. Your constituents must be able to easily identify with the burning problem or "the big pain."[55]

Step 3: What emotions does the "big pain" evoke? In Garage's case, it's the entrepreneur's fear of failing. Find the predominant emotion associated with the "big pain."[56] Garage used the following list to identify the predominant emotion.

Marketing's Role in Raising Finances for Your New Venture **Module 2** 43

> **"Garage's 'Evoked Emotions' List**
>
> | | |
> |---|---|
> | Fear of the unknown | Dissatisfied |
> | Upset | Confused |
> | Anxious | Fear of missing the opportunity 'window' |
> | Fear of failing | |
> | Impatient | Baffled |
> | Frustrated by delays | Thrashing |
> | Overwhelmed | etc. etc. etc."[57] |

Step 4: Come up with your company's "*is* statement." It's important to create an "*is* statement" that captures the investor's interest without giving anything away. Garage's "*is* statement" is: "Garage Technology Ventures is *the* leading venture capital investment bank . . . "[58]

Step 5: Add to the "*is* statement" the *for* clause—where you define a specific and identifiable market—and the *who* clause—where you define the primary and compelling need based on the "big pain."[59]

Step 6: Put it all together to finalize your market definition. "Garage Technology Ventures is *the* leading venture capital investment bank *for* premier high-technology startups seeking value-added investors *who* fear failure due to the inefficient fundraising process."[60]

Value Proposition

In your value proposition you clearly define the unique benefits of your product or service to the potential customer.[61]

Garage's Value Proposition. "Garage Technology Ventures delivers mission-critical private placement services *that* provide the most efficient and effective means for entrepreneurs to refine and build their companies, *which* will allow them to secure the very best investors."[62]

Garage advocates taking these five steps when developing a value proposition.

Step 1: Ask the management team what they really do. In Garage's case, the following list resulted.

> "Bullet-proof business plan   Partnerships/alliances
> Presentation coaching   Key customers
> Valuation guidance   Filling out the team
> Identify and pitch investors   Perfecting positioning
> Work within the current   Business structure
>   funding environment   Marketing/buzz
> Challenge/perfect business   etc. etc. etc."[63]
>   assumptions

44   Entrepreneurial Marketing

Step 2: Determine the composite essence of what you really do in a concise summarized statement. The composite essence of what Garage really does is: deliver mission-critical private placement services.[64]

Step 3: Compose your company's position parameters. The "*that* clause" for Garage is: "*that* provide the most efficient and effective means for entrepreneurs to refine and build their companies. . . ."[65]

Step 4: Compose the next portion of your value statement, the "*which* clause." The "*which* clause" is where an entrepreneurial marketer should ask, "so what?" Focus on the benefits or results of your business. Garage's "*which* clause" is: "*which* will allow them to secure the very best investors."[66]

Step 5: Combine the composite essence with the *that* and *which* clauses. This should be the hardest sentence you ever write! Garage's value proposition is: "Garage Technology Ventures delivers mission-critical private placement services *that* provide the most efficient and effective means for entrepreneurs to refine and build their companies *which* will allow them to secure the very best investors."[67]

The market definition and value proposition are the foundation for the sales portion of the entrepreneurial marketing campaign. The sales portion comprises the marketing materials you use to close a deal with a potential investor. Those materials can include the elevator pitch, the executive summary, and the corporate overview presentation. It's important as you develop these additional positioning materials that you stay focused on the core message and meaning behind one's market definition and value proposition.

Remember that entrepreneurs are visionary people and it will be the entrepreneurial marketer's mission to keep the founding team focused on the positioning outlined in the market definition and value proposition. Losing focus is one of the main reasons new ventures fail. Honing the precise message behind the market definition and value proposition is a good strategy for a marketer who is seeking financing.

A business plan may also incorporate the sales positioning materials. Since the business plan is generally not the sole responsibility of the entrepreneurial marketer, it is beyond the scope of this book.

Elevator Pitch

Many years ago the elevator pitch was called a cocktail party pitch, and one could go on for at least a minute before losing a potential investor's attention. Prospects listened out of social courtesy. People today still attend business cocktail parties but attention spans have decreased. The elevator pitch is a modern derivative of the cocktail party pitch with a much shorter time frame. Courtesy no longer requires the suffering of fools. You can expect to have about 30 seconds to gain the interest of the prospect—about the length of time it takes to travel a few floors in an elevator.

The term originated in Silicon Valley, where entrepreneurs would wait one floor below the floor their prospect worked on, and would attempt to meet their prospect as they left work. As such, one had only a matter of floors (The Valley is somewhat devoid of high-rise buildings) to capture the prospect's interest. There are four objectives to accomplish in an elevator pitch:

1. Gain the prospective investor's attention.

2. Generate a level of interest in what you are saying.

> **Mentor Insight**
>
> Stay focused

3. Gain a desire in your prospective investor to know more.
4. Get commitment to follow up.

    The first sentence of your elevator pitch is the hook. It should gain the interest of your prospect, as well as make a claim or ask a critical question that leads to a claim. Next, quickly follow up with a series of statements sufficient to give the prospect permission to believe your initial claim. Now, let the prospect know what is in the deal for him: make him an offer highlighting what you will do for him and clearly state what you need from him to make it possible. Finally, close! Get agreement to talk further and to open communications. Have a plan as to how you would like to proceed, but acquiesce quickly if the prospect offers another method by which you can make contact.

    The hook is 100 percent customized based on who you are approaching for an investment. You need pre-approach planning prior to developing your hook. In the pre-approach you should have researched your prospect to gain an understanding of her interests on what intrigues her about an investment opportunity. You can acquire the pre-approach understanding in several ways. One way is to have a face-to-face meeting with an entrepreneur from a company in which your targeted investor has previously invested. Not only can you learn important information for formulating your elevator pitch from this person, but you can also see if he is willing to pave the way with an introduction to your prospect. You can also go to **http://www.edgar-online.com** to read the S1s (SEC-required filings of financial statements) of publicly traded companies that your investor is involved with. S1s reveal an enormous amount of information and can give you some real insights into what sectors excite your prospect. You can also use electronic databases such as Dow Jones Interactive, LexisNexis Academic, and Moody's FIS Online to search for relevant information on your prospect's previous investments and on her career background.

Garage's Elevator Pitch for Companies Seeking Funding.

"Garage Technology Ventures: Capital for Innovation

Venture capital fundraising is a challenging process. As a venture capital investment bank, Garage Technology Ventures is uniquely positioned to provide valuable services to help early-stage technology companies raise funds.

    Our expertise lies in arranging private equity funding for technology companies raising between $2 million and $15 million in their first or second institutional round. We work with experienced venture capital, corporate, and individual investors to secure funding from the best investors for each client.

    Our venture finance team is organized into three sectors: communications and emerging technologies, network infrastructure, and enterprise software. This focus enables us to develop deep expertise in each of these sectors. Our sector experts understand the technology, they know the competitive landscape, and they have relationships with active investors in that sector. The result is better deal flow for our investors and higher quality investors for our portfolio companies."[68]

Garage's Elevator Pitch for Investors. (The five steps in this pitch are conceptualized in Mentor Method 2.1 and elaborated on in the text that follows.)

"**Garage Technology Ventures: Capital for Innovation**

[Hook] Investors rely on Garage Technology Ventures as a source of high-quality startup investment opportunities. We actively seek out the most promising companies, with the most cutting-edge technology, through our relationships with universities, research institutes, professional service firms, Garage's member investors, and Garage clients. Our venture finance team, which is organized into three sectors—communications and emerging technologies, network infrastructure, and enterprise software—understands the technology, knows the competitive landscape, and builds relationships with active investors in each sector. [Claim] The result is high-quality deal flow for investors.

[Permission to believe] Garage helps investors expand their bandwidth by providing portfolio companies with business development assistance, dedicated recruiters, marketing guidance, and advice on a wide range of management and operational issues.

Garage has built a network of member investors who derive benefits from participation in our active community of technologists and other investors. We sponsor events such as state-of-the-art and showcase breakfasts, which stimulate discussion and co-investment opportunities among venture capital, corporate, and individual investors.

[Close] If you are an accredited investor interested in early-stage technology investment opportunities and are not yet involved with Garage Technology Ventures, please read the Frequently Asked Questions and then apply for membership.

In addition to traditional methods, Garage provides member investors access to investment opportunities in a password-protected area on the web. Members may log in for access to the password-protected area of our site."[69]

We suggest you use a five-step process (see Mentor Method 2.1) in developing your elevator pitch. We've used Garage's elevator pitch for investors to illustrate the steps.

Mentor Method 2.1

Elevator Pitch 5-Step Development Process[70]

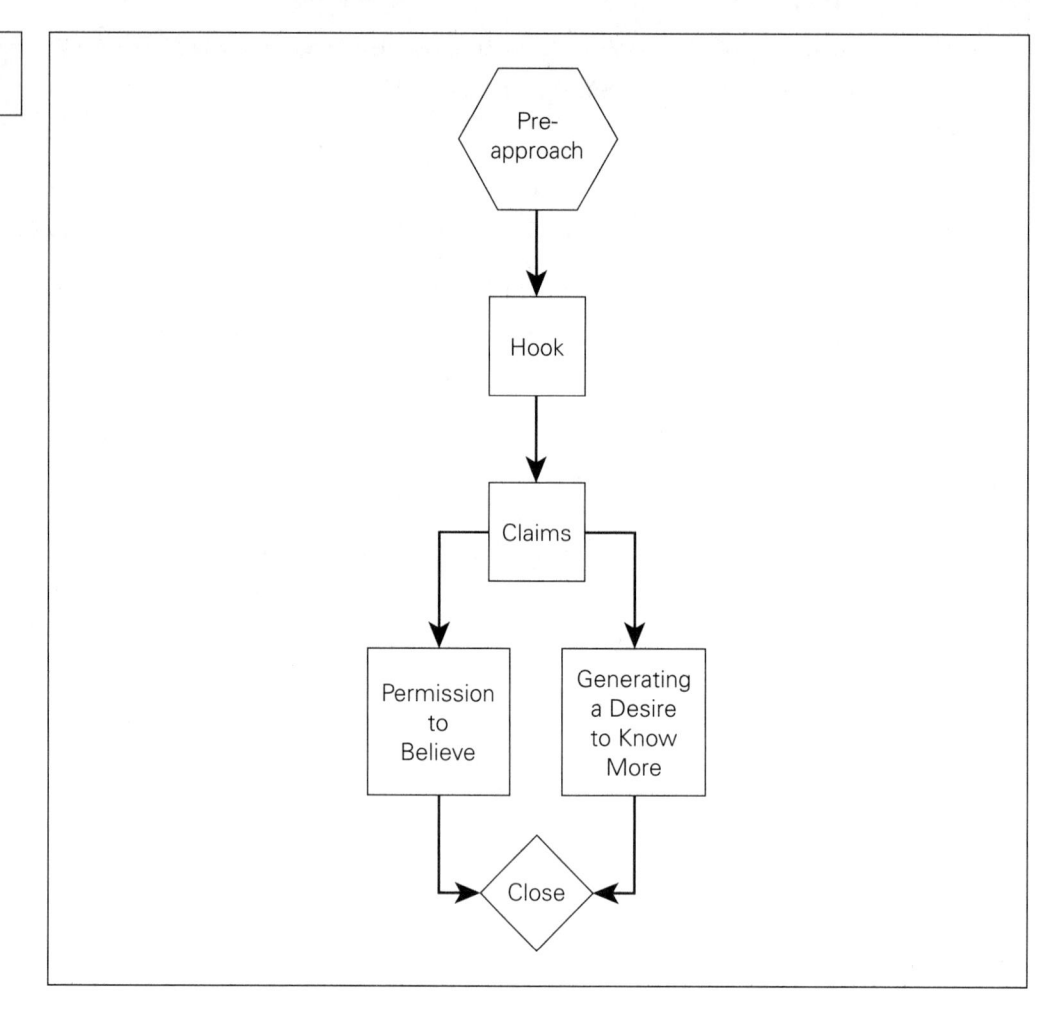

```
         Pre-approach
              ↓
            Hook
              ↓
           Claims
          ↙      ↘
  Permission   Generating
      to       a Desire
   Believe    to Know More
          ↘      ↙
           Close
```

Step 1: Pre-approach. Since this part of the elevator approach is completely customizable, we don't have a specific example to share with you. Consider the research methods suggested previously.

Step 2: The Hook. Take your pre-approach research and apply it to get your prospect excited about your pitch.

Step 3: The Claim. Make the statement behind your hook. The essence of this statement is the core attribute of your venture.

Step 4: Permission to believe. Offer statements that validate the elevator pitch. In the example of Garage's elevator pitch, these statements are mostly generalities that make credible assertions that give the prospect the comfort level to support the pitch. It's important to both make an argument that gives the prospect permission to believe and simultaneously omit the details so that you leave the prospect with a desire to know more. Guy is able to give investors permission to believe and interest in supporting Garage's portfolio of products in part because of the proprietary technology he incorporates. Incorporating proprietary technology creates powerful barriers to entry that help stave off the competition and captures the interest of investors who know that a blockbuster technology translates into profitable returns on their investment.

Mentor Insights

Give permission to believe

Incorporate proprietary technology

> *Today, circa 2001, the best advice I can give an entrepreneur is to develop hard-core technology, build a team of serial entrepreneurs, and get some customers to pay for your product. These are the most important factors today: technology, team, and traction.*
>
> *This may sound like a "duh-ism" now, but from 1997 through 2000 investors weren't that concerned with the three Ts.[71]*
>
> *– Guy Kawasaki*

Notice that Guy places technology first in his list of three key principles in becoming a successful entrepreneur.

Step 5: Generating a desire to know more. Generating interest is a natural segue to your close. The close is where you set up a specific time and place to continue a more detailed discussion with your potential investor. Garage has a virtual close on its online elevator pitch to investors. The most common oversight in an elevator pitch is forgetting to close. We suggest you make it a rule not to end your elevator pitch until you have a handshake on the time and place of the follow-up meeting.

Executive Summary

Once you have secured a time and place to further pitch your venture to an investor, you need a concise yet impactful two-page executive summary. For an example of Garage's Executive Summary, see pp. 53–54. There are mountains of literature on how to craft an effective executive summary. An executive summary summarizes your venture's business plan; you shouldn't write it until you have fully completed your business plan. It's the entrepreneurial marketer's mission and responsibility to make sure that the executive summary is a sales showpiece. Just as the elevator pitch generates the interest of the prospective investor to set a meeting time to learn more, the executive summary should entice the prospect to ask to see the entire business plan. A traditional executive summary consists of the following headings.

- Company Description
- Statement of Mission
- Assessment of Market Opportunity
- Knowledge of Customers
- Products and/or Services
- Target Markets
- Marketing Strategy
- Competitive Analysis
- Management Team

- Operational Processes
- Financials
- Long-term Goals

The executive summary, like the other materials of the entrepreneurial marketing campaign, should be updated continuously. Remember you are summarizing the highlights. The details of your plan belong in the business plan and in addenda at the back of the business plan. For example, include just the name and title of your management team in the executive summary; the bios and resumes of your team belong in an addendum, and key attributes of your management team go in your business plan.

Don't underestimate the importance of a strong management team. Anyone underwriting your venture must be comfortable, even convinced, that the management team is highly skilled and talented. Management prospects must be sold on a shared vision, motivated with the promise of an exciting life, and then convinced to join your team. The chance to work with a group of like-minded people is often sufficient motivation. Here are some additional suggestions.

> **Mentor Insight**
> Develop a strong management team

Helpful Hints on Developing a Winning Start-up Management Team

- Attend networking functions.
- Ask acquaintances and colleagues to refer you to potential management team candidates.
- Do extensive research on where to find others who are like-minded.
- Read publications focused on the area of interest that your new venture will follow and search for names of potential candidates.
- Go to universities that teach courses on entrepreneurship and see if any of the students are a match for your management team.
- Attend user group or special interest group (SIG) meetings to meet potential candidates and build your network.
- Tell everyone you are looking for referrals.
- Attend conferences that are related to your venture and seek out matches for your management team.
- Never turn your searching radar off.
- Enlist the support of recruiters and executive search agencies.
- Showcase your skill sets for the new venture and use your background as a magnet to attract other high-flyers to your team.
- Above all, find someone who embodies the entrepreneurial spirit.

Keep in mind as you develop the entrepreneurial marketing campaign materials that you need to actively evaluate your prospects just as they are evaluating you. The "investor target list" should be continuously revised as you finalize and customize your executive summary.

The following is a list of criteria to use to choose investors wisely.

> **Mentor Insight**
> Choose your investors wisely

> "Chemistry
> Treat it like a marriage
> Perform due diligence on firm & partner
> - Ask for references
> - Use your network
>
> Active vs. passive
> Lead or follow
> Industry knowledge
> How busy are they?
> Talk to other funded entrepreneurs
> - Successes
> - Failures
>
> What were they like during the tough times?
> Board meeting attendance?
> Returning phone calls
> Track record
> 'Hat trick' of experience
> - Technology
> - Management/leadership
> - Investor
>
> Do they actually have $$$ to invest?
> Where does their money come from?
> Are their interests aligned with yours?"[72]

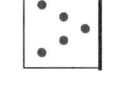

Mentor Insight
Seek angel investors

A brief letter to your targeted investor list should accompany your executive summary. This letter explains how much money you are seeking and for what purpose you plan to use these solicited finances. The letter should be customized to the type of investor you are seeking. If you are approaching an angel investor, and we recommend that you do, you still need the entrepreneurial marketing campaign materials. When seeking an angel investor, try to find people who are:

- "Pure. The personal satisfaction of helping the cause is the best motivation for an angel. Financial returns, power, and prestige are undesirable reasons.

- **Experienced.** Angels have built organizations and gained experience with a wide variety of causes. This enables them to help [you] avoid repeating mistakes of others.

- **Realistic.** Angels can assess what you can realistically accomplish. They have an understanding of what is desirable and possible for your organization.

- **Outspoken.** Experience and realism aren't enough. Angels dare to confront—even create conflict—to prevent your organization from going astray.

- **Connected.** Angels have influential and powerful friends, such as executives, venture capitalists, and foundations. This enables angels to help your organization raise money, cut through bureaucracy, and gain credibility."[73]

Guy's Words of Wisdom on How to Find Angels

All the evangelists that I talked to found their angels through pavement-pounding, brute effort. This is because good angels are hard to find, and when you find them, they are usually busy with other causes. There are, however, ways to improve your chances of both finding them and converting them.

The best places to find angels for social causes are foundations and the community action programs of large corporations. Frequently the charter of these organizations is to help causes and to operate grant programs, so the angels you find here are experienced. The best places to find angels for businesses are in the boardrooms of successful companies and among retired executives. These people often have a strong desire to help new people, pay back the industry, and stay young.[74]

– Guy Kawasaki

Garage has a strong executive summary because the company's positioning statement, market definition, value proposition, and elevator pitch serve as a good foundation for developing the business plan from which the executive summary is derived.

"Garage's Executive Summary"

Company Description

Garage Technology Ventures is a venture capital investment bank that provides private placement services for high technology companies and investors. Garage Technology Ventures serves companies in the communications and emerging technologies, network infrastructure, and enterprise software sectors that seek to raise up to $20 million in an institutional financing round. Since 1999, Garage has raised over $365 million in venture capital for its clients in 85 transactions through its broker/dealer subsidiary, Garage Securities, Inc.

Garage Technology Ventures is a hybrid of a venture capital firm and an investment bank. Like a VC firm, we have an equity relationship with our portfolio companies. We work together in long-term partnership to encourage their success. Like an investment bank, we syndicate venture investments with high quality investors from our member investor network—a network that's among the broadest in the industry. It is the strength of this network, and our ability to target the right investors for each of our portfolio companies, that has allowed us to raise funding successfully for our clients in this challenging environment.

Statement of Mission

To help entrepreneurs and investors build great technology companies.

Products and Services

- **Improved Access to Capital**
  Our venture capital investment banking services provide high technology companies with an efficient and effective means of raising venture capital from value-added investors. Our team of industry experts works in partnership with each portfolio client to target the investors that are most appropriate for their company. We leverage our strong network of member investors to syndicate financing.

- **Strategic and Operational Guidance**
  Garage Technology Ventures helps guide companies through the venture capital funding process. We provide information about current trends in venture finance. We assist companies in preparing investor road shows and learning to effectively communicate their investment opportunities to venture capital, corporate, and individual investors.

- **Business Development**
  Our network extends beyond investors to include business partners, analysts, and industry influencers.

Target Markets

We focus on companies in the communications and emerging technologies, network infrastructure, and enterprise software sectors. This focus enables us to develop deep expertise in each of these areas. Our sector experts understand the technology, they know the competitive landscape, and they have relationships with active investors in that sector. The result is better deal flow for our investors and higher quality investors for our portfolio companies.

(continues)

Marketing Strategy

Garage has built a network of member investors who derive benefits from participation in our active community of technologists and other investors. We sponsor events such as State of the Art and Showcase Breakfast, which stimulate discussion and co-investment opportunities among venture capital, corporate, and individual investors.

Competitive Analysis

Clients can use Garage or go it alone.

Competitive Advantages and Distinctions

Venture capital fundraising is a challenging process. As a venture capital investment bank, Garage Technology Ventures is uniquely positioned to provide valuable services to help early-stage technology companies raise funds. Our expertise lies in arranging private equity funding for technology companies raising up to $20 million in institutional rounds. We work with experienced venture capital, corporate, and individual investors to secure funding from the best investors for each client.

Management Team

Guy Kawasaki, Managing Director
Melissa Freidman, Marketing
Gideon Marks, Managing Director
Bill Joos, Entrepreneur Development
Bill Reichert, Managing Director
Natasha Srulowitz, Northwest Region
Mohnajit Jolly, Network Infrastructure
Matt Horton, Network Infrastructure

Operations for Investors

To seek out the most promising companies, with the most cutting-edge technology, through our relationships with universities, research institutes, professional service firms, and Garage clients. We meet with more startups, earlier than almost anyone else. We conduct analysis of market segments and talk to startups' current and potential customers. We are uniquely positioned to acquire knowledge about emerging technologies and trends among early-stage companies. We use this knowledge to rigorously screen and evaluate companies, ensuring the highest caliber of investment options. And we share this expertise with our Member Investors to help them make informed investment decisions.

Operations for Startups

Our services provide high technology companies with an efficient and effective means of raising venture capital from value-added investors. Our team of industry experts works in partnership with each portfolio client to target the investors that are appropriate for their company. We leverage our strong network of member investors to syndicate financing. Our process helps our clients obtain financing from the right investors in a timely manner.

Financials

[Garage's are proprietary. This is where you would include a summary of 3 years of forecasts of the venture's balance sheets. This is the most important part of the executive summary.]

Long-term Goals

To outlast the downturn in the investment markets. To create a strong portfolio of companies in the communications and emerging technologies, network infrastructure, and enterprise software sectors so that when the sun shines again on the market, Garage will be there with suntan lotion and Ray Bans to soak up the sun."[75]

Corporate Overview Presentation

The Corporate Overview Presentation is a very important component of the meeting you will have with a potential investor on the heels of your successful elevator pitch. Traditionally, these meetings take place in your prospect's conference room with your sensational PowerPoint presentation. Here are some important considerations for that presentation.

Helpful Hints for a Corporate Overview Presentation

- Strive for ten to fifteen PowerPoint slides. More than fifteen is too many.
- Enlist the assistance of a graphics professional to help you conceptualize your message in graphs, pie charts, tables, metrics, and other diagrams that will visually summarize your material; avoid a pure text presentation.
- Review literature about effective presentations. Remember, it's not just the content but also how you package that content that really counts.
- Cover the items in Mentor Method 2.1, from p. 48, supporting each process with summarized data.
- Dedicate the bulk of your presentation to the finances. This is what the people on the other end of the table are waiting to hear about.
- Be prepared for an onslaught of unfriendly questions designed to trip you up. Don't lose your cool. And don't be disturbed by the poker faces at the opposite end of the table. Investors typically try to make you feel like dirt so that they can invest in your company at a fraction of what you had hoped.
- Your presenting team is also being evaluated. The prospects want to make sure you are good people to work with through thick and thin.
- Remember, the presentation is a two-way street. You should also ask questions of your prospects and make sure they have more to offer than just cash.

Garage advocates using the following 12-slide presentation format when seeking financing.

Garage's PowerPoint Slide Content Suggestions

"Slide 1: Title; Speaker intro; how much money you are after
Slide 2: Company overview and elevator pitch; Mission statement
Slide 3: Problem buy-in; Market and opportunity size
Slide 4: Your solution and products; with benefits
Slide 5: More solution details
Slide 6: Technologies
Slide 7: Competition
Slide 8: Marketing and leverage points

Slide 9:   Success metrics; Revenue projections
Slide 10: [Management] Team
Slide 11: Status: Timeline; Use of funds
Slide 12: Why us? Call-to-action"[76]

That Was Then This is Now

> [Excerpt from recent *San Francisco Business Times* Interview with Guy Kawasaki.]
>
> "**Q:** There's a sense today that a few years ago all you had to do was sit down for a cup of coffee with a VC, jot down a business plan on the back of an envelope and you could walk out with a check for $30 million. Is that a myth?
>
> Well, it wasn't that easy. You also had to boot PowerPoint, but that's it. (laughs)"[77]

> **Mentor Insight**
>
> Bootstrap your business

Today's corporate overview presentation no longer can be just hype. During the dot-com era of the late 1990s, new ventures were judged by the extravagance of the business receptions they held and their luxurious office space. Investors today are looking for sound financial revenue projections that are based on existing customer history. Investors are also looking for companies that have been frugal and have redirected revenues back into developing the venture, not into having lavish parties and office space. Today's investors are looking for founders who know how to bootstrap their enterprise.

Things to Keep in Mind

As you prepare your marketing materials, try to ensure that they reflect your approach and accomplishments so far, particularly the strength of your management and your responsible financial attitude (your ability to bootstrap).

Guy Kawasaki bootstraps Garage by having affordable offices and forming alliances to help deliver services rather than making cash outlays solely from Garage's bank account. An entrepreneurial marketer who has been part of a team that has bootstrapped its business can enter into first-time investor negotiations from a point of greater leverage, for the following reasons:

1. Ownership—While the company may not be the size it could be, it's all yours. Ownership is not diluted, nor are future profits.

2. Control—Because ownership is not diluted, no outsiders can gain a foothold and therefore cannot squeeze the current team out of control.

3. Concentration on the Business Focus
4. Minimizing Risk—You are risking only your own personal assets. Once you get an investor involved, you have taken on additional risk—not only for yourself but also for the investor.
5. Maintaining your Vision—Investors might insist you alter the vision of your venture.

Bootstrapping has been the hallmark of some of the most financially successful entrepreneurs today.

Key Question—Should Our Firm Seek Venture Capital?

> **Mentor Insight**
> Seek venture capital financing when qualified

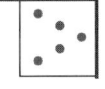

As an entrepreneurial marketer, you will be responsible for making sure the venture does not waste time going after venture capital financing when it does not qualify for this type of investment. Guy Kawasaki holds valuable training seminars to help entrepreneurs and investors ensure this doesn't happen.

Many start-ups waste valuable time trying to obtain VC financing when, in fact, they never would have qualified for this financing no matter how many "hoops" they jumped through. Here is a checklist to help you understand VC's expectations.

The Ten Qualifying Criteria for Obtaining Venture Capital Financing

1. Have you raised two rounds of financing? Have you raised close to $1 million from friends and family and your first round from an institutional investor for close to $10 million?
2. Have you forecast, with credible assumptions, a hockey stick revenue growth of more than $1 billion after three years?
3. Do you break even by the third year showing a sustainable profit?
4. Do at least two members of your executive team have a significant track record in your business?
5. Do you have the entrepreneurial marketing campaign materials?
6. Do you have documented in your business plan a provable business model that clearly and concisely communicates what you are doing?
7. Do you have credibility?
8. Is your timing perfect for the business you are in?
9. Are you the type of person with whom a venture capitalist would want to work closely?
10. Do you have a nest egg that will sustain you through nine months of a venture capitalist stringing you along before they actually give you a check or write a term sheet?

The criteria are daunting but don't despair. Here are Guy Kawasaki's ten tips for raising capital that you can utilize to raise finances for your venture.

- "Don't outsmart yourself. Keep your corporate structure simple and use service pros (lawyers, accountants, bankers) who always do high-tech startup work. Uncle Joe, the divorce lawyer, might be cheaper, but you'll regret using him.
- Don't be paranoid. If you're concerned about a competing investment, explain the basics of your company and ask potential investors if there is going to be any overlap. Corollary: Take money from people you like. You're going to be working together for a long time, so 'chemistry' counts.
- Be brief. These are the metrics: one-page introductory e-mail (no attachments); 20-page business plan; 12-slide PowerPoint presentation; and 40-minute presentation plus 20 minutes for discussion.
- Acknowledge the competition. If you tell potential investors that you have no competition, they will conclude one of two things: There's no market or you're clueless. Both are not conducive to getting funded.
- Look for value, not valuation. All money is not created equal. Take money from investors who 'get it' and have relevant experience and connections.
- Eat when served. This is the wisdom of Eugene Kleiner (of Kleiner Perkins Caufield & Byers). When people want to give you money, take it. Lots of things can happen between now and the next time you need to raise money.
- Keep 'burn rates' low and cash balances high. Keep enough capital on hand to last a year so that you can change your business model. Watch, don't buy, Super Bowl ads.
- Ask for 'less' than you need. If there is anything investors hate more than bad deals, it's being locked out of good deals. Ask for less than you need so that you can declare victory as soon as possible. Then, graciously 'let' others get in the deal.
- Let a thousand flowers bloom. Sometimes the most 'logical' investors won't bite. On the other hand, investors in unrelated fields might. Don't be proud: Take the money.
- Don't let the bozos grind you down. Some of the most successful entrepreneurs couldn't raise money for months. The founders of Cisco are one example. Frankly, if you give up, you aren't an entrepreneur."[78]

Republished with permission of San Francisco Chronicle, from Golden Rules to Attract Angel Investors, Peter Sinton, February 9, 2000, p. B-3, © 2000 San Francisco Chronicle; permission conveyed through Copyright Clearance Center, Inc.

Mentorography Conclusion

We've provided you with the criteria that a venture capitalist uses to make its investment decision. By studying Mentor Method 2.2, Arrow Dynamics of VC Investing Criteria, you can gain the necessary insights into what criteria you are being evaluated against to be in the running for an investment check. This conceptual model is based on an arrow because the entrepreneurial marketer will have to aim the entrepreneurial marketing materials precisely to hit the investment bull's-eye in Mentor Method 2.3.

Mentor Method 2.3 represents the stages an entrepreneurial marketer will have to suffer through before she can hope to hit the center of the dartboard. The center of the dartboard is illustrated as "money in bank" and known as the investment bull's-eye. An entrepreneurial marketer who takes careful aim by creating a well-calibrated entrepreneurial marketing campaign increases the new venture's odds of hitting that target.

Mentor Method 2.2

Arrow Dynamics of VC Investing Criteria[79]

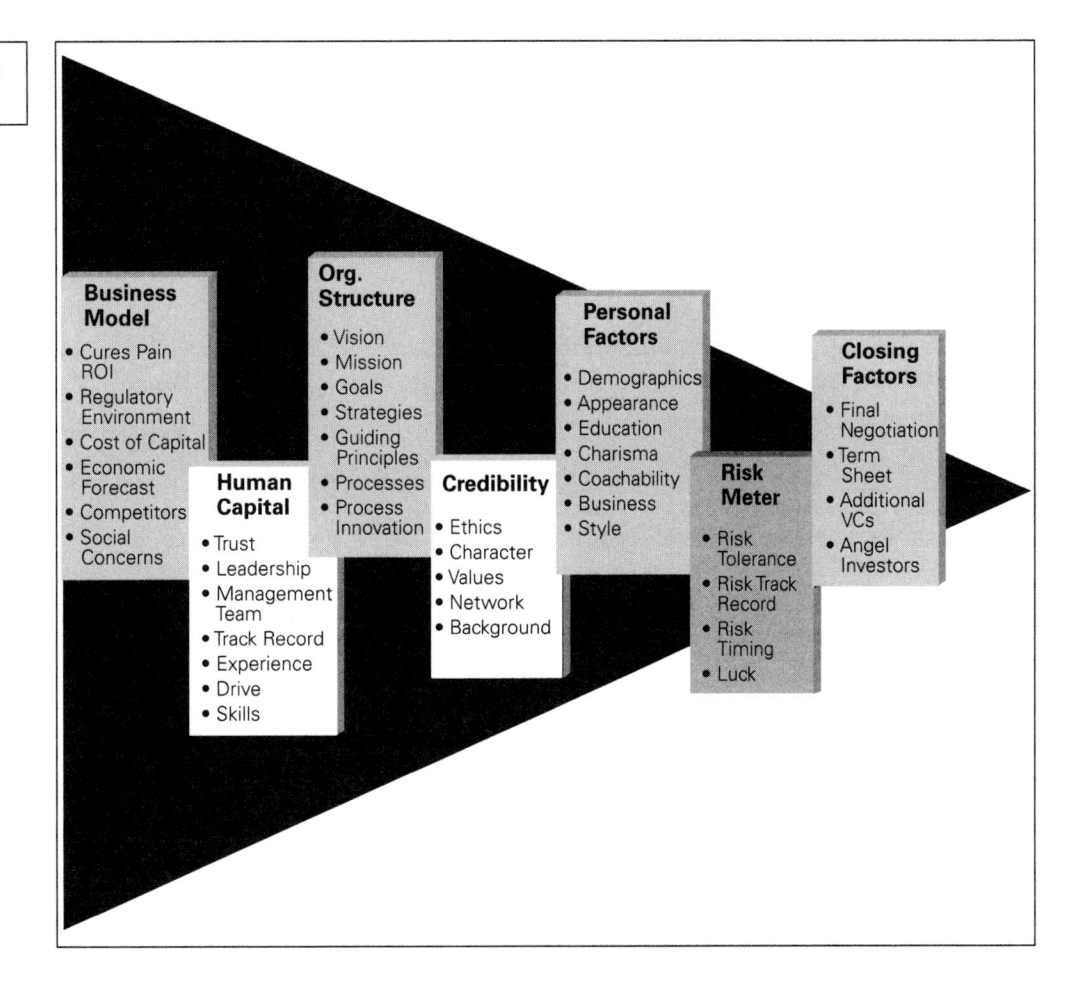

Business Model
- Cures Pain ROI
- Regulatory Environment
- Cost of Capital
- Economic Forecast
- Competitors
- Social Concerns

Human Capital
- Trust
- Leadership
- Management Team
- Track Record
- Experience
- Drive
- Skills

Org. Structure
- Vision
- Mission
- Goals
- Strategies
- Guiding Principles
- Processes
- Process Innovation

Credibility
- Ethics
- Character
- Values
- Network
- Background

Personal Factors
- Demographics
- Appearance
- Education
- Charisma
- Coachability
- Business Style

Risk Meter
- Risk Tolerance
- Risk Track Record
- Risk Timing
- Luck

Closing Factors
- Final Negotiation
- Term Sheet
- Additional VCs
- Angel Investors

Mentor Method 2.3

Investment Bull's-Eye[80]

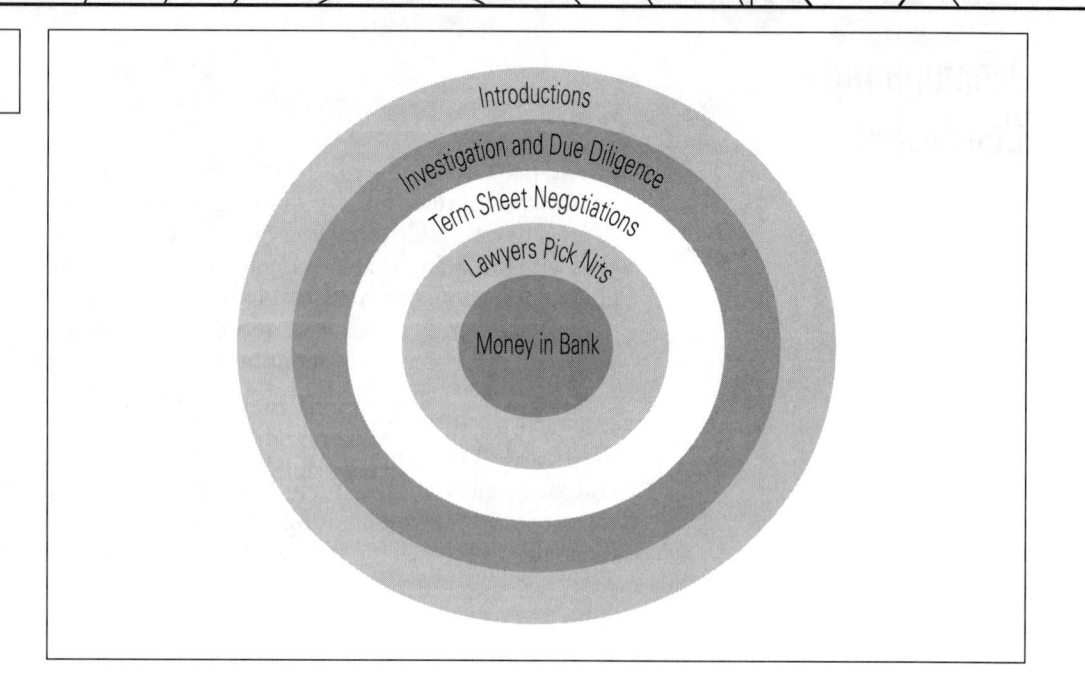

- Introductions
- Investigation and Due Diligence
- Term Sheet Negotiations
- Lawyers Pick Nits
- Money in Bank

In this chapter, we examined what lessons we can learn from the Mentor Insights that are key to marketing's role in raising financing for your new venture. Those Mentor Insights are:

Mentor Insights

- Give permission to believe
- Have passion for your venture
- Focus on customers
- Stay focused
- Incorporate proprietary technology
- Develop a strong management team
- Choose your investors wisely
- Seek angel investors
- Bootstrap your business
- Seek venture capital financing when qualified

We remind you to never forget the importance of marketing's role in seeking finances to sustain your business venture through the inevitable growing pains.

Mentorography Questions

1. Analyze the entrepreneurial marketing campaign of a new venture to determine if you would invest in this new venture. What criteria would you use to evaluate the entrepreneurial marketing campaign of this business?

2. Conduct an interview with a real-life entrepreneurial marketer to find out how they developed their entrepreneurial marketing campaign.

3. Write an elevator pitch for a hypothetical new venture. Present this elevator pitch to your class and have your classmates evaluate whether they would invest in your new venture.

Endnotes

[1] Definition of entrepreneurial evangelist developed by Molly Lavik, June 12, 2002.

[2] Jon Swartz, "Guy Kawasaki: Apple polisher writers of errors of others' ways.," *The Business Journal*, April 22, 1991, Vol. 9, n1, p. 12.

[3] Guy Kawasaki, *Selling the Dream: How to Promote Your Product, Company, or Ideas—and Make a Difference—Using Everyday Evangelism*, (HarperBusiness, a Division of HarperCollins Publishers, New York, 1992).

[4] Guy Kawasaki, *How to Drive Your Competition Crazy: Creating Disruption for Fun and Profit*, (Hyperion, New York, 1995).

[5] Guy Kawasaki, *Rules for Revolutionaries: The Capitalist Manifesto for Creating and Marketing New Products and Services*, (HarperBusiness, an Imprint of HarperCollins Publishers, New York, 2000).

[6] Guy Kawasaki, *The Macintosh Way: The Art of Guerilla Management*, (HarperPerennial, a Division of HarperCollins Publishers, New York, 1990).

[7] Guy Kawasaki interview conducted by Molly Lavik, February 21, 2003.

[8] Jim Carlton, *Apple: The Inside Story of Intrigue, Egomania, and Business Blunders*, (HarperBusiness, a Division of HarperCollins Publishers, New York, 1998), p. 24.

[9] Guy Kawasaki interview conducted by Molly Lavik, February 21, 2003.

[10] Jim Carlton, *Apple: The Inside Story of Intrigue, Egomania, and Business Blunders*, (HarperBusiness, a Division of HarperCollins Publishers, New York, 1998), p. 24.

[11] This feature first appeared in *Up Magazine*, May 2001, Adrian Murdoch, "Business is Served, One guy in a garage," *Up Magazine*, May 2001.

[12] Guy Kawasaki interview conducted by Molly Lavik, February 21, 2003.

[13] Ibid.

[14] Jim Carlton, *Apple: The Inside Story of Intrigue, Egomania, and Business Blunders*, (HarperBusiness, a Division of HarperCollins Publishers, New York, 1998), p. 374.

[15] Ibid.

[16] Guy Kawasaki, "Hindsight," Palo Alto High School Baccalaureate Speech, June 11, 1995.

[17] © 1998 by The New York Times Co. Reprinted by permission, Roy Furchgott, "Private Sector; Financier to the Garage Start-Up," *The New York Times*, Money and Business/Financial Desk, October 18, 1998.

[18] Ibid.

[19] Definition of vulture capitalists developed by Bruce Buskirk, June 7, 2002.

[20] This feature first appeared in *Up Magazine*, May 2001, Adrian Murdoch, "Business is Served, One guy in a garage," *Up Magazine*, May 2001.

[21] © 1998 by The New York Times Co. Reprinted by permission, Roy Furchgott, "Private Sector; Financier to the Garage Start-Up," *The New York Times*, Money and Business/Financial Desk, October 18, 1998.

[22] Guy Kawasaki e-mail response to questions posed by Molly Lavik, December 4, 2001.

[23] © 1998 by The New York Times Co. Reprinted by permission, Roy Furchgott, "Private Sector; Financier to the Garage Start-Up," *The New York Times*, Money and Business/Financial Desk, October 18, 1998.

[24] PricewaterhouseCoopers/Thomson Venture Economics/National Venture Capital Association MoneyTree™ Survey.

[25] This feature first appeared in *Up Magazine*, May 2001, Adrian Murdoch, "Business is Served, One guy in a garage," *Up Magazine*, May 2001.

[26] Ibid.

[27] Ibid.

[28] Courtesy of Guy Kawasaki, Founder and CEO, Garage Technology Ventures, Inc., December 16, 2002.

[29] Courtesy of Guy Kawasaki, Founder and CEO, Garage Technology Ventures, Inc., July 25, 2002.

[30] This feature first appeared in *Up Magazine*, May 2001, Adrian Murdoch, "Business is Served, One guy in a garage,"*Up Magazine*, May 2001.

[31] Definition of an angel investor developed by Bruce Buskirk, June 7, 2002.

[32] Guy Kawasaki, *Selling the Dream: How to Promote Your Product, Company, or Ideas—and Make a Difference—Using Everyday Evangelism*, (HarperBusiness, a Division of HarperCollins Publishers, New York, 1992), p. 33.

[33] This feature first appeared in *Up Magazine*, May 2001, Adrian Murdoch, "Business is Served, One guy in a garage," *Up Magazine*, May 2001.

[34] Reprinted with permission of The Conference Board, Melissa Master, "Guy Kawasaki offers a start-up mentality to big business.," *Across the Board*, March/April 2001, Vol. 38, Issue 2, pp. 17–18, 2p., 1c.

[35] This feature first appeared in *Up Magazine*, May 2001, Adrian Murdoch, "Business is Served, One guy in a garage," *Up Magazine*, May 2001.

[36] Ibid.

[37] Reprinted and adapted with permission from *Private Equity Week*, October 22, 2001. © 2001 Thomson Financial. All Rights Reserved. Danielle Fugazy, "Garage Tries To Adapt In Post-Dotcom World," *Private Equity Week*, October 22, 2001.

[38] Ibid.

[39] Ibid.

[40] Courtesy of Guy Kawasaki, Founder and CEO, Garage Technology Ventures, Inc., December 16, 2002.

[41] "Welcome to CalPERS On-Line!," http://www.calpers.ca.gov, accessed on June 12, 2002.

[42] Reprinted and adapted with permission from *Private Equity Week*, October 22, 2001. © 2001 Thomson Financial. All Rights Reserved. Danielle Fugazy, "Garage Tries To Adapt In Post-Dotcom World," *Private Equity Week*, October 22, 2001.

[43] Courtesy of Guy Kawasaki, Founder and CEO, Garage Technology Ventures, Inc., December 16, 2002.

[44] Reprinted and adapted with permission from *Private Equity Week*, October 22, 2001. © 2001 Thomson Financial. All Rights Reserved. Danielle Fugazy, "Garage Tries To Adapt In Post-Dotcom World," *Private Equity Week*, October 22, 2001.

[45] Ibid.

[46] Courtesy of Guy Kawasaki, Founder and CEO, Garage Technology Ventures, Inc., December 4, 2002.

[47] "Startup Strategies 2002," http://www.startupstrategies2002.com, accessed June 12, 2002.

[48] Reprinted by permission of FORBES ASAP Magazine. © 2002 Forbes Inc. "Guy Kawasaki's Karmic Code, " *Forbes ASAP*, November 27, 2000, Vol. 166, Issue 14, p. 112.

[49] Guy Kawasaki e-mail response to questions posed by Molly Lavik, December 4, 2001.

[50] Ibid.

[51] Definition of market definition developed by Bruce Buskirk, June 13, 2002.

[52] © 2002 Garage Technology Ventures, "Perfecting Your Positioning Workshop," Developed by Garage Technology Ventures, June 25, 2002.

[53] Ibid.

[54] Guy Kawasaki, *How to Drive Your Competition Crazy: Creating Disruption for Fun and Profit*, (Hyperion, New York, 1995), p. 59.

[55] © 2002 Garage Technology Ventures, "Perfecting Your Positioning Workshop," Developed by Garage Technology Ventures, June 25, 2002.

[56] Ibid.

[57] Ibid.

[58] Ibid.

[59] Ibid.

[60] Ibid.

[61] Definition of value proposition developed by Bruce Buskirk, June 13, 2002.

[62] © 2002 Garage Technology Ventures, "Perfecting Your Positioning Workshop," Developed by Garage Technology Ventures, June 25, 2002.

[63] Ibid.

[64] Ibid.

[65] Ibid.

[66] Ibid.

[67] Ibid.

[68] Courtesy of Guy Kawasaki, Founder and CEO, Garage Technology Ventures, Inc., August 2, 2002.

[69] Ibid.

[70] Elevator Pitch 5-Step Development Process developed by Bruce Buskirk, June 13, 2002.

[71] Guy Kawasaki e-mail response to questions posed by Molly Lavik, December 4, 2001.

[72] Jay Humphlett, "VC 101," Fall 2001.

[73] Guy Kawasaki, *Selling the Dream: How to Promote Your Product, Company, or Ideas—and Make a Difference—Using Everyday Evangelism*, (HarperBusiness, a Division of HarperCollins Publishers, New York, 1992), p. 34.

[74] Ibid, p. 33.

[75] Reprinted with permission, Garage Technology Ventures, Inc.

[76] Startup Strategies 2002, "Use About a Dozen Slides!", Power Point Presentation, June 25, 2002.

[77] Daniel S. Levine, "One-on-one with Guy Kawasaki, CEO, Garage Technology Ventures," *San Francisco Business Times*, March 29, 2002.

[78] Republished with permission of San Francisco Chronicle, from Golden Rules to Attract Angel Investors, Peter Sinton, February 9, 2000, p. B-3, © 2000 San Francisco Chronicle; permission conveyed through Copyright Clearance Center, Inc., Peter Sinton, "Golden Rules to Attract Angel Investors," *San Francisco Chronicle*, February 9, 2000, p. B-3.

[79] Arrow Dynamics of VC Investing Criteria developed by Bruce Buskirk, June 15, 2002.

[80] Investment Bull's-Eye developed by Bruce Buskirk, June 15, 2002.

BRANDING MENTOR MODULE

Branding That Works

LEONARD ARMATO
Founder, Management Plus Enterprises and Commissioner, AVP Pro Beach Volleyball Tour

Mentorography Part I

Entrepreneurial marketer Leonard Armato has repeatedly created world-recognized brands. We illustrate real-world branding practices using Leonard's strategies to build the public images of the elite athletes and celebrities he represents. Branding is a commonly used marketing term that refers to a distinctive image, usually in the form of a logo or company mark that represents a company or product. In recent years, a company's brand has become an asset with a financial worth known as brand equity. Leonard provides valuable insights into brand creation. This module will examine the origins of the Branding That Works Mentor Insights by chronicling Leonard Armato's career in managing elite athletes. Those Mentor Insights are as follows:

Mentor Insights

- Possess ironclad perseverance
- Seize the day
- Forge corporate partnership alliances
- Invest in brand equity
- Develop the brand advantage
- Use star power to boost your brand
- Utilize an integrated marketing communications approach
- Develop brand resilience
- Exude a positive mental attitude
- Be an extraordinary brand ambassador

Who Is Leonard Armato?

Leonard's extreme drive manifests itself in nearly all aspects of his life; one of his major strengths has been his ability to find equally driven business colleagues. Leonard's career includes accomplishments in the entertainment, sports, and music industries.

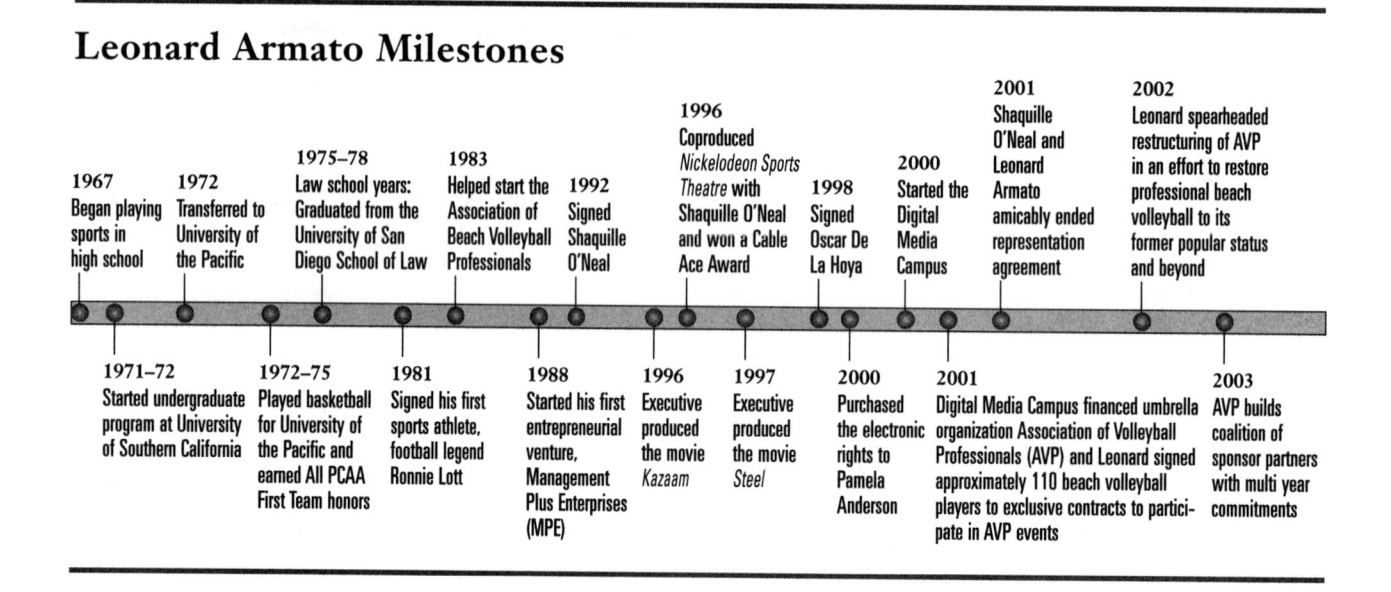

Leonard Armato Milestones

1967 Began playing sports in high school

1971–72 Started undergraduate program at University of Southern California

1972 Transferred to University of the Pacific

1972–75 Played basketball for University of the Pacific and earned All PCAA First Team honors

1975–78 Law school years: Graduated from the University of San Diego School of Law

1981 Signed his first sports athlete, football legend Ronnie Lott

1983 Helped start the Association of Beach Volleyball Professionals

1988 Started his first entrepreneurial venture, Management Plus Enterprises (MPE)

1992 Signed Shaquille O'Neal

1996 Coproduced *Nickelodeon Sports Theatre* with Shaquille O'Neal and won a Cable Ace Award

1996 Executive produced the movie *Kazaam*

1997 Executive produced the movie *Steel*

1998 Signed Oscar De La Hoya

2000 Started the Digital Media Campus

2000 Purchased the electronic rights to Pamela Anderson

2001 Shaquille O'Neal and Leonard Armato amicably ended representation agreement

2001 Digital Media Campus financed umbrella organization Association of Volleyball Professionals (AVP) and Leonard signed approximately 110 beach volleyball players to exclusive contracts to participate in AVP events

2002 Leonard spearheaded restructuring of AVP in an effort to restore professional beach volleyball to its former popular status and beyond

2003 AVP builds coalition of sponsor partners with multi year commitments

Entrepreneurial Marketing

Leonard's Background

Leonard's family is a talented, close-knit Italian-American family residing in Manhattan Beach, California. They tend to be successful artists and professionals whose first priority is to the family. They have weekly family dinners where each member shares his accomplishments in return for critical feedback. Leonard's father, Sam Armato, Ph.D., a professor emeritus of English at the University of Southern California, has been a driving force in Leonard's life, and an inspiration and adviser over the years. For example, Dr. Armato tutored Shaquille O'Neal during Shaq's 2000 quest to complete his undergraduate degree from LSU. Leonard and his father are not the only people in his immediate family to work with prominent people. Leonard's family also includes a songwriting younger sister, Antonina Armato, who has had her songs performed by Brenda K. Starr, Sheena Easton, Mariah Carey, and Barbra Streisand among others.[1] His brother, Dr. John Peter Armato, is an internal medicine specialist with an elite clientele.

Leonard was a dedicated high school athlete and ultimately became a successful collegiate scholar athlete as an All PCAA basketball player at University of the Pacific. However, he recognized that he lacked the raw talent required to be a professional athlete in the NBA. In the mid-1970s Armato began playing beach volleyball as a supplement to his basketball training and became an enthusiast of the sport. After graduating from the University of San Diego School of Law, Leonard channeled his love of sports into his career aspiration to represent elite athletes. His first break came through extreme determination when he boldly approached football superstar Ronnie Lott about becoming his agent. Ronnie knew Leonard from Leonard's earlier sports background and asked him what competitive advantage Leonard, a young law school graduate, could give him over other agents. Leonard promised Ronnie the most important resource of all, his exclusive time. Since Leonard had no previous experience or other clients, he explained, he was free to spend 100 percent of his time on Ronnie's career. The strategy paid off and Leonard signed his first client.

> **Mentor Insight**
> Possess ironclad perseverance

Where Does His Drive Emanate From?

The son of an English professor fond of classics, Leonard derives his wisdom from great literature. Leonard will often kick off his meetings and presentations with quotes from the great minds of the past. One of his favorites is from Shakespeare's *Julius Caesar*.

> There is a tide in the affairs of men
> Which, taken at the flood, leads on to fortune;
> Omitted, all the voyage of their life
> Is bound in shallows and in miseries.
> On such a full sea are we now afloat;
> And we must take the current when it serve
> Or lose our ventures.
>
> – Brutus, from *Julius Caesar*, Act 4, Scene III

Mentor Insight

Seize the day

To Leonard, this quote means that one must not sit back and let opportunity pass by. Leonard feels it is crucial to seize every opportunity as it presents itself. By drawing on his pioneering practices in branding, Leonard has the uncanny ability to recognize opportunities and shape these opportunities into successful ventures. Leonard Armato is an exceptional entrepreneur seizing each day to the fullest. For example, Leonard successfully developed beach volleyball into a $15 million a year industry in the 1980s and early 1990s, by starting the Association of Volleyball Professionals and serving as its executive director. Leonard reflects on this period in his career.

> It was a very interesting experience because what it did was utilize my skills as a representative of athletes. I organized them collectively to gain more power with the organizers of the tour at the time. And we ultimately became the group that took over management of the tour so, after two years of representing the players collectively, we secured for the AVP the right to promote the entire tour and in 1985 signed a historic agreement with the Miller Brewing Company to do that. Then there were other companies that immediately wanted to help sponsor this tour such as Fila, Bally's, Pepsi, and Taco Bell. We had a lot of different companies that supported the growth of beach volleyball. Jose Cuervo was a big factor during that period. It gave me a lot of experience with player representation, organizing, and providing a vision and foundation for the growth of the sport. We administered television, sponsorships, ancillary rights, and all kinds of different things from our offices. And I was still carrying on a law practice and representing athletes and other companies. It was a busy time.[2]
>
> – Leonard Armato

Mentor Insight

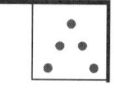

Forge corporate partnership alliances

In the 1990s Leonard shifted his focus away from the Association of Volleyball Professionals because he became very busy with his responsibilities as a lawyer, a sports agent, and a marketer.

Superstar Agent

Beyond Leonard's abilities in forging corporate partnerships, he knows how to attract, motivate, and develop world-class talent. In the 1990s Leonard became a superstar agent of elite athletes, representing sports stars such as Kareem Abdul-Jabbar, Hakeem Olajuwon, and Ahmad Rashad. His company, Management Plus, continues to represent many sports legends including pro-boxing champion Oscar De La Hoya and WNBA star of the Los Angeles Sparks Lisa Leslie; until October of 2001 he represented NBA MVP Shaquille O'Neal. As AVP commissioner, Leonard does not represent his wife, Holly McPeak, a women's professional beach volleyball champion and beach volleyball Olympian, because he considers this a "conflict of interest."

Over the years, Leonard fine-tuned his sports management offerings and pioneered new processes in sports marketing. Specifically, Leonard

Entrepreneurial Marketing

> **Mentor Insight**
> Invest in brand equity

introduced the concept of branding an elite athlete so that his career continues to flourish after retirement. His pitch was straightforward and simple—he offered elite athletes "equity for the long term." Leonard offered his clients a branding campaign complete with a mission statement and founded Management Plus Enterprises (MPE) to implement his sports branding campaigns. The mission statement for MPE is as follows:

"MPE manages sports and entertainment clients that have the potential to transcend celebrity status and become global brands. MPE will also create, develop, acquire, produce, and market (1) programming, (2) events, and (3) other tangible assets related or unrelated to the clients it manages. The Company will expand its capability to engage in such activities by securing appropriate relationships and financial resources to stimulate that expansion and facilitate the most profitable exploitation of those assets."[3]

MPE's mission develops the brand advantage of elite athletes.

> **Mentor Insight**
> Develop the brand advantage

The following sections on "Shaq Brand History," "Shaq as a Global Icon," and "The Coalition" were part of the Shaq Brand Marketing Communications Plan that MPE developed in 1998. These sections give insights into how MPE developed the brand advantage for Shaquille O'Neal.

> ### "Shaq Brand History
> The Shaq brand was launched ... [in approximately the mid 1990s]. This launch was based upon the theory that a coalition of companies with the common interest of exploiting Shaq, consistent with a singular Brand Positioning Statement, would create a powerful force in the marketplace."[4]

> **Mentor Insight**
> Use star power to boost your brand

"Shaq as a Global Icon

Shaq's performance as an NBA superstar—and his multimedia personality and talent—coupled with the power of ... [Leonard and MPE's] marketing coalition, transformed Shaq into a global icon. When the coalition was formed, the companies comprising it were traditional sporting goods and related companies and the focus of ... [MPE's] marketing was on Shaq's ability to inspire kids in general. [It became] ... time for Shaq to expand his demographic and reposition his Brand. [When Shaq was] ... 26, he ... [moved] into the prime of his career as a basketball player and in his other areas of interest."[5]

A key component of the Shaq Brand Marketing Communications Plan was the coalition technique developed by Leonard. Specifically, Leonard strategically approached companies to join a marketing coalition formed for each of his elite athletes he represented. For Shaq, Leonard approached organizations such as Pepsi, Reebok, the NBA, Spalding Sports Worldwide, and Electronic Arts. Executives from each of the companies would collaborate to creatively explore the vision from their own individual marketing perspectives, and these ideas were combined to create an effective marketing campaign. Leonard called this approach Marketing Coalition Systems™ (MCS™). Leonard elaborates on his MCS concept in the Shaq Brand Marketing Communications Plan:

The Coalition

We are in the process of organizing a coalition of global companies that have the common goal of using Shaq's new "technology" Brand [P]ositioning to image their own brands. Our initial inquiries have determined resoundingly that this is perfect positioning for Shaq as we enter the millennium and that companies grounded in technology are eager to explore becoming coalition members.

For example, we are in final discussions to build Shaq Learning Centers in Boys & Girls Clubs around the country.

These Centers will be supported by companies such as Microsoft, Digital, and Tandy and will provide the technology to assist under-privileged children in accessing the latest educational opportunities.

The number of charter coalition members will be limited. These select companies will be compatible with each other and will be the only companies permitted to do television, radio, or print ads featuring Shaq for commercial purposes.[6]

– Leonard Armato

Leonard developed the marketing coalition concept in order to avoid the initial negative impact of media fragmentation. Leonard felt that new brands could and should leverage and exploit existing brands and their vast marketing resources in order to supplement the tiny marketing budget of the new brand. Leonard's formation of a powerful marketing coalition helped to preserve the importance of television as a place to promote and advertise an elite athlete despite the erosion of TV ratings and diminished impact caused by media fragmentation.

The World of New Media Convergence

In 1995, Leonard entered the world of new media convergence by forging a relationship between Shaq and Microsoft whereby Shaq's Web site, Shaq World, would reside on the Microsoft Network (MSN). "Shaq and Bill Gates announced this partnership together at a Microsoft developer's meeting in Long Beach[, California]. When MSN discontinued their original programming, Shaq World moved to SportsLine and through its relationship with Shaq, SportsLine gained instant credibility and ultimately became a public company. Shaq was the first sports celebrity to house his Website on SportsLine, and athletes including Michael Jordan and Tiger Woods quickly followed suit."[7]

The Entertainment Arena

In July of 1996, Leonard and Shaq executive produced the feature film *Kazaam*. "Casting basketball star Shaquille O'Neal as a genie who offers a beleaguered 12-year-old boy three wishes . . ."[8]

Shaq also composed a rap track for the *Kazaam*'s music score which included tracks that were featured on the radio.[9]

Kazaam extended Shaq's brand into the audience of filmgoers and rap enthusiasts. Clearly Leonard was implementing the MPE mission to "create, develop, acquire, produce, and market (1) programming of the clients it manages."[10]

In mid-July of 1996, Shaquille O'Neal departed the Orlando Magic and signed a contract with the Los Angeles Lakers. Leonard brokered the deal. Shaq's superior athleticism combined with MPE's branding campaign clearly was making an impact.

Leonard is a powerful businessman who enjoys challenges and playing on complicated new ground.

The Digital Media Campus

Leonard combined his passion, energy, and ability to take extreme chances to seize the opportunities that came with the onset of the new media industry. In Manhattan Beach, California, in 2000, Leonard founded the Digital Media Campus, an enterprise whose mission was to be the "next-generation developer of sports, music, and entertainment-related interactive and new technology business models. [The Digital Media Campus] . . . combine[d] seed capital with premier service providers, world class advisors, experienced operating management, and a rich technology infrastructure to provide leading entrepreneurs with all the tools for a rapid and successful launch."[11]

The Digital Media Campus was initially an incubator. The concept behind an incubator was to give new media venture founders the operational and mentoring support they needed to increase their chances of success. An incubator basically offered clusters of founders from primarily new media ventures an all-inclusive office package as well as access to high-level business mentors for a reduced or waived fee. In return, the mentors would own part of the new venture. The Digital Media Campus could best be described as an office utopia for a small business venture. The original Digital Media Campus featured an office environment furnished completely with the finest Herman Miller furniture and boasted soaring ceilings and a seating area reminiscent of a football field. (See Module 2 on financing p. 35 for Guy Kawasaki's comments on the "Come-to-my-palace" mentality as an alternative viewpoint.) The Digital Media Campus showcased technology innovations to automate office systems, combined with top-tier technicians available 24 hours a day.

The Demise of the First Iteration of the Digital Media Campus

The opulent office environment symbolized the misplaced priorities of the dot-com spending era. The bubble had already burst on the dot-com industry by July of 2000, when the Digital Media Campus opened its doors, and the Digital Media Campus was unable to rent the majority of its luxurious office space. Leonard, a man who does not believe in failure, was undaunted by the vaporization of the new media industry.

Market Downturn

Responding to market conditions, the Digital Media Campus relocated in July of 2001, to cut monthly expenditures and downsize so the company could operate profitably and without dissipating capital at such a dramatic rate.

As mentioned, the public market for companies like the first iteration of the Digital Media Campus as an incubator had completely evaporated by July of 2000. The Digital Media Campus survival strategy by the summer of 2001 was to make wise investments in assets that could grow in value and therefore protect shareholder value.[12] Despite a setback to the Digital Media Campus by the downturn in the economy and the shift in focus, scope, and location of the Digital Media Campus, that same summer Leonard was able to manage Shaq when he achieved his second consecutive NBA team championship and was selected the most valuable player of the NBA for the second consecutive year.

Recognizing Market Opportunity

In 2001, Leonard's focus shifted back to professional volleyball. "Agent Leonard Armato is close to buying two competing beach volleyball tours and merging them into one, marking the latest effort to reverse the sport's fortunes. Armato . . . would unify the Assn. Of Volleyball Professionals and the newer Beach Volleyball America, which have been at odds in the last year."[13]

He feels that pro beach volleyball has enormous growth potential as well as all the elements to become a long-term global mainstream sport. Its great athleticism, wonderful lifestyle association, geographic beauty, and great sex appeal make beach volleyball well suited to become a mass televised sport success.

Leonard recalls that in the 1980s he didn't have "ownership" to grow his involvement in the Beach Volleyball tour. After the 2000 Olympics in Sydney where beach volleyball was the hottest ticket, Leonard had the opportunity to acquire both the men's and women's tours, which at the time were floundering. Leonard acquired the men's and women's tours, putting them under the umbrella of the AVP. Everything had come full circle for Leonard.

The Digital Media Campus put up the capital and resources to help rebuild beach volleyball.

Leonard believes he and his team can expand beach volleyball across all the fragmented media, from interactive to traditional, from network television to cable television and wireless, and from print to radio.

On the heels of acquiring the men's and women's pro beach volleyball tour, Leonard recently faced getting the 120-plus professional athletes who were part of the tour to sign on to continue their involvement. Leonard describes the process:

> "We picked it up [in the] ER last year," Armato said. "We had to resuscitate a dying body. It was survival."[14]
>
> – Leonard Armato

Mentor Insight

Utilize an integrated marketing communications approach

> It's difficult to convince 120-plus people to be of one mind, to get them on the same page, to unify their interests. We were able to do that, not easily, but we were able to do that. Now that everyone is on the same page and acting as a community, I think we have a great chance to make this thing work . . . think the players have been through a tumultuous ten years. They were on top of the world, at least a high growth curve, and then all of a sudden, it all came crumbling down. And I think that they have confidence that we have an expertise and the contacts and skills to manage the sport appropriately and they put their confidence in us [that we] understand exactly what it takes to make this sport grow. I think they would like to be part of that, as would we.[15]
>
> – Leonard Armato

> *"Once we set ourselves and our credibility, we have a place at NBC where we can grow,"* Armato said. *"There's certainly the opportunity for us if we perform well."*[17]
>
> *– Leonard Armato*

"The AVP kicks off its seven-stop tour Friday [Spring 2002] with the Huntington Beach Open. On the plus side, the AVP is back on NBC for the first time since 1997, with live coverage of the Manhattan Beach and Chicago tournaments in August [2002]. However, the AVP is not being paid broadcast rights fees by NBC, which will lose the NBA after this season and this summer is conducting an audition of sorts for lesser-known sports, including arena football. Regardless, Armato hopes that the national exposure will pay off. Last year, AVP tournaments were shown solely tape-delayed on Fox Sports Net, usually three or four weeks after actual tournament dates."[16]

Making a Splash on the Radio Waves
"AVP HITS THE RADIO WAVES
AVP
6/14/2002

The Association of Volleyball Professionals and Los Angeles sports radio station KMPC (1540 AM) announced an agreement to broadcast one-hour AVP Hour radio show to air live on Thursdays 7–8 p.m. (PST) running May 23–August 8. The jointly promoted program features stars from the AVP as well as other sports personalities in an open talk-show format and is hosted by Sinjin Smith, Karch Kiraly and the Voice of AVP Chris "Geeter" McGee.

The show can be heard via the Internet at radio.sportingnews.com/losangeles.

One of Southern California's premiere sports radio stations, KMPC features a line-up of top programming, which when combined with the prestige and imagery of the AVP, create a reputable and highly anticipated radio show for a vast and diverse audience.

'This agreement between the AVP and KMPC further elevates the AVP and it's sponsors by providing a weekly forum and sounding board where individuals and products can be introduced to a large and sought after audience,' said AVP commissioner Leonard Armato. 'The AVP is committed to partnering with reputable sponsors like KMPC as we continue to move forward with returning the AVP to its place as the nation's premiere volleyball tour.'"[18]

Grassroots Activities Matter

Grassroots activities are just as important to building a brand as radio and television broadcasts. The grassroots program known as AVPNext was launched to help the AVP under Commissioner Armato's guidance.

> ## "The grassroots hub of the AVP
> AVP
> 4/23/2002
>
> The AVP is proud to announce the addition of its nationwide grassroots development program, AVPNext. AVPNext is a national network of amateur volleyball associations sanctioned by the AVP. Its mission is to increase and enhance volleyball participation throughout the United States. The program establishes a direct link between the *next* generation of volleyball players and the AVP professional tour. Not only does AVPNext support America's youth and recreational level players by delivering ample opportunities for play and instruction but AVPNext also grants AVP hopefuls the opportunity of earning AVP points to obtain a higher seed in the qualifiers or even direct main draw entry into AVP tournaments. Select AVPNext associations have already started promoting and running these Open (AAA) level events that abide by the 2002 AVP competition rules that include rally-scoring, official AVP Wilson volleyball, AVP-certified court size and award AVP points."[19]

In June 2002 at the Hermosa Beach Open, word of a newly announced AVP weekly radio show, the national television broadcasts, and the AVPNext grassroots campaign were having an impact on the revamped sport.

Leonard's and the Digital Media Campus's actions in revamping the failing AVP are an example of how to develop brand resilience. Brand resilience is defined as being able to restore a declining brand back to its former position of popularity and widespread awareness. We will discuss this in greater detail in Part II of this Mentor Module.

Leonard Armato exudes positive energy in the face of adversity. He actually thrives on solving complicated problems and challenges such as developing a new focus for the Digital Media Campus in the wake of a downturned economy and revitalizing the floundering men's and women's professional beach volleyball tours. Where most people would give up, Leonard basks in the sunshine. He practices what he preaches to the elite athletes that he represents; his coaching on positive mental attitude starts with his example. Leonard resists negative energy. His high standard of excellence and his long-term credibility are hallmarks of his own outstanding brand. Leonard epitomizes what it means to be an extraordinary brand ambassador. Leonard is an entrepreneur with ironclad perseverance, a useful tool for anyone engaged in the business of branding new ventures.

Mentor Insights

Develop brand resilience

Exude a positive mental attitude

Mentor Insight

Be an extraordinary brand ambassador

Mentorography Part II

In this half of the chapter we will explore Leonard Armato's craft behind creating brands that work. We will analyze the Branding That Works Mentor Insights:

Mentor Insights

- Possess ironclad perseverance
- Seize the day
- Forge corporate partnership alliances
- Invest in brand equity
- Develop the brand advantage
- Use star power to boost your brand
- Utilize an integrated marketing communications approach
- Develop brand resilience
- Exude a positive mental attitude
- Be an extraordinary brand ambassador

The Origins of the Term *Branding*

It's helpful to understand the origins of the term *branding* before we analyze Leonard Armato's craft behind branding that works. The marketing use of the word *brand* is borrowed from the process of burning a rancher's mark into a calf for identification purposes.

"Branding livestock is an essential piece of work performed by ranchers and . . . [cowhands]. A brand is the special mark or identifying design owned by a rancher and used in registering and identifying his cattle and horses. A branding iron is the handmade iron or steel tool that applies the mark to the . . . [cow]. The end with the owner's brand is pressed against the side of the animal after being heated to red hot in a fire in the corral. The earliest 'irons,' as they are called in Nevada, were simple initials, figures, or numbers, but the designs grew intricate and ingenious as generations passed and conflicts arose over duplications of simple figures. The iron designs are recorded in a statewide brand book published by the Nevada Department of Agriculture, which often provides the ultimate evidence of ownership in disputes. The brands are illustrated, previous owners are listed, and the location of the mark on the animal is given. Brand books also indicate other ownership marks—wattles and ear notches. 'Irons' are serious business."[20]

Branding as a marketing term became widely utilized in the 1930s when companies as well as the military developed logos as a way to distinguish their products or purposes. In the late 1970s the term *branding* took on greater significance as companies began to attach a financial value, known as brand equity, to brands. Today there are thousands of companies dedicated to helping marketing professionals develop their brand equity. The brand equity is the "feel-good" benefits directly attributed to a business venture's image.

The identifying design in a cow-herding brand is known in business circles today as a logo. In this module we concentrate on managing your brand rather than the graphic development of your brand. (See Module 7 on new products on p. 184 for more discussion on developing a logo.) Additionally, we urge you to develop logos and graphic images that are user friendly and reflect the true image of your venture.

Leonard's Competitive Side

> **Mentor Insight**
> Possess ironclad perseverance

The elite athletes Leonard represents have to respect Leonard's competitive nature: his drive and perseverance match or exceed theirs. This is perhaps Leonard's strongest personality trait. It allows him to repeatedly brand the sports icons he represents, a process that takes a tenacious spirit. The tactics that Leonard utilizes are:

1. Leonard is most demanding of himself. He holds himself accountable to high standards of speech, knowledge, dress, and professionalism. His prime drive seems to be to deliver the best possible product in "himself." He is a man driven to perfect himself as well as those under his tutelage.

2. Leonard surrounds himself with people, like himself, for whom personal drive is the most crucial component. Leonard knows the importance of being a "winner," and of keeping the company of "winners."

3. It's never about the money. It's about transforming the people he represents into masterpieces worthy of encore standing ovations.

4. Leonard adheres to a high standard of excellence. He understands that achieving quality comes from attention to detail.

Carpe Diem!

> **Mentor Insight**
> Seize the day

Ironclad perseverance is not the only ingredient necessary to successfully build widely recognized and admired brands for new ventures. The entrepreneurial marketer needs to move quickly to take advantage of a potential opportunity before her competitors do. Leonard's guiding philosophy is "Seize the day." When professional beach volleyball needed a savior, Leonard quickly stepped in to lead the revamping and revitalization of the sport. Leonard has had ventures that didn't perform as originally intended, such as the Digital Media Campus, but he has been able consistently to evolve his new ventures to meet the demands of a changing environment. The AVP now under Leonard's direction is a prime example of responding to a changing environment. Because Management Plus Enterprises is composed of a small yet gifted staff and is a lean small business, Leonard and his team are able to be nimble and agile in quickly seizing opportunities before their competitors even realize that there are looming possibilities on the horizon.

Photo provided courtesy of the AVP

Branding on a Shoestring—AVP Applies MCS™

How can a new small business mount an impressive and effective branding campaign on a limited or nonexistent budget? One way is to apply the same principles of MCS™ that Leonard used in building the Shaq Brand. The net effect is that you can use other people's money (OPM) by forging corporate alliances and requiring those corporate partners to support/fund your marketing initiatives. Leonard has utilized this strategy again in securing AVP's new found coalition of marketing partners. How can you create corporate partnership alliances? Below is a list of helpful hints.

Helpful Hints for Forging Corporate Partnership Alliances

- **Package the unique selling proposition** of your product or service.

- **Make your product or service the definitive solution** to your targeted corporate partner alliance's problems.

- **Pitch to the decision-maker.** Getting to the decision-maker can be tedious and arduous but pitching to anyone else can hinder your ability to close the deal and receive a sponsorship check.

- **Run a thorough sales process.** Tenacity and ironclad perseverance are necessary attributes for not giving up during the lengthy sales process that accompanies any successful corporate partnership negotiation.

- **It's a quality, not quantity, game.** Remember that time is much better spent approaching a few well-qualified corporate partnership alliance prospects. Valuable time can be lost going after prospects that wouldn't normally participate in the corporate partnership alliance deal you are pitching.

> **Mentor Insight**
>
> Forge corporate partnership alliances

- **Allocate resources.** This doesn't necessarily mean hard cash. Understand that closing a deal with a corporate partner requires a significant time commitment. Not allocating the people to work on the sales process means you won't be successful in closing the deal.

- **Put a golden Rolodex to work.** If you don't have a Rolodex of key prospects then affiliate yourself with someone who does. A prior business relationship or even a weak link to a key influencer or internal champion at a company can mean the difference between success and failure in forging corporate partnership alliances. Learn how to take advantage of others' contacts in a professional yet tenacious way.

- **Have passion for what you are pitching.** If you can't be enthusiastic about the alliance you are pitching, you can't expect a prospect to get excited about the pitch either.

- **Be available 24/7/365.** You must be available to answer the prospect's questions when they arise even if it's on a weekend, evening, or holiday. The team or person pitching the alliance has to be readily accessible at all times.

- **Be open and flexible.** The deal you end up brokering may not be what you originally planned. However, by incorporating a prospect's needs and wishes into your pitch, your chances of moving forward increase dramatically.

- **Don't give up.** Just when you are frustrated, exhausted, and burnt out is about the time that you are most likely to break down your prospect's barriers.

Events are another way to mount an impressive branding campaign for your new venture on a limited budget. Producing and publicizing events takes an enormous amount of detailed work by a management team, but it doesn't necessarily take large fiscal resources. In fact, corporate sponsorships such as the type the AVP is serving up for its tournaments can go a long way toward covering the expenses for producing an event. The brand awareness and publicity generated by events can be powerful marketing tools. NBC's nationally televised coverage of the AVP's Manhattan Beach and Chicago tournaments are valuable examples of how you can build, or restore, a brand to epic proportions.

Another way to build a brand of substantial magnitude on a limited budget is through grassroots efforts. The AVPNext grassroots campaign gives hopeful amateurs an inroad to the professional volleyball circuit by providing instruction as well as the opportunity to earn points toward professional qualification. This national program costs the AVP nothing while it drives word-of-mouth excitement. (See the Viral Marketing Module for more on this topic.)

Corporate partnership alliances, highly publicized events, and grassroots campaigns are not just ways to build your brand on a shoestring. They are also ways to invest in your brand equity. Brand equity is the "feel-good" benefits, the goodwill associated with a product or service's image. This concept is significant for the success of your overall entrepreneurial marketing program. You must stay focused on building your brand equity as an entrepreneurial marketer.

Mentor Insight

Invest in brand equity

Entrepreneurial Marketing

The Brand Advantage

> **Mentor Insight**
>
> Develop the brand advantage

Yet there is still more to be done toward effectively implementing your brand. Developing and publicizing your brand's advantages are important aspects of any branding campaign. Brand advantages are the key attributes of a venture's image that set it apart from others. To develop or identify your brand advantages, start with an understanding of the essence of your venture's key image attributes. In the AVP's case, the key image attributes are: great athleticism, wonderful lifestyle association, geographic beauty, and great sex appeal.

Understanding the Essence of Brand Advantages

The following questions are helpful when you are trying to understand the essence of your brand advantages. Leonard is adept at understanding his brand advantages and communicating them to his sports-loving audience. He makes this complicated process seem easy. Don't be fooled. This process is hard work and takes many hours of reviewing these questions to ascertain the brand's key advantages. Communicating brand advantages is a powerful weapon in understanding how to motivate your customer base to embrace a new venture's brand.

- What is distinctive about the brand?
- What differentiates this brand from the competitor's?
- How do customers perceive the brand?
- What emotions does the brand evoke?
- Who appreciates the brand? Why?
- What do customers get from the brand?
- What do customers wish were different about the brand?
- Where do customers go to find the brand?
- What compels repeat customers of the brand?
- What do customers see in the brand that the founders didn't?

Once you have analyzed the answers to the questions above, we suggest you turn your brand advantage into a story. Leonard did this by playing a heroic role in the rise and later resurgence of the AVP. Leonard emphasizes the resurgence of the AVP story in his brand marketing campaign. Brand advantages that tell a story can become legendary.

Star Power

> **Mentor Insight**
>
> Use star power to boost your brand

Using star power is building a brand by standing, figuratively, on the shoulders of a celebrity's notoriety. Using star power to boost a brand is a proven method to ensure brand appeal. Leonard is uniquely positioned to use this strategy because he manages the careers of elite athletes and celebrities. For example, Leonard represents an array of championship professional volleyball players whom he can highlight as focal points to the AVP brand. But, what if you don't have access to stars? What if you don't have the marketing budget of Nicolas G. Hayek, who uses Cindy Crawford and Anna Kournikova in his marketing campaign as discussed in Mentor Module 8 on public relations? Don't despair. There are celebrities in every market space. Entrepreneurial marketers who work hard and are strategic in their efforts are able to forge partnerships with well-known celebrities. Celebrities occasionally seek media associations as much as the entrepreneurial marketer does. The following is a list of ways to attract celebrity endorsements for your brand campaign.

Helpful Hints for Finding a Celebrity Brand Endorsement

- Identify a celebrity who may be in transition. These celebrities are more likely to be amenable to lending their image to a brand.

- If your brand is attached to a worthwhile cause, you may find a celebrity behind this cause who would like to assist you.

- Contact the Writers Guild of America (WGA), the Directors Guild of America (DGA), and other guilds to identify potential celebrities. You will be working through a third party but you may get access to people through normally inaccessible channels.

- Introductions can go a long way. If you are fortunate enough to have a mutual friend or internal champion, ask for his help. You may be pleasantly surprised at the end result.

- If you have corporate partnership alliances, your liaison with the corporate partnership can help make a celebrity endorser part of their sponsorship. Or perhaps these corporate partners can introduce you to someone who can help.

- As always, be tenacious. This is not the time to be shy about cold calling to reach your objective.

- Adopt Leonard's ironclad perseverance. You may very well need this if you are on a limited or non-existent budget. Remember, throughout the history of marketing, utilizing star power to build your brand has proved a winning strategy.

Integrated Marketing Communications

Another way to build momentum for a brand is through the use of integrated marketing communications (IMC). IMC is the methodology for assuring that the messages in a venture's marketing campaign are distributed in multiple media outlets for the purpose of maximizing a product's or service's image awareness and profitability.

Origins of IMC

IMC grew out of a period when large firms would have both a traditional advertising agency and a direct marketing agency. Often, the two would not communicate well with each other. What typically happened was that the direct marketing business was so small, originally, that it was too much bother for the traditional ad agency so they sent their clients out to a direct marketing agency. Direct marketing agencies became very successful by delivering measurable results and grew to a point where they challenged the revenues of traditional agencies. At this point, many traditional agencies decided that they wanted access to the direct business, so they hired direct departments and used the concept of IMC to argue that their clients should have only one agency—theirs. Regardless of its origin, IMC is a sound and viable way to build a brand.

Leonard is a master at marketing his sport icons through an integrated marketing communications approach. For example, in the first half of this module we saw that Shaq is marketed online and offline, via the radio airwaves with his rap music, and on the big screen in *Kazaam*.

The Building Brand Equity graph (see Mentor Method 3.1) represents the positive impact brand momentum makers have on brand equity worth. A company's brand equity worth will most likely rise as you introduce greater combinations of brand momentum makers into your entrepreneurial marketing campaign. Examples of activities that are known as brand momentum makers include:

- Forging corporate partnership alliances
- Publicizing events
- Creating grassroots campaigns
- Publicizing brand advantages and their correlating stories
- Using star power
- Using integrated marketing communications campaigns

> **Mentor Insight**
>
> Utilize an integrated marketing communications approach

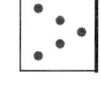

Mentor Method 3.1

Building Brand Equity[21]

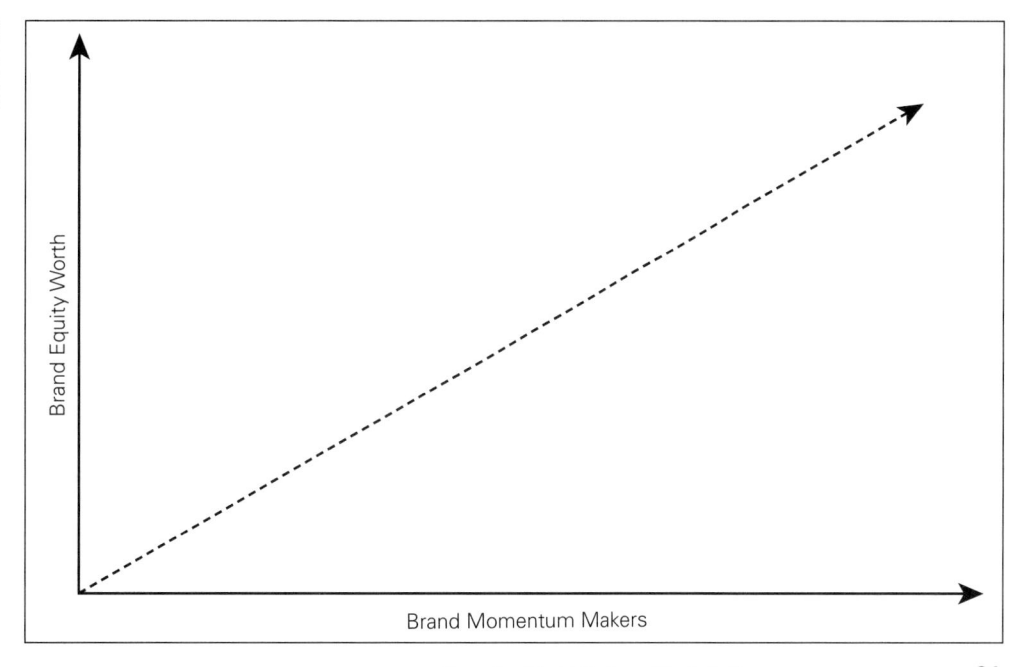

Branding That Works **Module 3**

Developing Brand Resilience

Mentor Insight

Develop brand resilience

Brand resilience is your ability to implement tactics that will allow the brand of a venture to survive the ongoing onslaught of adverse environmental factors. Leonard is adept at creating brand resilience. His products demonstrate this by having withstood the adverse impact of the marketplace. Leonard's use of world-renowned icons to represent brands is key in helping Leonard establish brand resilience. Additionally, Leonard is able to revitalize the AVP brand because he recognized the exact moment (the gold medal-winning professional beach volleyball team in the 2000 Olympics) when the market was ripe for a savior of the sport. See Mentor Method 3.2 below.

Mentor Method 3.2

The Brand Resilience Cycle[22]

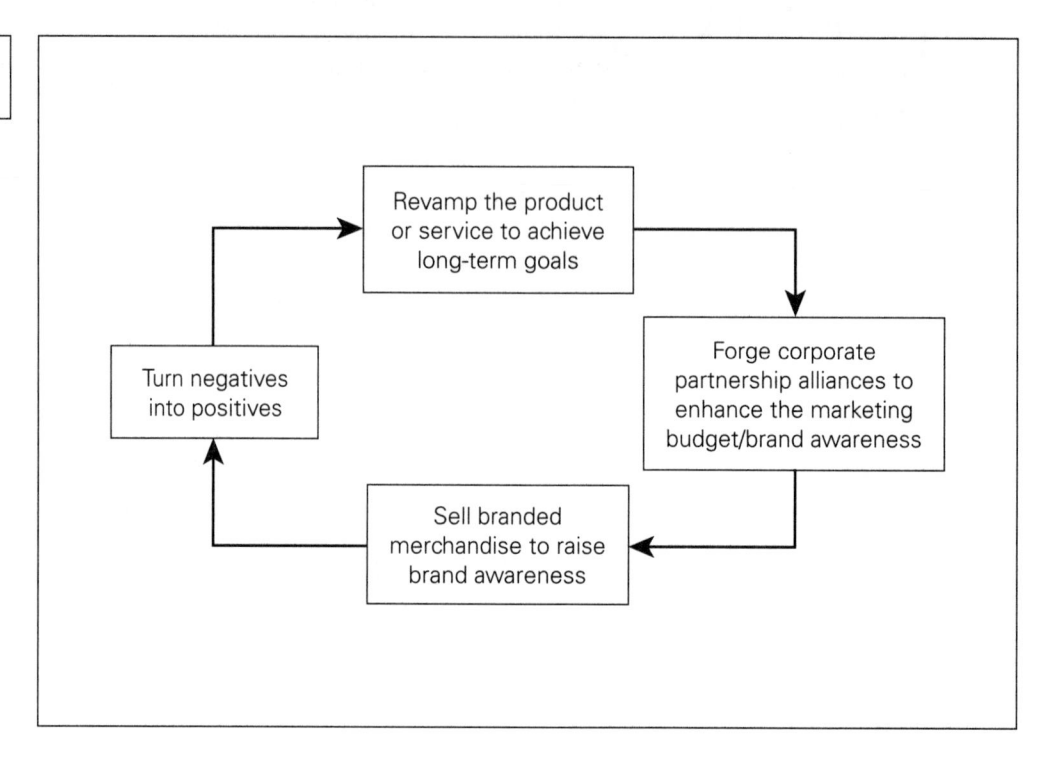

```
         Revamp the product
         or service to achieve  ──────┐
    ┌──▶ long-term goals              │
    │                                 ▼
Turn negatives              Forge corporate
into positives              partnership alliances to
    ▲                       enhance the marketing
    │                       budget/brand awareness
    │                                 │
    └────── Sell branded ◀────────────┘
            merchandise to raise
            brand awareness
```

The brand resilience cycle starts with revamping the product or service to achieve long-term goals. As the new commissioner of the AVP, Leonard is in the driver's seat for creating programs and excitement around the tour. Examples of his efforts are his ability to attract new sponsors, negotiate national television coverage, initiate a weekly radio program and AVPNext.

The next part of the cycle is forging corporate partnership alliances. In July of 2002 the AVP had an array of corporate sponsorships that included Wilson as the official ball of the AVP, KINeSYS sport as the official sunscreen of the AVP, and Paul Mitchell, Aquafina, ClubMed, Michelob Light, XBox, and Gatorade also as sponsors. Leonard and the AVP are not only augmenting the marketing budget with these corporate partnership sponsorship dollars but also raising the stakes with more prize money from sponsorship dollars. More prize money means eventually more tournaments and ultimately more brand awareness for the AVP.[23]

The brand resilience cycle continues with selling branded merchandise. Selling branded merchandise means more people wearing items with the AVP mark prominently displayed. AVP fans can purchase a wide variety of AVP–logo items that include T-shirts, visors, and sunscreen at the new AVP online store. AVP branded merchandise raises awareness of the AVP brand.

Photo provided courtesy of the AVP

Photo provided courtesy of the AVP

The final part of the brand resilience cycle is to turn negatives into positives. Leonard has taken the floundering professional beach volleyball industry and is breathing new life into the sport by improving the marketing and management of the AVP. Leonard publicizes the positive image attributes of the AVP, from the superior athleticism to the sex appeal of the sport, to transform the AVP's image into a positive. A brand resilience cycle is not complete until what caused the brand's decline has been turned into a positive.

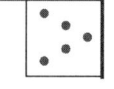

Positive Mental Attitude

> **Mentor Insight**
> Exude a positive mental attitude

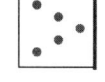

Leonard needs a positive mental attitude to navigate the chaotic waters of brand resilience for the AVP. Successfully building the brand of a new venture or an expansion of an existing enterprise also takes a positive mental attitude. A positive mental attitude will help you attract and retain the type of following you need to build a brand, even if you are on a limited budget.

Brand Ambassadorship

> **Mentor Insight**
> Be an extraordinary brand ambassador

There is one final, critical element in developing branding that really works: You. Leonard Armato understands this. It's rare to find him in any condition other than professionally impeccable. Leonard understands that at the end of the day it all comes down to the need to be an extraordinary brand ambassador of a venture's image. Here is a list of practices to consider adopting to enhance your own brand ambassadorship diplomacy.

Branding That Works **Module 3** 83

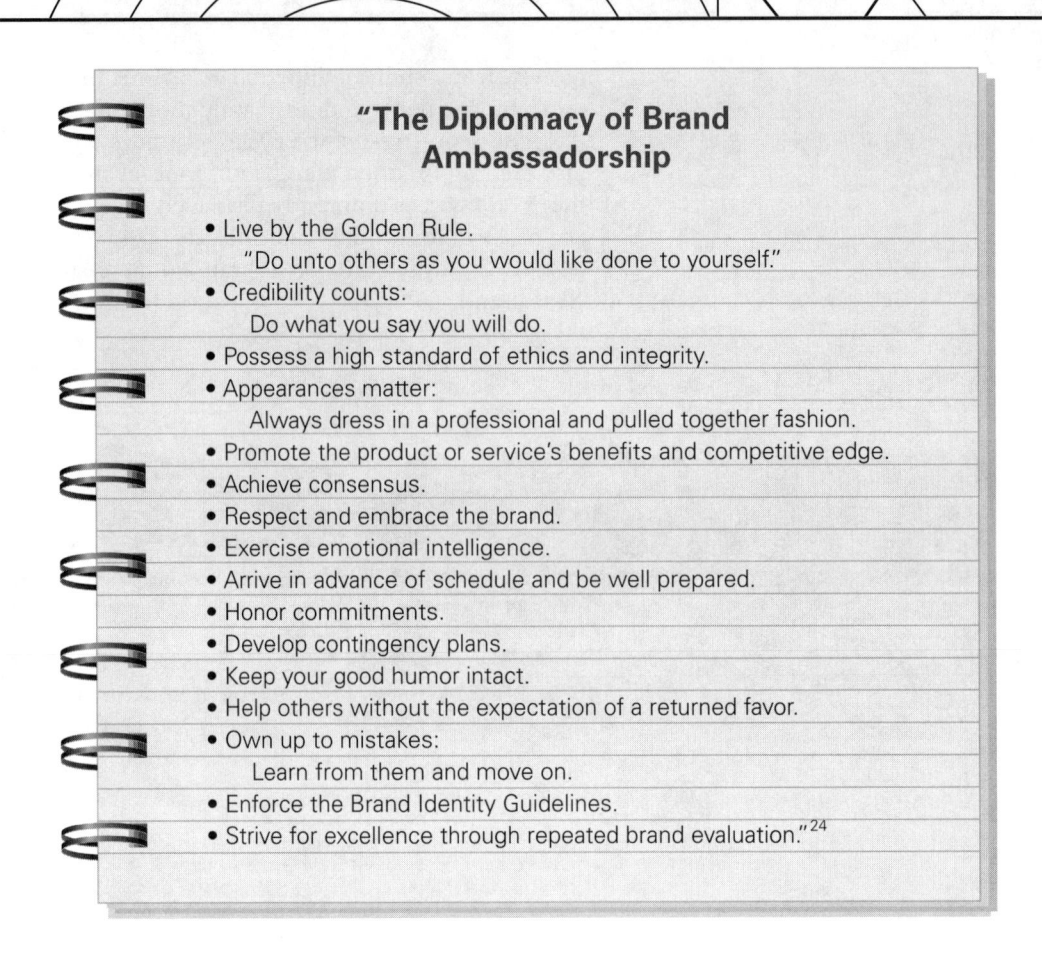

> ### "The Diplomacy of Brand Ambassadorship"
>
> - Live by the Golden Rule.
>   "Do unto others as you would like done to yourself."
> - Credibility counts:
>   Do what you say you will do.
> - Possess a high standard of ethics and integrity.
> - Appearances matter:
>   Always dress in a professional and pulled together fashion.
> - Promote the product or service's benefits and competitive edge.
> - Achieve consensus.
> - Respect and embrace the brand.
> - Exercise emotional intelligence.
> - Arrive in advance of schedule and be well prepared.
> - Honor commitments.
> - Develop contingency plans.
> - Keep your good humor intact.
> - Help others without the expectation of a returned favor.
> - Own up to mistakes:
>   Learn from them and move on.
> - Enforce the Brand Identity Guidelines.
> - Strive for excellence through repeated brand evaluation."[24]

Following these guidelines will help you be an extraordinary brand ambassador.

Leonard makes a good role model for ways to implement extraordinary brand ambassadorship techniques. For instance, Leonard lives by the **Golden Rule**; he makes sure he treats others in a manner he would want to be treated.

Leonard has a **track record** with the AVP that helps him attract the sponsorship dollars and negotiate the contracts that are needed to restore the AVP to its former prominence.

Ethics and integrity are at the forefront of Leonard's activities. He also makes sure that he hires co-workers with a high standard of ethics.

As mentioned before, Leonard and his team are **professionally pulled together** at all times. His staff is also comprised of sports enthusiasts who keep in good physical condition.

Leonard **promotes the benefits** of the AVP at every stage of his entrepreneurial marketing game.

Leonard **achieves consensus** in challenging situations. For example, he convinced the professional beach volleyball players to sign with his representation.

He and his team clearly **revere the brand** of the AVP.

Exercising emotional intelligence means being able to put yourself in someone else's shoes to understand and sympathize with where they are coming from. This is easier said than done. However, Leonard has had to

exercise his emotional intelligence on multiple occasions to get consensus and persuade others to help with restoring the AVP back to its original prominence.

You can **set your watch on Leonard's arrival**. Being late, being unprepared, or not honoring commitments are words that aren't in Leonard's vocabulary.

Leonard built his career on his credibility by making sure he **honored commitments** once they were made.

Leonard is strategic in his branding campaigns. When the Digital Media Campus didn't take off as a new media incubator he quickly refocused his attentions on the AVP that is financed by the new iteration of the Digital Media Campus (**contingency plan**).

If you spend time around Leonard you will hear him laugh and maybe even see him do something that is reminiscent of childlike behavior. Leonard **keeps his good humor** no matter what the situation is at hand.

Leonard has a long history of being a good corporate citizen by helping disadvantaged youth. **He helps others without expecting anything in return**.

When something is going wrong, Leonard is not one to cover it up or to exaggerate the problem to meet his advantage. Leonard **owns up to his mistakes**. When the first iteration of The Digital Media Campus was not working, Leonard freely admitted that he didn't have the answers but that he was trying to find them.

The last two tenets of brand ambassadorship are the most challenging to implement in a new venture. These last two tenets are: **to enforce the brand identity guidelines** and **to strive for excellence through repeated brand evaluation**.

Brand Identity Guide (Enforce the Brand Identity Guidelines)

A brand identity guide is a key part of brand ambassadorship diplomacy. A brand mark is publicized successfully through rigorous enforcement of the correct use of the logo and image. Well-recognized branded companies like Kinko's have teams of people who administer their company's brand marks making sure that if a logo is used, it's used in the proper way, with the correct color ink, in the correct size, and in the correct page layout when used in conjunction with other logos. Many companies (including Kinko's, Inc.), refer users to their style guide, which provides tools and guidelines when referencing their identity acceptably. As an entrepreneurial marketer, you will be responsible for developing your brand's identity guide and to enforce the use of your mark. A perusal of AVP logo items and the media the AVP mark appears on gives an indication that someone is paying close attention to the AVP brand identity guidelines.

The Final Brand Element—Evaluation

Last, but not least, striving for excellence at every turn of a brand's development is possible only through ongoing evaluation of a branding campaign. You can evaluate a branding campaign by measuring the size of your customer base. If the customer base isn't growing then most likely the brand equity is declining. Market research techniques such as focus groups, in-depth telephone interviews, questionnaires, surveys, and audits are good tactics to utilize to continuously evaluate a brand's effectiveness. Making mid-term corrections to a branding campaign based on customer feedback is something every entrepreneurial marketer should be willing to do. Time will tell if Leonard's efforts to restore the AVP brand to its former prominence will succeed.

Mentorography Conclusion

In Part II of this Mentor Module we have explored the methods behind Leonard Armato's representation of elite athletes and his attempts to save the AVP brand. We have analyzed the Branding That Works Mentor Insights:

Mentor Insights

- Possess ironclad perseverance
- Seize the day
- Forge corporate partnership alliances
- Invest in brand equity
- Develop the brand advantage
- Use star power to boost your brand
- Utilize an integrated marketing communications approach
- Develop brand resilience
- Exude a positive mental attitude
- Be an extraordinary brand ambassador

Mentorography Questions

1. Devise a strategy to create a successful brand on a limited or nonexistent budget.
2. Describe the branding techniques Leonard Armato is using to restore the AVP brand to its former prominence.
3. Name a new venture or an expansion of an existing enterprise that is engaged in a brand resilience campaign. What strategies is this company utilizing to restore brand interest?
4. When you develop a brand for a new venture, what diplomacy will you engage in to be an extraordinary brand ambassador?
5. Evaluate how Commissioner Leonard Armato is doing with the AVP brand.

Endnotes

[1] Courtesy of Leonard Armato, Founder, Management Plus Enterprises and Commissioner, AVP, December 13, 2002.

[2] Leonard Armato interview conducted by Molly Lavik, April 2001.

[3] Reprinted with permission of Leonard Armato, Founder, Management Plus Enterprises and Commissioner, AVP.

[4] Reprinted with permission of Leonard Armato, Shaq Brand Marketing Communications Plan by Management Plus Enterprises, March 1998.

[5] Ibid.

[6] Ibid.

[7] Reprinted with permission of Leonard Armato. "Leonard Armato's Management Bio," http://www.thecampus.com/CO_swf.asp (website now defunct), accessed March 21, 2001.

[8] Godfrey Cheshire, *Kazaam* Review, *Daily Variety*, July 17, 1996.

[9] Courtesy of Leonard Armato, Founder, Management Plus Enterprises and Commissioner, AVP, February 28, 2003.

[10] Reprinted with permission of Leonard Armato, Management Plus Enterprises Mission Statement.

[11] Reprinted with permission of Leonard Armato. "Company overview," http://www.thecampus.com (website now defunct), accessed March 23, 2001.

[12] Leonard Armato interview conducted by Molly Lavik, July 13, 2001.

[13] © 2001 The Los Angeles Times. Reprinted by permission. Mike Bresnahan, "Pro Volleyball Deal May Spike Interest," *Los Angeles Times*, April 19, 2001.

[14] © 2002 The Los Angeles Times. Reprinted by permission. Mike Bresnahan, "Beach Volleyball; 'New' AVP Tackles Some Old Problems," *Los Angeles Times*, May 23, 2002.

[15] Leonard Armato interview conducted by Molly Lavik, July 13, 2001.

[16] © 2002 The Los Angeles Times. Reprinted by permission. Mike Bresnahan, "Beach Volleyball; 'New' AVP Tackles Some Old Problems," *Los Angeles Times*, May 23, 2002.

[17] Ibid.

[18] Reprinted by permission of Leonard Armato. "AVP Hits the Radio Waves," http://www.avp.com/content.asp?ArticleID=1261, accessed June 14, 2002.

[19] Reprinted by permission of Leonard Armato. "The grassroots hub of the AVP," http://store.avp.com/content.asp?MenuID=1071&ArticleID=1196, accessed July 13, 2002.

[20] Howard W. Marshall, "Buckaroos in Paradise," *Publications of the American Folklife Center*, (Library of Congress, Washington, D.C., 1980), No. 6.

[21] Developed by Molly Lavik, July 13, 2002.

[22] Ibid.

[23] Reprinted with permission of Leonard Armato, sponsor listings from http://www.avp.com, accessed July 2002.

[24] Developed by Molly Lavik, July 13, 2002.

VIRAL MARKETING MENTOR MODULE

Crafting a Viral Marketing Phenomenon

ANITA RODDICK OBE
Non-Executive Director and Founder,
The Body Shop

Mentorography Part I

This is the story of a storyteller. This module explores how a first-generation immigrant born into a working-class family founded one of the most renowned and socially responsible international companies of our time. Today, Anita Roddick, founder of The Body Shop, still serves on the company's board as Non-Executive Director.

This exploration into Anita Roddick's background and The Body Shop will reveal a fascinating example of the viral marketing phenomenon. The definition of viral marketing is the concept of triggering an epidemic in customer purchases of a venture's products or services driven by enthusiastically shared messages. The use of the word *epidemic* does not refer to the spread of a disease but rather the widespread occurrence of exponentially multiplying amounts of customer purchases.[1]

The word *viral* is analogous to something that is caused by a virus. A virus is "an ultramicroscopic (20 to 300 nm in diameter), metabolically inert, infectious agent that replicates only within the cells of living hosts, mainly bacteria, plants, and animals; composed of an RNA or DNA core, a protein coat, and, in more complex types, a surrounding envelope."[2] In the case of viral marketing, the *infectious agents* are individual people who are so motivated about the product or service that they tell their friends and family about the wonders of the product. This dialogue by the *infectious agents* to their circle of acquaintances (the hosts) does not occur because of expensive advertisements and traditional marketing campaigns. This occurrence is purely motivated by individuals who are so enamored with a purchase that they feel compelled to share the product or services' endearing attributes in a word-of-mouth way that translates into their circle of friends making purchases and in turn telling their particular circle of friends about their incredible new acquisition.[3]

Because new ventures or expanding enterprises tend not to have the marketing resources necessary to raise brand awareness while motivating prospects to make purchases, entrepreneurial marketing often requires viral marketing. Entrepreneurial marketers must find ways to market products while spending little or no money. This may sound impossible, but it's not. This module shares the techniques used to craft a viral marketing phenomenon as demonstrated in the insights of Anita Roddick during the time she led The Body Shop. The following viral marketing Mentor Insights have been ascertained from this story:

Mentor Insights

- Place principle before profit
- Utilize creative storytelling
- Incorporate customer feedback
- Have passion for your work
- Make communications the essential tool of leadership
- Dispel myths
- Be guided by love, care, and intuition
- Solve other people's problems
- Ignite customer demand
- Kindle a word-of-mouth occurrence

Anita Roddick Milestones[4]

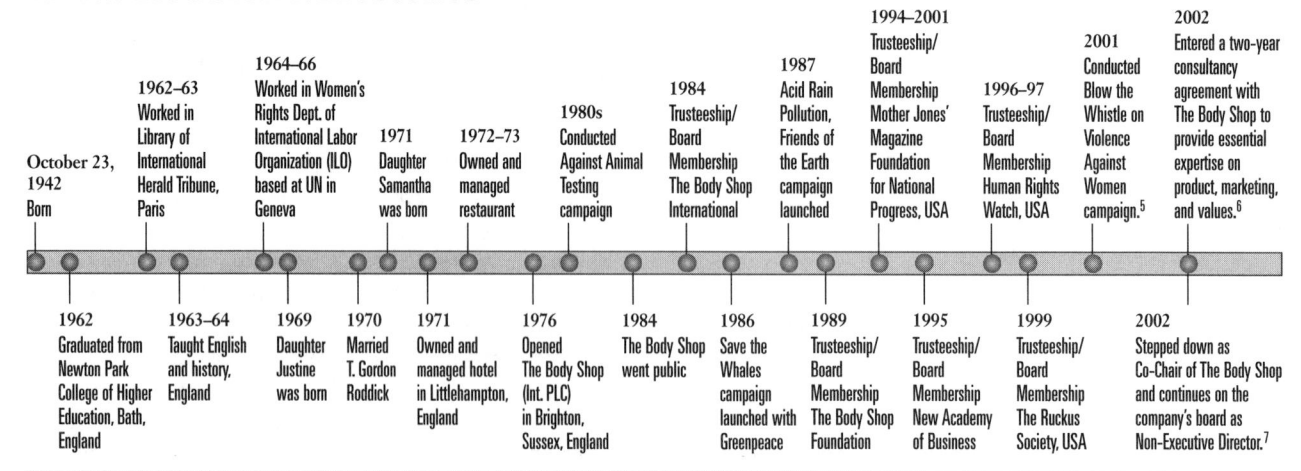

October 23, 1942 Born

1962 Graduated from Newton Park College of Higher Education, Bath, England

1962–63 Worked in Library of International Herald Tribune, Paris

1963–64 Taught English and history, England

1964–66 Worked in Women's Rights Dept. of International Labor Organization (ILO) based at UN in Geneva

1969 Daughter Justine was born

1970 Married T. Gordon Roddick

1971 Daughter Samantha was born

1971 Owned and managed hotel in Littlehampton, England

1972–73 Owned and managed restaurant

1976 Opened The Body Shop (Int. PLC) in Brighton, Sussex, England

1980s Conducted Against Animal Testing campaign

1984 The Body Shop went public

1984 Trusteeship/Board Membership The Body Shop International

1986 Save the Whales campaign launched with Greenpeace

1987 Acid Rain Pollution, Friends of the Earth campaign launched

1989 Trusteeship/Board Membership The Body Shop Foundation

1994–2001 Trusteeship/Board Membership Mother Jones' Magazine Foundation for National Progress, USA

1995 Trusteeship/Board Membership New Academy of Business

1996–97 Trusteeship/Board Membership Human Rights Watch, USA

1999 Trusteeship/Board Membership The Ruckus Society, USA

2001 Conducted Blow the Whistle on Violence Against Women campaign.[5]

2002 Entered a two-year consultancy agreement with The Body Shop to provide essential expertise on product, marketing, and values.[6]

2002 Stepped down as Co-Chair of The Body Shop and continues on the company's board as Non-Executive Director.[7]

Anita Roddick Describes Who She Is

I was born Oct. 23, 1942 to Italian immigrant parents in the tiny hamlet of Littlehampton in the south of England. My mother, Gilda Perella, still lives in the terraced house where I was born. Even when I was little I could tell my family was different: we were noisy—always screaming and shouting and playing music loudly—and we ate pasta and smelled of garlic.

My family was very much working class—my parents and grandparents ran a cafe in Littlehampton, where all the children were expected to pitch in washing dishes, buttering bread and tending the till after school and on weekends. We all slept in the same room and rented the other bedrooms out to boarders for extra money.

It was at age 10 that I found my sense of moral outrage when I read a book on the Holocaust. My face was in books so often, my mother would tell me, "You shouldn't-a read so much, you'll-a hurt your brain."

Eventually I would go on to college to study education, and became a schoolteacher. But I soon got itchy feet and began traveling, eventually finding myself talking my way into a job at the United Nations in Geneva where I worked in the women's rights division of the International Labor Organization. After an eye-opening year, I was off to travel the globe, from Tahiti to Australia to Mauritius and beyond. When the money ran out, I scraped together enough for a ticket home.

As soon as I arrived, my mother introduced me to Gordon Roddick. Gordon was a poet and children's story writer and a grand fan of international travel. We had an instant rapport. Within three years, we had Justine, Samantha, and were married, not necessarily in that order.

Gordon and I made several stabs at entrepreneurship in those early years. Gordon opened a picture framing shop, then we opened a restaurant, and later a hotel. It was hard work, and tough to get ahead. After several years of grueling hours and short pay, we packed it in.

That's when Gordon decided he had to finally attempt his dream—to travel on horseback from Argentina to New York, after the style of Swiss explorer Aimé Tschiffley. And that's when I got the idea for The Body Shop.

When I opened that first shop on a tiny street in Brighton in 1976, I had no visions of international success; I was simply frustrated that I could not buy small sizes of everyday cosmetics, and that I was spending a lot of the purchase price for fancy packaging I didn't need. So I decided to whip up my own range of cosmetics using natural ingredients in the cheapest possible plastic bottles.

By the time The Body Shop went public in 1984, Gordon and I realized that rather than just being an innovative skin and hair care company, The Body Shop had the potential and power to do good.

That's why the company's Mission Statement opens with the overriding commitment, "dedicate our business to the pursuit of social and environmental change."

And that's what we've been doing ever since.[8]

– Anita Roddick

Mentor Insight

Place principle before profit

Anita's Entrepreneurial Spirit

For Anita, becoming an entrepreneur enabled her to express her ideas about personal freedom. She is a self-professed closet anthropologist. While working for the United Nations, Anita had an opportunity to travel throughout the world. She likens traveling to a "university without walls." Anita remembers gathering stories from women about their rituals during these travels. These stories had a profound impact on Anita. She would later use stories about these rituals in her marketing of The Body Shop.

When she returned from her travels, Anita met Gordon Roddick. Together they began experimenting with various entrepreneurial endeavors. Anita explains that her business knowledge did not develop while at a business university, but through testing various products with customers. She believes you can't teach entrepreneurship. In fact, it was several years into her business before she even came across the word *entrepreneurship*. She feels that true entrepreneurs are born out of a great need and that the entrepreneurial spirit develops only when one's "back is against the wall." True entrepreneurs, to Anita, have a keen sense of what it means to bootstrap. She underscores the importance of being an outsider as a key ingredient in the development of the entrepreneurial character. Anita felt as if she was an outsider because her parents were Italian immigrants who settled in Sussex, England.

> **Mentor Insight**
> Utilize creative storytelling

The difference between a crazy person and a successful entrepreneur is, of course, that the latter can convince others to share the vision. That force of will is fundamental to entrepreneurship. Like a genie in a bottle, the idea is nothing unless someone can exploit it, which is another thing that separates entrepreneurs from everyone else. They act on what they see, think, and feel. And why are they that way?

Blame the dark side of entrepreneurship. If the entrepreneurs I'm familiar with didn't have disadvantaged childhoods, they were at least pushed into adulthood early on. They all share a sense of loss, which only deepens as the companies they create grow up and away from them. That, in turn, compounds the feeling of isolation.[9]

– Anita Roddick

An Entrepreneur Born Out of Necessity

With two young children and a husband who had embarked on an epic horseback riding adventure in a faraway land, Anita realized she needed a livelihood. She co-founded The Body Shop with her husband as a way to support her family. Growing up during World War II, Anita learned from her mother the importance of frugality and conservation. The core value of frugality was the foundation of The Body Shop. Building on these values, Anita made her products natural and packaging reusable and gave incentives for the reuse of containers. She did no traditional marketing for the first 18 years of The Body Shop. Instead Anita created products that were enhanced by her developing stories about the origins of the products.

> **Mentor Insight**
> Utilize creative storytelling

Entrepreneurial Marketing

She used interesting anecdotes and communicated her product offerings in creative ways. For example, the products were sold in small sizes so customers were not wasteful. Selling her products in five sizes gave The Body Shop an edge. Customers had the ability to choose the quantity of product they wanted instead of having to purchase a quantity that didn't meet their needs. She also gave her customers small trial samples of different products. All her products were packaged in the cheapest bottles she could find and were sold without excessive packaging. In the beginning, Anita even handwrote The Body Shop product labels. She did this until economies of scale made printing the labels cost-effective. The Body Shop customers respected Anita's values and understood when the handwritten labels smeared in the shower.

An Evolving Product Offering

Anita had learned while working with her husband in their first entrepreneurial endeavor that, when a product wasn't what customers wanted, you simply changed products until you found one they did want. For example, Anita and Gordon had started a restaurant featuring their favorite cuisine, Indian food. It never dawned on Anita and Gordon that customers would not be as enthusiastic about this type of cuisine as they were. Undaunted when no one came to the restaurant, they modified the fare until they came up with a restaurant format that was popular and successful. Anita learned that incorporating customer feedback into your product offering could mean the difference between success and failure.

> **Mentor Insight**
> Incorporate customer feedback

Anita Adopts a Socially Responsible Company Culture

Everything was seamless to Anita. Her work at The Body Shop was heartfelt. She was passionate about her work and about her activism. Growing up as an outsider, Anita feels it's important to stand up and question the status quo. She naturally gravitates toward those who are activists.

At The Body Shop, she attracted activists and people who were deeply concerned about social responsibility. She fostered a workplace community of activists and like-minded individuals who were not dedicated solely to the quest for profitability.

To help foster change in the status quo, Anita built a child development center for employees. In addition, she budgeted money for employees to take educational courses, even if the courses didn't relate to their jobs.

Anita hates hierarchy. When she was leading The Body Shop, she created a horizontally structured company and launched programs like the "red letter" program, where any employee can bypass their supervisor and send suggestions directly to managers.

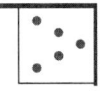

> **Mentor Insights**
> Have passion for your work
>
> Place principle before profit

Storytelling

Anita remembers, dating back to when she worked in the family café, how compelling it was for the family to tell stories to the customers and she has incorporated storytelling throughout her business adventures. Storytelling

> **Mentor Insight**
> Utilize creative storytelling

has been a powerful and often used tactic at The Body Shop. Anita and her team had used storytelling to communicate to employees, in marketing materials, and as part of her public speaking on social responsibility. Books that Anita has published or that include excerpts from Anita have fascinating stories woven into them to engage the reader.

Anita embraced free-flowing communication at The Body Shop, exemplified not just by the "red letter" program, but by numerous communications on many topics that employees received. Topics included background information on the products, how the products were produced, good uses for the products, causes Anita supported, as well as the unfortunate myths that other cosmetic companies perpetrate on consumers. Anita feels strongly that communication is the essential tool of leadership.

Anita ran The Body Shop with her heart and a strong dose of empathy.

Anita is known for her use of irreverent humor. A keen knowledge of current social and political issues is required to fully appreciate her message. Whether it's in her books, her communications to her employees, a presentation, or a chance conversation, Anita is fond of employing shocking yet humorous dialogue to engage the listener and motivate them to understand the deeper meaning.

> **Mentor Insights**
>
> Make communications the essential tool of leadership
>
> Dispel myths
>
> Be guided by love, care, and intuition

Staying True to Her Beliefs

When Anita decided to advertise on the sides of The Body Shop delivery trucks, the advertisements did not expound the merits of The Body Shop products. Instead they showed the faces of missing children with a number to call with any information. More recently the trucks have been used to spread messages about other campaigns, such as an Esso boycott. Anita has had a loyal following of customers who admire her commitment to solving other people's problems.

When the Gulf War began in the early 1990s, Anita used every billboard she could access to place antiwar messages stressing that war wasn't the answer. For example, The Body Shop at that time was headquartered in Littlehampton where they have billboards erected on the premises. Anita utilized these billboards to communicate important issues instead of using them for advertising purposes. When someone from The Body Shop accused Anita of going too far with her use of The Body Shop funds to communicate personal messages, the board of directors decided it was time to take down the billboards. Anita was outraged and threatened to resign. She put everything on the line for her beliefs. Anita decided her feelings about war would be best communicated by two employees who had survived war. These employees addressed the board, describing the true nature of what it means to fight in a war. The directors allowed the billboards to stay up.

> **Mentor Insight**
>
> Solve other people's problems

The Trade Principle

Anita learned the basics of business working in the family café. She believes that business should be based on fair trade. Fair trade is the buying and selling of goods in an ethical way. For example, Anita believes that

> **Mentor Insight**
>
> Dispel myths

94   Entrepreneurial Marketing

the cosmetic industry's myth that cosmetics can reverse the effects of time is unfair to women and she attempts to dispel it at every opportunity.

"Outraged" doesn't begin to cover how Anita feels about the exploitation of workers in economically challenged parts of third-world countries. She has traveled the globe speaking out against the atrocities inflicted by multinational companies on the weak and the frail. She has seen firsthand the aftermath of the pollution and waste caused by globalization. She has met babies born severely mutated from these pollutants. She has visited sweatshops that pay slave wages to those who need money desperately.

In the 1980s, Anita came up with an alternative way of trading. She set up trading relationships with disadvantaged communities she encountered on her travels around the world. By trading as closely as possible with the primary producers and cutting out the middleman, she made sure that the people who actually made the products benefited from the trade.

> **Mentor Insight**
> Solve other people's problems

These trading relationships have evolved into a program now known as the Community Trade program. In a nutshell, The Body Shop buys accessories and natural ingredients from poor or disadvantaged communities. The Body Shop receives good quality products while communities obtain a sustained source of income. The income can be invested as well as used to improve education or sanitation, to build homes, or to modernize farming methods.

> *Our customers get the highest quality product and an opportunity to support these communities; suppliers benefit from fair pricing and support in trying to meet their wider community goals; The Body Shop has a better way to do business which provides a model of ethical trading for other businesses.*[10]
> – Anita Roddick

- "We've established relationships based on trust and respect that enable communities to achieve social and economic independence."[11]
- Farmers in Ghana have extracted cocoa beans from pods for cocoa butter.[12]
- Women break babassu nuts in Brazil for babassu oil.[13]
- "Women in India print cotton bags for The Body Shop."[14]

Bringing in Customers

> **Mentor Insight**
> Ignite customer demand

Anita has helped ignite customer demand for products at The Body Shop by enabling people to have more control over their lives and futures and by focusing on helping others. Anita has done more than make great products; she has taken socially responsible stances via her business practices and it hasn't gone unnoticed. Socially responsible consumers and franchisees are fiercely loyal. These consumers are not only lining up to purchase products at The Body Shop, but they are also spreading the word, like wildfire, about the humanitarian work of the company. Anita and the humanitarian practices of The Body Shop are the catalyst of the viral marketing phenomenon that made The Body Shop a successful global corporation. We will analyze in-depth the reasons behind this phenomenon in the second half of this module.

Fiercely loyal customers have been essential to sustaining The Body Shop business in recent years. This is because in the past few years The Body Shop has been through a very tough competitive period due to more companies now offering natural cosmetic products. These competitors pose new challenges unlike the ones The Body Shop faced in the entrepreneurial stage of development when it dominated a market niche.

Anita's socially responsible practices are highly relevant to inspiring a viral marketing phenomenon. Humanitarian followers of The Body Shop serve as infectious agents by communicating to their circle of acquaintances (the hosts) the importance of supporting The Body Shop. In turn, this circle of acquaintances spreads the word to their circle of humanitarian acquaintances. In essence, the socially responsible practices of The Body Shop are the spark that has ignited demand for the company's products and incited many people who are motivated to buy into Anita's franchise model. A viral marketing phenomenon cannot occur without a spark that can quickly be fanned into a flame by a highly motivated and loyal customer base, and a larger target customer base predisposed to the message.

Anita's socially responsible stance is not a contrived or temporary practice at The Body Shop. Over the years Anita has remained true to her beliefs. She recently published two books that are important reading for anyone running an ethical business. She seeks to foster a business environment where business people place principles before their drive to increase the bottom line.

In 1991, Anita published *Body and Soul: Profits with Principals—The Amazing Success Story of Anita Roddick & The Body Shop*.[15] *Body and Soul* chronicles Anita's life story and the first ten years of her leadership at The Body Shop. In 2000, she published *Business as Unusual: The Triumph of Anita Roddick*[16], which details the last ten years of Anita's leadership at The Body Shop. *Business as Unusual* gives a firsthand account of Anita's revolutionary life. It's full of great material on how businesses can be socially responsible. In 2001, she published *Take It Personally: How to Make Conscious Choices to Change the World*,[17] a practical how-to guide to practicing vigilant awareness against the atrocities caused by globalization.

> **Mentor Insight**
> Place principle before profit

Principles before Profit

Anita's mantra of placing principles before profits was exemplified by her actions when she ran The Body Shop. She believed in principles before profit.

> **Mentor Insight**
> Place principle before profit

"... As legend has it, Roddick started The Body Shop in 1976 in Brighton, England, by mixing natural elixirs and pouring them into ... [small] ... bottles, which were all she could afford at the time. The stores quickly caught on, and Roddick became the 'It' entrepreneur, famous for espousing a new way of doing business. She promoted buying from indigenous people and refused to let her products be tested on animals. The world watched her trade nut oil with Indians in the Brazilian rain forest and receive an honor from the Queen of England."[18]

Dispelling the Beauty Myth

> **Mentor Insight**
> Dispel myths

One central reason that Anita was able to enlist a large core following was her direct honesty with her customers. While most in the cosmetics industry go to great lengths to espouse the merits of their products, preaching that by using such-and-such product one can reverse the process of aging, Anita was straight with her customers—not exaggerating or misrepresenting the benefits of her products. She stayed true to this concept in everything she did. She saluted women who were comfortable with who they are

Entrepreneurial Marketing

rather than strive to achieve unreal concepts of beauty represented in airbrushed and retouched glamour magazines. She remained consistent with this message when she was leading The Body Shop.

> *While I was waiting in the Denver airport for a connecting flight to Santa Barbara, I popped into the restroom and there before me was a woman with a beard. Not just facial fuzz, but a full jaw's breadth of manicured hair. My natural assumption was that this person was a man who'd gone through the wrong door, until we got to talking.*
>
> *Instantly, my mind raced to put her into context: you see bearded ladies at circuses, not airport loos. But it turned out Jennifer did, in fact, work in a circus—her own: 12 people, one ring.*
>
> *But that is the only predictable element in her story, a story she told me right there among the rushing travelers and flushing toilets.*
>
> *Jennifer was raised by her mother and grandmother, both dynamic, non-conformist educators, to believe that it was important and beautiful to be who you are. So when she first grew a little facial hair in her late teens, she left it and withstood the stares and whispers. At 20, a brush with electrolysis felt like self-mutilation and strengthened Jennifer's conviction that her beard was a learning curve, rather than a curse.*
>
> *Now Jennifer is in her mid-30s. Unsurprisingly, life has not been easy. She withdrew from the mainstream world in her 20s, turning her back on college and career paths. So she is ill-equipped to follow in her mother's footsteps and teach, much as she'd like to.*
>
> *Besides, the beard would make it hard, just as it turns public places into an ordeal. Jennifer has taken to using the men's bathroom—fewer questions asked. Or she'll take a female friend into the ladies' room so people will hear her talking and know from her voice that she's a woman.*
>
> *I can sense you thinking, why bother? Just shave the damn thing off and life would be so much easier. I thought of the women I met in Japan who shave their faces every day with tiny little pink razors, to ensure smoothness and grip for their foundation. If they can shave every day for so little a perceived social benefit, why wouldn't Jennifer do the same to ease the social strain?*
>
> *Well, she has . . . once or twice. She says the experience left her feeling even more self-conscious, as though she would be perceived as vain, trying to hide her imperfections and not really doing a very good job of it.*
>
> *As she is, Jennifer is absolutely herself, just the way God planned her, and profoundly independent and dignified with it, though you'll also be pleased to know she has a sense of humor about her lot in life and isn't boringly earnest about it.*
>
> *I loved her take on her life, and I felt lucky as we parted that, in my 50s, I could learn something from the way this seemingly radically different woman has chosen to express herself as a feminist . . .* [19]
>
> – Anita Roddick

> **Mentor Insight**
>
> Kindle a word-of-mouth occurrence

This story, posted on Anita's personal Web site, has a strong "be true to yourself" message that is not what we typically expect to see as published material from a former CEO of a global corporation. However, it's just the type of message that endears Anita and The Body Shop to its clientele. It's also the type of message that kindles a word-of-mouth occurrence. As an entrepreneurial marketer, you can spend millions upon millions of dollars trying to create a word-of-mouth occurrence to raise awareness of your business and not get as much as one mumble. Kindle a word-of-mouth occurrence by giving your clientele something they can relate to like the dramatic example of how to be true to yourself in Anita's story. Anita is the first owner of a cosmetic company to say, "Hey, it's O.K. to be who you are," a dramatically different message than other cosmetic company owners. The end result is that Anita has made a direct impression on people who buy cosmetics that she is trustworthy and isn't preaching an unachievable message. Anita has given her clientele something to talk about and spread the word about. A viral marketing phenomenon about your venture is historically preceded by a word-of-mouth occurrence.

Take It Personally

> *Some corporations maraud countries looking for the cheapest labor and the most passive and docile workers, and they go into countries that have no human rights standards and hardly any environmental regulations. In my opinion, greed's collective insanity has taken hold . . . The only developed emotions now are fear and greed, and these shortcomings have to be exposed.*[20]
>
> – Anita Roddick

While Anita ran The Body Shop, she encouraged employees to be innovative, daring, and radical and to display those traits in their daily work. She sought to hire employees who shared her passions about corporate social responsibility and environmental issues. In hiring interviews she asked unusual questions to gauge if people would fit in with the family community at The Body Shop.

Anita passionately implores us all to become vigilant consumers to curtail the damage caused by multinational corporations extending their power through globalization.

Anita created an effective viral marketing campaign for The Body Shop by creating a strong and long lasting bond with her customers reaching beyond their wallets and into their hearts. She gathered very loyal customers who were happy to loudly proclaim the reasons to shop at The Body Shop. Anita has stayed true to her guiding principles of social responsibility. She continues to alert consumers of the current and looming dangers of globalization. This is one story that Anita is doing everything in her power to give a happy ending.

Mentorography Part II

In Part II of the Viral Marketing Mentor Module we will analyze the Mentor Insights behind the viral marketing phenomenon that propelled The Body Shop into the spotlight as a dominant force in the cosmetic industry. Those Mentor Insights are:

Mentor Insights

- Place principle before profit
- Utilize creative storytelling
- Incorporate customer feedback
- Have passion for your work
- Make communications the essential tool of leadership
- Dispel myths
- Be guided by love, care, and intuition
- Solve other people's problems
- Ignite customer demand
- Kindle a word-of-mouth occurrence

Genesis of Viral Marketing Phenomenon at The Body Shop

How has The Body Shop created an intriguing message their customers find worth repeating? The phenomenon started with The Body Shop's mission:

"our reason for being
mission statement

The Body Shop International plc
 – a company with a difference

- To dedicate our business to the pursuit of social and environmental change.

- To creatively balance the financial and human needs of our stakeholders: employees, customers, franchisees, suppliers and shareholders.

- To courageously ensure that our business is ecologically sustainable: meeting the needs of the present without compromising the future.

- To meaningfully contribute to local, national and international communities in which we trade, by adopting a code of conduct which ensures care, honesty, fairness and respect.

- To passionately campaign for the protection of the environment, human and civil rights, and against animal testing within the cosmetics and toiletries industry.

- To tirelessly work to narrow the gap between principle and practice, whilst making fun, passion and care part of our daily lives." [21]

And continues with the values of The Body Shop:

| "AGAINST ANIMAL TESTING" [22] | "SUPPORT COMMUNITY TRADE" [23] | "ACTIVATE SELF ESTEEM" [24] | "DEFEND HUMAN RIGHTS" [25] | "PROTECT OUR PLANET" [26] |

Mentor Insight
Place principle before profit

The Body Shop has a mission that is outside today's norm. No other cosmetics company has values that include the five core values of The Body Shop. Anita created a company culture that puts principle before profit by starting with a mission statement and values connected to the values of a caring group of consumer advocates. The Body Shop clientele began sharing the company's message with their friends because the product line stands for something that has been forgotten in most businesses today. Customers spread this message because they want to help make the world a better place. The loyal customer following that Anita and The Body Shop enjoy has as much to do with the connection that The Body Shop has with its customers as with the products.

The Viral Marketing Message

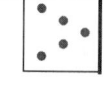

Mentor Insight
Utilize creative storytelling

Simply having customers as advocates is not enough to cause the viral marketing phenomenon. You need a clearly articulated and memorable message in order for your company's message to reach exponential rates of return in viral marketing. Anita called upon her ability as a creative storyteller to help The Body Shop craft these memorable messages. For example: "Celebrate Natural Beauty"[27] is the tag line of a memorable marketing campaign, which tells about the disgust people should have for events like beauty contests that offer distorted ideals of a women's figure. "Celebrate Natural Beauty" empowered women to be happy with their figures. The campaign boosted women's self-esteem while providing a memorable story for the carriers of The Body Shop message.

Staying in the Loop

Mentor Insight
Incorporate customer feedback

Even a memorable message isn't enough to trigger a viral marketing phenomenon. As an entrepreneurial marketer, you must make sure that the product or service is continuously updated with customer feedback. Otherwise, you risk creating a product or service that quickly goes stale with the customer base. To stay in the loop with customers, The Body Shop has a program known as The Body Shop at Home. Some 3,000 consultants hold on average 100,000 parties with more than 1 million customers each year. From these parties The Body Shop consultants obtain customer anecdotes, spontaneous reactions, and stories.

> *Nothing, but nothing, in the history of this company has been more profound or focused as the two-way conversation in people's homes in terms of letting us know whether or not we are living up to our customer's expectations.[28]*
>
> – Anita Roddick

The People on the Front Line

We've discussed the importance of having strong advocates spreading your memorable message about a product line that continuously incorporates customer feedback. Accomplishing this takes you only about halfway toward triggering a viral marketing phenomenon.

Another critical element is the people who face your customers during the sales process. Anita understands this, and made sure employees of The Body Shop shared her passion for the company mission. An absence of passion for your work can derail a viral marketing program before it starts.

Anita extended The Body Shop reach by taking on franchisees who were passionate to be selected because Anita's socially responsible work goals were consistent with their own beliefs.

There are three strong reasons for adopting a franchising growth strategy:

1. Need for capital investment
2. Need for able management
3. Need to grow into a market segment before a large competitor pre-empts your growth

The Body Shop had all three reasons to adopt franchising, but the most interesting factor was Anita's concept of "able management." Anita personally interviewed all the early applicants for The Body Shop franchises. Many people who by most standards would have been outstanding franchisees were turned down while others who might not have met traditional standards were chosen. Anita asked many typical questions, but she always asked a few unpredictable, outlandish questions to ensure that the people she worked with put principle before profits. She wanted people with a passion for her mission. In her selection process, which some described as seeking people like herself, she selected a team of managers who were the ideal team for viral marketing. They sold the concept of a store that delivered the benefit, "Feel good about yourself, for you are a good, caring, contributing citizen of the world."

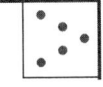

> **Mentor Insight**
> Have passion for your work

Leadership Counts

Triggering a viral marketing phenomenon is no small accomplishment. The leadership of the venture plays a critical role. As the one wearing the entrepreneurial marketing hat, you are responsible for making sure that

> **Mentor Insight**
> Make communications the essential tool of leadership

communication flowing within your internal organization is as powerful and openly communicated as the external messages.

The Body Shop is structured in a manner that encourages communication. As previously mentioned, The Body Shop's "red letter" system keeps communication flowing throughout every level of the company. The way the system works today is that the staff may communicate directly to the CEO or Human Resources Director by writing down their communications and placing them in an envelope they can mark "red letter." The Body Shop once had "idea boards" at 12 company locations where employees could share their ideas. The "idea boards" are no longer permanent fixtures and currently exist for key initiatives. Selections from the ideas submitted are sent to the board for potential integration. "Idea boards" make it possible for multiple levels of the company to have a role in business development, unlike in most companies, which subscribe to a hierarchical approach. No areas are off-limits to The Body Shop employees: in fact, even the cleaners are able to use The Body Shop's executive boardroom for meetings if they choose.

It's easier for small start-ups than larger firms to incorporate these ideas, but even start-ups face internal communications challenges. Start-up founders are often so busy with founding the new venture that internal communications is at risk. Open communications is especially important for start-ups to engage in from the beginning because a new venture requires underpaid and risk-taking employees, and these people could easily work elsewhere. The loyalty and trust you create in your corporate culture will help ensure employees stay on board as your start-up begins to lift off. In the earlier days of The Body Shop, there were late-night "mind-blowing" conversations with staff that broke down the barriers between boss and employee and abandoned taboos that limit who can talk to whom about what. The Body Shop also held family days and company days to familiarize staff with their co-workers as well as with the activities in other areas of the company. Today The Body Shop continues to foster a positive and innovative company culture by offering:

- "Love scheme for personal development—£100 a year toward courses, alternative therapy, etc.
- Choices—opportunity to buy more holiday
- Advocates—staff advocates scheme (independent staff advocates who are trained)
- Values Champions—an individual in each department tasked with raising awareness on values issues
- Global company—taking advantage of the ability to share experience from different markets"[30]

> *The key to handling problems and conflict within an organization is to keep the channels of communication wide open.*[29]
> – Anita Roddick

Mentor Insight

Make communications the essential tool of leadership

It's important to recognize that some of the best *infectious agents* for spreading the message in a viral marketing phenomenon are co-workers. Remember to make communications the essential tool of leadership.

The Beauty Myth

> ### "The Beauty Myth
> The Beauty Myth is that the effects of aging on women can be reversed by using cosmetics. That wrinkles can disappear by using certain creams. That cosmetics can rejuvenate your body and skin to regain the same appearance that existed in one's youth. This is the Beauty Myth." [31]

> *In the factory, we make cosmetics; in the store, we sell hope.*[32]
>
> – Charles Revson (Revlon Inc.)

The relationship of women and cosmetics appears to be first documented on the walls of ancient Egyptian ruins. Helen of Troy, the face that launched a thousand ships, is one of our first documented cases of the media setting unreal standards of beauty for women, and relegating their worth as people to be correlated with their appearance. Charles Revson may have been the first to acknowledge the true benefit of cosmetics to be "hope"; he was not the first to sell the benefit rather than the attribute.

Most people who use cosmetics seek glamour, beauty, and social status. Anita Roddick sells self-worth. From a traditional marketing standpoint, Anita did everything wrong by not perpetuating the beauty myth. By not doing anything like a large cosmetics corporation, she positioned her stores and products well away from the mainstream. The market segment she targeted was not large, but it had been ignored and was tired of the "business as usual" cosmetics industry offerings. The people in this segment were frustrated by their inability to personally affect their environment and world. The beliefs and values of youth of the sixties and seventies toward the environment and the ethical treatment of people and animals were often compromised by the demands of career and family. Compromising ones' beliefs and values leads to lower self-esteem. The Body Shop gave people a way to live in harmony with their beliefs and values, which in turn allowed them to have higher self-esteem. Buying hope is a fleeting treatment for the symptoms of low self-esteem. By dispelling the long-perpetrated Beauty Myth, The Body Shop has provided a valuable tool for creating the viral marketing phenomenon.

Mentor Insight
Dispel myths

Ethics Matters

At no other time in global corporate history has ethics been so much in the forefront of business ventures as it is today. Corporate leaders, possibly motivated by greed, have forgotten that customers do care about the ethics of a company and the products and services they are purchasing. As an entrepreneurial marketer, you need to play a role in upholding the ethical practices of the venture. You also need to communicate these ethical practices to customers.

Malcolm Gladwell in his national bestseller, *The Tipping Point*,[33] describes in detail "how little things can make a big difference." Paying attention to these little things are the key reasons Malcolm attributes for reaching the tipping point. The tipping point is that moment in time when a viral marketing phenomenon occurs.[34]

Anita Roddick understands how small things like having an ethical stance running through every aspect of your business can make a big difference. As seen in the H.E.R.O. pyramid in Mentor Method 4.1 below, Anita founded The Body Shop based on these core-guiding principles. She did this by being guided by love, care, and intuition. Love, care, and intuition are values that are often forgotten in today's greed-motivated corporate world.

> **Mentor Insight**
>
> Be guided by love, care, and intuition

Mentor Method 4.1

Hierarchy of Ethics Role in an Optimum Organization (H.E.R.O.) Pyramid[35]

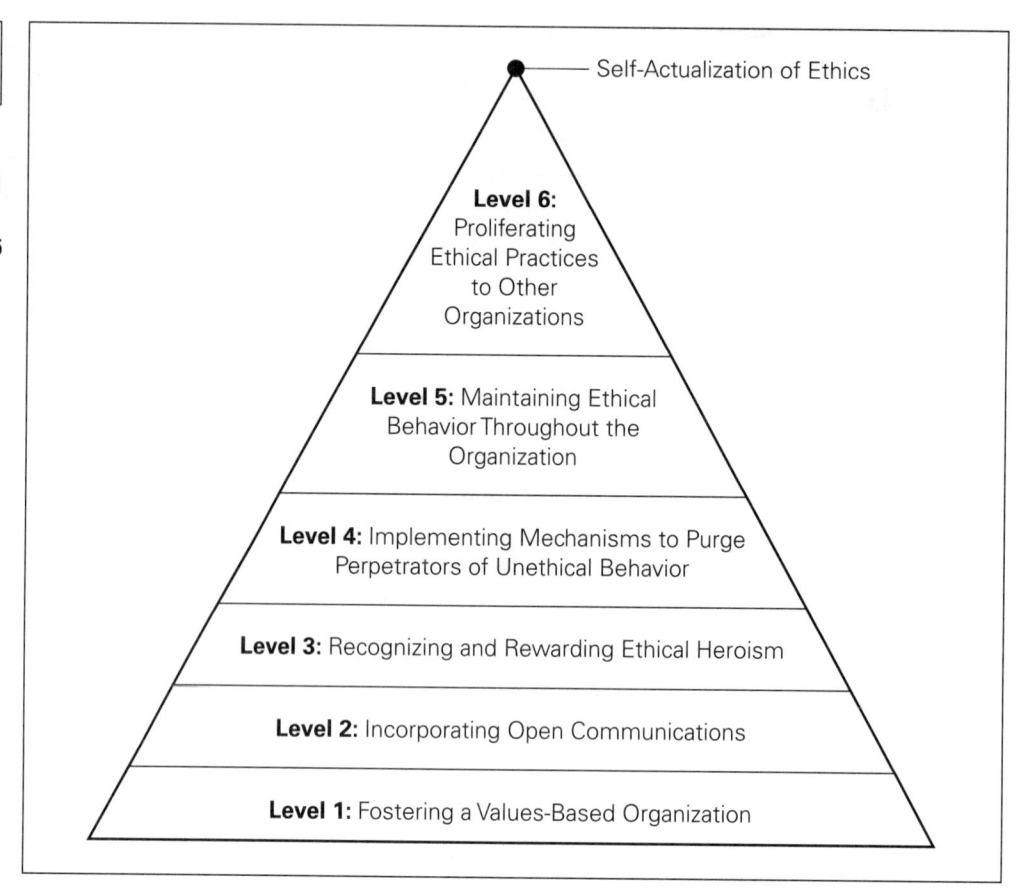

- Self-Actualization of Ethics
- **Level 6:** Proliferating Ethical Practices to Other Organizations
- **Level 5:** Maintaining Ethical Behavior Throughout the Organization
- **Level 4:** Implementing Mechanisms to Purge Perpetrators of Unethical Behavior
- **Level 3:** Recognizing and Rewarding Ethical Heroism
- **Level 2:** Incorporating Open Communications
- **Level 1:** Fostering a Values-Based Organization

Anita and The Body Shop epitomize The H.E.R.O. pyramid for the following reasons:

- **H.E.R.O. Pyramid Level 1**: Anita's use of love, care, and intuition throughout the organization allowed the company culture to be values-based. Anita incorporates empathy on a daily basis in her business practices. The Body Shop mission statement includes the words "To tirelessly work to narrow the gap between principle and practice, whilst making fun, passion and care part of our daily lives."[36]

Entrepreneurial Marketing

- **H.E.R.O. Pyramid Level 2:** The Body Shop uses communications as the essential tool of leadership. New ventures that lack open, free-flowing communications are inadvertently creating fertile ground for unethical behavior. Closed-door meetings can spark employees' covert behavior. Repressing information can silence whistle-blowers.

- **H.E.R.O. Pyramid Level 3**: Recognizing and rewarding ethical heroism is a norm at The Body Shop. A start-up venture can go a long way toward ensuring the creation of an ethical corporate culture by rewarding ethical heroism rather than punishing those who aren't consumed with making their employer richer.

- **H.E.R.O. Pyramid Level 4:** If you can't trust someone in your new venture, show him or her the door. There is too much at stake to do anything less. As the entrepreneurial marketer of the venture, you must have the courage to carry out the dismissal of these individuals. Anita created such a loving, caring organization that unethical behavior would have no place to hide.

- **H.E.R.O. Pyramid Level 5**: This is undoubtedly the most challenging part of achieving continual ethical behavior within an organization. Many well-intentioned new ventures have started heading in the ethical direction only to wake up one morning to find themselves on the wrong side of the ethical behavior line. Anita had implemented some processes at The Body Shop that help the company stay ethical. She calls these processes ethical auditing and she described this process in her book, *Business as Unusual: The Triumph of Anita Roddick*. "'Ethical auditing' is an all-encompassing term that describes social and environmental auditing and any other ethics-related auditing that we may do, such as animal-protection auditing. We began it as an independently verified assessment of the company's performance against our stated values, and in 1995 we produced our first Values Report. The latter involved in-depth interviews and wide-scale surveys with all our stakeholders, ranging from employees to shareholders, from suppliers to local communities."[37]

- **H.E.R.O. Pyramid Level 6:** The Body Shop is one of the best examples of a business that successfully proliferates ethical practices to other organizations. The company does this by raising consumer awareness of businesses that have inhumane labor practices. Anita does this because, in her own words, " . . . I am opposed to maximizing profit to satisfy investors and I believe you should care for your employees and care for your suppliers. You should tell the truth to your public and your customers. Only then can you conduct your business in a profitable way."[38]

- **The Self-Actualization of Ethics Point:** Self-Actualization of Ethics is when H.E.R.O. pyramid levels 1–6 have been achieved. The Body Shop during Anita's leadership achieved what most businesses don't even dream of doing: the self-actualization of ethics point. This point is only achievable through a long-term commitment to the six levels of the H.E.R.O. pyramid. Hitting the self-actualization of ethics point can permanently ingratiate you with your customers. This can also light the spark needed to start a viral marketing phenomenon.

Solving Other People's Problems Solves Your Own

Mentor Insight

Solve other people's problems

In the past, The Body Shop has used the sides of its company trucks to advertise missing children, not The Body Shop products. Today the trucks are used to spread other up-to-the-minute campaign messages. Anita has used her own billboards to give visibility to raising the awareness about inhumane activities. Anita has purchased directly from impoverished laborers the goods she uses at her shops so that laborers can benefit directly from their work. The Body Shop is actively engaged in helping others solve their problems on a regular basis and spearheads campaigns about everything listed in the company's values (see p. 100). Solving other people's problems is often overshadowed in the corporate world. As the founder of a new venture, you have the flexibility necessary to solve other people's problems. Solving other people's problems creates an enormous amount of goodwill for your venture, and goodwill is another spark that can ignite customer demand.

Igniting Customer Demand

Mentor Insight

Ignite customer demand

The Body Shop has figuratively lit many sparks to ignite customer demand. These sparks include running the organization with love, care and intuition, having a strong ethical stance, and generating an enormous amount of goodwill with the clientele. What role does igniting customer demand play in the viral marketing phenomenon process? Mentor Method 4.2 helps answer this question.[39]

Mentor Method 4.2

The Symmetric Pattern of Purchases Driven by Viral Marketing[40, 41] (A Bell-Shaped Curve)

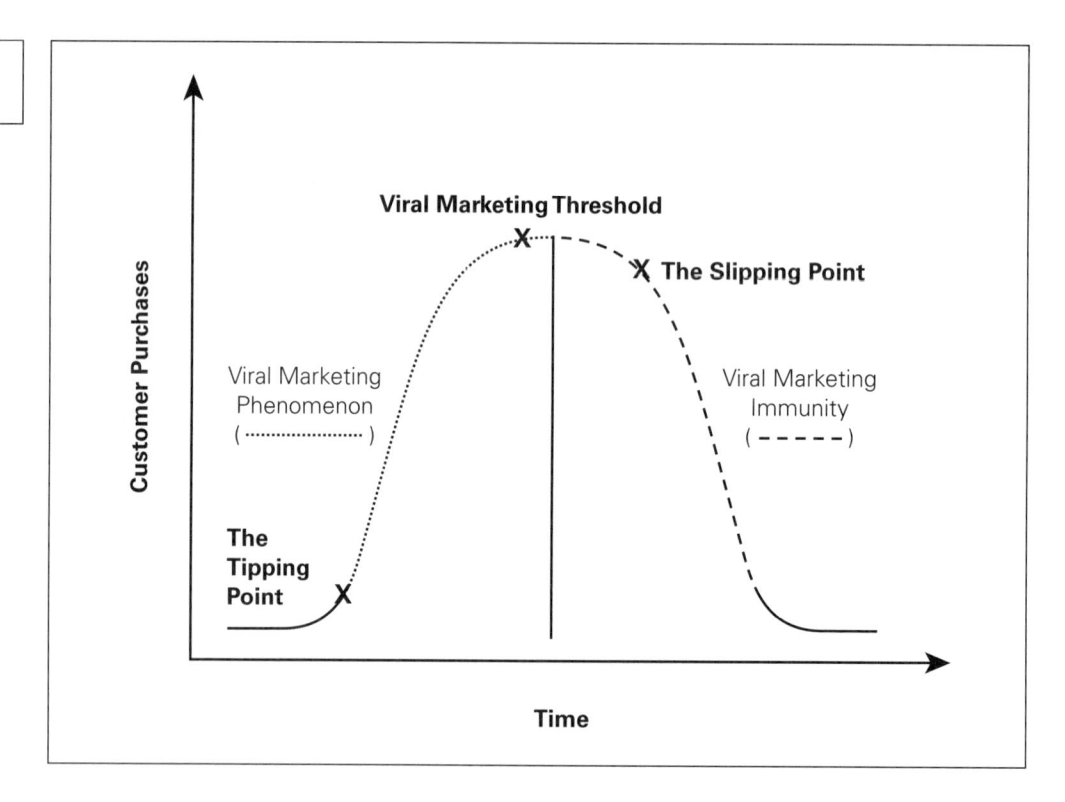

[Graph showing Customer Purchases vs Time as a bell-shaped curve, with labels: "Viral Marketing Threshold" at the peak, "The Tipping Point" at the start of the rise, "The Slipping Point" on the descent, "Viral Marketing Phenomenon (..........)" on the ascending dotted portion, and "Viral Marketing Immunity (- - - - -)" on the descending dashed portion.]

106   Entrepreneurial Marketing

> **Mentor Insight**
>
> Ignite customer demand

Igniting customer demand to the point of triggering a viral marketing phenomenon is a major challenge to accomplish. There is no amount of money, time or contriving that can guarantee this process. During Anita Roddick's socially responsible and ethical leadership, this phenomenon occurred repeatedly. There was a magic moment in time when Anita went from manufacturing by hand in reused tiny bottles with ink-drawn labels her first cosmetic products to when customer demand skyrocketed. We've discussed in-depth what fueled this occurrence with The Body Shop. When that magic moment occurred is when the tipping point happened. The skyrocketing sales of the product line featured at The Body Shop, in an almost 90 degree vertical ascent, marks the viral marketing phenomenon.[42]

It's important to note though that the viral marketing phenomenon is a double-edged sword. What goes up must come down. The best way to remember this important lesson is to understand that viral marketing is an extremely effective tool for entrepreneurial marketers to engage in because the phenomenon doesn't require a heavy outlay of cash. With that said, the very velocity that propels the occurrence of viral marketing will also cause its descent. Best to think of viral marketing and the purchasing behavior of customers driven by this occurrence as a symmetric pattern. A time will inevitably arrive when the company's message hits the viral marketing threshold. This is the point where in the absence of no new message about a product that has the impact of the previous messages, the process is headed for the slipping point. The slipping point is when a descent of equal magnitude to the ascent will occur. What has occurred is that the marketing message no longer triggers further viral marketing phenomena. Instead, the message has developed immunity with one's customer base. The infectious agent affect has been cured. Viral marketing immunity has set in and in essence inoculated the viral marketing phenomenon.[43]

As an entrepreneurial marketer who may have enjoyed the tipping point, it's best to understand that a long-term strategy is needed to continue to reap the benefits of the exponential increase of customer demand.[44] When Anita Roddick and her team were running The Body Shop they had been able to successfully trigger continual customer demand by having new and improved products as well as introducing new activism campaigns. A recent example of a new activism campaign can be found on The Body Shop web site.

". . . Choose Positive Energy

The Body Shop and Greenpeace International have joined forces in a global campaign to combat global warming.

Global warming is the most serious environmental threat we face today. One solution is to switch to renewable energy such as solar, wind, and wave power. The Choose Positive Energy campaign is about making the switch at home in the UK and demanding access to renewable energy for 2 billion people in developing nations who are currently without access to energy.

(continues)

What Can You Do To Help?

At Home: to switch to renewable energy at home, pick up a leaflet in store or sign up at a The Body Shop at Home party, fill it out and post it to Greenpeace. Greenpeace will send you information on a local renewable energy provider including Ecotricity and Juice.

Globally: You . . . [could have signed] a petition in store and urge[d] world leaders at the next World Summit on Sustainable Development in Johannesburg [that occurred] in August 2002, to commit to providing 2 billion people with access to renewable energy. Or . . . [have signed] the petition on the campaign website at: www.choose-positive-energy.org.

The Choose Positive Energy campaign . . . [ran] at The Body Shop in 31 countries until September 2002.

Green Electricity

In January 2001, The Body Shop Head Offices and 134 UK stores switched to renewable energy.

One step The Body Shop has taken to slow the effect of global warming, is the switch to renewable energy provider, Ecotricity. The energy from Ecotricity is sourced from wind, solar, small-scale hydropower, landfill gas and biomass. Making the switch will save The Body Shop 6800 tonnes of carbon dioxide per year, or the equivalent of emissions from 4660 houses.

Anita recently challenged other retailers to make the switch; 'Climate change is the biggest environmental issue we face today and The Body Shop wants to do everything it can to address this head on. With no extra cost, there's no earthly reason why other high street retailers shouldn't switch to Ecotricity. In fact, the Earth demands it, I challenge them to follow our lead . . .'"[45]

John Morrison, Head of Campaigns for The Body Shop International, elaborates further on the Choose Positive Energy campaign in August of 2002.

"The Body Shop is using grassroots communication to explain why we should CHOOSE POSITIVE ENERGY. The Body Shop and Greenpeace's joint CHOOSE POSITIVE ENERGY Campaign aims to secure a commitment at the World Summit on Sustainable Development (WSSD) in Johannesburg in September 2002 to bring renewable energy to two billion of the world's poorest people, many of whom are without access to any form of electricity, within ten years. Over 1.6 million customers have signed our Choose Positive Energy petition. The great level of customer support reflects the commitment and enthusiasm of our shop staff across the world who have spread the message. Our commitment to shopfloor campaigning remains unique in the business world."[46]

The Magic Ingredient

Mentor Insight

Kindle a word-of-mouth occurrence

The effects of viral marketing will not drive customer purchases without a buzz being generated regarding the product. The generation of a loud din of excitement about a product is what is commonly referred to as the word-of-mouth occurrence. The origins of a word-of-mouth occurrence can be traced back to the very definition of viral marketing. As seen in Mentor Method 4.3 Word-of-Mouth Occurrence Diagram, it only takes one person, usually known as a trendsetter, to enthusiastically raise attention to their circle of friends about a product to start the viral marketing process in motion.[47] The word-of-mouth occurrence diagram conceptualizes this process.

Mentor Method 4.3

Word-of-Mouth Occurrence Diagram[48]

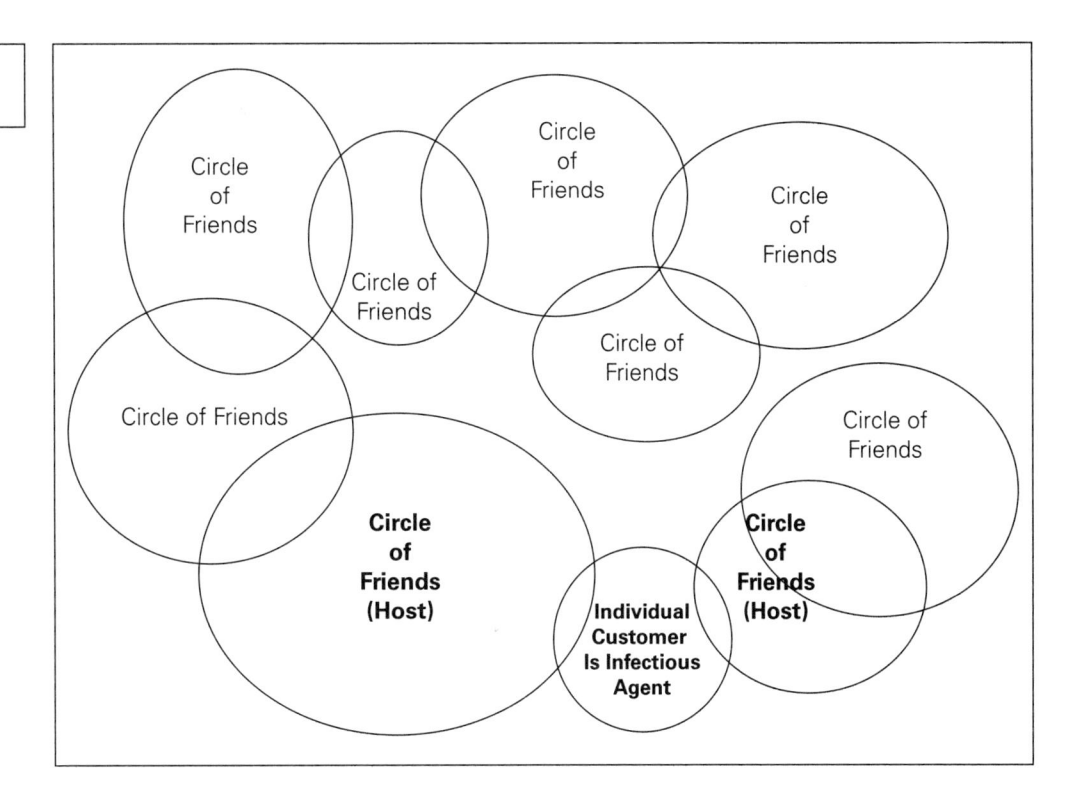

- Circle of Friends
- Circle of Friends
- Circle of Friends
- Circle of Friends
- Circle of Friends
- Circle of Friends
- Circle of Friends
- Circle of Friends
- **Circle of Friends (Host)**
- **Circle of Friends (Host)**
- **Individual Customer Is Infectious Agent**

Word-of-Mouth Occurrence[49]

Once the viral marketing process is set in motion by the word-of-mouth occurrence the message will not be communicated to the scope of people necessary to reach the tipping point unless there are multiple circles of friends' host groups. The message will go no further if the trendsetter tells a circle of friends who does not in turn disseminate the message to multiple circles of friends. How then does an entrepreneurial marketer ensure that the trendsetter will infect multiple circles of friends' host groups?[50] The answer can be found in the well-documented diffusion of innovation process (Mentor Method 4.4).

Mentor Method 4.4

Viral Marketing Phenomenon Occurs When Infectious Agent's Circle of Friends Belongs to Multiple Product Adoption Sectors[51]

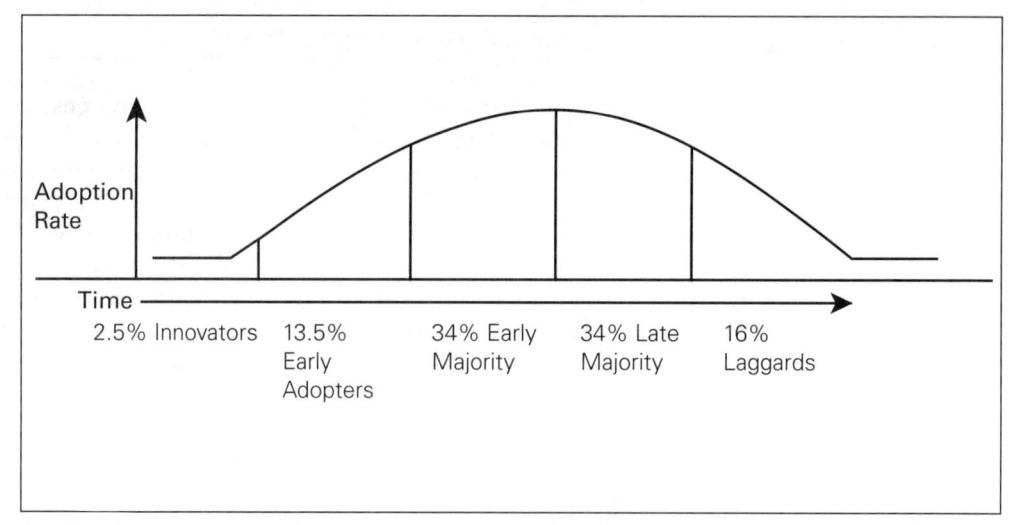

Adoption Rate

Time

2.5% Innovators | 13.5% Early Adopters | 34% Early Majority | 34% Late Majority | 16% Laggards

Reprinted and redrawn with the permission of The Free Press, a Division of Simon & Schuster Adult Publishing Group, from DIFFUSION OF INNOVATIONS, Fourth Edition by Everett M. Rogers. Copyright © 1995 by Everett M. Rogers. Copyright © 1962, 1971, 1983 by The Free Press. Reprinted and redrawn from "Adopter categorization on the basis of innovativeness," Figure 7.2, DIFFUSION of INNOVATIONS, Fourth Edition, p. 262.

DIFFUSION OF INNOVATIONS, (as reprinted and redrawn in Mentor Method 4.4), breaks people's product adoption behaviors into sectors. An innovator begins using a product before the instruction manual has even been printed. These people thrive on teaching themselves how to use complicated products before they are even completed. Early adopters are usually the first people to start using a new product. They are experimenters who prefer using new products before others. Early majority adopters are mainstream customers known as fast followers of early adopters. They are typically not the first people to use a product but they are a close second. Late majority adopters are mainstream customers who adopt new products after others have worked out the bugs and problems. Lastly, there are laggards, slow followers who typically don't adopt a new product till after it has moved out of the new product arena.

As an entrepreneurial marketer, you should group your prospective customers into these categories because doing so will help you understand the motivations behind the sectors you are targeting. The easiest sector to market to and capture the interest of is the innovators. Start-up ventures that begin with targeting innovators can count on the word-of-mouth occurrence. As the marketing guru Geoffrey A. Moore states, "One of the keys in breaking into a new market is to establish a strong word-of-mouth reputation among buyers . . . [F]or word-of-mouth to develop in any particular marketplace, there must be a critical mass of informed individuals who meet from time to time and, in exchanging views, reinforce the product's or the company's positioning. That's how word-of-mouth spreads."[52] Notably there is a massive "chasm to cross" in order to migrate word-of-mouth occurrences from one category to the next. This can be accomplished if you have memorable messages worth repeating. Memorable messages, like the messaging articulated by Anita and The Body Shop, are the secret ingredient that bridges multiple sectors and kindles the word-of-mouth occurrence creating the viral marketing phenomenon.

Mentor Insight

Kindle a word-of-mouth occurrence

110   Entrepreneurial Marketing

Mentorography Conclusion

In this Mentor Module on viral marketing we have discussed the Mentor Insights behind Anita Roddick's craft in creating The Body Shop. Those Mentor Insights are:

Mentor Insights

- Place principle before profit
- Utilize creative storytelling
- Incorporate customer feedback
- Have passion for your work
- Make communications the essential tool of leadership
- Dispel myths
- Be guided by love, care, and intuition
- Solve other people's problems
- Ignite customer demand
- Kindle a word-of-mouth occurrence

Mentorography Questions

1. What is the viral marketing phenomenon? Give several examples of ventures that have utilized this marketing technique successfully as well as examples of those that tried and failed. Why did they succeed or fail?
2. Why was Anita Roddick able to utilize viral marketing techniques effectively at The Body Shop?
3. How does one cause a word-of-mouth occurrence?
4. What are the benefits to an entrepreneurial marketer in triggering a viral marketing phenomenon?

Endnotes

[1] Adapted by permission of Malcolm Gladwell from *The Tipping Point: How Little Things Can Make a Big Difference*, Malcolm Gladwell, *The Tipping Point: How Little Things Can Make a Big Difference*, (Back Bay Books, New York, 2002), (Originally published in hardcover by Little, Brown and Company—now a division of AOL Time Warner Book Group, New York, 2000), pp. 7–9.

[2] *Random House Webster's College Dictionary*, (Random House, Inc., New York, 1992, 1991), p. 1489.

[3] Adapted by permission of Malcolm Gladwell from *The Tipping Point: How Little Things Can Make a Big Difference*, Malcolm Gladwell, *The Tipping Point: How Little Things Can Make a Big Difference*, (Back Bay Books, New York, 2002), (Originally published in hardcover by Little, Brown and Company–now a division of AOL Time Warner Book Group, New York, 2000), pp. 91–96.

[4] All the Anita Roddick Milestones unless otherwise stated are from Anita Lucia Roddick OBE, Founder of The Body Shop, profile and curriculum vitae, Anita Roddick Publications Ltd.

[5] Reproduced with kind permission of The Body Shop International plc, "Blow the Whistle on Violence Against Women" Brochure, Distributed by The Body Shop Stores in 2001.

[6] "The Body Shop International plc, The Body Shop Terminates Offer Discussions and Announces Board Changes," official announcement, February 12, 2002, Courtesy Bill Eyres, Head of Global Corporate Public Relations, The Body Shop International plc.

[7] Ibid.

[8] Reproduced with kind permission of Anita Roddick Publications Ltd., "EVERYTHING you ever wanted to know about Anita," About Anita Roddick page, http://www.anitaroddick.com/aboutanita/, accessed November 3, 2001.

[9] Reproduced with kind permission of Anita Roddick Publications Ltd., "Entrepreneurship, Constructive Lunacy," BUSINESS > ENTREPRENEURSHIP page, http://www.anitaroddick.com/weblog/weblogdetail.jsp?title=Entrepreneurship&id=58, accessed November 4, 2001.

[10] Reproduced with kind permission of The Body Shop International plc, "COMMUNITY TRADE: What you buy can make a difference" Brochure, Distributed by The Body Shop Stores in 2001.

[11] Ibid.

[12] Ibid.

[13] Ibid.

[14] Ibid.

[15] Anita Roddick, *Profits with Principals—The Amazing Success Story of Anita Roddick & The Body Shop*, (Crown Publishing, New York, 1991).

[16] Anita Roddick, *Business as Unusual: The Triumph of Anita Roddick*, (Thorsons, London, 2000).

[17] Anita Roddick, *Take It Personally: How to Make Conscious Choices to Change the World*, (Conari Press, Berkeley, 2001).

[18] Carlye Adler, "The Disenfranchised," *Fortune*, September 17, 2001, pp. 200C–200H.

[19] Reproduced with kind permission of Anita Roddick Publications Ltd., "Jennifer, the Bearded Lady," SELF-ESTEEM page, http://www.anitaroddick.com/weblog/weblogdetail.jsp?title=null&id=57, accessed November 4, 2001.

[20] Anita Roddick presentation held at Midnight Special Bookstore, October 15, 2001.

[21] Reproduced with kind permission of The Body Shop International plc, "The Body Shop International plc – a company with a difference.," our reason for being page, http://www.thebodyshop.com/web/tbsgl/about_reason.jsp, accessed February 23, 2003.

[22] Reproduced with kind permission of The Body Shop International plc, our values page, http://www.thebodyshop.com/web/tbsgl/values.jsp, accessed February 23, 2003.

[23] Ibid.

[24] Ibid.

[25] Ibid.

[26] Ibid.

[27] Anita Roddick, *Business as Unusual: The Triumph of Anita Roddick*, (Thorsons, London, 2000), p. 97.

[28] Ibid, p. 86.

[29] Ibid, p. 83.

[30] Courtesy of Bill Eyres, Head of Global Corporate Public Relations, The Body Shop International plc, September 11, 2002.

[31] An elaboration on The Beauty Myth developed by Molly Lavik, June 23, 2002.

[32] Andrew Tobias, *FIRE AND ICE: The Story of Charles Revson—the Man Who Built the Revlon Empire*, (William Morrow and Company, Inc., New York, 1976), p. 107.

[33] Adapted by permission of Malcolm Gladwell, from *The Tipping Point: How Little Things Can Make a Big Difference*, Malcolm Gladwell, *The Tipping Point: How Little Things Can Make a Big Difference*, (Back Bay Books, New York, 2002), (Originally published in hardcover by Little, Brown and Company—now a division of AOL Time Warner Book Group, New York, 2000).

[34] Ibid, pp. 7–14.

[35] Hierarchy of Ethics Role in an Optimum Organization developed by Molly Lavik, June 22, 2002.

[36] Reproduced with kind permission of The Body Shop International plc, "The Body Shop International plc – a company with a difference.," our reason for being page, http://www.thebodyshop.com/web/tbsgl/about_reason.jsp, accessed February 23, 2003.

[37] Anita Roddick, *Business as Unusual: The Triumph of Anita Roddick*, (Thorsons, London, 2000), p. 68.

[38] Ibid, p. 17.

[39] Adapted by permission of Malcolm Gladwell from *The Tipping Point: How Little Things Can Make a Big Difference*, Malcolm Gladwell, *The Tipping Point: How Little Things Can Make a Big Difference*, (Back Bay Books, New York, 2002), (Originally published in hardcover by Little, Brown and Company—now a division of AOL Time Warner Book Group, New York, 2000), p. 12.

[40] The Symmetric Pattern of Purchases Driven by Viral Marketing developed by Molly Lavik, June 22, 2002.

[41] Adapted by permission of Malcolm Gladwell from *The Tipping Point: How Little Things Can Make a Big Difference*, Malcolm Gladwell, *The Tipping Point: How Little Things Can Make a Big Difference*, (Back Bay Books, New York, 2002), (Originally published in hardcover by Little, Brown and Company—now a division of AOL Time Warner Book Group, New York, 2000), pp. 7–14, 271–275.

[42] Ibid, pp. 7–14.

[43] Ibid, pp. 271–275.

[44] Ibid, pp. 7–14.

[45] Reproduced with kind permission of The Body Shop International plc, "whats happening in the UK," protect our planet page, http://www.uk.thebodyshop.com/web/tbsuk/values_pop.jsp, accessed November 17, 2002.

[46] Quote by John Morrison, Head of Campaigns, The Body Shop International plc, Courtesy Bill Eyres, Head of Global Corporate Public Relations, The Body Shop International plc, August 23, 2002.

[47] Adapted by permission of Malcolm Gladwell from *The Tipping Point: How Little Things Can Make a Big Difference*, Malcolm Gladwell, *The Tipping Point: How Little Things Can Make a Big Difference*, (Back Bay Books, New York, 2002), (Originally published in hardcover by Little, Brown and Company—now a division of AOL Time Warner Book Group, New York, 2000), pp. 30–34, 69–70, 91–92.

[48] Ibid.

[49] This variation of a word-of-mouth occurrence concept developed by Molly Lavik, June 22, 2002.

[50] Adapted by permission of Malcolm Gladwell from *The Tipping Point: How Little Things Can Make a Big Difference*, Malcolm Gladwell, *The Tipping Point: How Little Things Can Make a Big Difference*, (Back Bay Books, New York, 2002), (Originally published in hardcover by Little, Brown and Company—now a division of AOL Time Warner Book Group, New York, 2000), pp. 30–88.

[51] Reprinted and redrawn with the permission of The Free Press, a Division of Simon & Schuster Adult Publishing Group, from DIFFUSION OF INNOVATIONS, Fourth Edition by Everett M. Rogers. Copyright © 1995 by Everett M. Rogers. Copyright © 1962, 1971, 1983 by The Free Press, Everett M. Rogers, "Adopter categorization on the basis of innovativeness," Figure 7.2, DIFFUSION OF INNOVATIONS, Fourth Edition, (The Free Press, a Division of Simon & Schuster Adult Publishing Group, New York, 1995), p. 262.

[52] Geoffrey A. Moore, *Crossing the Chasm: Marketing and Selling High-Tech Products to Mainstream Customers*, (HarperBusiness, a division of HarperCollins Publishers, New York, 1995), p. 69.

CRM MENTOR MODULE

Creating a Company Culture That Fosters Effective Customer Relationship Management (CRM)

PAUL ORFALEA
Founder, Kinko's, Inc.

Mentorography Part I

Paul Orfalea, founder and chairperson emeritus of Kinko's, Inc., is a fascinating study and a true modern adventurer. In this module, we will explore how to found a business with an exceptional company culture for fostering Customer Relationship Management (CRM). Effective CRM is essential for new venture success. CRM refers to the methods marketers use to understand the behaviors and actions needed to motivate a customer to form a loyal attachment and repeatedly purchase a company's products or services. Marketers use this understanding of the customer to create customer loyalty programs that drive profitable sales for the business venture.[1] Building customer relationships in the new venture arena calls for a broad shift from database marketing to true customer relationship management.

Paul Orfalea and his management team at Kinko's had a profound understanding of CRM. In this module, we will explore Paul's insights about creating a company culture effective in helping customer relationship management thrive. We will examine how CRM transformed Kinko's into a business masterpiece. The CRM Mentor Insights we will focus on are the following:

Mentor Insights

- Treat people as equals
- Have integrity
- Depend on others for skills that aren't your strengths
- Achieve a balance between work and personal life
- Subscribe to lifelong learning
- Encourage innovation, creativity, and experimentation
- Identify, acquire, and retain profitable customers
- Strive for 110 percent customer satisfaction
- Be proactive
- Make quality a priority

This module highlights how one man overcame obstacles that most would categorize as insurmountable, and by doing so, sheds light on the origins of Paul Orfalea's CRM Mentor Insights.

Paul Orfalea Milestones

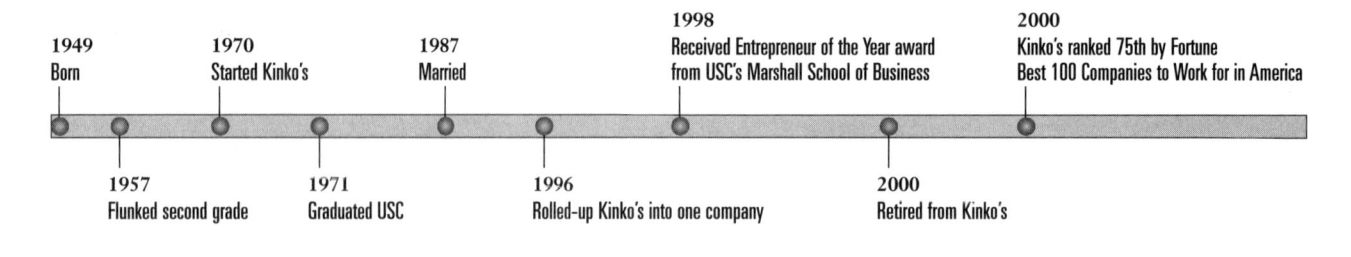

- 1949 — Born
- 1957 — Flunked second grade
- 1970 — Started Kinko's
- 1971 — Graduated USC
- 1987 — Married
- 1996 — Rolled-up Kinko's into one company
- 1998 — Received Entrepreneur of the Year award from USC's Marshall School of Business
- 2000 — Retired from Kinko's
- 2000 — Kinko's ranked 75th by Fortune Best 100 Companies to Work for in America

Paul's Early Years

Born to loving and nurturing parents, Paul Orfalea is the youngest of three children. Mr. and Mrs. Al Orfalea were Lebanese immigrants whose extended family are all business owners of one kind or another. The idea of working for other people was not part of the landscape in Paul's family. He has 17 first cousins who all have their own businesses. Paul's first lesson in management came from conversations taking place around the dinner table.

116   Entrepreneurial Marketing

> *To a dyslexic, a sentence is not like Egyptian hieroglyphics or a cryptogram. It's more like a road map with mouse holes or coffee stains in critical places.[2]*
>
> *– Paul Orfalea*

Hiding a Secret

Paul made it to second grade before one of his teachers realized that he not only couldn't read, but also couldn't even really make out the alphabet. In the fifties, when Paul attended grammar school, dyslexia was not yet identified as a disorder; the symptoms were considered a character flaw. As his classmates in second grade recited paragraphs and wrote the alphabet, Paul managed to memorize patterns.

Paul was relegated to a special area where he would be "nailed" regularly for not writing clearly and on time. After failing second grade, Paul was sent to a special school with mentally impaired and Down's Syndrome students where he felt out of place. Paul's mother was always trying to find some solution for his reading problems and eventually she would take him to have his IQ tested. It was then discovered that he had an IQ of 130; this allowed him to return to regular school. Paul developed survival skills and became a visual learner to help overcome his dyslexia.

> *People with dyslexia are highly intuitive. They learn to listen and sharpen their memories. They avoid writing if they can and develop unique survival skills in what would otherwise be a hostile universe. If management is the art of avoiding obstacles, they manage their way around their condition.[3]*
>
> *– Paul Orfalea*

The Impact of a Caring Mother and Father

Mentor Insights

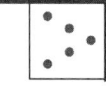

- Treat people as equals
- Have integrity
- Depend on others for skills that aren't your strengths

Having caring and nurturing parents minimized the negative impact of Paul's dyslexia on his self-esteem. In high school, Paul's mother never chastised him for his low grades. Instead, she instilled in him the notion that with hard work he could be and do anything. She encouraged Paul to attend college. His parents' attitude taught Paul the power of treating people right and as equals.

Paul also received strong support from his father, who was not only nurturing, but also a successful businessman willing to share his work ethic. Paul remembers vividly his father always working hard. Paul would carry his father's sense of integrity into his own business ventures.

Paul's father was in the women's apparel industry in Los Angeles and although he had some great ideas, he was too busy operating the company to implement them. For example, Paul's father wanted to label denim jeans, but never managed to get around to it. He also spoke of liquidating the business and buying real estate in Malibu, but he never did. Paul recalls that his dad was a man of great ideas who could have been very successful if he had only removed himself from the daily operation of the company. Later in life, Paul would be very careful not to make this same mistake with Kinko's. Paul claims he never officially ran Kinko's. Instead, he hired talented co-workers, the term Paul uses for employees, who knew how to make the company successful. Paul also credits his dyslexia with his realization that he had to depend on others to do the things he couldn't excel at himself. "Anyone else can do it better" was his motto.

The Impact of the Mundane

Due to his father's unfortunate inability to remove himself from the mundane aspects of his business, Paul made sure to balance his own career between work, love, and play. Paul works hard, but when 5:00 p.m. comes around, it is time for him to be with family or relax. He believes that if you can't finish your work by quitting time, you probably aren't working efficiently. Long hours prevent you from having really great ideas because long hours make you feel tired.

> **Mentor Insight**
> Achieve a balance between work and personal life

It's What You Save That Counts

While in high school, Paul opened a vegetable stand to earn extra money. The stand served him as a business case. He learned the magic of selling his vegetables at a reduced price. He saw the impact of selling high-quality fresh corn. He also became aware of the drawbacks of his involvement with the minutiae of running this business. On days he spent arranging displays, he wouldn't be able to get to the newspaper office in time to place the advertisements for help that he badly needed. Further, Paul developed a keen eye for the bottom line and learned to measure his success by how much money he could put into savings each week. Paul adopted frugal habits in order to save.

News Junkie

While growing up, Paul was a self-professed news junkie. Every day after school he would watch the news from 4:30 p.m. to 7:30 p.m. He was consumed with current events. To this day, Paul feels that a keen awareness of current events is an integral part of any successful business. He believes staying on top of emerging trends can help you better predict and understand your customers' needs.

College Days

Paul made his parents proud by attending college. For him, it was an easy decision. His visual image of Vietnam—backpacks, guns, high humidity, mosquitoes, and body bags—motivated him. Paul attended Los Angeles Valley Community College before going on to business school at the University of Southern California.

> **Mentor Insight**
> Have integrity

> *Although my professors' disdain was sometimes harsh, I knew they were right. Maybe I didn't belong, but that didn't mean I wasn't in for the long haul. I had decided that college wasn't as much fun as my mother had suggested, but getting a degree was worthwhile. Whatever I may have learned or not learned in college because I am a poor reader, I had already learned the value of following through with what I had started. I was learning how to manage myself.[4]*
>
> – Paul Orfalea

Entrepreneurial Marketing

> **Mentor Insight**
> Subscribe to life-long learning

Paul always planned to start his own business. Business school was loaded with important and fascinating information that he planned to use one day in his own business. While the students around Paul were cramming for exams, Paul had used his razor-sharp memory to retain business lessons. At USC Paul discovered that he had a real affinity for math and that he loved the stories behind financial statements. Paul recognized the importance of education because he understood the relevance of learning for an entrepreneur.

On the Brink of Brilliance

A terrifying moment for Paul at USC came while he was in a class taught by Dr. Trefze. A good educator, who presided over the classes he taught with frigid dignity, Dr. Trefze was known for the terror he imposed on those who dozed off in class. He had a reputation for asking complex questions and accepting no excuses from the timid or tardy. This daunting professor discovered that Paul could barely read and spoke to Paul's tutor. Paul to this day isn't sure exactly what his tutor told this professor, but he will never forget the outcome of their discussion.

> *To this day, I don't know exactly what my tutor told Dr. Trefze. She was an honest woman and I'm sure she wouldn't lie about the reading ability I didn't have, but she must have said something to change his opinion of me.*
>
> *At the next class session, Trefze called on me at the end of class. I shuddered at his mention of my name, preparing myself for the exposure and denunciation that would come. I wondered if students were ever lynched for entering college under false pretenses. I could not deny my guilt; yet felt that I was too young to die.*
>
> *Suddenly, what I heard was not a blast of outrage but a compliment so extravagant and unexpected that to this day, I smile when I think of it. Trefze announced to my undoubtedly astonished fellow students and without a trace of sarcasm, "I am told Mr. Orfalea is on the brink of brilliance."[5]*
>
> – Paul Orfalea

> **Mentor Insight**
> Encourage innovation, creativity, and experimentation

Paul is very mindful of the motivating power of a well-placed compliment. He knows firsthand the power of praise, even when it seems misplaced. This lesson played a role in Paul's learning to foster a company culture that encourages experimentation. People won't be inclined to be innovative, creative, or experimental if they don't receive some encouragement along the way.

> **Mentor Insight**
> Identify, acquire, and retain profitable customers

Kinko's Is Born

Paul started Kinko's while a senior at USC. He chose Santa Barbara, California, as the location for two reasons: His girlfriend at the time attended the University of California, Santa Barbara (UCSB), and he had seen a copy store near USC that had been doing a brisk business. At that time, the photocopier was a new innovation. Despite its recent arrival, the photocopier became an overnight necessity in the academic world. Students, for example, needed copies of everything from class notes to textbook chapters. Professors needed multiple copies of everything they distributed in the classroom—from the course syllabus to exams. Paul noted that in Isla Vista, where UCSB is located, students were constantly traipsing down the street to school. Paul saw this heavy foot traffic as a stream of potential customers.

> *Students could make copies at the university library for ten cents a copy. I figured I could sell them for four cents and still make a profit—the way I had sold fresh vegetables from an outdoor stand a couple of summers earlier and beat the price of the local supermarkets. I might be a bad reader and dangerous to machinery, but I knew I could peddle things to other students.*
>
> *With my dad as cosigner, I borrowed $5,000 from the Bank of America, and for $100 a month rented a converted lunchroom so small that I had to lug the copy machine out on the sidewalk each business day. The copier, of course, was rented too. On the first day of school I offered film processing as an additional service and hawked spiral notebooks, pens and pencils, not in the store, but on the curb, because I figured that, especially on the first day of school, every student needed a notebook and a pen and I knew from experience that a college bookstore where students usually purchase supplies was always a mob scene during the first week of term.*
>
> *Not every student did need a notebook—at least not from me—but during those first weeks of operation I was selling $2,000 worth of school supplies a day, as well as selling copies.*[6]
>
> – Paul Orfalea

Mentor Insight

Strive for 110 percent customer satisfaction

Paul located his first outlet in a convenient spot for his targeted customers and sold his copy products for less than 50 percent of his competitor's price. With his convenient location and low prices, Paul created very satisfied customers. Satisfied customers translated into an instantly profitable new business venture.

The Early Days of Kinko's

With Kinko's profitable from its first month of operation, Paul experienced firsthand the positive side of having a business with an innovative technology product.

The UCSB Kinko's was the only Kinko's for the first two years of the company's existence. After two years Paul experimented with a blueprinting business, but he quickly found out it was not a profitable venture. Paul had learned in business school that the life of an entrepreneur was fraught with ups and downs. He discontinued the blueprinting to focus on Kinko's photocopying products that were in demand.

Paul opened the second Kinko's near the University of California, Irvine. It, too, was profitable from the start.

Kinko's Expands

During the 1970s, Kinko's expanded further. Paul decided not to use a traditional franchise model for expansion. Instead he grew the business by taking on partners, which brought about slow, steady growth.

Paul's Role at Kinko's

Paul's role at Kinko's was that of a "happy wanderer." The partnership method of growth allowed Paul to invest little money in the new stores. By forming partnerships, Paul was able to distribute the risk as well as infuse the business with talented and motivated individuals. He figured that partners would be less likely to eventually compete against him and potentially wipe him out. Paul would eventually take on about 120 partners. Forming partnerships gave Paul the freedom to do what he did best: experiment with the company. Paul was rarely to be found in his office, and as the years went by, he became less and less accessible. His thinking was that if you couldn't find him readily, you would be more inclined to make your own decisions and take care of your own problems. So, instead of working in his office, Paul would wander about at different Kinko's stores, talking to customers, getting their input and feedback, and testing out new ideas. Although Paul administrated accounting practices, his ability to not get bogged down in the details of running Kinko's allowed him to be a great visionary behind the company's success.

Paul saw his management role as the remover of obstacles. He focused his energy on removing obstacles from his co-workers' paths. He did this through the "happy wandering" that allowed him and others to experiment with unique solutions to customer challenges.

As a partner, Paul motivated his partners to work hard by giving them a piece of the action; they shared the rewards as well as the risks. Additionally, Paul was very appreciative of his co-workers. He was amazed that anyone would work for him given his disabilities, and often asked, "When someone came to work for me, do you think I slapped their hands or kissed their hands?"[7]

"By 1980 . . . [Kinko's] had over 120 stores nationwide . . ."[8] By the early 1980s, there were 400 Kinko's branches. The company was experiencing a steady growth curve. During this time, Paul lived a frugal existence that meant he was able to reinvest everything he made back into Kinko's.

Mentor Insights

Strive for 110 percent customer satisfaction

Identify, acquire, and retain profitable customers

Mentor Insight

Encourage innovation, creativity, and experimentation

Creating a Company Culture That Fosters Effective CRM **Module 5**

> **Mentor Insights**
>
> Treat people as equals
>
> Strive for 110 percent customer satisfaction

During the seventies and eighties, Paul fine-tuned his management skills. He strongly believed in empowering his co-workers and demonstrated that trust by leaving his co-workers alone to do their jobs. Paul was a pioneer in adopting employee empowerment techniques. By treating his staff as equals, Paul created very satisfied employees—internal customers.

Paul realized in the early eighties that the Kinko's management structure needed to expand to support the company's growth. Kinko's Service Corporation was formed out of the need to serve Paul's partners and branches better. The Service Corporation proved to be an outstanding way to "provide administrative services to . . . [Kinko's] partners."[9]

During the 1980s, Kinko's began a company initiative to work toward the goal of standardizing the store environment. A brand image and colors were discussed. During these discussions, the foundation for more structure was begun throughout the company. The results of these discussions would eventually lead to standardizing the interior design of each Kinko's branch so that the customer would experience uniform look and feel no matter which Kinko's she frequented. Brand identity guidelines began to be formalized so that each store had consistent Kinko's logo usage and signage. Eventually, the color blue was selected for the interior of the Kinko's stores, because blue is a calming color that offers a soothing balm to the Kinko's customer, who was often rushed and unsure of his needs.

Customers would eventually come to depend on Kinko's for the same product line at every Kinko's, in much the same way we expect the same French fries at any McDonald's we visit. This consistent product offering at Kinko's would lead to the solidifying of customer loyalty.

Game Plan for Expansion of Kinko's

The game plan was very simple.

New partners → New stores → Innovation → More business

Prominent Partnerships

During the late 1980s and early 1990s, Kinko's expansion was aided by a series of strategic alliances with companies that had similar corporate cultures and commercial interests.

In 1993, Kinko's partnered with Sprint to add videoconferencing to Kinko's branch services. Kinko's videoconferencing quickly developed into a network of more than 150 public videoconference rooms. Kinko's provided reliable, easy-to-use, high-quality videoconferences empowering users to share full-color presentations, charts, and graphics, as well as connect to a laptop to access the Internet.[10]

In 1997, Kinko's forged a joint venture with the Virgin Group, enabling Kinko's to open its first store in London. This partnership gave Kinko's, a previously domestic U.S. company, the expertise and marketing savvy to go global.[11]

As a company, Kinko's could have simply enjoyed the profits from its copying business. Instead, Kinko's, nurtured by the happy wandering of Paul Orfalea, continued to forge new ground by adding innovative technologies through partnerships with companies like Sprint. Paul and Kinko's always took a proactive approach to business by understanding their customers' needs and rolling out innovative products to meet these needs.

> **Mentor Insight**
>
> Be proactive

> *Back then we didn't think of Kinko's as either "corporate" or a "culture." Just a cool way to do things.*
>
> *Back then, if we were tied into any culture at all, it was that of the college campus.*[12]
>
> – Paul Orfalea

"The Company Picnic"

Paul was not only proactive in understanding his external customers' needs, but also in understanding his internal customers' (co-workers') needs. For example, Kinko's has an annual picnic which, in the beginning, was a one-day affair in a park in Goleta, California. The picnic consisted of beer, hot dogs, and beans. The activities included listening to music, playing volleyball, and sharing ideas. The event brought together every member of the Kinko's management team.

Photo courtesy of Kinko's, Inc.

As the years went by, the "Company Picnic" began to transform itself to better reflect the changes at Kinko's. Eventually the "Company Picnic" (now called the "Kick-off Meeting") became a five-day event with a focus on business issues and a limited amount of recreation. The event now focuses on training and sharing ideas and directions, with the final day remaining a picnic celebration.

The Kinko's Philosophy

Kinko's, as a company, is consistently able to greatly exceed customer expectations. One reason for this is the guiding principles behind the visionary philosophy of Kinko's. Paul didn't merely have a company philosophy for Kinko's, he had a credo by which the company was run, and every action at Kinko's had to live up to this credo. Additionally, many of the Mentor Insights that are critical for effective CRM are clearly articulated in the original version of the Kinko's philosophy:

Mentor Insights

Make quality a priority

Strive for 110 percent customer satisfaction

Encourage innovation, creativity, and experimentation

Treat people as equals

Achieve a balance between work and personal life

Kinko's Philosophy: The Vision and Blueprint for the Company

"Our primary objective is to take care of our customer.

We are proud of our ability to serve him or her in a timely and helpful manner, and to provide high quality at a reasonable price. We develop long-term relationships that promote mutual growth and prosperity.

We value creativity, productivity and loyalty, and we encourage independent thinking and teamwork. Our co-workers are the foundation of our success. We consider ourselves part of the Kinko's family.

We trust and care for each other, and treat everyone with respect. We openly communicate our accomplishments and mistakes so we can learn from each other.

We strive to live balanced lives in work, love, and play. We are confident of our future and point with pride to the way we run our business, care for our environment, and treat each other."[13]

The vision and blueprint of Kinko's is incorporated in the way Kinko's is run as a business and the way people are treated at the company.

Mentor Insights

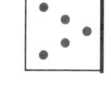

Subscribe to life-long learning

Make quality a priority

Strive for 110 percent customer satisfaction

Kinko's has never been about machines; it has always been about people, their wants and needs and how best to serve them. In the beginning, the head of a store was a person who was comfortable with machines. Nowadays we prize co-workers with excellent people skills. We do more than prize them; we train them to have those skills.

How serious are we about good customer relations? Serious enough to invest millions in training, testing, and more training. In the future no one is going to touch a customer until he or she has had two weeks in the classroom.

Someone has said, "When the vision is clear, decisions become easier," and we have found that to be true. Whether it is determining where to locate a store, what services to offer, or what hours to operate, customer service has always been our first concern.

... For us, service relates to three primary customer concerns: the quality of the service, its timeliness, and its cost. If one is missing, the customer has not been well served.[14]

– Paul Orfalea

Long-term Relationships

Kinko's has always been committed to long-term relationships—with our customers and with our co-workers.

Kinko's is a for profit organization. Of course we want to make money. But we also recognize that profitability depends on establishing long-term relationships with customers: this means service and products that are consistent. It means promises kept, and it means going the extra mile when there is an opportunity. At Kinko's quality of service must be predictable. A company that sacrifices long-term commitment to customers for short-term profit advantage is a company working its way out of business.[15]

– Paul Orfalea

Obsessed with Quality

Paul and the management team made quality a priority at Kinko's, which could be seen in many ways at the Kinko's outlets. Under Paul's leadership, Kinko's branches were always sparkling clean from countertop to copy service. The continuously trained staff at Kinko's were well equipped to offer the best in service to hurried and stressed customers. In fact, Kinko's staff were known for helping to solve challenging projects. Many people came to depend on the Kinko's team for their own start-up ventures. Kinko's obsession with providing a high-quality product and service instilled loyalty in the hearts and minds of their customers.

Turning a Negative into a Positive

The lawsuit came as a real shock. Although my partners and I went into the copy business to earn a living, we had always felt that we were also providing a service—to a segment of the population, students and teachers, who needed all the help they could get. Our whole corporate philosophy was service oriented. We thought of ourselves as the good guys, on the side of the angels.[16]

– Paul Orfalea

A lawsuit was brought against Kinko's in 1989. The lawsuit claimed copyright infringement. Specifically, Kinko's allegedly provided the means for professors and students to obtain copies of copyrighted materials for use in their classes without approval from the publishers. The lawsuit came from a group of publishing houses asserting that 12 of their copyrighted works had been infringed in the copying of course packets.[17]

Kinko's, as a copy shop, had always been mindful to respect copyright laws. Kinko's fought the course packet lawsuit, believing that the copying of course packets for use in classrooms was permissible as a "fair use" under the copyright laws, which specifically exclude from liability the copying of certain copyrightable materials for educational use. However, Kinko's voluntarily entered into an agreement with the publishing houses to establish new procedures for its course packet business, after a judge ruled against Kinko's. The result changed the way Kinko's did business. The new procedures meant that Kinko's could no longer copy certain chapters and long passages from textbooks for students' educational purposes without getting approval from the publishers.[18] This type of copying had been a major part of Kinko's business.

The lawsuit had a major impact, greatly reducing Kinko's course packet business.[19] Kinko's implemented new training for its frontline employees to ensure that no copyright protected material was being copied. Perhaps the most significant outcome of the lawsuit was that Kinko's had to seek a new niche outside of the college market. As luck would have it, the timing coincided with a shift in the needs of business people. The home-office trend was emerging and people needed Kinko's type services to complete their work. Paul describes these shifting times and the impact of this new trend on Kinko's.

> *The key was the combination of technological change, economic hard times, and the American dream of a more flexible lifestyle. During the 1990s, economic recession led to downsizing in hundreds of businesses. Thousands of white-collar workers suddenly found themselves on the street competing for jobs that were too few and, in many cases too unchallenging and unrewarding. At the same time, thousands of workers were voluntarily leaving large corporations to start businesses of their own, small businesses motivated by the entrepreneurial spirit. More co-workers of large corporations were being sent home to work; more and more projects were being outsourced. Even within companies, offices were being streamlined, re-engineered, and reconceptualized.*
>
> *An office was no longer just a place.*
>
> *It was a state of activity.*
>
> *It was access to resources, a verb, and an action word.*
>
> *It was a revolution in the workplace, a revolution largely made possible by technology and by imagination untrammeled by traditional paradigms of work.*
>
> *In 1992, we targeted this new customer base with a marketing campaign called "Your Branch Office."*[20]
>
> *– Paul Orfalea*

The enormous success of the overall advertising effort proved that Kinko's had effectively identified, acquired and retained profitable customers by getting a substantial return from their marketing investment.

And just like that, Paul and Kinko's had taken a negative (the copyright infringement lawsuit) and turned it into a real positive by having new target markets such as the home office segment to sell their products and services to. Kinko's had identified a large market opportunity—the displaced worker/home worker—and transformed the company to provide services for this expanded customer base. This shift in business focus turned out to be very lucrative for Kinko's.

Kinko's Takes a Capital Investment

As Kinko's expanded globally, it became apparent that the company needed to keep pace with the latest developments in copy technology. This latest development in copy technology was known as digital communication. A large amount of cash was needed not only to invest in digital technology, but also to pay for a technology upgrade necessary for information to move smoothly from one Kinko's store to another. The stores needed to have the same operating procedures and standardized equipment. The continued incremental growth of Kinko's didn't necessarily provide the resources for a large-scale upgrade to standardized and innovative equipment.

In 1996, it was decided to roll-up Kinko's into one big company where partners would become shareholders, the company would be restructured, and additional capital would be sought. The New York private investment firm of Clayton, Dubilier & Rice (CDR) made a significant investment in Kinko's to make this "roll-up" possible.

All change is met with a certain amount of resistance and uneasiness. Kinko's as a company survived the transition that follows sweeping changes. These changes led the way for Kinko's to create a scalable line of product offerings and for the company to become even more profitable.

Moving On

In 2000, Paul decided it was time for him to leave Kinko's. He had worked very hard on Kinko's for three decades and was 50 years old; he believed that when you were in your 50s it was time to enjoy life. He felt it was time to continue his happy wanderings elsewhere. Paul assumed the role of chairperson emeritus for Kinko's, Inc., and is no longer involved with Kinko's day-to-day operations. He now devotes much of his time to other business ventures and teaching.

One of his ventures is the Orfalea Family Foundation, which supports various philanthropic efforts, but specifically spotlights early childcare and education, caregiver training, and intergenerational programs. Orfalea, his family, and Kinko's have a long history of supporting educational initiatives including scholarships and child development programs with efforts concentrated in California.[21] Paul speaks out on the need for family-friendly business practices through work-life policies, and shares his insight on learning challenges—that everyone learns differently.

Paul's Three Rules on Business

"Liquidity, Liquidity, Liquidity"[22]

Paul's Theory About Life

In your 20s you should try it all.

In your 30s you should figure out what you do best.

In your 40s you make money at what you do best.

In your 50s you just don't "do," it's when you should enjoy life.[23]

– Paul Orfalea

These words are from a saying that Paul's mother had that Paul adopted in the way he lives his life. Paul is fond of sharing this saying with others.

This has been the background of a great entrepreneur, a person who proved that you can achieve anything in life, even, and perhaps especially, in the face of challenges. Paul Orfalea created a very successful global corporation in Kinko's. He developed a company whose core guiding philosophy centered on creating a company culture that fosters effective CRM. We have explored in this half of the chapter the origins of the Mentor Insights that can be learned from studying Paul and Kinko's history.

Mentorography Part II

In this half of the module we will analyze the Mentor Insights that Paul utilized to create a company culture that fosters effective CRM. Those Mentor Insights are:

Mentor Insights

- Treat people as equals
- Have integrity
- Depend on others for skills that aren't your strengths
- Achieve a balance between work and personal life
- Encourage innovation, creativity, and experimentation
- Identify, acquire, and retain profitable customers
- Strive for 110 percent customer satisfaction
- Be proactive
- Make quality a priority
- Subscribe to lifelong learning

> *I attribute the foundation of our success to good customer relations achieved by our co-workers being sensitive to customer needs.*[24]
>
> – Paul Orfalea

Paul and Kinko's team's unwavering focus on fostering lasting customer relationships led Kinko's to achieve a customer base that is not only profitable but also enduring.

A dissection of the work processes Paul and Kinko's utilized will give us greater insights into the techniques that can produce effective CRM. It is helpful to first analyze the Kinko's business market space.

Brief Analysis of the Kinko's Business Market Space

Paul understands how highly people value the work that they bring into Kinko's. Paul realized that there was a segment of customers for whom no amount of care was enough. These customers helped Paul realize that there was a market for high-end document preparation services. What especially attracted Paul to this segment was that he sensed that customers in this segment were willing to spend more than customers looking for the standard copying service. Further, he realized the need to replace part of the university segment of business he lost when Kinko's lost the copyright infringement lawsuit.

With the increase of home computers and the reluctance of many businesses to invest in high-quality printers, the market for high-quality color replication and report generation rapidly grew. The business expanded from just making copies of existing print documents to printing final output for people who had the software, but not the printer, to produce quality documents.

Paul also noticed that the use of quality output devices increased at night. A little investigation found a need in the market for Kinko's stores to be open all night. Kinko's again expanded its concept to providing a 24-hour office to traveling executives and salespeople who needed perfect presentations ready at 8:00 A.M. in a distant city. The 24-hour service is a major competitive edge for Kinko's. It has attracted some of the business's most loyal customers. Hotels have been very slow to meet business travelers' document needs and have often priced them as an emergency service. Further, business centers in hotels are open only during business hours and tend to be in the most expensive hotels.

Partners, Not Franchisees

Mentor Insight

Treat people as equals

Paul was able to create rapid growth in sales by forming partnerships rather than establishing franchises. Forging multiple partnerships is not easy. Paul accomplished this in part by treating people well. Paul is a firm believer in giving every co-worker the greatest respect, and treating each co-worker as a valuable asset to the company. This is consistent with how Paul treats everyone he meets, and it is doubly important to Paul to treat co-workers well, since he believes that how you treat co-workers will be reflected in how they treat customers.

Consistent with his views about the treatment of others, Paul decided at the very beginning of his growth period, in the late 1970s, that he wished to have the benefits of franchising, but was uncomfortable with the relationship under the standard franchise contract. To Paul, a franchisee is a friend for a fee. Typically, a franchisee undertakes to conduct a business or sell a product or service the way the franchiser wants him to. The franchiser assists the franchisee through advertising and marketing and other services and does it for a specific sum each month over and above the franchisee's original investment. There's no risk to the franchiser; that's passed on to the franchisee. Instead, Paul preferred a collaborative format of ". . . making money with people rather than off of them."[25] So Paul entered into partnerships with each individual who managed an area of expansion for Kinko's. Each unit, which traditionally represented a Kinko's store outlet, was set up as an individual partnership with Paul. Paul states that he looked for three major factors in screening business partners:

1. They must be able to save money.
2. They must be able to balance their checkbook.
3. They must value their parents. Paul would avoid a partnership with someone who had relationship issues with their parents. This is because he believed that those who value their parents have the moral integrity that he sought in business partners.

The partnership agreement assigned operations tasks to the field partner and financial operations to Paul. Paul wanted every one of his partners to feel equal in the relationship.

> During the late seventies we continued to expand. By now I realized that the best way to grow was to take in partners, not sell franchises like most chains. I realized that if I gave up half of the equity in a local operation I gave up half of the headaches, and I didn't need headaches. I would be satisfied with slow, steady profit from holding a half interest. Half of something good is better than more than half of something bad.[26]
>
> – Paul Orfalea

Slow, Continuous Growth

In 2002, the dot-com days of inflating a company's valuation to attract venture capital dollars were over. In April of 2000, the world experienced the fallout of venture capital dollars fueling companies that had no sustainable business model. Before that time, a decade of MBA students and entrepreneurial-spirited people were driven by a hockey-stick revenue growth goal. The hockey-stick revenue growth model is the idea that after a brief period of time a start-up aided by a large infusion of venture capital financing can have an immediate upward vertical climb for revenue growth. The few companies that actually were on a hockey-stick trajectory may have had an upward vertical record of revenue growth, but their costs far outweighed their income. These businesses and their venture capital backers were not perpetuating a sustainable business model. The net effect of this type of activity was the bubble bursting on the new media industry. By 2002, the bubble burst had spread to traditional businesses, causing a recession felt worldwide.

Kinko's was different. Kinko's had been built on a concept that was not being taught in most MBA classrooms: slow, continuous growth. Kinko's had started in the seventies and had grown as a profitable business because it had a sustainable business model based on selling products and services that customers want. The profits from these customers were put back into the business. Kinko's grew under Paul's leadership because of the emphasis placed on bootstrapping and frugality. Paul did not grow the business initially based on large infusions of capital. The resources to grow Kinko's came slowly and continuously from the company's customer base and from partners. These partners initially invested as little as $5,000 each, because the partners' investments were about showing commitment and loyalty, not raising large sums to falsely inflate the valuation of Kinko's. Paul and the Kinko's team were growing the business in a slow, continuous growth pattern (see Mentor Method 5.1).

Mentor Method 5.1

Slow, Continuous Growth Graph[27]

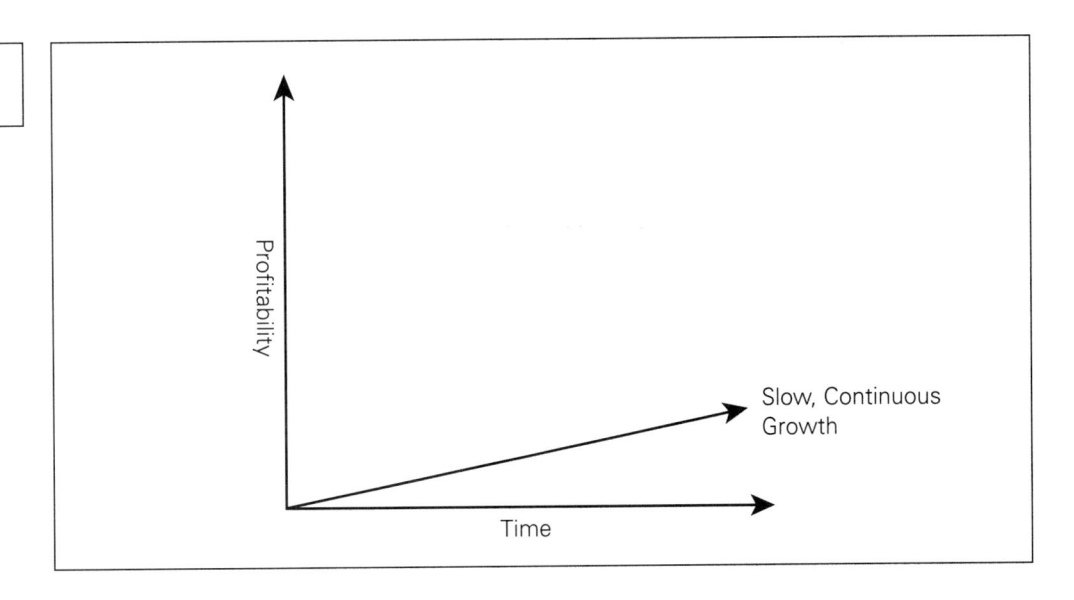

The slow, continuous growth process is when business owners have a sustainable business model maintained by profits derived from their customers' purchases. These profits are reinvested into the company. Payables for the business growth are kept at a minimum. Over time, often for 10 to 30 years, the business slowly grows. The bulk of the ownership remains with the founders. This is so that bottom-line driven accounting types, as found in the venture capital community, don't drive the direction of the

> **Mentor Insight**
> Have integrity

company to force a company to overspend and move into directions that don't meet the expectations of its customers. Greed is a dangerous ingredient in a new venture. Paul and his management team understood this and were careful to practice the slow, continuous growth method of business development. Paul and his team maintained their integrity through the development and growth of Kinko's business model. Be wary of greed—it can topple your CRM systems.

Empowering Others

> **Mentor Insight**
> Depend on others for skills that aren't your strengths

The very personality traits that constitute an entrepreneurial-minded individual are not necessarily the best traits for empowering those around you to help with managing the business. People who are visionary, focused, passionate, and driven problem-solvers are not necessarily best at delegating. "Crazy Founder Syndrome" is when a visionary founder needs to step aside from managing day-to-day operations. Although founders have great ideas, they usually aren't equipped to run the day-to-day operations of a growing business. The reins are usually handed over to operationally savvy managers who are superior implementers but often lack the charisma and vision of the founder. Paul Orfalea was able to successfully lead Kinko's for many years and avoid "Crazy Founder Syndrome" in part because he knew the value of depending on others for the skills and mechanical ability that he lacked. His dyslexia was in fact a mixed blessing. Paul had no alternative—he had to depend on others to accomplish what he could not.

Empowering those around you is an essential ingredient of success when executing an effective CRM program. Effective customer relationship management takes a tremendous understanding of what drives your customers' buying decisions. An entrepreneurial marketer must delegate some of this responsibility in order to continuously build loyal customers. In addition, when an entrepreneurial marketer empowers those around him, that marketer has more time to understand and research where the customer is coming from. For example, Paul was able to spend his time interacting at the Kinko's stores with customers because he empowered those around him. He treated his co-workers with high regard. He valued his co-workers' assistance and support. The insights Paul gained from this time spent staying close to the customer proved to be extremely valuable as he led Kinko's to greater profits.

The Balancing Act

> **Mentor Insight**
> Achieve a balance between work and personal life

Empowering others also helped Paul to head home by 5:00 P.M. on most days while he was at Kinko's. Entrepreneurial marketers engaged in the hockey-stick revenue growth model have one thing in common: burnout. The old saying "slow and steady wins the race" may be cliché but you should take it to heart. Balancing your work life with your personal life is not easy. The temptation as an entrepreneurial marketer will be to put your personal life on the back burner. Don't. Paul was successful in leading Kinko's through many stressful challenges and also with his personal life. Paul even included this premise in the Kinko's philosophy statement: "We strive to live balanced lives in work, love, and play."[28]

We suggest you earmark for repeated review the following list of ideas on how to achieve a balance between personal life and work.

**Helpful Hints for Achieving a Balance
Between Your Personal Life and Work:
A Guide to Creating an Enduring Entrepreneurial Marketer**

1. Start each workday with a list of to-do items. Put the list in priority order. Have a contingency plan for priority items that you are unable to finish before it's time to go home for the day. Set a "lights off" time to end your day so that you don't end up staying past the time you need to transition into your personal life.

2. During your workday, keep personal phone calls and e-mails to a five-minute time limit. During your personal time, keep work calls and e-mails to a five-minute time limit.

3. Set up separate areas for doing work (even if you work from home) and for enjoying your personal time. If you work from home you will never get to unplug from work if you are surrounded by your work. If you bring work home to do, keep it somewhere separate from where you spend your personal time.

4. Set boundaries so that others can't extend your workday. Learn the power of saying no.

5. Take a series of five-minute work breaks during the day to stretch and clear your mind.

6. Follow a healthy diet. Eating a nutritionally balanced diet on a regular basis can help keep your energy level up.

7. Drink plenty of water daily.

8. Exercise on a regular basis can also help keep your energy level up as well as potentially improve your concentration.

9. Attempt to get at least six and a half hours of sleep a night. If this isn't possible, take a 30-minute nap when you get home from work.

10. Breathe correctly. Learn how to breathe deeply. Take Yoga.

11. Keep a calendar of personal activities, not just work activities.

12. Practice time management on a daily basis. If you aren't sure how, read about it.

13. Learn how to under promise and over deliver in your work and personal life.

14. Meditate.

15. Play music. It's a wonderful motivator for both your work and personal life. Wear a headset at work if your cubicle community prohibits music listening.

16. Make personal life an equal priority to your work life.

17. Live in the moment. Stay in the now, not the past or future.

18. Take vacations for more than three days. It often takes three days to just unwind from a hectic work life. Don't check your voice mail and e-mail while you are on vacation.

19. Have a crisis management plan for work as well as for your personal life.

20. If you are losing the battle between managing your personal life with work, get help. There is an infinite amount of help available out there. All you have to do is look. The Internet search engines are a place to begin finding this advice.

Why is this balancing act so important? To identify, acquire, and retain profitable customers is an almost impossible challenge. It requires a team of people who are in good physical and psychological condition. CRM done well requires endurance and perseverance as well as a large dose of creativity. Truly creative people know how to quiet the constant chatter of their inner voice so that new ideas can bubble up into their consciousness.

Let Innovation Reign

> **Mentor Insight**
> Encourage innovation, creativity, and experimentation

Paul was also good at creating an innovative company culture. Innovative products usually create a sustainable competitive advantage, have a customer base that is inclined to purchase them, and create products and services that are successful in raising brand awareness to your targeted customers. In Module 1, Formulating Killer Strategies for Your Business, we shared with you a checklist for fostering innovation. In this module we would like to suggest that you take innovation to the next level. The next level is performing an analysis to measure how innovative your new venture company culture is. You can accomplish this by performing a 360-degree analysis of your company culture. Below are the guidelines.

"Guidelines for Performing a 360-Degree Analysis of Your Company Culture Innovation Rating

A 360-degree analysis means that you expand your survey beyond just the founding management team. You should survey your customers, potential customers, people who will never be your customers, your employees, your receptionist if you are lucky enough to have one, and your board members.

On a scale of 1 to 10 rate the new venture's company culture for fostering innovation. Circle 10 if you strongly agree with the statement; circle 1 if you strongly disagree. A rating of 1 equals a nonexistent innovation rating and 10 equals an extremely impressive amount of innovation. Tally the scores from all the respondents and average the results.

1. The product or service offered is not the same as anything you have encountered before.   1 2 3 4 5 6 7 8 9 10 (circle one)

2. There is a way that an employee, customer, or shareholder can make suggestions for enhancements to the product.   1 2 3 4 5 6 7 8 9 10 (circle one)

3. Employees are able to make mistakes without the fear of termination or disciplinary measures.   1 2 3 4 5 6 7 8 9 10 (circle one)

(continues)

4. The company seems to have co-workers who lead balanced personal and work lives. 1 2 3 4 5 6 7 8 9 10 (circle one)

5. The product or service incorporates a technology in it. 1 2 3 4 5 6 7 8 9 10 (circle one)

6. The company is not overly structured in its work processes. 1 2 3 4 5 6 7 8 9 10 (circle one)

7. The employees of the company reflect diverse educational backgrounds, skill sets, and demeanors. 1 2 3 4 5 6 7 8 9 10 (circle one)

8. Thinking outside of the box is encouraged. 1 2 3 4 5 6 7 8 9 10 (circle one)

9. There appear to be resources allocated for ongoing research and development of the product or service. 1 2 3 4 5 6 7 8 9 10 (circle one)

10. The new venture seems innovative. 1 2 3 4 5 6 7 8 9 10 (circle one)

An average score of 80 or above means you have fostered an innovative company culture.

An average score of 60–79 means you have an above-average tendency for innovation in your company culture.

An average score of 40–59 means you have an average tendency for innovation in your company culture.

A score of 39 or below means you have some serious work to do if you want to foster innovation in your company's culture."[29]

Mentor Insight

Identify, acquire, and retain profitable customers

The Kinko's that existed under Paul's leadership would score 100 on this analysis. The innovative company culture at Kinko's was a lightning rod for producing effective CRM.

Paul and his management team at Kinko's were not only good at creating innovative company cultures for fostering CRM activities; they were also good at identifying, acquiring, and retaining profitable customers. Identifying, acquiring, and retaining profitable customers are the main components of CRM. In fact, the key to CRM is identifying what creates value for the customer and then delivering it in much the same way as Kinko's delivered a superior product for business, home-office, and personal supply services.

While individual customers have different views of value, there are many common value concepts. In the real world a new venture must satisfy the common value concepts for each customer group and communicate and deliver them to each of the targeted customer groups. Kinko's did this by targeting the college student and faculty member and then expanding to the home-office customer.

The key CRM tasks can be distilled down to the following activities:

1. "Identifying those consumer values that are pertinent to a particular business
2. Understanding the relative importance of those values to each customer segment
3. Determining if delivery of those values will affect the bottom line in a positive manner
4. Communicating and delivering the appropriate values to each customer segment in ways *the customer* wants to receive the information
5. Measuring results and proving return on investment"[30]

Customer Satisfaction

Customer satisfaction is the uniting theme of Kinko's business practices. Exceeding customers' expectations is not a goal for Kinko's, it's the Holy Grail, as evidenced by Kinko's philosophy, company culture, and loyal customer base. Customers don't think of Kinko's as just a place to get copies made. Instead, Kinko's is where they go to have their resumes made to get their dream job. It's the place they go to have their business cards made. For holidays, it's where people go to have a calendar made of their children for a grandparents' gift. Kinko's is where they turn when they need presentation booklets to be made in bulk at the last minute for the board of directors meeting. In short, Kinko's is a place where dreams are accomplished and business goals are met. Kinko's is where you go for a middle-of-the-night business crisis. Kinko's is one of the few places where you can be treated equally as a customer whether you are the President of the United States or a homeless person. It makes no difference; your job will be ready in the order it was received. It's one of the last bastions of global democracy. For these customer satisfaction reasons, Kinko's customers are usually more than 110 percent satisfied.

> **Mentor Insight**
>
> Strive for 110 percent customer satisfaction

Market Research

Market research is another method Paul used to create satisfied customers. Paul has a very simple model of market research: Look for long lines, and then explore what the line is about. The methodology is simple and has the side benefit of keeping Paul out of any market that isn't already proven.

Paul is an entrepreneur, but he is not a leader in bringing major technological breakthroughs to the marketplace. When Paul sees a business with a long line of customers, he assumes that the present providers are not keeping up with demand and may be vulnerable to competition. This fits with his business creed of never being first in a market, but rather being a fast follower. He chooses to learn from the mistakes of the market pioneers and perfect his business plan to win the established customer base whose needs are under satisfied. This has proven a great strategy for Kinko's in creating highly satisfied customers.

> **Mentor Insight**
>
> Encourage innovation, creativity, and experimentation

Paul says keeping customer focus is something that you intuitively know how to do. Paul's major complaint about large corporations' management is that they do not get out of their offices and interact with the front-line workers meeting with the customers. Paul is known as a great wanderer who regularly made visits to the Kinko's stores, not to chastise his co-workers, but to see what each Kinko's was doing right—what clever new ideas the individuals at Kinko's were devising to satisfy their customers. Paul felt it was his responsibility to communicate these innovative ideas to the other people at Kinko's so that other branches could adopt a good idea. Throughout his tenure at Kinko's, Paul was known as an extremely "hands-on" leader who was keenly focused on providing customer satisfaction. Paul and the Kinko's team developed 14 principles of customer service.

Paul's Principles of Customer Service

"1. Listen! . . .
2. Maintain an attractive environment . . .
3. Adopt a professional look . . .
4. Be proactive . . .
5. Value your customer's time . . .
6. Treat your customers as guests . . .
7. Make training an ongoing commitment . . .
8. Be positive with customers, even when they're wrong! . . .
9. Don't forget the little things . . .
10. Make quality a priority . . .
11. Take the long view of customer satisfaction . . .
12. Don't promise what you can't or won't deliver . . .
13. Reward outstanding customer service . . .
14. Shoot for 110 percent customer satisfaction . . ."[31]

Taking a Proactive Posture

> **Mentor Insight**
>
> Be proactive

Paul instituted a "closed door" policy for himself after a day when a store manager called him to ask him what should be done with a bounced check. He realized that by being readily accessible, he was preventing the manager from coming up with a solution. He also realized that when he sat in his office he became a reactive manager, reacting to events of the day. Paul felt that he was being prevented from getting information firsthand. Paul is adamant about keeping levels of administration to a minimum. He feels that layers of management remove the manager from the reality of the business and promote misinformation and non-communication. Paul had a lean, horizontal management structure at Kinko's, which allowed him the freedom to divorce himself from the minutiae of running a business and to take a proactive stance in marketing and customer relationship

> *I was an idea man. My talent wasn't keeping my nose to the grindstone. It was finding new grindstones for someone else's nose.*[32]
>
> – Paul Orfalea

Mentor Insight

Make quality a priority

management issues. Paul was repeatedly proactive in his business practices at Kinko's, from migrating the copy technology to the state-of-the-art digital copier systems to offering videoconferencing services.

Paul was ultimately able to be proactive because he is a wanderer, a modern-day adventurer. While this is a liability in most business situations, for Paul it was an asset. He spent his time seeing things firsthand, coming up with remarkable ideas and experimenting with these ideas until he figured things out. This process allowed him to grow his business based on opportunities that presented themselves and opportunities that evolved over time.

Paul's great ideas were implemented at Kinko's with the highest quality in mind, from state-of-the-art photocopiers to the latest computers. Discerning customers notice the quality behind your product or service.

Paul's greatest emphasis on quality, however, was nurturing quality people. The logic behind focusing on developing quality people is well articulated by Donald G. Reinertsen in his book *Managing The Design Factory: A Product Developer's Toolkit*:

> **"Respect the People**
>
> There has been a dangerous tendency in the quality movement to attribute all problems to the system rather than the people. While the intentions of this approach are good, its side effects are dangerous. If you believe that the primary determinant of outcomes is the system, this is where you will focus your time and attention. You will try to create a system that can be operated by fools.
>
> An alternative view is that success is equally dependent on creating a workable system and populating this system with excellent people . . ."[33]

Under Paul's leadership and tutelage, the staff at Kinko's became more than employees. Paul treated staff as equals and provided them with continuous improvement, empowerment, and training to make them the valuable asset that attracted and retained Kinko's customers. The Kinko's co-worker behind the counter was a trusted problem solver for many customers. He or she collaborated with the customer to make sure the final product met and exceeded the customer's needs.

> **Mentor Insight**
>
> Subscribe to lifelong learning

Lifelong Learners

Every day at Kinko's marks the beginning of a fresh battle to stay ahead of the customer's needs. As a happy wanderer, risk-loving experimenter, and lifelong learner, Paul has the right personality for continuously seeking the knowledge necessary to keep Kinko's customers satisfied. He made sure that Kinko's co-workers were continuously trained in what they needed to know to retain a satisfied customer. Today you won't find Paul at the helm of Kinko's but you will find him in the classroom, teaching entrepreneurial-spirited people the lifelong lessons he has learned.

Mentorography Conclusion

Paul and the Kinko's team are great examples of how to create a company culture that fosters effective Customer Relationship Management techniques. In this module we have focused on these CRM-related Mentor Insights:

Mentor Insights

- Treat people as equals
- Have integrity
- Depend on others for skills that aren't your strengths
- Achieve a balance between work and personal life
- Encourage innovation, creativity, and experimentation
- Identify, acquire, and retain profitable customers
- Strive for 110 percent customer satisfaction
- Be proactive
- Make quality a priority
- Subscribe to lifelong learning

If you need an ongoing refresher course on crafting CRM processes for your new venture, we recommend a trip to your local Kinko's.

Mentorography Questions

1. How can one turn severe dyslexia or any disability into an asset in business?

2. Are parents an entrepreneur's first mentors? To what extent can your parents influence you as an entrepreneurial marketer?

3. Analyze a company that has grown from reinvesting its profits derived from slow steady growth. How has the founder of that business fared? (Helpful hint: you may want to search for these people on the Internet or in *Entrepreneur* magazine.)

4. What does it take to identify, attract, and retain a profitable customer to your new venture?

Endnotes

[1] This variation of the definition of CRM developed by Molly Lavik, June 9, 2002.

[2] Paul Orfalea with Leonard Tourney, *Making Better Best: Achieving Balance in Business and Life*, (Unpublished manuscript), p. 14.

[3] Ibid, p. 11.

[4] Ibid, p. 37.

[5] Ibid, p. 39.

[6] Ibid, pp. 47–48.

[7] Paul Orfalea interview conducted by Molly Lavik and Bruce Buskirk, November 7, 2001.

[8] Paul Orfalea with Leonard Tourney, *Making Better Best: Achieving Balance in Business and Life*, (Unpublished manuscript), p. 53.

[9] Ibid, p. 62.

[10] "Kinko's Videoconferencing Offers Travel Alternative: High-tech Solution Offers a Simple Way to Save Valuable Time, Money and Resources," News Release, September 28, 2001. http://www.kinkos.com/pr/pr_sept282001.php, accessed May 15, 2002 with updates provided courtesy of Kinko's, Inc. Public Relations, August 8, 2002.

[11] Courtesy of Kinko's, Inc. Public Relations, August 8, 2002.

[12] Paul Orfalea with Leonard Tourney, *Making Better Best: Achieving Balance in Business and Life*, (Unpublished manuscript), p. 66.

[13] Ibid, p. 69.

[14] Ibid, pp. 71–72.

[15] Ibid, p. 72.

[16] Ibid, p. 79.

[17] Courtesy of Kinko's, Inc. Public Relations, August 12, 2002.

[18] Ibid.

[19] Ibid.

[20] Paul Orfalea with Leonard Tourney, *Making Better Best: Achieving Balance in Business and Life*, (Unpublished manuscript), pp. 80–81.

[21] Profile, Paul J. Orfalea, Founder and Chairperson Emeritus, Kinko's Inc., courtesy of Lois Mitchell, Executive Director, Orfalea Family Foundation, November 8, 2001.

[22] Paul Orfalea interview conducted by Molly Lavik and Bruce Buskirk, November 7, 2001.

[23] Ibid.

[24] Paul Orfalea with Leonard Tourney, *Making Better Best: Achieving Balance in Business and Life*, (Unpublished manuscript), p. 63.

[25] Ibid, p. 57.

[26] Ibid, p. 52.

[27] Developed by Molly Lavik, May 25, 2002.

[28] Paul Orfalea with Leonard Tourney, *Making Better Best: Achieving Balance in Business and Life*, (Unpublished manuscript), p. 69.

[29] Developed by Molly Lavik, May 26, 2002.

[30] Frederick Newell, *Loyalty.com: Customer Relationship Management in the New Era of Internet Marketing*, (McGraw-Hill, New York, 2000), pp. 11–12.

[31] Paul Orfalea with Leonard Tourney, *Making Better Best: Achieving Balance in Business and Life*, (Unpublished manuscript), pp. 209–222.

[32] Ibid, p. 52.

[33] Donald G. Reinertsen, *Managing The Design Factory: A Product Developer's Toolkit*, (The Free Press–a Divsion of Simon & Schuster Inc., New York, 1997), p. 249.

DISTRIBUTION MENTOR MODULE

Devising Distribution-Dominating Tactics

KEN PARK
Founder and President, BBM. HyperCD

Mentorography Part I

This is the story of an emerging entrepreneurial marketer named Ken Park. Ken is a pioneer behind an innovative distribution technique that is transforming the way some products and services are distributed and the way marketing communication messages are disseminated.

As a point of reference for this module, we underscore that when we use the word *distribution* we mean marketing channels and the manner in which a product "touches" its target customers. Distribution or marketing channels are the means by which products are transported physically, inventoried, and delivered to customers, as well as the flow of information to and from those customers.

Ken Park is a competitive, spirited entrepreneur who was a top-ten professional skateboarder for the last half of the 1980s before he began a series of career pursuits that converged around the dawning Internet industry. Skateboarding taught Ken that when you fall down, you get back up. In fact, in skateboarding as in entrepreneurial marketing, falling is an essential step on the path to "nailing the stunt." Ken's competitive spirit from his skateboarding days has been refined in his business practices. He aspires to win in his current arena: small business start-ups.

Ken is a pioneer in an industry so new it hasn't been named; for now we will call it the connected-disc industry. Connected discs are web-enabled CD-ROMs that allow the video stored on the CD-ROM (or any optical memory media) to be viewed in a high-quality format via the Internet. The connected-disc industry is having a major impact on methods of distribution.

In Part I of this module we will explore the origins of the Mentor Insights behind the distribution-dominating tactics that Ken Park is best known for. They are as follows:

Mentor Insights

- Empower direct customer distribution
- Disrupt the status quo
- Hold business relationships sacred
- Embrace the Internet's capabilities
- Incorporate distribution evaluation methods
- Tap into connected constituencies
- Bypass traditional channels
- Partner with key influencers
- Capitalize on the impact of word-of-mouth
- Utilize virtual marketing arenas

Ken Park Milestones

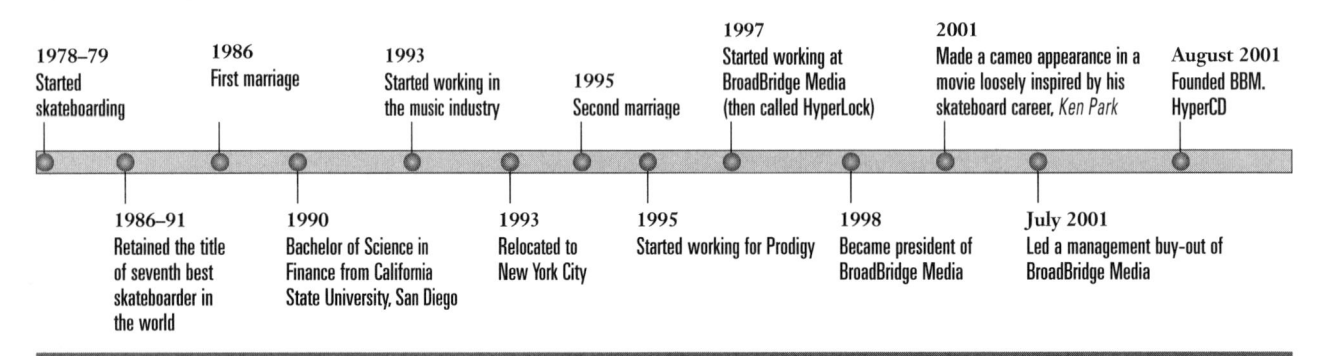

1978–79 Started skateboarding

1986 First marriage

1986–91 Retained the title of seventh best skateboarder in the world

1990 Bachelor of Science in Finance from California State University, San Diego

1993 Started working in the music industry

1993 Relocated to New York City

1995 Second marriage

1995 Started working for Prodigy

1997 Started working at BroadBridge Media (then called HyperLock)

1998 Became president of BroadBridge Media

2001 Made a cameo appearance in a movie loosely inspired by his skateboard career, *Ken Park*

July 2001 Led a management buy-out of BroadBridge Media

August 2001 Founded BBM. HyperCD

In the Beginning

Ken's childhood was strongly influenced by his father's profession in sales. His father's job with Levi-Strauss and Barco kept the family moving, from Los Angeles to Montana to Michigan and then to San Diego. Ken, an extrovert by nature, learned to use athletics and a bold personality to make

Entrepreneurial Marketing

friends quickly. Frequent relocation impressed upon Ken the importance of building close relationships with others. Ken's early years led him to become a self-professed "jock" and an intensely competitive person.

Ken's move to San Diego, in the seventh grade, introduced him to skateboarding way before the sport gained popularity. Ken enjoyed the individuality and freedom of expression of skateboarding, embracing a sport whose limits were self-imposed. The team sports in which Ken had participated, such as baseball, didn't offer the independence Ken sought. He also appreciated how some skateboarding legends had been able to create signature skateboards, selling them directly to skateboarders through skate shops and marketing themselves via tournaments. Growing up in skate parks, Ken developed an appreciation for direct customer distribution tactics. Skateboarding marked the beginning of Ken's interest in empowering direct customer distribution.

> **Mentor Insight**
>
> Empower direct customer distribution

Ken devoted several hours daily to skateboarding. His first mentor was Steve Sherman, a professional skateboarder and son of a family friend. Ken's mom hired Steve to teach Ken some tips, which made Ken a laughingstock at the skate park. The idea of skateboarding lessons went against the spirit of the sport.

Ken remembers when skateboarding suddenly became popular: many companies tried to cash in. Ken could see a dark side in the way in which companies put quick profits before products that were true to the skateboard movement. Ken learned to spot opportunities, as well as understand what made for a profitable business model. Further, he discovered that the skateboarders who made the most money weren't necessarily the most talented. He found that a skateboarder's earning potential correlated directly with his ability to develop a personal "brand" and build a personality via antics both on and off the skate ramps. Ken realized that a skateboarder's success was contingent on the skateboarder's willingness to disrupt the status quo with a unique style of creativity.

> **Mentor Insight**
>
> Disrupt the status quo

As a professional skater, Ken was often chosen to be the on-camera spokesperson for the industry and he became comfortable speaking on camera. Ken eventually emceed some of the skateboard contests, starred in company sponsored videos, and became involved in running skateboarding camps.

A memorable moment in Ken's life came when he received a phone call from the mother of one of his skateboarding campers. She informed Ken that her son had been killed in an automobile accident, and she wanted Ken to know that her son had never been as happy as he was when he was with Ken at camp. Time and time again, Ken reflected on this event as an underscore to the importance of everyday interactions. This is a concept that became fundamental to his philosophy of business.

> **Mentor Insight**
>
> Hold business relationships sacred

To this day, Ken considers each meeting he may have with a person, however brief, a potential building block for a long-term relationship even years later. He recognizes that every person holds the potential to play a significant role in his life and business dealings.

Ken's parents were less than excited about his choice of a skateboarding career. Ken's father told him repeatedly that skateboarding was a waste of his talent and time and a hardship for Ken's mother to get Ken to the skate park because it was 45 minutes away. In contrast, Ken fondly remembers skateboarder Tony Hawk's father. Ken had never met a man so completely supportive of his child's sport. Tony's father participated in all aspects of Tony's skateboarding and was equally enthusiastic and supportive of all his other children. Years later, when Ken became a father himself, he understood the significance of Tony's father's involvement compared with his own parents' lack of support.

By 17, Ken had moved away from home, and by the time he was 19 years old he was married. He was financially independent at an early age. He chose to attend California State University, San Diego, over the University of California, Berkeley for two reasons. First, he had to pay his own way through school. Berkeley was more expensive. Second, attending Berkeley would have required him to shelve his skateboarding career for the moment as his attention would have been focused entirely on school given the cost and relocation. Ken became the first college graduate in his family. After graduation, he moved from San Diego to Boulder, Colorado, where he started two skateboard companies—one on a $5,000 investment from a friend and the other by convincing an overseas angel investor of the value of starting "One More Skate Company." His businesses thrived until the economy soured in the early 1990s and he suffered from severe under capitalization as his two companies began to grow. Shortly thereafter, he divorced his first wife and was faced with the decision whether to stay in the skateboarding industry and reap the benefits of his established stature or reinvent himself. He chose the latter.

Ken moved to New York City and pursued the music industry for his next career. A friend suggested that Ken target a small but influential company in the music industry while starting over in an entry-level position. Ken followed his friend's advice and took an entry-level job in sales at *CMJ* (*College Music Journal*), a magazine about emerging alternative music acts. Simultaneously, he became consumed with a passion for the marketing power and potential reach of the Internet.

Mentor Insight

Embrace the Internet's capabilities

Ken is a self-taught computer graphic artist and an early adopter of technologies. Ken understands that his work in the music industry was a good preparation for what he is doing today. Ken had spent his time trying to find ways to get music into the marketplace. Today he spends time finding ways to commercialize technology into the marketplace.

Ken designed *CMJ*'s Internet strategy. He went on to work at Prodigy in its music and entertainment division. While working at Prodigy, Ken received a call from an executive of HyperLock (which later became BroadBridge Media) offering him a job. Ken took a risk leaving his stable job at Prodigy to join a small start-up business. Only after he had resigned from Prodigy did Ken discover that the person he had been negotiating with didn't have the final say in his job offer: the offer was contingent upon the approval of the board of directors. Ken showed up in Chicago expecting a welcoming committee and was instead thrust into a final interview. This required a spontaneous pitch to the HyperLock board of directors and shareholders on the power and potential of the connected disc. That was Ken's first successful sales presentation of the HyperCD technology.

A HyperCD is a way to circumvent the problems with Internet streaming video in order to deliver high-quality video images in conjunction with a web site, regardless of the speed of the computer's connection to the Internet. The HyperCD provides copy protection of the video from the provider's web site.

> *The two things that drew me to the web were the fact that it is a fabulous tool to introduce and differentiate a product to a highly targeted audience in an extremely cost efficient way. The other aspect that I loved was its ability to establish and build direct one-on-one communication with a given community of like-minded consumers.[1]*
>
> – Ken Park

> **Mentor Insight**
>
> Incorporate distribution evaluation methods

Tracking users is a significant byproduct for evaluating the distribution tactics implemented.

Ken's first update to the HyperCD technology occurred when he worked with the company's R&D team to ensure that the technology worked on Mac®OS as well as Windows® platforms. A platform can be any established system in the marketplace that one can receive a product on, such as game systems. Artists create primarily on Macs, so the addition of the cross-platform feature to the HyperCD technology was seen as an impressive and necessary product extension. In fact, the cross-platform functionality of HyperCD technologies became and still is a real competitive edge for HyperCD over its competitors in the connected-disc market space. The reason for this is that most of the other competitors in the connected-disc marketplace focused their R&D and thus their product on Microsoft technology, which relegated them to supporting the PC platform only, and not the Mac®OS (Operating System).

> **Mentor Insight**
>
> Tap into connected constituencies

Ken led the efforts to rename the company from HyperLock to the more user-friendly BroadBridge Media. He also spearheaded the company's headquarters relocation from Chicago to New York City, where many media companies are headquartered. Understanding the importance of tapping into connected constituencies, he targeted the key players that existed in the New York City media industry. Ken had learned this lesson from the tight-knit skateboard community. Knowing the significance and strength of a connected body of like-minded people representing an industry, he concentrated on building awareness with key executives who were well known in an industry. Also, having seen firsthand the positive impact of skateboard fans on the rise in popularity of the skateboard industry, Ken targeted projects that would reach large consumer markets. While New York City may house the media industry, it is far from the technology hub of the U.S., so R&D was relocated to San Jose, California. Additionally, a team of top-tier employees was recruited to join the company. Ken worked his way up from vice president of business development at HyperLock to president of BroadBridge Media. BroadBridge Media boasted clients like HBO, BMG, Warner Music Group, CDNOW, and a variety of sports franchises.

As president of BroadBridge Media, Ken began helping fellow entrepreneurial marketers by providing them with the HyperCD platform. Ken

---

Ken's Aspiration for Marketers

What Jim Clark (founder of Silicon Graphics, Inc., Netscape Communications Corporation and Healtheon/WebMD) is good at . . .
I aspire to accomplish from a different perspective. Jim took what he saw as a market or as a group of under respected individuals, engineers, and made them the focal point of an emerging industry. When you read his history—that is what he did. It inspired me.

I also want to reach out and take an under respected group of people in the form of marketers and make them a focal point of industry. . . In a time where the Internet is looking for solutions, there is no doubt in my mind that those solutions and the next wave of innovation will come from marketing minded people with a new vision on how to create direct product-to-consumer relationships.[2]

– Ken Park

developed a deep respect for entrepreneurial marketers and believes they are undervalued in their organizations. Today, Ken dedicates himself to helping fellow entrepreneurial marketers reach their goals.

Ken Empowers Direct Customer Distribution

In December of 1999, Ken began helping an independent producer distribute the content for a television program concept directly to the customer. Thanks to Ken, a team of very talented people, and the HyperCD technology platform, an independent producer was able to mail to the National Association of Television Program Executives (NATPE) a HyperCD of a television show concept, called "The Digital Diary." The HyperCD was shrink-wrapped to the front cover of the NATPE bi-monthly newsletter. Ken was able to help develop a product that enabled daily tracking of usage patterns for specific targeted markets. Each HyperCD includes an audience profiling Web site which provides, on a 24-hour basis, access to the number of visitors to each segment of the program featured on the HyperCD as well as the duration and time of day of each visitor. Direct feedback arrived via e-mail messages from recipients of the NATPE mailing. These feedback systems helped further develop and evaluate the "The Digital Diary" HyperCD television program concept. A sample of the targeted customer usage patterns of "The Digital Diary" HyperCD follows.

Urchin®,[3]

Reprinted with permission from Urchin Software Corporation.
Use of Urchin® trademark and logo courtesy of Urchin Software Corporation. Urchin, Urchin Software Corporation and the Urchin logo are all registered marks of Urchin Software Corporation.

"The reports below were created by Urchin, a popular web analytics package produced by Urchin Software Corporation. Urchin is among the most widely deployed software systems of this type, and is currently used on millions of web sites worldwide. For more information about Urchin, see **http://www.urchin.com**."[4]

Mentor Method 6.1

Profile of "The Digital Diary™" Targeted Customer Usage Profile[5, 6]

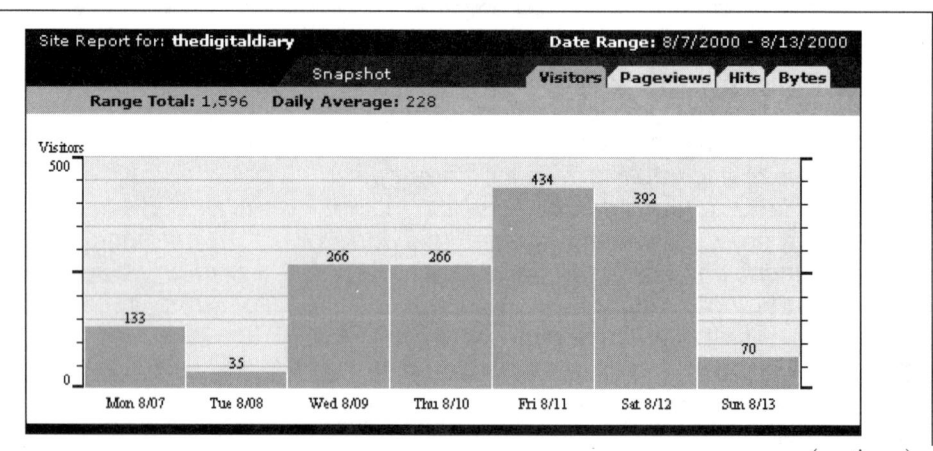

Site Report for: thedigitaldiary Date Range: 8/7/2000 - 8/13/2000
Snapshot — Visitors | Pageviews | Hits | Bytes
Range Total: 1,596   Daily Average: 228

Day	Visitors
Mon 8/07	133
Tue 8/08	35
Wed 8/09	266
Thu 8/10	266
Fri 8/11	434
Sat 8/12	392
Sun 8/13	70

(continues)

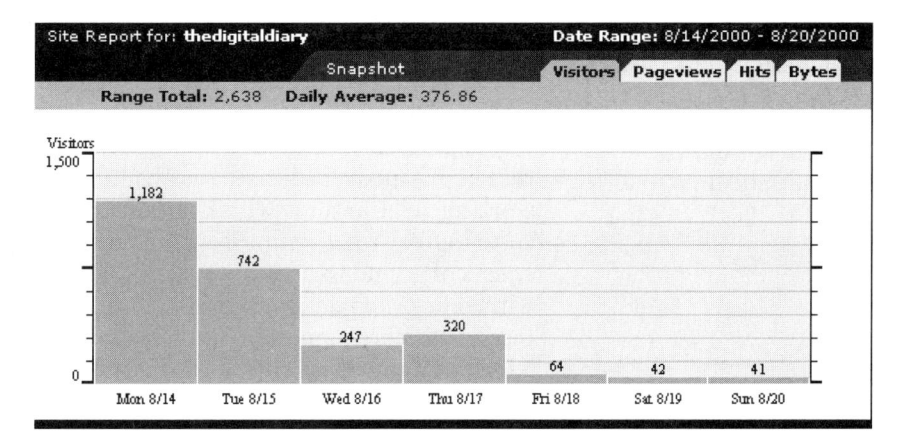

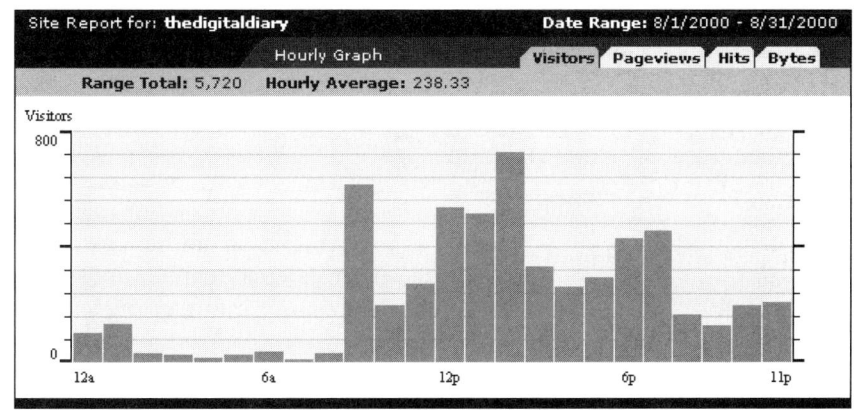

Site Report for: thedigitaldiary	Date Range: 8/14/2000 - 8/20/2000
Snapshot	Visitors / Pageviews / Hits / Bytes
Range Total: 2,638　Daily Average: 376.86	

Visitors
- Mon 8/14: 1,182
- Tue 8/15: 742
- Wed 8/16: 247
- Thu 8/17: 320
- Fri 8/18: 64
- Sat 8/19: 42
- Sun 8/20: 41

Site Report for: thedigitaldiary	Date Range: 8/1/2000 - 8/31/2000
Hourly Graph	Visitors / Pageviews / Hits / Bytes
Range Total: 5,720　Hourly Average: 238.33	

Site Report for: thedigitaldiary	Date Range: 8/1/2000 - 8/31/2000
Summary	
Total Visitors	5,720
Total Pageviews	59,035
Total Hits	132,698
Total Bytes Transferred	450.4MB
Average Visitors Per Day	184
Average Pageviews Per Day	1,904
Average Hits Per Day	4,280
Average Bytes Transferred Per Day	14.53MB
Average Pageviews Per Visitor	10
Average Hits Per Visitor	23
Average Bytes Per Visitor	82,560
Average Length of Visit	472sec

Reprinted with permission. Reporting software courtesy of Urchin Software Corporation. Urchin, Urchin Software Corporation and the Urchin logo are all registered marks of Urchin Software Corporation.

Mentor Insight

Bypass traditional channels

"The immediate results of 'The Digital Diary' HyperCD mailing was that a worldwide sales agent for independent television producers was potentially interested in representing the concept. However, 'The Digital Diary' concept is currently on hold waiting for the economy to improve."[7]

The independent producer behind "The Digital Diary" was just one of many people Ken Park personally helped to adopt the HyperCD platform as a tactic to bypass the traditional distribution channels.

> **Mentor Insight**
> Partner with key influencers

Ken had specifically sought out an alliance with the person behind "The Digital Diary" concept because Ken thought the program idea had merit. Ken also felt that participating in the development of a product such as "The Digital Diary," that profiled pioneering icons in digital leadership, would give him a firsthand opportunity to partner with key influencers of the digital media industry. Ken had found that forging strong bonds and working relationships with key influencers is something that takes a concerted effort to accomplish. In his experience, people that are key influencers of an industry or business marketplace typically are hard to connect with. These people often have staff that act as gatekeepers to keep away the masses who are pounding on their door. Identifying projects that yield the added benefit of creating circumstances where you can develop a bond with highly influential people is a rare opportunity. Ken inherently understood the benefits and impact that working with people who were key influencers in the digital media industry could have on the HyperCD product line. Ken also understood from his skateboarding days the value of building a customer base by partnering with key influencers.

> **Mentor Insight**
> Capitalize on the impact of word-of-mouth

"The Digital Diary" HyperCD had an important effect on its target market. "The Digital Diary" HyperCD drove interest and communication with the television program creator's targeted customers even though it was developed on an almost nonexistent budget. The creator began to receive e-mails directly from her customer base. The HyperCD platform had enabled an independent producer to capitalize on a word-of-mouth occurrence. For more information on word-of-mouth please refer to the Viral Marketing Mentor Module and Part II of this module.

Despite all the goodwill generated by Ken's efforts and the benefits of the HyperCD product, BroadBridge Media went into bankruptcy when the downturn in the economy began to negatively impact small Internet-related businesses in 2001.

Ten Minutes to Go

The most stressful minutes of Ken Park's life were not when he attempted a 540° McTwist on his skateboard and found himself plummeting head-first, nor were they when he faced a divorce before his 30th birthday, nor when he faced his parents' disappointment in his decision to become a professional skateboarder. The most stressful minutes in Ken's life were the ten minutes between 2:50 P.M. and 3:00 P.M. on July 18, 2001. These were the final minutes before Ken would find out if he had been able to purchase all the assets of BroadBridge Media. Ken understood in the final minutes before the results of the BroadBridge Media liquidation auction were announced that he faced the very real possibility of not being able to purchase the HyperCD assets and more importantly not being able to pursue his passion and vision for the connected-disc marketplace.

At 3:00 P.M. on July 18 Ken and the six investors he had feverishly assembled were triumphant—the assets from the now defunct BroadBridge Media became the property of Ken and several of the former BroadBridge Media executives. After a management buy-out, Ken became the CEO as well as president of BBM. HyperCD. This was a dream come true for Ken. Ken and the management team now owned the small business that they had all built from scratch not more than three years before. Ken and a small staff had survived the economic downturn and the end of the first iteration of the Internet industry.

One of the first things Ken did after the buy-out was change the company name to BBM. HyperCD. Ken named the parent company of BBM. HyperCD John Galt Media after a character in one of his favorite books, *Atlas Shrugged*[8] by Ayn Rand. Ken feels that Rand's writings exemplify attitudes in the emerging digital media marketing industry.

> *Never before have I been so moved by the theoretical stance of any one person in my life. I think that [Rand's] theories are so fundamentally sound. I identify with the idea that we all can be very selfish and steadfast in the pursuit of vision and goals, treating business as our art and our own accomplishments as our rewards—all without negatively impacting or trampling those along our paths.*[9]
>
> – Ken Park

Mentor Insights

Bypass traditional channels

Empower direct customer distribution

BBM. HyperCD designs, develops, and implements new forms of distribution methodologies and provides powerful forms of empowerment to entrepreneurs to start their own businesses. Specifically, BBM. HyperCD is the world's leading provider of connected-disc strategies, with proven success in the fields of consumer entertainment, advertising, direct marketing, customer relations, market research, online training and learning, and more.

The HyperCD technology empowers independent producers of content such as musicians and film producers with the ability to bypass the traditional middlemen (record labels and the movie studios, for example) to self-distribute their intellectual property. By bypassing traditional channels musicians and independent producers can put their creative works directly in the path of customers and seek subsidized distribution through corporate promotions and consumer product packaging without having to factor in the often impenetrable processes and resources needed to secure movie studio distribution deals or record label contracts.

"BBM. HyperCD's proprietary digital rights management (DRM) and customer relationship management (CRM) solutions empower a new generation of media and marketing distribution by directly addressing the barriers to success that continue to plague the Internet—namely limited bandwidth, digital piracy, lackluster click-through rates, and ill-conceived online revenue models."[10]

Ken Park's involvement with the HyperCD proprietary technology, which enables users to have direct customer distribution, also gave him innovative insights into new ways of looking at distribution.

Ken's Insights on Distribution

As far as the distribution itself, I think that the marketplace has helped us validate our predictions as proven fact...We saw something and we took a position that was necessary. I think that you have to take a position in this market—sometimes you are right and sometimes you are wrong. You have to take chances, be disruptive, and implement brazen strategies that take a whole new approach. That is what a HyperCD enables. HyperCD has now proven itself and more importantly the connected-disc platform has really positioned itself as a solution for a very significant problem that has nothing to do with streaming and it really has nothing to do with bandwidth. It has to do with how we are going to make money on the Web? How is the Web going to sustain a business model in this growth period when it doesn't have that massive audience? When it doesn't have that mass medium impact of television. How do we educate companies that have content? How do we educate companies that are in the distribution piece and how do we educate consumers most of all on the opportunities that a media-rich web environment is going to offer?

The HyperCD technology is a solution to these questions. The HyperCD technology embraces:

- All of the best aspects of print
- All of the best aspects of publications
- All of the best aspects of television
- All of the best aspects of the web
- All of the best aspects of interactivity

And the technology is ubiquitous in its use. It provides the same high-quality video experience to those dialing in on a 28.8 modem as it does those accessing it via a high-speed Internet connection. That's a very critical, important part of our message. This is a way to serve bandwidth on a much more economic and a much higher quality foundation.[11]

– Ken Park

Mentor Insight
Disrupt the status quo

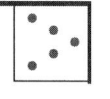

Mentor Insight
Incorporate distribution evaluation methods

Under Ken's Watch

With Ken at the helm, HyperCDs are becoming prevalent in music, training and distance-learning, recruitment, sports fan clubs, virtual trade shows, webzines, clothing hang tags, and trading cards and as commemorative memorabilia. There are an infinite amount of possibilities for the use of HyperCDs as a distribution platform. Ken and his team continue to explore new options for the HyperCD technology platform.

Ken feels one of the biggest benefits of the HyperCD is that it allows you to track, monitor, and document the usage patterns constantly, file-by-file consumption, media trends, and brand behavior of your targeted audience. The HyperCD product offers solutions on how to sustain a business model in a media-rich web environment.

Virtual Marketing Arenas

> **Mentor Insight**
> Utilize virtual marketing arenas

Ken and his team are conducting research and development on the potential HyperCD opportunities in virtual marketing arenas. Virtual marketing arenas are marketplaces that exist outside face-to-face interactions and include:

- Online auctions
- Web sites that feature e-commerce functionality
- Online communities of interest that unite customers for the purpose of raising awareness of products and services as well as making group purchases
- Web environments powered by robust database capabilities
- E-mail and instant messenger systems used for surveying, selling, and disseminating information on products or services in conjunction with the HyperCD product line
- Interactive DVDs that create an interactive online product while enabling large amounts of video to be utilized in a product known as a HyperDVD

Under Ken's leadership, HyperCD and its underlying technology have been utilized to create virtual marketing arenas for companies such as Major League Soccer, the New England Patriots, and Spalding Sports Worldwide, Inc. Web-enabled video uniquely directed at soccer and football fans places sports enthusiasts in a playback environment that fosters communication and promotes the purchase of branded merchandise from these sport franchises.

The distribution flexibility of the HyperCD is what makes it infinitely valuable to the marketplace. There is no limitation. There is no set distribution channel and no governing body other than the party that is distributing it. Each HyperCD establishes a private label media network that supports the overall marketing and branding objectives of its host company's products or goods. It seamlessly supports and is defined by the marketing campaign. So instead of looking at the distribution as a challenge, I look at it as the enabler. I look at it as new revenue potential, new consumer relationships and new direct market feedback. I look at it as multi-transactional profit potential. I look at it as adding personality and humanity to the physical product—a consumer concierge if you will. A tool for measuring brand behavior of proven consumers and a platform for new viral marketing opportunities. If you look at it from that standpoint then physical distribution becomes critical to the success of the product.

. . . Our focal point now at BBM. HyperCD is to empower and enable entrepreneurial spirited people to go out and open up new media marketing categories based upon their unique vertical market expertise. It is amazing how many content producing companies don't realize the potential of repackaging their unique offering and bringing it to more consumers worldwide. Content is still king and the best new channels are those that are right in front of our nose.[12]

– Ken Park

Mentorography Part II

In Part II of this module, we will analyze the craft behind the distribution-dominating tactics that Ken Park utilizes with his HyperCD platform and his business practices as a guide for entrepreneurial marketers.

The Mentor Insights we will further explore are as follows:

Mentor Insights

- Empower direct customer distribution
- Disrupt the status quo
- Hold business relationships sacred
- Embrace the Internet's capabilities
- Incorporate distribution evaluation methods
- Tap into connected constituencies
- Bypass traditional channels
- Partner with key influencers
- Capitalize on the impact of word-of-mouth
- Utilize virtual marketing arenas

The Business of Small Businesses

Ken Park is a small business entrepreneur whose focus is on assisting fellow founders with devising their distribution tactics utilizing the HyperCD platform. Ken knows that a common error of small businesses in the start-up mode is to forget to build a distribution model. This process should not be postponed. Instead, entrepreneurial marketers need to devise distribution tactics early in the company or product lifecycle. Postponing devising distribution tactics can lead to a product that has no way to reach its intended customer.

Ken attempts to help companies of all sizes, but small businesses in particular, avoid distribution dilemmas. Distribution dilemmas arise because of the pressure on small businesses to accomplish multiple priorities. It's crucial to emphasize the importance of distribution tactics in the planning stage of the business. Small start-up businesses usually don't have the financial resources to access the traditional distribution channels to reach their targeted markets.

Additionally, most entrepreneurs tend to be smaller ventures, unable to dominate the traditional major channels of distribution, and more than likely unable to penetrate the established distribution channels. That is why Ken believes wholeheartedly in empowering direct customer distribution. How can the newer, smaller firm gain a foothold? One way is by learning from Ken, who has been in the trenches helping other entrepreneurs do just that.

Mentor Insight

Empower direct customer distribution

154   Entrepreneurial Marketing

Helpful Hints on Distribution for Small Businesses

- **"Pay attention to the customer you are targeting.** Understand the mind-set of the user of your products. Ask yourself what is exciting about your product and/or what offering could excite and entice customers.
- **Strive for cooperative promotions that are synergistic partnerships.** Target companies that already have established channels and brand affinity with the targeted customer. Brand affinity is a predisposition to like or be attracted to a company or product's image. A cooperative promotion can usually be accomplished free of charge or for little resources—in some cases with the other company paying you money. These copromotions extend your marketing reach.
- **Create cooperative promotions by**
  - Possessing or quickly establishing key business contacts in the area of your targeted audience.
  - Diligently attending all the networking events related to your targeted audience.
  - Developing your marketing message to capture the attention of your targeted market.
  - Creating a compelling pitch to attract cooperative partners.
  - Remembering that creating cooperative promotions is very challenging but the rewards can make it worth the effort.
- **Slowly grow your business into a success.** Grow your business slowly. Grow your business by reinvesting sales revenue into your new venture's development.
- **Focus on niche markets.** Start small by catering to a specific niche audience. This positions the small business to become a larger entity with deep market support.
- **Choose the right manufacturing company.** Ken advocates doing this by
  - Understanding the personality of the company you are dealing with.
  - Finding a company that will partner with you instead of treating you as simply a vendor. Is the company you are considering willing to empower you to go after exciting business opportunities? Will they support you in creative financing options, for example, extending the time you have to pay them back so you can go after that exciting opportunity?
  - Establishing a strong bond with a manufacturer so that you are able to schedule with the principal of the manufacturing organization an in person or phone meeting if and when this is necessary.
  - Negotiating for the manufacturer to front your product for a cut of future revenues when an exciting opportunity arises.
- **Thoroughly establish the metrics of your business model before launching into the next level.** It's important not to move on to the next stage of your business development prematurely."[13]

Distribution-Dominance Solar System Model

Another way that newer, smaller firms can gain a foothold in the market is to strive to devise distribution-dominating tactics using the Mentor Insights in this module. Distribution-dominating tactics are methods that an entrepreneurial marketer can use to get their product, service or marketing message to a customer without necessarily having to invest expensive resources. This method allows the venture to accomplish these goals in a way that can be superior to the competition. These tactics can be devised by following the Distribution-Dominance Solar System Model analogy shown in Mentor Method 6.2.

Mentor Method 6.2

Distribution-Dominance Solar System Model[14]

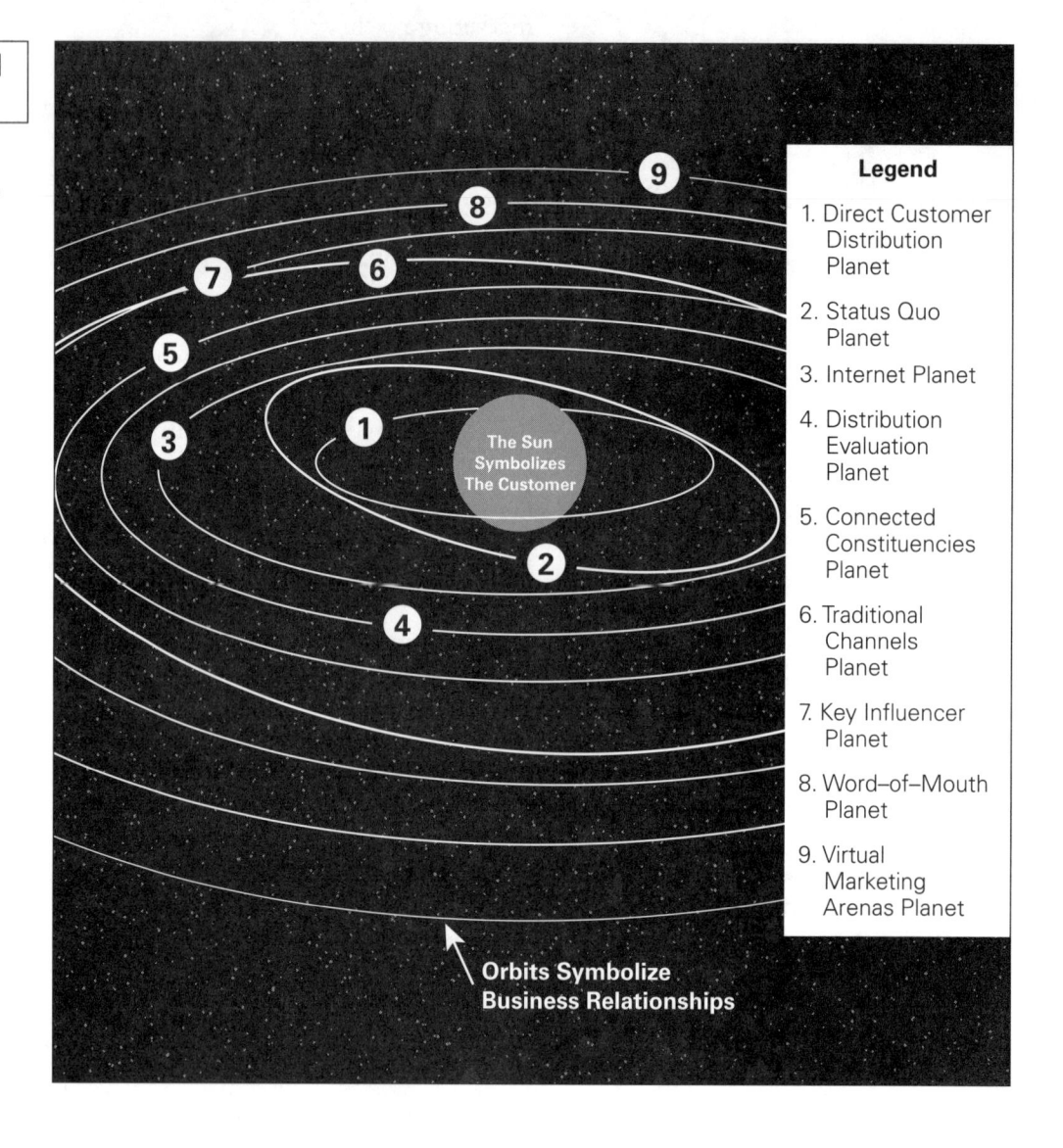

Legend

1. Direct Customer Distribution Planet
2. Status Quo Planet
3. Internet Planet
4. Distribution Evaluation Planet
5. Connected Constituencies Planet
6. Traditional Channels Planet
7. Key Influencer Planet
8. Word–of–Mouth Planet
9. Virtual Marketing Arenas Planet

The Sun Symbolizes The Customer

Orbits Symbolize Business Relationships

156   Entrepreneurial Marketing

The Distribution-Dominance Solar System Model symbolizes the analogy of the sun orbited by planets. (Please review the Distribution-Dominance Solar System Model before continuing with this module.)

Elaboration on the Distribution-Dominance Solar System Model

In the Distribution-Dominance Solar System Model each planet corresponds with one of the key components of the distribution-dominance Mentor Insights. The center and focal point of this analogy is the sun, which symbolizes the customer. In this analogy everything revolves around the sun. As an entrepreneurial marketer, the customer, like the sun, is the life force of a new venture or expansion of an existing enterprise. Distribution strategies that are devised with the customer as the focal point are positioned for long-term stability.

In the remaining pages of this module we will further elaborate on the Solar System analogy by describing the planets and their relationship to the sun.

The first planet closest to the sun is analogous to direct customer distribution. "The Digital Diary" HyperCD covered in Part I of this Mentorography serves as a good example of how an independent producer was empowered by HyperCD to directly distribute a television program concept to the customers of such a product without having to dedicate funds to pay for the traditional methods of this type of distribution.

The second planet closest to the sun, Status Quo, is represented as a troubled planet in an unstable orbit because maintaining the status quo with distribution tactics is an expensive place to be. Instead, an entrepreneurial marketer should strive to disrupt the status quo.

"The Digital Diary" HyperCD disrupted the status quo of how television pilots are distributed and marketed for sales. The traditional method for television content creators had previously been to shop for an agent or worldwide licensor to broker a program deal with a television network, cable station, or syndicator. The orbits of the other planets in the Solar System Model perturb the Status Quo Planet. This is because using status quo distribution tactics isn't often an option for entrepreneurial marketers. For example, signing with an agent for brokering a television deal is an expensive proposition for an independent producer who most likely doesn't have the leverage of a track record. An independent producer would have to turn over at least 15 percent of any revenues to an agent.

Another example of direct distribution via the HyperCD platform is the distribution of an electronic application kit for potential university student enrollment. Previously application kits were sent via direct mail. These application kits were enclosed in expensively designed brochures commonly referred to at universities as "View Book" brochures for prospective students. An electronic version means that a potential student can use their computer to fill in and submit an enrollment application.[15]

Electronic Application Kit. Pepperdine University's Graziadio School of Business and Management recently released a Web-enabled interactive HyperCD to market its full-time graduate business programs to prospective students. The HyperCD delivers instantaneous, full-motion video

---

> **Mentor Insight**
> Empower direct customer distribution

> **Mentor Insight**
> Disrupt the status quo

regardless of the user's Internet connection speed. The HyperCD performs as an information-rich, electronic application kit to enhance enrollment.[16]

The Graziadio School is excited to be the first university business school to use the HyperCD technology platform for student recruitment, as developed by BBM. HyperCD. More than 50 percent of prospective students learn about the Graziadio's accredited business school via the Internet, so the HyperCD was a natural choice to enhance their traditional marketing channels of communication. Since fewer than 11 percent of all Internet users have broadband access, the HyperCD's unique ability to deliver instantaneous video addresses a growing need as well.[17]

The Marketing Message Behind the Electronic Application Kit. The Graziadio School's HyperCD is being distributed to prospective students, corporate executives, and academic leaders throughout the world. The HyperCD features the Graziadio School's programs, philosophy and the achievements of many outstanding alumni. Targeted initially to prospective graduate students, the HyperCD interactively provides detailed, full-motion video information about the full-time MBA, JD/MBA and Master of International Business programs. The Graziadio School recruits students from around the globe, and the HyperCD is a powerful tool to attract international students.[18]

Hold Business Relationships Sacred

In the Distribution-Dominance Solar System Model, business relationships are represented as the planets' orbits. In the conceptual model, business relationships are the glue that encircles, enables and holds together many of the strategies needed to achieve a new venture's distribution tactics. In this model, each planet's orbiting path has one thing in common. The sun, which symbolizes the customer, is always at the center of each planet's orbit. We can't stress enough the importance of holding business relationships as the central and sacred theme in the entrepreneurial marketer's quest for successful distribution tactics. As mentioned, Ken Park holds business relationships sacred because he never knows when someone he met a long time ago is about to have a major impact on his life.

In the HyperCD applications for "The Digital Diary" and Pepperdine's Graziadio School, both tools were utilized to enhance business relationships. In the case of "The Digital Diary" HyperCD the product creators were able to showcase a television program concept to thousands of people in an innovative and creative way that was underscored by the vehicle of distribution. In the case of the Graziadio application kit, the HyperCD was mailed to key stakeholders.

> **Mentor Insight**
>
> Hold business relationships sacred

Ken Park's Gamble

Ken, for an over-the-top risk taker on a skateboard, has taken a conservative gamble in the HyperCD platform that utilizes the Internet. His technology has the greatest value to those who have slow Internet speed connections. This is a safe gamble until high-speed Internet connections are adopted worldwide. The HyperCD product provides low-tech solutions to high-tech distribution problems. Ken disrupts the status quo by embracing the Internet's capabilities. The Internet is the third planet shown in the model.

The Internet's Impact on Distribution

> **Mentor Insight**
> Embrace the Internet's capabilities

Prior to the emergence of the Internet many entrepreneurs were blocked from reaching their potential customers by crowded retail shelves, tradeshows attended by fragmented audiences, and the high cost of advertising. Many entrepreneurial marketers started their business through direct mail, simply because it was the only cost-effective way to reach customers. The large, existing manufacturers often aggressively blocked other paths. The advent of the Internet created a marketing channel and distribution method open to all.

The Internet has had two major effects on distribution. The delivery of intellectual properties is perhaps the most disruptive. Napster changed the music industry and gave notice to any intellectual property producers that their channel of distribution is changing. Music, books, videos, software, or any other product that can be digitized can be delivered via the Internet. Look for entrepreneurial marketers to make changes in these industries as they find that the shortest path between the source of the intellectual property and its end user is the Internet. The second effect of the Internet is the easy communications between users. Word-of-mouth on almost any topic is readily available on the Internet. Product reviews are easily acquired. Further, the Internet is being used to organize consumers into buying groups. Consumers are using this ease of communication to organize buyer groups that are able to negotiate lower prices by placing larger orders.

The fourth planet in the solar system analogy is known as the Distribution Evaluation Planet. As an entrepreneurial marketer you must

> It's important to evaluate one's distribution by asking:
> What impact did this distribution that I just did have on establishing the image of my business as something truly unique for my target market?
> What reaction did the customers have to the product?[19]
>
> – Ken Park

> **Mentor Insight**
> Incorporate distribution evaluation methods

incorporate distribution evaluation methods as often as possible so that you can quickly evaluate the effectiveness of one's distribution tactics. The Internet has additional functionality that is conceptualized with the Distribution Evaluation Methods Puzzle Pieces diagram as seen in Mentor Method 6.3.

Mentor Method 6.3

The Distribution Evaluation Methods Puzzle Pieces[20]

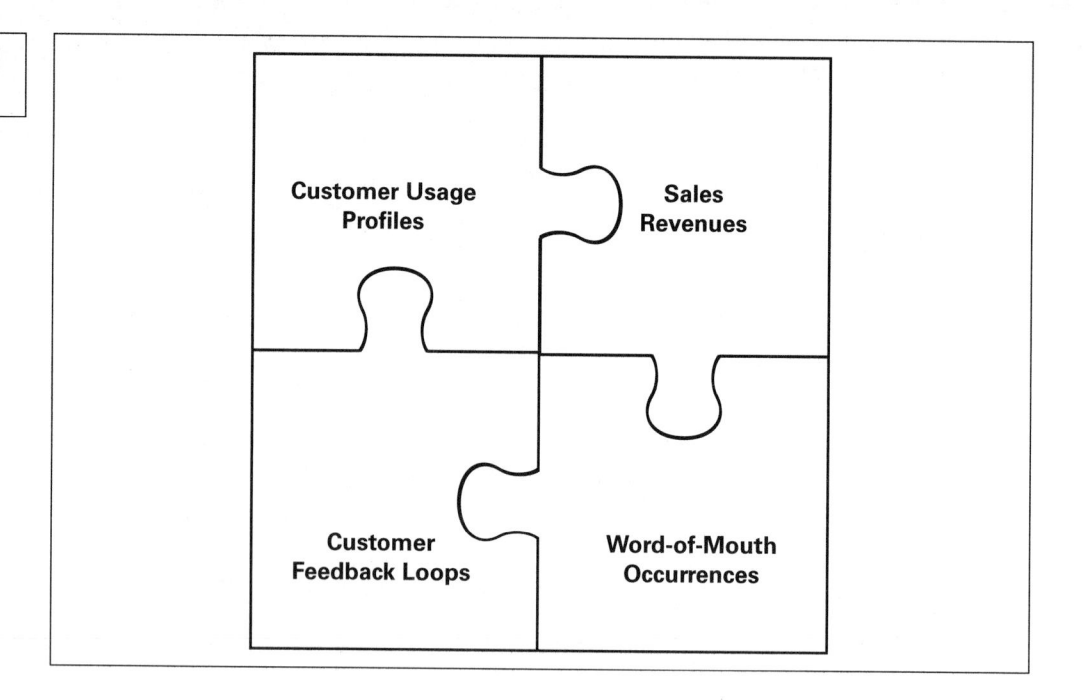

```
┌─────────────────────┬─────────────────────┐
│                     │                     │
│  Customer Usage     │      Sales          │
│     Profiles        │    Revenues         │
│                     │                     │
├─────────────────────┼─────────────────────┤
│                     │                     │
│    Customer         │   Word-of-Mouth     │
│  Feedback Loops     │    Occurrences      │
│                     │                     │
└─────────────────────┴─────────────────────┘
```

Customer Usage Profiles

Ken is a fan of the Internet because it can distribute marketing messages and certain products while collecting data on the usage patterns of your targeted customer. Earlier distribution techniques such as direct mail didn't offer marketers insights into how a customer was using a product. Marketers never even knew if a customer opened the envelope. The Internet and accompanying software allow the marketer to track the time of day that a message or product is consumed and whether the message reached the targeted recipient.

Sales Revenues

Certain types of products and services such as concert tickets, software, music, film clips, and training material can be distributed and sold via the Internet, typically allowing the entrepreneurial marketer continuous, instantaneous access to sales revenue data without having to calculate the information manually. This automates the sales data collection process and saves an entrepreneurial marketer time and often resources. Ken feels an important evaluation tool is constant access to continuously updated sales figures. Sales revenues tell the story of the implied success of a product or service. Web-enabled databases serve as repositories of key sales information that can be used to your advantage in a marketing campaign.

Customer Feedback Loops

In the past, customers have communicated with manufacturers through toll-free phone numbers or by filling out a feedback card. These processes are neither convenient nor efficient for the customer. Distribution platforms on the Internet and wireless phones with two-way communication

Entrepreneurial Marketing

capabilities have transformed customer feedback loops. Now customers can send an e-mail or an instant electronic message directly to the business to receive instant answers to their questions and comments. The business can capture valuable customer comments and save them in databases that archive and organize these comments for further analysis and trend identification.

Word-of-Mouth Occurrences

Today's economically challenged entrepreneurial marketer relies on the positive impact of word-of-mouth advertising to disseminate promotional messages via marketing channels. Ken has a particular strategy for making a word-of-mouth occurrence happen during the distribution process. He specifically goes after tastemakers in his key audiences. A tastemaker is someone who has the respect of others and who influences others by recommending a product or service. Ken feels the viral recommendation is the most powerful form of marketing that exists. For more on word-of-mouth occurrences see Module 4, Crafting a Viral Marketing Phenomenon.

Analyzing distribution evaluation data may help you identify interesting trends and potentially realize that you have tapped into a connected constituency.

Connected Constituencies

> **Mentor Insight**
> Tap into connected constituencies

In Mentor Method 6.2, the Distribution-Dominance Solar System Model, Connected Constituencies is the fifth planet away from the sun. Finding connected constituencies is often a function of having a strong business relationship with someone who provides access to the community. Examples of connected constituencies are people of similar political persuasions, athletes of the same sport, people who work at the same business or in the same industry, and artists in the same medium. The list of potentially connected constituencies is infinite. Recognizing connected constituencies and ways to tap into these groups can enhance your distribution.

Ken Park is always on the lookout for opportunities to work with connected constituencies. He develops distribution channels that tap into connected constituencies whenever he can.

Traditional Channels

The Traditional Channels Planet is the sixth planet from the sun. The Traditional Channels Planet is the other troubled planet in our model. The planet is represented with an unstable and perturbed orbit as conceptualized in Mentor Method 6.2.

Today's entrepreneurial marketers need to develop innovative distribution models that don't carry a costly overhead. Gaining distribution through traditional channels can be quite difficult for the entrepreneurial marketer, since members of traditional distribution systems have little reason to change their presently profitable way of doing business. This means it's very challenging if not almost impossible for an entrepreneurial marketer to obtain the distribution channels that she needs. That is why the Traditional Channels Planet's orbit is described as unstable and perturbed. New products carry risk that traditional distribution channels have little need to bear. Indeed, there is a long list of products that retailers took a chance on and gave shelf space to, which did not sell for one reason or another.

Existing competitors often block traditional distribution and marketing channels. New firms face massive resistance from retailers and other members of existing channels since traditional distributors have little to gain from being a part of new product introductions.

Ken, a person who enjoys finding solutions to difficult problems, embraces the Internet as a distribution problem-solving technique. The Internet represents a method by which smaller firms can bypass traditional channels and disrupt established distribution channels. Disruptive distribution methods take imagination and ingenuity to create. Disruptive distribution represents great opportunities to entrepreneurial marketers looking to gain access to markets that they're presently blocked from. The functionality of the Internet empowers new ventures to reach customers directly, and to market to them on a one-to-one basis, either through the Internet or another medium in combination with the Internet.

> **Mentor Insight**
>
> Bypass traditional channels

Partnering with Key Influencers

> **Mentor Insight**
>
> Partner with key influencers

The seventh planet away from the sun is known in our analogy as the Key Influencer Planet. This is because a method for an entrepreneurial marketer to accelerate and enhance distribution opportunities is to partner with key influencers of the process. That is what Major League Soccer (MLS) did when they put their trust in the HyperCD platform.

Under Ken's leadership in 2001, The MLS Electronic Information Guide was distributed via the HyperCD platform. This product . . . "was developed as a very targeted, groundbreaking media relations vehicle to promote the league's upcoming season and its various strategic goals on and off the field. The discs were distributed shortly before the 2001 [marketing] campaign began to 1,200 media members across the United States who regularly cover the league. The MLS HyperCD contained 12 exclusive video files that can be viewed instantaneously within a live web environment."[21] The disc's web interface is seamlessly integrated into the league's official site, **http://www.MLSnet.com**, so users can access real-time stats, news, and information about the league throughout the season and beyond, giving the disc an extended shelf life.

The response rate was impressive. The HyperCD audience profiling software showed that 81 percent of the 1,200 disseminated discs were accessed for an average of 6 minutes and 24 seconds.[22] MLS was able to replace the traditional postal mail system of distributing press information with this eye-catching, rich media technique. The disc publicized ticket sales for upcoming soccer matches as well as sold MLS merchandise. The MLS league was able to experience firsthand the power of a partnership with a key influencer of an innovative distribution technique.

162 Entrepreneurial Marketing

> **Mentor Insight**
> Capitalize on the impact of word-of-mouth

Byproduct of the MLS HyperCD

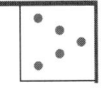

The media increased its coverage of the MLS after the release of the MLS Electronic Information Guide. The MLS was able to capitalize on the dialogue generated by this media coverage. The eighth planet away from the sun in our analogy is represented as the Word-of-Mouth Planet. Generating a word-of-mouth occurrence has a positive impact on distribution. Capitalizing on that occurrence has a long lasting impact that can make even the smallest or newest venture rise above its competition.

Utilize Virtual Marketing Arenas

> **Mentor Insight**
> Utilize virtual marketing arenas

We have described three virtual marketing arenas created with the HyperCD platform: "The Digital Diary" for program buyers, Pepperdine University's Electronic Application Kit for prospective students, and the 2001 Major League Soccer Electronic Information Guide for media members who cover the league. The Virtual Marketing Arenas Planet is the ninth and outermost planet in the Distribution-Dominance Solar System Model.

Another example of a potential virtual marketing arena is training. Corporate and motivational training is often consumed virtually, rather than in person. Today, to accommodate attendees' busy lifestyles and add convenience, trainees now have the option to learn via their computer. This type of training revolves around people's schedules, interests, and aspirations. Ken and another executive at BBM. HyperCD have collaborated to develop a product that will exist in a virtual marketing arena to take advantage of the growing trend of learning linked to personal pursuits.

"BBM AND INNERSPORTS, INC. TO JOINTLY DEVELOP A SERIES OF COLLECTIBLE HYPERCD TRAINING CARDS FOR SEVERAL 'PASSION' SPORTS (11/26/01)

After months of discussions and planning, NY based InnerSports, Inc. and BBM solidified a relationship that will result in the development of a series of collectible sports training cards specific to various passion or lifestyle sports like soccer, skateboarding, personal fitness, golf, to name a few. Each series will feature top professional athletes and/or notable trainers and will provide in upwards of 30 minutes of game highlights, individual interviews and perspectives, and detailed training tips designed to educate and assist the aspiring athlete to excel in their chosen sport.

The two companies are currently solidifying discussions with content partners and sponsors for the first series which is expected to focus on soccer and be available at the end of the first quarter of 2002 through local soccer shops, [bundled in soccer ball packaging] leagues and sponsorship channels."[23]

Mentor Method 6.4

Soccer Skilz Digital Trading Cards [24, 25, 26, 27, 28, 29, 30]

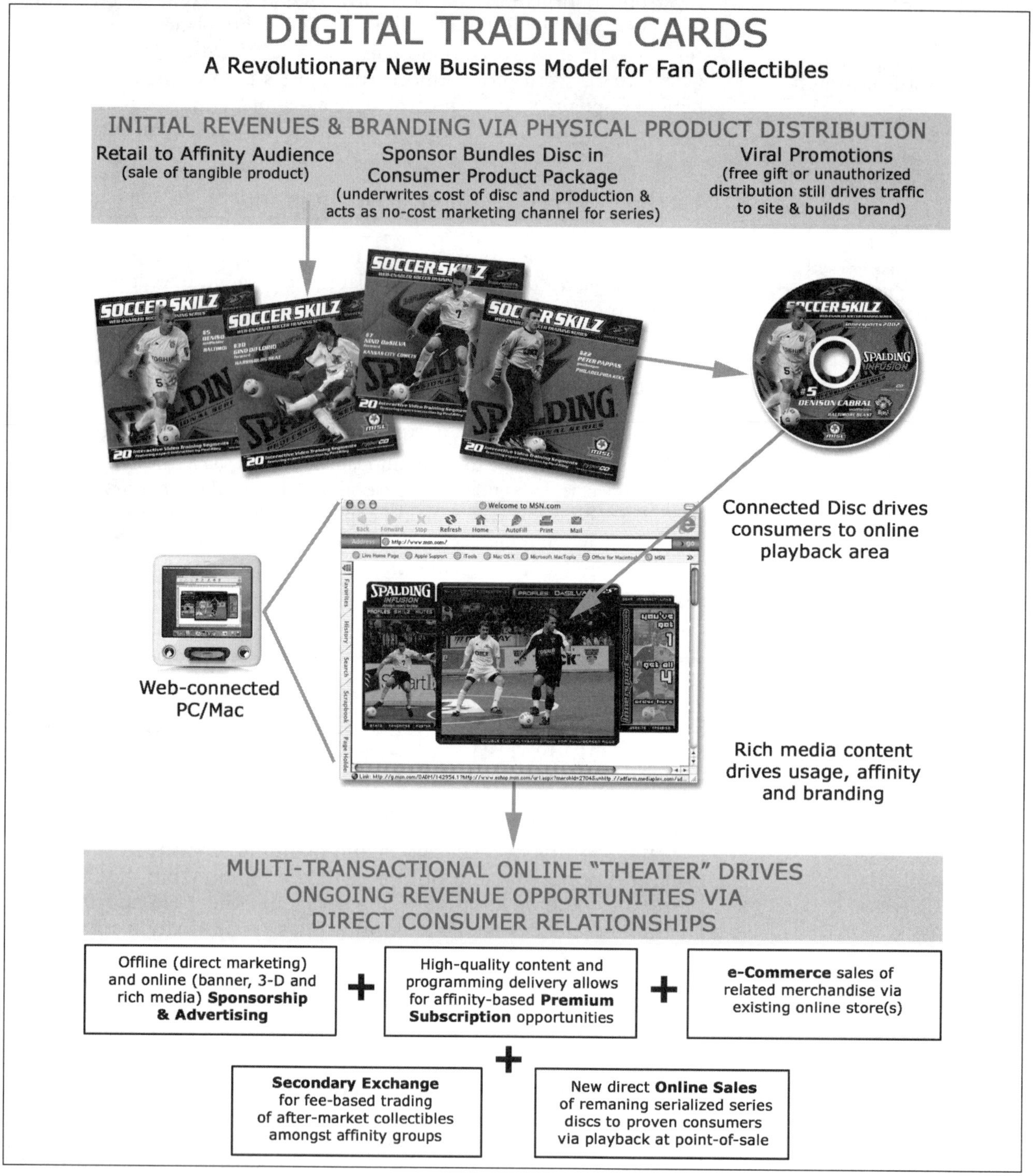

DIGITAL TRADING CARDS
A Revolutionary New Business Model for Fan Collectibles

INITIAL REVENUES & BRANDING VIA PHYSICAL PRODUCT DISTRIBUTION

- **Retail to Affinity Audience** (sale of tangible product)
- **Sponsor Bundles Disc in Consumer Product Package** (underwrites cost of disc and production & acts as no-cost marketing channel for series)
- **Viral Promotions** (free gift or unauthorized distribution still drives traffic to site & builds brand)

Connected Disc drives consumers to online playback area

Web-connected PC/Mac

Rich media content drives usage, affinity and branding

MULTI-TRANSACTIONAL ONLINE "THEATER" DRIVES ONGOING REVENUE OPPORTUNITIES VIA DIRECT CONSUMER RELATIONSHIPS

- Offline (direct marketing) and online (banner, 3-D and rich media) **Sponsorship & Advertising**
- **+** High-quality content and programming delivery allows for affinity-based **Premium Subscription** opportunities
- **+** **e-Commerce** sales of related merchandise via existing online store(s)

+

- **Secondary Exchange** for fee-based trading of after-market collectibles amongst affinity groups
- New direct **Online Sales** of remaning serialized series discs to proven consumers via playback at point-of-sale

Reprinted with permission of Denison Cabral, Baltimore Blast. Reprinted with permission of Gino DiFlorio, Harrisburg Heat, (formerly Baltimore Blast). Reprinted with permission of Peter Pappas, Philadelphia KiXX. Reprinted with permission of Nino DaSilva, Kansas City Comets.
Reprinted with permission from Major Indoor Soccer League.
Use of SPALDING® trademark and logo courtesy of Spalding Sports Worldwide, Inc.
Created by Ken Park, founder, BBM. HyperCD for *Entrepreneurial Marketing: Real Stories and Survival Strategies*.

Entrepreneurial Marketing

These collectible sport trading cards serve as yet another example of how one can create as well as utilize virtual marketing arenas. See Mentor Method 6.4 on page 164 for elaboration of how the InnerSports product line will function in the marketplace.

Mentorography Conclusion

In closing, we recommend that as an entrepreneurial marketer you don't postpone devising your distribution strategy. Instead, immediately begin devising your own style of distribution-dominating tactics. The Mentor Insights that were covered in this module and conceptualized in Mentor Method 6.2, the Distribution-Dominance Solar System Model analogy, are a good starting point for devising your own tactics. The Mentor Insights are as follows:

Mentor Insights

- Empower direct customer distribution
- Disrupt the status quo
- Hold business relationships sacred
- Embrace the Internet's capabilities
- Incorporate distribution evaluation methods
- Tap into connected constituencies
- Bypass traditional channels
- Partner with key influencers
- Capitalize on the impact of word-of-mouth
- Utilize virtual marketing arenas

Mentorography Questions

1. Hypothetically speaking, what tactics are needed to enhance one's distribution strategy in a small business? What are the hurdles in a small business that one needs to overcome to have a successful distribution strategy?

2. Describe the distribution platform application featured in the diagram in Mentor Method 6.5 (see page 166). How does this HyperCD application differ from the other applications described in this module?

Mentor Method 6.5

Digital Hang Tags/Premiums[31]

DIGITAL HANG TAGS/PREMIUMS
Turning the Consumer Product Package into a New Media, Marketing & CRM Channel

ADDED VALUE PREMIUM BUNDLED WITH PACKAGE OFFERS SOLUTION FOR CORPORATE PARALYSIS & NON-SYNERGISTIC SILOS CENTERED AROUND BRAND AND PRODUCT LINE

Design & Manufacturing
(new role in media & marketing planning)

Marketing
(enforces and extends brand through proven consumers)

Business Development
(Use company brands to introduce & cross-promote other brands)

Advertising
(new revenue center)

CRM/Market Research
(low-cost channel for direct feedback)

PROJECT FUNDING
- Reallocated advertising dollars
- 3rd sponsorship/ad sales
- Promotional dollars from new or related brands
- Paid by market research or CRM department
- Bury costs within COGS

ROI FROM PROJECT
- Viral brand promotion via proven consumers
- Measurable usage & response rates
- Empirical data capture regarding brand behavior
- Brand controlled media channel
- Direct-to-consumer communication channel
- Revenues from ad & sponsorship sales

Created by Ken Park, founder, BBM. HyperCD for *Entrepreneurial Marketing: Real Stories and Survival Strategies.*

3. Develop your own idea for a HyperCD application. Describe your product, the main goals of your project, the target market, planned market research techniques you will implement to validate your idea, how you will distribute the HyperCD, and the methods you will use to evaluate the distribution's success.

4. Devise and describe additional planets for the Distribution-Dominance Solar System Model.

Endnotes

[1] Ken Park interview conducted by Molly Lavik, April 2, 2001.

[2] Ibid.

[3] Reprinted with permission from Urchin Software Corporation. Use of Urchin® trademark and logo courtesy of Urchin Software Corporation. Urchin, Urchin Software Corporation, and the Urchin logo are all registered marks of Urchin Software Corporation.

[4] Courtesy of Brett Crosby, Vice President, Business Development, Urchin Software Corporation.

[5] Reprinted with permission from the creator of "The Digital Diary."

[6] Reprinted with permission. Reporting software courtesy of Urchin Software Corporation. Urchin, Urchin Software Corporation, and the Urchin logo are all registered marks of Urchin Software Corporation.

[7] Reprinted with permission from the creator of "The Digital Diary."

[8] Ayn Rand, *Atlas Shrugged*, 35th Anniversary edition, (Dutton, New York, 1992).

[9] Ken Park phone interview conducted by Molly Lavik, September 6, 2002.

[10] Welcome page, http://www.hypercd.com/home.html, accessed September 3, 2001.

[11] Ken Park interview conducted by Molly Lavik, April 2, 2001.

[12] Ibid.

[13] Ken Park phone interview conducted by Molly Lavik, September 6, 2002.

[14] Developed by Molly Lavik, July 30, 2002.

[15] Reprinted with permission from the Graziadio School of Business and Management, Pepperdine University.

[16] "Pepperdine University's Graziadio School of Business and Management Launches New HyperCD Technology," Press Release, September 10, 2001, Reprinted with permission, courtesy of the Graziadio School of Business and Management, Pepperdine University.

[17] Ibid.

[18] Ibid.

[19] Ken Park phone interview conducted by Molly Lavik, September 6, 2002.

[20] Developed by Bruce Buskirk and Molly Lavik, July 20, 2002.

[21] "2001 Major League Soccer Electronic Information Guide HyperCD," Marketing Sheet, created by BBM. HyperCD, Reprinted with permission of Major League Soccer.

[22] Ibid.

[23] "BBM AND INNERSPORTS, INC. TO JOINTLY DEVELOP A SERIES OF COLLECTIBLE HYPERCD TRAINING CARDS FOR SEVERAL 'PASSION' SPORTS," Press Release, November 26, 2001, courtesy of BBM. HyperCD.

[24] Reprinted with permission of Denison Cabral, Baltimore Blast.

[25] Reprinted with permission of Gino DiFlorio, Harrisburg Heat, (formerly Baltimore Blast).

[26] Reprinted with permission of Peter Pappas, Philadelphia KiXX.

[27] Reprinted with permission of Nino DaSilva, Kansas City Comets.

[28] Reprinted with permission from Major Indoor Soccer League.

[29] Use of SPALDING® trademark and logo courtesy of Spalding Sports Worldwide, Inc.

[30] Created by Ken Park, founder, BBM. HyperCD for *Entrepreneurial Marketing: Real Stories and Survival Strategies*.

[31] Ibid.

NEW PRODUCTS MENTOR MODULE

Savvy Strategies for Marketing New Products

DIRK GATES
Founder, Xircom—An Intel Company

Mentorography Part I

This is the story of a young entrepreneur, Dirk Gates, who founded a company, Xircom, that was at the intersection of two high-growth market spaces: local area networking and mobile computing.

Under Dirk's leadership, mobile computer professionals around the world learned to rely upon Xircom for access to their information anytime and anywhere. Xircom designed and developed innovative solutions that connected mobile users worldwide to corporate networks, the Internet, Intranets and other online resources. Xircom sold and supported its products in over 100 countries through distributors, resellers, electronic channels, and global OEM (Original Equipment Manufacturer) partnerships.

The sale of Xircom was reported in an article on March 3, 2001 stating that "Santa Clara-based Intel is purchasing Xircom for $748 million in cash."[1] In 2001, when the stock market had seen a major downturn, this sale was significant. The sale represented a young entrepreneur who had the vision and foresight in the 1980s to create a product line around the growing necessity of the laptop.

Dirk Gates is an entrepreneur who demonstrates the key strategies required to successfully market new products. Part I of the module examines the origins of the Mentor Insights that predisposed Dirk Gates to successfully market new products. They are as follows:

Mentor Insights

- Recognize market opportunity
- Establish a clear-cut vision
- Brand the product with a distinctive logo mark
- Initiate firsthand market research
- Get the product to market
- Build an "all-star cast" for the board
- Strive for operational excellence
- Develop new product strategies
- Place the product engineer in front of the customer
- Exceed customer's needs with the product

Dirk Gates Milestones

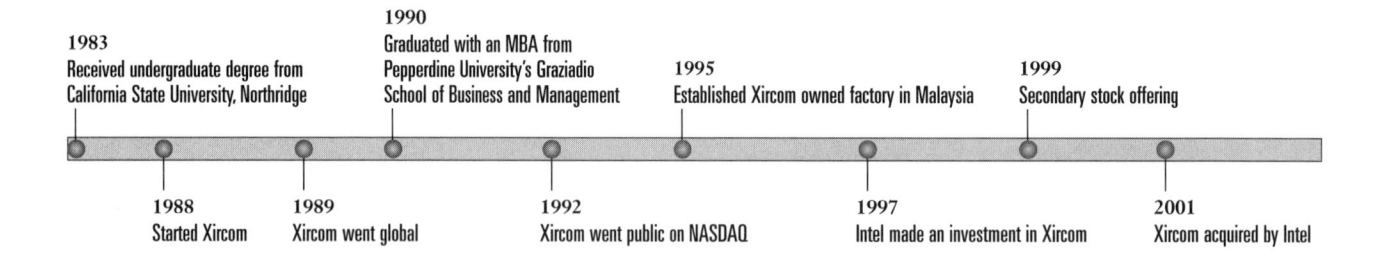

1983 — Received undergraduate degree from California State University, Northridge

1988 — Started Xircom

1989 — Xircom went global

1990 — Graduated with an MBA from Pepperdine University's Graziadio School of Business and Management

1992 — Xircom went public on NASDAQ

1995 — Established Xircom owned factory in Malaysia

1997 — Intel made an investment in Xircom

1999 — Secondary stock offering

2001 — Xircom acquired by Intel

In the Beginning

Dirk enjoyed a normal childhood growing up in Southern California. His father was an aerospace engineer at TRW (a global company in the automotive, aerospace and information technology markets) who shared with Dirk his plans to start a business in retirement. Dirk's dad passed away in 1986 shortly before his retirement unable to live out his retirement dream.

Dirk originally worked for a company called Pertron (which was later acquired by Square D). After reaching his frustration limit over what he describes as a "culture clash," Dirk decided to leave and start his own business with Kirk Mathews, founder of Pertron, who was 20 years his senior. Dirk and Kirk made a commitment of one year of their time and energy to starting their business. The first thing they did, on the advice of a

A Gleam in His Father's Eyes

We always talked about building computers in the '70s. I remember tinkering with my old Heath Kit computer in college and upgrading to an 8086 processing board. We always talked about my dad wanting to start his own business building personal computer products of some sort. But unfortunately, in 1986, he passed away. He did not get to see Xircom. He would have been proud and would have most likely found a way to help out.[2]

– Dirk Gates

business acquaintance, was to rent office space. The friend had explained to them the importance of having an office to go to each day as opposed to working out of their garages or homes, even if they sat at the office all day not accomplishing anything. This suggestion turned out to be worthwhile because it eventually provided Dirk and Kirk with the inspiration for their new business venture.

For the first three weeks Dirk and Kirk brainstormed multiple new business venture ideas until they began to settle on a concept that incorporated solving a problem that they themselves were experiencing. Specifically Dirk and Kirk were early adopters of laptop computers. In 1986 it was expensive to connect a laptop to a network. Dirk and Kirk wanted to bring their laptops to the office and network them so that they could share information and data. They began to consider creating products that enabled a laptop to connect to a network in a more affordable manner. That is how the company's initial product focus was conceived.

> **Mentor Insight**
>
> Recognize market opportunity

The Product Concept

The first product idea for the company was devising an inexpensive way to attach a laptop to a computer network via the printer port. Both of us had been looking for a way to put our laptops on a network in the office. Connecting laptops to the network used to cost about $2,500. We came up with a small device that could accomplish the same function. We produced these new devices inexpensively and sold them for between $600 and $700. People were purchasing them in volume because it saved a lot of money compared to the external device they previously purchased for $2,500. This quickly grew in its first full year—to $10 million in revenue. We suddenly realized that we had tapped into the intersection of both the rapidly growing mobile computing and networking markets.[3]

– Dirk Gates

Savvy Strategies for Marketing New Products **Module 7**

Dirk enrolled in Pepperdine's MBA program prior to starting his new venture. He decided to stay enrolled thinking it could help him with his new career focus. Dirk's Bachelor's degree is in engineering. He saw benefits in getting an education in business to complement his start-up aspirations. Dirk found that the knowledge he gained while working on obtaining his MBA was valuable to his start-up. The MBA program is where Dirk fine-tuned his skills in marketing, strategy, and operations. He had access to the insights of students and professors using Xircom as a real-world business case study.

The Educational Edge

I used the MBA program as a strategy to complement my knowledge base while running my first new venture. It turns out that was one of the best decisions I could have made. Every evening when I shifted my focus to school I was automatically forced to work on other areas of the business instead of just engineering. Kirk (my co-founder) and I were both engineers by training . . . So, for two years for 20K (tuition cost less than it does now), I had five or six other MBA students working on Xircom-focused group projects for me and I had all the advice and insights of the university faculty that reviewed and critiqued my initial business strategy. The educational edge I was getting from the MBA program helped the company achieve its first 10-million-dollar revenue year as I was graduating from the program.[4]

– Dirk Gates

Mentor Insight

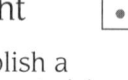

Establish a clear-cut vision

Xircom's Vision

Dirk's training stressed the need for a clear-cut vision statement as an important consideration in achieving success in business. Firms that follow a clear-cut vision through good as well as challenging times are the successful firms. In Dirk's case the company vision was one that was stumbled upon.

The Naming Process of Xircom

Xircom was originally called GMH DataCom for Gates, Mathews, and Hayes. The name was long, awkward, and unmemorable. (Good names are short, easy to pronounce, and easy to remember.) In February of 1988, Dirk and his team went looking for an advertising/public relations agency. As a small new business venture, people had a hard time taking the founders seriously because the business was so young and the initial product line was not yet readily identified in the marketplace as needed products. Dirk and the founding team chose a small advertising agency out of Simi Valley, California that was willing to create the company identity and a trade show booth and write some press releases for $30,000. As the ink was drying on the agreement with the advertising agency, the agency pro-

Mentor Insights

Establish a clear-cut vision

Recognize market opportunity

Striking Gold

The vision was simply to create a cash flow to bootstrap the business and give us time to come up with the really big idea. We really had no one vision in mind. We wanted to escape from Square D. We wanted to have some fun and build cool products. It was after the launch of the first product and its success that we started doing true research in terms of sizing the market. We realized this is more than just a great bootstrap product. This was a huge market space. There was long-term growth potential. It was then we realized that we had struck gold with this product. We hit the right markets and we have been focusing on that ever since.[5]

— Dirk Gates

vided the feedback that the product was great but the company name was awful. The agency had them fill out a corporate name survey. Dirk remembers thinking at the time that with only four employees filling out the survey was a pretty "silly exercise." With the help of this advertising agency, a list of a hundred names was compiled.

They Used the KISS Method (Keep It Simple, Stupid)

We agreed that [GMH Datacom] was not the best name. In search of a brand name we actually did a corporate culture survey. There were only three or four of us at the time and some of the guys thought it was rather silly, but my organizational behavior classes had taught me the value of this process. It was actually a rather interesting survey that sparked some ideas and we agreed to come in on a Saturday to wrap up the naming process. We spent the entire day trying to come up with a name. Finally at the very end of the day—about 6 o'clock—we were all tired and a little punchy. One of the guys said, 'OK, I give up. Let's name the company Xirk after Dirk and Kirk.' Kirk really liked the idea. He actually wanted one of the guys to sketch a logo for the company. I shook my head. Another guy said, 'No, we can fix this, let's throw com on the end for communications.' We dropped the 'k' and called it Xircom for Dirk and Kirk Communications.

Everyone was in agreement that this worked. The final piece was the logo. It was suggested that the name of the company be the logo and not to add a separate graphic element. This would lead to stronger name recognition as we invested in building the brand. A small triangle was used above the 'i' to turn the name into a logo.[6]

— Dirk Gates

Savvy Strategies for Marketing New Products **Module 7**

> **Mentor Insight**
>
> Brand the product with a distinctive logo mark

> **Mentor Insight**
>
> Initiate firsthand market research

> **Mentor Insight**
>
> Get the product to market

By developing the name Xircom and incorporating the letters of the company's name in the mark, the new venture was branding its products with a distinctive logo mark. This was a concept stressed by one of Dirk's mentors that had been coaching him as a new CEO.

In 1988, Dirk and his team attended a technology innovation trade show called Comdex for market research purposes. After canvassing the trade show floor, they were relieved to find that no one else seemed to have products competing with Xircom's. While attending this trade show, Dirk signed up for the next trade show, to be held in Chicago in April 1989. This was a significant moment in the new venture's history because it forced Dirk and his team to develop a product in time for the next trade show.

Just in Time

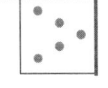

We signed up for a 10-by-10-foot booth for the upcoming trade show in Chicago. We had a product idea but that was it. The product was not built or functioning yet. The deadline pressures to be prepared with a working product gave us the motivation and drive to finish the product's development. Miraculously, we were able to produce samples of a functioning product in time for the trade show along with a corporate identity for the new business. We made the deadline and debuted our new product in April of 1989 at the Chicago trade show.[7]

– Dirk Gates

Making a Very Small Business Seem Larger

One of Xircom's first marketing strategies for the company was to sell through distributors and give the company an image that made it seem a lot larger than it really was.

In the years that followed, Xircom saw explosive growth in its market, revenues, and profit margins. Dirk had started Xircom with Kirk Mathews. In the beginning the company was a very tight team that worked well together. In the early days, everyone knew what he was responsible for and there wasn't a need to write it down formally. Kirk was responsible for the operations and sales of the business and Dirk ran the engineering and marketing.

> *Our original business plan was wrapped around a cash flow model. We were assuming that we could sell hundreds of these units through the backs of magazines a little bit at a time. Suddenly, it became very clear that we did not understand how to launch and distribute a product. I had not taken a sales management class yet. So, as we went to distributors, we learned very quickly. We somehow got through that phase and got our product to market.*
>
> *It turned out that by using these methods we sold thousands of units. Thinking about brand, we tried to make sure the company looked much larger than life.*
>
> *First we ran an ad in the front of* LAN Magazine. *The ad was a full page and in full color, and really quite expensive for a start-up. Then we ran an ad in* PC Magazine. *So back in those days, we were seven to eight guys in a small office in Woodland Hills and people would call up and talk to us on the phone or see us at trade shows and we were always very coy about the size of the company. Those who figured it out could not believe that a small group of guys had created a company image that gave the impression of being a large-sized operation.[8]*
>
> – Dirk Gates

The Right Venture Capitalists

> **Mentor Insight**
>
> Build an "all-star cast" for the board

The first venture capitalist to invest in Xircom was Roger Evans who was the founder and CEO of Micom. Roger joined Graylock (a venture capital firm) as a venture capitalist. Dirk was impressed with Roger because of his operating experience. Roger joined the board of Xircom in 1990 and was instrumental in helping Dirk build his first management team as well as helping build an "all-star cast" for his board of directors. These outside directors included Bill Shroeder, Vice Chairman of Connor Peripherals; Bruce Edwards, CFO of AST; Del Yocam, former COO of Apple; Gary Bowen, VP Sales and Marketing of Bay Networks; and Michael Ashby, CFO of Pacific Telesis Enterprises.

Mentors to Dirk

Kirk was Dirk's mentor for Xircom from 0–10 million dollars in operating profit and Roger Evans became Dirk's mentor from 10–100 million dollars. The board of directors became mentors to Dirk as well at 100+ million.

Nine months after the company went public in 1992, Kirk retired and Dirk took over running the business.

Kirk and Roger Were Active Mentors in Dirk's Career

Kirk and I spent a considerable amount of time working together. I learned a lot about running a business from working with him. He introduced me to most of the operations and sales methods because he had experience in those areas. With Roger, it was quite different . . . He would come in once a week and spend a day with us. In some cases, he would actually come in and sit in the staff meetings. He would sit quietly and then give me feedback afterwards. He helped us with some key strategic decisions. Once a quarter, we would go on a strategic retreat offsite. We would discuss our strategies for Xircom.[9]

– Dirk Gates

Implementing Key Strategies

From 1995 to 1997, Xircom was engaged in a painful market share war with 3Com. Xircom saw a dip in their market share of 70–80 percent to as low as 15 percent. To combat the price wars with 3Com's products, Xircom implemented two key strategies. The first was one of operational excellence. Xircom created an Advanced Manufacturing group. The Advanced Manufacturing group worked with product designers to simultaneously have a design tested for manufacturability during development. The end result allowed the pre-production processes to occur at the same time that a new product was designed so that the product could move immediately into manufacturing. The concept of an Advanced Manufacturing group shortens the time it takes to get a new product to market.

The second key strategy was to return to focusing on creating products that were thought of as major innovations. Creating innovative products was the guiding principle upon which the company had been founded. The need was great for Xircom to become more innovative again because of the competition. What hurt Xircom was the X-Jack (a tiny spring-loaded socket that pops out of the side of 3Com's modem cards). Mobile laptop users disliked carrying modem leads. The X-Jack instead provided an easier method for allowing people to utilize the standard telephone cable to transmit the data between a phone and a computer.

To combat 3Com's X-Jack, Xircom developed an innovative new product. Xircom created its own method using a standard cable between a phone and laptop computer. The full height of the PC Card slot was utilized allowing laptop users to connect to the Internet and/or a computer network using standard connections. Xircom patented the new PC Card connector and named this product, RealPort^{TM}, shutting out 3Com from this innovation.

The new product strategies of implementing operational excellence combined with bringing innovative new products, like the RealPort^{TM}, to market allowed Xircom to recover 30 percent to 40 percent of the market share it had lost to 3Com.

Mentor Insight
Strive for operational excellence

Mentor Insight
Develop new product strategies

Entrepreneurial Marketing

At the Helm . . .

I ended up running the company at that point [when the company went public], which worked out pretty well. Even in those days, running a $40 million company was done in a pretty loose manner. We were well over $100 million when we started doing business with ISO for the certification process. It was 1995 when we brought in our first true VP of Engineering, so that we could run multiple complex projects at the same time. We also brought in our first COO. These two hires helped us establish the proper processes that larger companies need.

. . . The more efficient the process we achieved, the better the prospect became for success. . . . I have enjoyed broadening my responsibilities from developing only the technological aspect of the product to other aspects of new product management including product marketing and customer research that emphasizes understanding what the customer wants to see in the product.

Typically, engineers get blamed for wanting to engineer a product for the engineer's sake, and if you keep the engineers from the customers—they will do that. But I have found that if you get engineers out in front of customers, they better understand the customers and their needs. It is actually very rewarding to solve customers' problems. Engineers really just have advanced degrees in problem solving and it is fun when you actually get out there and do it. The growth of Xircom was a sequence of problem solving. I didn't miss the technical side of product development because I derived so much more joy in the process of creating a successful product in the market because that product solved a customer's needs.[10]

– Dirk Gates

> **Mentor Insight**
>
> Place the product engineer in front of the customer

Innovative New Products

As Xircom grew in revenue and size, so did its list of product innovations. In 1997 and 1998, Xircom experienced significant growth that was enhanced by a 1997 investment from Intel Corporation. Xircom and Intel had many reasons for working together. The primary reasons included Intel's need to access the customers and connections that Xircom had amassed with its regional headquarters in Belgium, Japan, and Singapore. Xircom needed a discounted price on the silicon chips that were needed to power the computer laptop accessories they were having manufactured.

Highlights of Xircom's Product Innovations from 1997 to 2001

1997   Xircom announces the industry's first combination PC Card with 100Mbps Ethernet and 56k modem speed. The company also shipped PC Cards that enabled wireless data communications.[11]

1998   Xircom introduces the RealPort™ family of integrated PC Cards and later that same year announces a wireless data connection kit for this product.[12]

Xircom was also awarded a patent for its revolutionary RealPort™ Integrated PC Card.[13]

1999   Xircom held a secondary stock offering. This investment continued to fuel Xircom's growth. Additionally, Xircom entered the broadband home networking markets with the PortStation™ System, which provided customizable mobile access solutions for small office/home office laptop users (SOHO market).[14]

2000   Patent wars continued to erupt between Xircom and 3Com.

"Xircom Inc. (Nasdaq: XIRC) filed a patent infringement suit Thursday [September 21, 2000] against 3Com Corp. (Nasdaq: COMS) in the U.S. District Court for the Central District of California. Xircom charges that 3Com's forthcoming Type III PC Cards infringe on patents for Xircom's RealPort PC Cards and should be barred from sale . . . The Xircom RealPort Integrated PC Card is a Type III PC Card that allows users to connect to their data networks without using fragile features that can easily be lost or broken . . ."[15]

Reprinted with permission of the Ventura County Star.

Xircom claimed it revolutionized the networking market when it released the RealPort™ Integrated PC Card.[16]

Previously a lawsuit had been served by 3Com against Xircom in which 3Com accused Xircom of using patented 3Com technology to make PC cards. Xircom denied these allegations and said it would fight these lawsuits vigorously.[17]

As the economy declined, Intel and 3Com made peace over these patent wars as in the end no one was profiting from the battles.

Patent wars and a downturned economy were not preventing Xircom from posting a healthy increase in their fiscal year that ended on September 30, 2000. "Net sales for the year [2000] were $496.2 million, a 17% increase over the $424.4 million reported last year. Net income was $25 million or 82 cents per share, compared with $37.9 million or $1.48 per share for fiscal 1999."[18]

The healthy revenue postings for Xircom in a declining economy solidified Dirk's view that Xircom was exceeding the mobile customer's needs.

In November Xircom introduced yet another product directed at customers' needs. Xircom introduced a 5mm-thin personal digital assistant. The goal of this new product was to find a new niche among PDA (Personal Digital Assistants) users. This handheld

---

Mentor Insight

Exceed customer's needs with the product

electronic device offered the ability to browse the Web offline and rolodex-style features while weighing only 1.4 ounces.[19]

2001 2001 was a landmark year for Xircom. It also marked the end of an independent Xircom. Early in 2001, Xircom expanded its wireless portfolio with the debut of a CreditCard™ GPRS (General Packet Radio Service) solution, which is a Type II PC Card that provides wireless wide-area network (WWAN) connectivity for laptop PC users. Using Xircom's CreditCard™ GPRS solution, mobile professionals were able to re-create their office environment at an airport, a hotel, or anywhere in the world there is GPRS coverage.[20]

A Serious Issue

Product innovations aside, there were serious concerns at Xircom about the ultimate future of the company, as it then existed. Overseas circuit board manufacturing companies were forcing Xircom to lower its prices, jeopardizing Xircom's position in the marketplace.

The integration of the Xircom networking communication cards has not hit the Motherboard of the laptop yet. Instead we were experiencing an intermediate step. The PC Card slot, which had been on the side of the laptop, was moving to a PCI Slot on the bottom of the laptop. If you flip over a laptop and look at the bottom side there is a little slot with a trap door that flips up. This opening is where you can now drop in the communication card. A lot of the computer manufacturers have shifted to using this slot. This obscure slot location for the communication card meant that Xircom was removed from having any branding power or any point of differentiation with our product. This shifted the power to the PC OEM manufacturers: the Dells, the Compaqs, and the guys building the machines. They would spec out if they wanted an Ethernet or modem on this card.

We found ourselves competing with the guys in Taiwan who inexpensively put together cards. Silicon manufacturers like Intel and Lucent were gladly supplying silicon chips to these firms in Taiwan who operate as board manufacturers who were then supplying their boards to laptop manufacturers. It was a real challenge. We were now all in the same boat in that we were all buying silicon chips from Intel and Lucent for the same price.

We were working closely with Dell Computers. We tuned our supply chain with Dell. We set up our warehouses next to Dell's facilities. We integrated our manufacturing software and we tied our systems together with Dell. Yet Dell was still hanging over our heads these small Chinese manufacturing houses forcing us to be price competitive with them. So we were forced to compete on price.

It became clear that we had to own the silicon chips. We had to own that core intellectual property. That's when it made sense to say, 'Hey, Intel, we want to become part of you.' Otherwise we were going to just end up being a board-manufacturing house.[21]

– Dirk Gates

To deal with this situation, Dirk and his team needed to become part of Intel. To accomplish this goal, Xircom was sold to Intel.

This sale was reported in an article on March 3, 2001 stating that "Santa Clara-based Intel is purchasing Xircom for $748 million in cash."[22]

The all-essential silicon chip that powered Xircom's products now cost Xircom—An Intel Company a fraction of what it cost before. This allowed Xircom—An Intel Company to be price competitive against the manufacturing houses overseas.

The March 3rd article went on to say, "Xircom will become part of Intel's Network Communications Group and will provide Intel with new products for notebook and mobile computing, Intel officials said. Xircom, which has about 1,900 employees worldwide and regional offices in Belgium, Japan, and Singapore, is in the midst of a planned move into a new corporate headquarters at the Conejo Spectrum, the new office and industrial complex being built on the former Northrop-Grumman property in Thousand Oaks."[24]

Reprinted with permission of the Ventura County Star.

> *Now that we are part of Intel we can purchase Ethernet chips for a transfer cost that is significantly lower than before. Likewise our cost for a Lucent DSP (now that we are part of Intel) is also significantly less. (DSP stands for Digital Signal Processors which are tiny silicon chips that enable voice recognition on computers.)*[23]
>
> – Dirk Gates

Despite the meshing of two different company cultures, Xircom's relationship with Intel has been a profitable one. Intel's purchase of Xircom marked the beginning of another era of product innovations. At the end of March of 2001, Xircom—An Intel Company launched a family of Bluetooth wireless accessory products, which provided simple and seamless interaction between mobile devices.[25]

New Phase of Career

With the Intel acquisition behind him, Dirk entered a new phase of his career. Dirk is enjoying this time in his career although you shouldn't be surprised if Dirk is behind some new product innovations in the future.

Mentorography Part II

In Part II of this module on savvy strategies for new product marketing, we will continue to explore and analyze the Mentor Insights demonstrated by Dirk Gates and Xircom. These are as follows:

Mentor Insights

- Recognize market opportunity
- Establish a clear-cut vision
- Brand the product with a distinctive logo mark
- Initiate firsthand market research
- Get the product to market
- Build an "all-star cast" for the board
- Place the product engineer in front of the customer
- Strive for operational excellence
- Develop new product strategies
- Exceed customer's needs with the product

The History of New Product Marketing

Prior to analyzing the Mentor Insights that Dirk Gates imparts in his business practices, it's helpful to understand the historic backdrop for new product marketing.

Traditionally products have emerged from scientific advances, technological advances, and invention. New product development is typically built upon some combination of these three. New product management is the area of business that has emerged out of the new product development process being too "product driven" rather than "market driven." New product management is a natural offspring of the adoption of the marketing concept. The marketing concept is finding a need and filling it, which was first widely espoused in the fifties. The leader in the field, by way of example, was Procter & Gamble, which is well known to be driven by market research when it debuted a stream of highly successful product introductions.

Recognizing Market Opportunity

Highly successful product introductions are derived from recognizing market opportunity. Dirk identified an unmet function in the marketplace in the late 1980s, and built Xircom upon that one market niche—laptop connection to other computer systems. How did he have the foresight to recognize this opportunity? Was it luck that placed him squarely at the intersection of two rapidly growing marketplaces: mobile computing and networked computers?

The foreword of this book discusses techniques for assessing market opportunity. It's essential that you as an entrepreneurial marketer recognize and understand the market opportunity. Dirk Gates may have stumbled onto the market opportunity that struck gold for him but once he began in this market he quickly recognized the possibilities. As exemplified by the building blocks in Mentor Method 7.1, Dirk's personality allowed him to recognize market opportunity.

Mentor Insight
Recognize market opportunity

- Dirk was an **early adopter of innovations**. He was using a laptop computer long before most people had even heard of them. He pioneered innovative product lines of laptop accessories. It takes a true pioneer to recognize market opportunities.

- Dirk's **hobbies became more fascinating to him over time**. As a youngster he built processing boards and as an adult he went on to design products that took processing boards to a whole new product innovation level. This enthusiasm and drive enabled Dirk to have the interest in an area that would develop into an exciting and lucrative market opportunity.

- Dirk's dad's interests inspired him to develop computer accessories. When his father passed away, Dirk had a **desire to fulfill his dad's dreams** and went on to found Xircom. Inspiration doesn't just happen; it has its roots from somewhere. In Dirk's case, he was inspired to explore new areas that led him on the path toward discovering a great market opportunity.

- Dirk has the rare ability to **transform adversity into opportunity**. He did this repeatedly throughout his career starting when

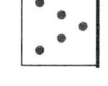

Mentor Method 7.1

Recognizing Market Opportunities Behavioral Building Blocks[26]

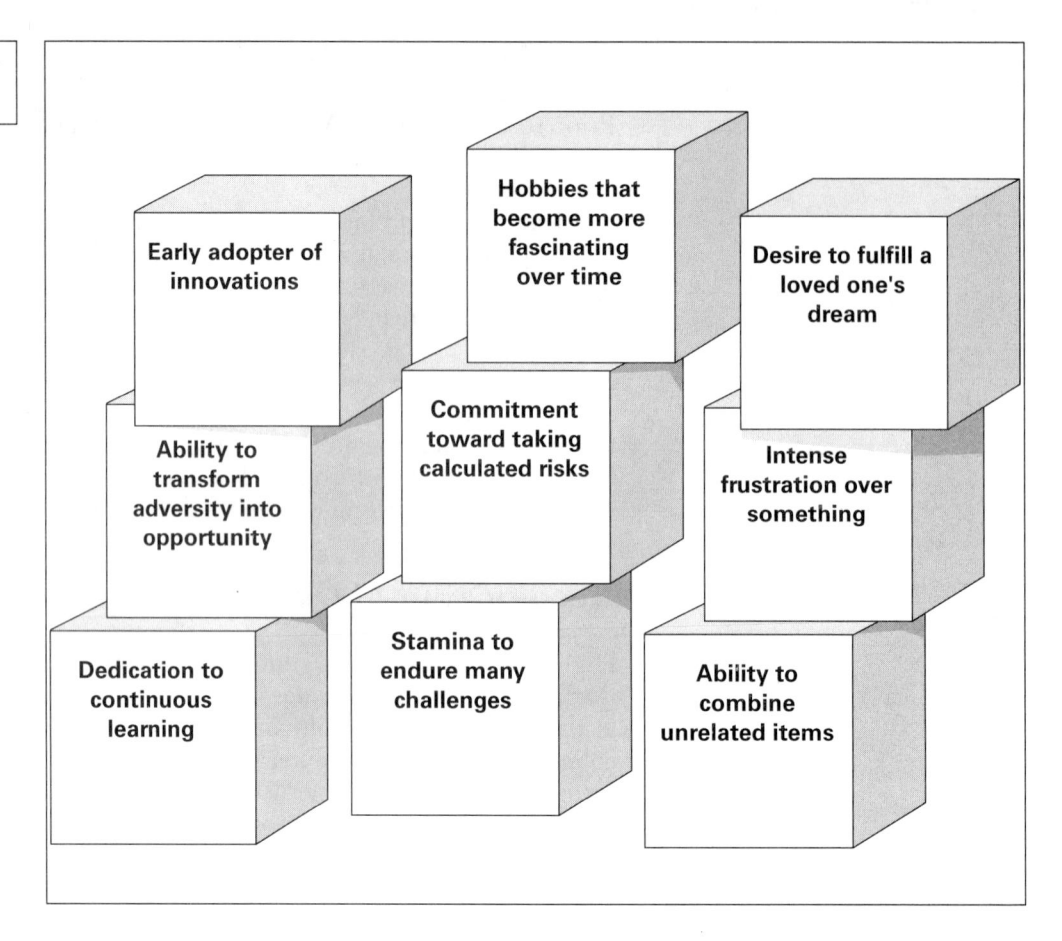

- Early adopter of innovations
- Hobbies that become more fascinating over time
- Desire to fulfill a loved one's dream
- Ability to transform adversity into opportunity
- Commitment toward taking calculated risks
- Intense frustration over something
- Dedication to continuous learning
- Stamina to endure many challenges
- Ability to combine unrelated items

he founded Xircom and was trying to find an inexpensive way to network his laptop. He continued to do this when Xircom filed a lawsuit against 3Com for patent infringement on the RealPort. It's especially true in Dirk's case that "necessity is the mother of all invention."

- Dirk is capable of a **commitment toward taking calculated risks**. For example, he did this when he started Xircom and committed to his partner to dedicate a year of his life's savings and time to the effort. Usually one has to take a risk to discover a market opportunity.

- Dirk's interest in starting his own new venture was fueled in part by an **intense frustration** at Square D of not seeing some of his product designs come to market after they had been fully developed. Dirk channeled his frustration into positive energy by starting Xircom to provide an environment where engineers' designs would be treated with higher regard. The high regard for engineers' designs at Xircom assisted the company in identifying the innovative products that had the greatest market opportunity.

- Dirk possesses a strong **dedication to continuous learning**. This is exemplified with how he remained in a demanding MBA program while starting his new business venture. This is also exempli-

Entrepreneurial Marketing

fied by how he surrounded himself with mentors who he learned from. This ongoing commitment toward developing his intellect led to Dirk being able to excel at engineering as well as marketing. These combined skills helped Dirk further recognize the market opportunity that existed in the space that Xircom occupied.

- Dirk has the **stamina to endure many challenges**. He was able to outlast and outwit 3Com in the laptop accessory war. Stamina and determination are prerequisites for successfully entering a new market space.

- Dirk has a rare and uncanny ability to **combine unrelated items** in recognizing a market opportunity. He did this when he focused the vision of Xircom at the nexus of mobile computers and laptop networking.

Vision

> **Mentor Insight**
>
> Establish a clear-cut vision

Although Dirk's original vision for his new business was to simply start a cash flow, he quickly expanded and fine-tuned that vision. Dirk's clear-cut vision was a necessary foundation for successfully marketing new products. How does one become a visionary like Dirk? And how does one develop a successful vision? Here are some helpful hints based on Dirk's new venture guide of establishing a clear-cut vision.

Helpful Hints for Establishing a Clear-cut Vision

- It matters not how you arrive at vision. What matters is that you discover what your venture can focus on that will drive long-term sales and profitability. Dirk stumbled into Xircom's vision but he quickly identified a long-term revenue stream.

- You need to be open to new frontiers and ways of doing things to arrive at a vision that others have missed. There are no bad ideas when establishing a vision; there are ideas that may not yield the results you are after. It's a journey of discovery to find a truly prolific vision.

- Others must easily understand your vision; otherwise you have more work ahead. A vision should be clear-cut and easily understood.

- Making a sale and manufacturing a product for a customer can help you fine-tune or establish a vision. A vision that exceeds customers' expectations should be seriously considered. The popularity of Dirk's first products was a great validation that his vision was on point.

- Stick with a vision for the long haul. Be sure to give your vision an opportunity to succeed. Any great vision takes a long-term commitment. Dirk was in for the long haul with Xircom and this solidified his company's vision in the marketplace.

Distinctive Logo Marks

> **Mentor Insight**
>
> Brand the product with a distinctive logo mark

Once a clear-cut vision for the venture is in place, focus on developing the image that brings life to the company's vision. Begin with creating the company's identity manual. The identity manual typically gives guidelines for how the new venture's logo mark and name should be publicly represented and published. The venture's new products are key to properly representing the company's identity and raising overall brand awareness. Having a distinctive logo mark is essential to creating brand awareness. Dirk and the first team at his new venture crafted a distinctive and memorable logo by making the letters of the company's name the logo. There are some additional techniques one can use to create a distinctive logo.

Helpful Hints for Creating a Distinctive Logo Mark

- **Use a distinctive typeface.** There exist today thousands upon thousands of typefaces. You can find distinctive fonts to use for free on the Internet. You can purchase inexpensive fonts from photo and image houses. If you have an abundance of money, you can commission an original typeface that only your company has permission to use.

- **Add a distinctive element to the logo.** In Dirk's case they placed a triangle over the letter "i" instead of a dot. This small, subtle update gave Xircom's logo mark a unique flair that made the logo memorable for anyone who saw it.

- **Make sure the mark stands out.** Put the draft of your logo next to your competitors' logos. Does your mark stand out? Will the mark stand out on a flyer with other logos on it? How does your mark compare to the others?

- **Tweak and tune the mark.** Once you have the logo mark in place, spend time refining the mark until you are more than 100 percent satisfied. Are the letters or the top edge of the mark in proportion and alignment? Is the kerning (space between the letters) proportional? Are there any letters in the font that you selected that don't resemble the letters of the alphabet that they are supposed to reflect? Does the mark have the appearance of being designed by a professional? Is there anything that bothers you about the mark that you want fixed? Remember, once you finalize the mark you will have to live with it for a very long time. If you decide to update it later you run the risk of losing the brand awareness that you have already established.

- **Trademark or service mark your logo.** You can do this yourself at **http://www.uspto.gov/**.[27] A registered trademark or service mark at the end of your logo mark not only gives you the right to stop others in the same business category from havng the same name but also adds credibility and prestige to your logo.

184   Entrepreneurial Marketing

Market Research for the Entrepreneur

> **Mentor Insight**
> Initiate firsthand market research

Market research plays a key role in creating savvy strategies for marketing new products. The early success of Xircom along with its sustained success of the business was accomplished in part through initiating firsthand market research. Starting with the very first trade show that Dirk attended, firsthand market research data collection was a main component at Xircom. As the company grew, the market research techniques were expanded.

History of Market Research

Market research probably has always had a place in business, as individuals investigated the worth of their business ventures. It was the advent of paid advertising media, however, that created the environment where market research first flourished. Advertisers had to be able to document the nature of their audience if they were to get top dollar. Advertisers, from the very start, valued reaching the "right" people with their ads. Market research first started developing in the 1920s at some of the larger magazines. The Depression and World War II delayed development of market research as a widespread tool of business. Market research came of age with the advent of the computer. The computer not only allowed for efficient tabulation and storage of data, but also was critical to the development of statistical tools necessary for advanced analysis.

Tips for Gathering Market Research

Step 1: Define your question. To begin with, answer why you want the information before you attempt to determine what information to gather. Remember:

- The most useful information can be the easiest and cheapest to acquire. There is no rationale that more expensive or difficult to acquire information should be more useful.

- Some information is unknowable. Don't get lost in a quest for finding information that is unattainable.

- Quantitative research is not necessarily superior to qualitative research. Bad research yields bad numbers. While numbers don't lie, they can be dead wrong.

Step 2: Once the problem has been clearly defined, start with secondary data. Secondary data comes to the manager secondhand from another source. This means the library, the Internet, trade organizations, information companies, government documents, any existing outside source.

Step 3: Get on the phone. Call the authors of any relevant articles you have found. Discover what they did not put in the article, what they have found since the article, their opinions on the subject, and the names and numbers of three more people who know more about the subject than they do. Call, call, call—the price is right.

Step 4: Conduct in-depth interviews of key members of your industry if questions remain. In-depth interviews can be phone calls, but are important enough to warrant a lunch or a bit of travel. While end-users are crucial, start in-depth interviews by interviewing key decision makers in your channel of distribution. Professional buyers who specialize in your area are great sources of information in two respects: You can discover the saliency of various features and benefits in the eyes of the buyer and you can profile the "personality" of the buyer. Interview potential manufacturers' representatives as if they were being considered to help sell the product.

Step 5: Identify the nature of the decision making unit (DMU). What roles do people play? Here are some possibilities.

- Decision makers
- Purchasers
- End-users
- Gatekeepers
- Influencers
- Initiators
- Approvers

Explore how your new venture meets or does not meet the needs of each of these roles in the purchase process. Define your model of the DMU. Develop a strategy for dealing with each role. Discover whether the relevant DMU is consistent between potential customers or whether it varies from customer to customer.

Step 6: Conduct a focus group if the defined problem has still not been addressed. Don't despair if you don't have the resources to spend on a traditional focus group. We suggest trying an informal focus group where you invite participants, you prepare the discussion points, and you are in the room asking the questions firsthand.

Dirk's New Product Philosophy

> **Mentor Insight**
>
> Get the product to market

Even with your clear-cut vision, distinctive logo mark, and market research findings in hand, there are still other items you need to successfully market your new products. You must have high regard for the people who are designing your products. Dirk understands firsthand the importance of design. He is an engineer's engineer:

To Live or Die...

If you want to kill the spirit of an engineer or an engineering team—let them get all the way through it and kill the product just before it sees the light of day. That was constantly demonstrated at my former company—too many times I would build a product and it would go nowhere. You are better off to let it go and fail in the market.[28]

– Dirk Gates

186　　　Entrepreneurial Marketing

He thrives on seeing product ideas implemented and has the highest regard for engineers' designs. Dirk believes it is wrong to create something and not put it into the marketplace. He would rather see a new idea killed up front than once it has been finished. He feels that once a product has been created it is better to put it out into the market and let the market decide if it should live or die rather than not giving the product its marketplace moment.

"All-Star" Board

> **Mentor Insight**
>
> Build an "all-star cast" for the board

If you have accomplished getting your product to market as Dirk Gates did, there is a much higher probability that you will be able to entice an "all-star cast" in forming your board of directors. Market research can also be used to identify and build an "all-star cast" for one's board of directors. The people you survey while you conduct market research can share the names you need to create an experienced board of directors. The biggest challenge for a new venture in obtaining a high-performing board often isn't convincing people to join but identifying whom to invite. Dirk conducted his market research firsthand for potential board members through his first board member and mentor, Roger Evans. Your customers may also be able to provide a list of potential candidates. Don't be bashful about inviting high-performing business leaders to join the board. There are many people like Dirk, who have achieved success and are seeking an opportunity to help others.

Why is it significant to have an "all-star cast" for the board of directors when marketing a new product? This is because you need to obtain the insights of experience quickly when marketing new products. There often is such extreme pressure to get products to market that the absence of good advice and seasoned knowledge can prove detrimental. Dirk assembled an "all-star cast" for his board of directors that was instrumental in Xircom's success and ability to market successful products repeatedly in the marketplace.

Tear Down the Walls

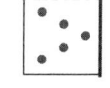

> **Mentor Insight**
>
> Place the product engineer in front of the customer

Dirk was careful when inviting people to join his "all-star cast" board of directors to make sure that no one joined who didn't have the same high regard for an engineer's work as he did. As mentioned in Part I, Dirk as an engineer understood not only the importance of getting a product to market but also the importance of putting the engineer or product designer in front of the customer to gather valuable insights. New ventures are often described as being technology driven or marketing driven. When a company is able to be both simultaneously, its products have a higher probability of being successful. Xircom serves as a good example of how a product can be successfully marketed when the firm balances technology processes with marketing processes. Having the design engineers out in front of the customers is one of the most natural and easiest ways for a new firm to be both marketing and technology driven.

Inspiring Operational Excellence

> **Mentor Insight**
> Strive for operational excellence

Engineers that aren't sheltered from customers' feedback are at times inspired to come up with new processes and standards for operational excellence. An entrepreneurial marketer can play a significant role in enhancing the chances of new product success by helping facilitate as well as striving for operational excellence.

Process mapping is a technique that an entrepreneurial marketer can utilize to achieve operational excellence in their new venture. The following is a step-by-step guide on a method for obtaining operational excellence.

New Venture Instructional Manual to Operational Excellence. Start by process mapping all of the organization's processes by creating a process log. Utilize a word processing software program which has auto shapes that feature a "flowchart." This will give you the software necessary for developing your process map. It does take a long time to process map the functions within an organization, even a newly formulated venture. It's time well spent.

Process Mapping Guide. There are many books and publications about process mapping and there are multiple ways to process map. We are going to focus here on showing you how to map the processes that make up new product development and marketing. We suggest the following:

- Assemble the people who are involved in the development and marketing of a new product at your organization.

- Brainstorm a list of the day-to-day steps that are taken to develop and market a new product.

- Review the list with your board, strategic alliance partners, mentors, vendors, and family members for items that may have been missed.

- Take the final list and divide it into two categories: repetitive processes and rare processes. Repetitive processes are steps that are taken repeatedly when developing and marketing a new product such as manufacturing the product. Rare processes occur infrequently.

- Analyze the rare processes list to see if any of the items mentioned can be combined with or woven into the repetitive processes. Rare processes can drain resources and are often not budgeted for. If you can combine a rare process with a repetitive process, you have taken a valuable step toward improving the operational excellence of your business. For example, the development of a distinctive logo mark is an important element for new product development. However, getting together for an entire day as Dirk's team did might have also been accomplished simultaneously with a board of directors meeting or mentor session to combine processes, save costs, and get additional thought leaders and idea generators engaged in the process. The Xircom name and logo was a success in the marketplace. However, it was also possible that one day of brainstorming may not have yielded such a positive outcome.

- Make a flowchart of the processes within your organization from the list that was prepared and fine-tuned. This is where you take what might be explained in several paragraphs of text and drill it down to several flowchart icons. For example, the development of the Xircom company name might be flowcharted as shown in Mentor Method 7.2.

Mentor Method 7.2

Process Mapping Diagram[29]

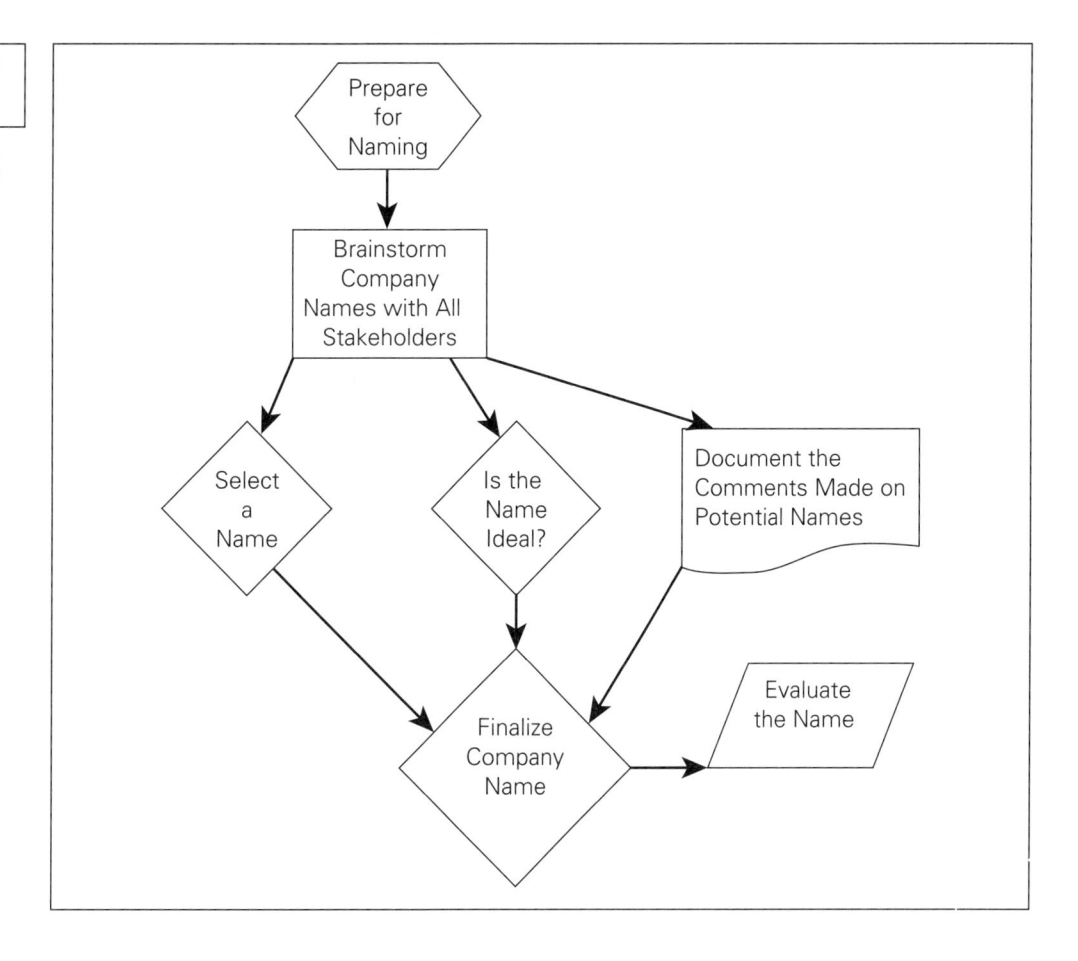

```
Prepare for Naming
        ↓
Brainstorm Company Names with All Stakeholders
    ↓       ↓           ↓
Select   Is the    Document the
a Name   Name      Comments Made on
         Ideal?    Potential Names
    ↓       ↓           ↓
         Finalize Company Name  →  Evaluate the Name
```

There is a growing trend for corporations to organize their management systems by processes instead of products. Large and mid-size corporations are making this shift to achieve cost savings.

Once you have completed your process log you must repeat the analysis phase. Gather your resident experts as well as some new mentors and outside board members to analyze the firm's processes. Look for current processes that could be streamlined. Because areas to streamline are difficult to see, keep re-examining what has been documented in the process log. Upon exhaustive examination of every possible streamlined scenario, the solution to achieving operational excellence will come into focus. Stay open and flexible to these new ideas.

Log the new process innovations. Embrace the new processes and apply them throughout the organization with the committed support of top management. This can be the most challenging step and requires a change management campaign. A change management campaign is the internal communication campaign that is targeted at a venture's employees regarding a shift in the way a business is managed. This means you have to take a hands-on role in communicating the changes throughout the organization, making sure that everyone understands the new game plan, and why it is necessary. Inevitably, some won't be willing to go along with the new program and you may need to help them find employment elsewhere. One negative person can delay the whole group's transformation.

Dirk demonstrated operational excellence while he was running Xircom. His Advanced Manufacturing processes, discussed in Part I, serve as just one example of how he successfully implemented operational excellence.

Devising New Product Strategies

> **Mentor Insight**
> Develop new product strategies

Striving for operational excellence is a new product strategy that played a big part in Xircom's success story. There are many new product strategies that need to be developed in a new venture or expanded enterprise.

Dirk had great marketing instincts for formulating new product strategies. Early in his product rollout, he made the decision to position the company in the marketplace so that it would seem to be larger than it actually was. This led him to a limited advertising program in terms of the number of ads. However, he made sure each of his ads was noticed by using full page and color in prime positions. An engineer without Dirk's instincts would have attempted to calculate the return on investment of each ad and attempted to maximize exposures per each dollar spent. Dirk made a move to build image and had faith that long-term sales for the company would eventually follow.

While not everyone is going to have the insights and abilities that Dirk possesses, anyone can devise a new product strategy. Learn from Dirk's techniques of formulating a new product strategy. For example, we can formulate a strategy to remove from the marketplace or "kill" a new product that isn't succeeding so that time and resources can be allocated toward focusing on marketing successful new products. For every new product that is successfully marketed there are numerous other new products that fail. Still, profits from successful launches tend to be far greater than losses from failed introductions.

Knowing when to remove a product from the marketplace is as difficult as knowing when to introduce it. The key factor is the identification of the cause of the poor performance. A sales decline alone may not be indicative of poor performance if the product's market share does not reflect a similar decline. Entire categories go into decline, as well as entire economies. If the cause is global economic forces, a firm may seek a survival strategy for the product. If the cause is the superior technology of a competitive product, the firm should consider an investment in the newer technology to attract customers who are quick to adopt innovative products. Marketers also need to examine if the product can be repositioned in its current market, or retargeted to new market segments. If a competitor has directly targeted your new product with disproportional marketing efforts, a direct counter offense to buy back lost market share may be possible. This was the case with the introduction of newly patented innovations at Xircom against 3Com whereby Xircom was able to battle back a good portion of the previously lost market share.

New products can be introduced that "solve" the marketplace deficiencies of an older product. Xircom accomplished this with its less expensive laptop networking devices, which launched the company into unprecedented success.

Lastly, firms can decide to "kill" the product when it is not profitable. In summary, potential tactics for an unsuccessful new product are:

- Wait out a poor economy.
- Harvest profits during a decline in the product category.
- Reposition the new product if consumers have shifted in the benefits they seek.
- Reformulate—improve the product to meet changing consumer shifts—and reposition.
- Introduce a replacement product while harvesting the former product.
- Kill the product.

Another new product strategy you can develop has to do with building a well-recognized brand. A new product launch event is a proven method even when resources are limited. Dirk launched his new product of laptop accessories at the industry trade show where his target audience was conveniently assembled. An event is a great way to build brand awareness. We recommend that you consider building, within your new product marketing campaign, a new product launch event plan.

New Product Launch Event Plan

Events organized around a new product launch are typically postponed or cancelled because the new product doesn't turn out as anticipated. Build this scenario into any planned event so that you can recoup some of the costs if the event needs to be cancelled.

Checklist for a New Product Launch Event

- Is the new product going to be fully functional in time for the event? What is your backup plan?
- Have you assembled a well-connected board of advisers to help with the production of the event?
- Have you determined your budget for the new product launch event? Is there anyone you can bring in to cosponsor the event to help defray the cost?
- Have you hired someone to be responsible for the myriad of details that must come together in order for a new product launch event to be called a success?
- Have you prepared a detailed spreadsheet, with deadlines, of all the items that need to take place for the event to come together and assigned each item to a responsible person?
- Have you devised the best forum for the new product launch event? Is the event scheduled during an industry trade show where everyone will already be assembled and you can easily fold your

event into the bigger show, leveraging all the resources available at that event?

- Have you outlined how you are going to communicate your new product message at the launch event? (There is nothing worse than producing an expensive new product launch event that everyone may enjoy but attendees leave not having any idea what brand was being promoted.)
- Have you invited your targeted press to cover the new product event?
- Do you have a contingency plan if few people respond to your invitation to the new product launch event?
- Do you have takeaway logo items, commonly referred to as premiums, for attendees so they can be reminded of the new product?
- Have you decided how you will measure and evaluate your brand-building strategy?

Fulfilling Customer Needs

One of the savviest strategies when marketing a new product is to have the product exceed the customer's needs. Dirk was a master in this department. Customers repeatedly bought his line of computer accessories for networked laptop users with profitable returns. He gave the customers what they wanted and they rewarded him by spending with Xircom, which ultimately led to Intel's purchase of the company.

The Mentor Method 7.3 diagram helps conceptualize what Dirk and Xircom accomplished by having their product line exceed their customers' needs.

Mentor Insight

Exceed customer's needs with the product

Mentor Method 7.3

New Product Hockey Stick[30]

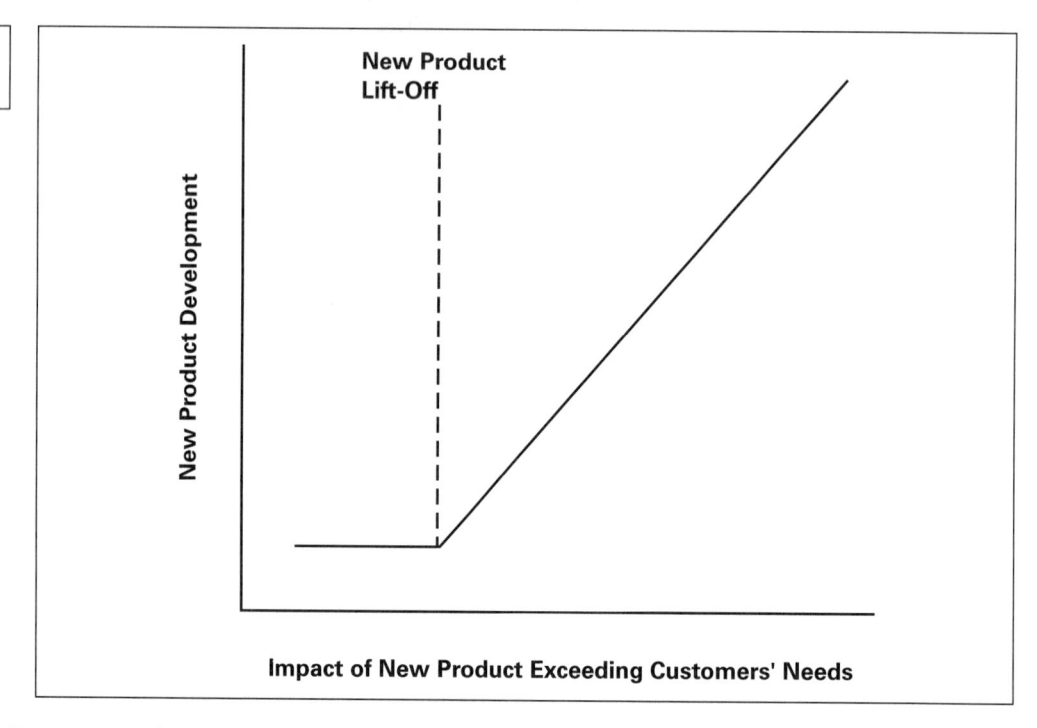

[Graph showing New Product Development on y-axis and Impact of New Product Exceeding Customers' Needs on x-axis, with a hockey stick curve and vertical dashed line labeled "New Product Lift-Off"]

192   Entrepreneurial Marketing

Mentor Method 7.3 depicts the impact on the volume of sales of a new product when a new product is developed with the goal of exceeding the targeted customer's needs. The graph shows that when a new product is launched initially there is a period of flat sales. This is when the firm is communicating with and educating the marketplace about the new product. This period can be short, as with Xircom's launch of its first product, or a new product can take months to resonate with the targeted customer. However, when you have devised a product that exceeds the customer's needs, the firm can anticipate a sharp vertical spike in sales for the new product. The point where customers realize that the product solves their problem is known as the new product lift-off. The new product lift-off creates the enviable New Product Hockey Stick spike.

Mentorography Conclusion

Whether Dirk is in the boardroom, at his desk, or elsewhere, he knows how to market his new products, a skill that has helped Dirk make a financial and personal success of Xircom. This has been the firsthand story of how Dirk Gates successfully marketed his products using a variety of techniques that imparted the following Mentor Insights:

Mentor Insights

- Recognize market opportunity
- Establish a clear-cut vision
- Brand the product with a distinctive logo mark
- Initiate firsthand market research
- Get the product to market
- Build an "all-star cast" for the board
- Place the product engineer in front of the customer
- Strive for operational excellence
- Develop new product strategies
- Exceed customer's needs with the product

Mentorography Questions

1. How does one formulate savvy strategies for new product introductions?

2. From a marketing standpoint, what strategies did Xircom utilize to position its new product introductions for explosive growth?

3. How does marketing a new product differ from marketing an existing product?

4. When is it appropriate to "kill" a new product that has been introduced in the marketplace?

5. What do you predict the future will be for new product introductions at Xircom—An Intel Company?

Endnotes

[1] Reprinted with permission of the Ventura County Star, "Intel Gets Xircom Approval," *Ventura County Star*, March 3, 2001.

[2] Dirk Gates interview conducted by Bruce Buskirk and Molly Lavik, May 7, 2001.

[3] Ibid.

[4] Ibid.

[5] Ibid.

[6] Ibid.

[7] Ibid.

[8] Ibid.

[9] Ibid.

[10] Ibid.

[11] Xircom Product News-Worldwide, Press Release Archive: 1997.

[12] Xircom Product News-Worldwide, Press Release Archive: 1998.

[13] Ibid.

[14] Ibid, 1999.

[15] Reprinted with permission of the Ventura County Star, "Xircom files suit," *Ventura County Star*, September 22, 2000.

[16] John Geralds, "Xircom files patent lawsuit against 3Com" *vnunet.com*, September 25, 2000.

[17] Ibid.

[18] © 2000 Los Angeles Times. Reprinted by permission. "Ventura County Earnings; Xircom Reports Record Revenues for Fiscal 2000," *Los Angeles Times*, October 31, 2000.

[19] E-mail correspondence from Dirk Gates, November 14, 2002.

[20] Xircom Product News-Worldwide, Press Release Archive: 2001.

[21] Dirk Gates interview conducted by Bruce Buskirk and Molly Lavik, May 7, 2001.

[22] Reprinted with permission of the Ventura County Star, "Intel Gets Xircom Approval," *Ventura County Star*, March 3, 2001.

[23] Dirk Gates interview conducted by Bruce Buskirk and Molly Lavik, May 7, 2001.

[24] Reprinted with permission of the Ventura County Star, "Intel Gets Xircom Approval," *Ventura County Star*, March 3, 2001.

[25] Xircom Product News-Worldwide, Press Release, "Xircom Launches Family of Bluetooth Wireless Access Products," March 22, 2001.

[26] Developed by Molly Lavik, October 6, 2002.

[27] United States Patent and Trademark Office home page, http://www.uspto.gov, accessed February 1, 2003.

[28] Dirk Gates interview conducted by Bruce Buskirk and Molly Lavik, May 7, 2001.

[29] Developed by Molly Lavik, October 6, 2002.

[30] Ibid.

PUBLIC RELATIONS MENTOR MODULE

The Art of Budget-Boosting Public Relations

NICOLAS G. HAYEK
Chairman of the Board,
The Swatch Group Ltd.

Mentorography Part I

> *The rarest resource on earth is [real] entrepreneurs in the top management. We have enough middle management. But not enough creative guys. Most people are lazy. It is idleness to say we can produce elsewhere and earn money here, in the long haul this doesn't pay off for any firm, for any country. And this generally applies for all of us. In Germany, above all in the big industry, mistakes are made. Many management members don't dare much anymore; don't make the necessary decisions, which could encounter opposition. There are too few people being self-confident, being courageous enough to say, 'I do the necessary (things) even if I lose my contract.'*[1]
>
> – Nicolas G. Hayek

Reprinted and translated with permission of © DIRK LEHRACH VERLAG e.K., Düsseldorf, 1999, Translation into English by Christian F. Munz (unpublished).

This chapter takes an in-depth look into the life and professional practices of Nicolas G. Hayek, Chairman of the Board, The Swatch Group Ltd., best known for saving the Swiss watchmaking industry. We'll explore Nicolas' extraordinary feats in the marketing arena: specifically his innovative approach to fostering public relations programs that enhance the bottom line. We will share with you Mentor Insights from Nicolas G. Hayek and the Swatch Group regarding entrepreneurial public relations practices. Molly Lavik coined the phrase budget-boosting public relations[2] to give meaning to the evolved practice of public relations in entrepreneurial marketing campaigns. Budget-boosting public relations is the ability to utilize public relations practices with a revenue-generating focus to positively impact a company's bottom line in the immediate future.[3] The Mentor Insights for budget-boosting public relations are as follows:

Mentor Insights

- Compete via innovation
- Have a credible, popular spokesperson
- Develop emotionally appealing products
- Continuously add beauty to every product
- Create a story to enhance your brand message
- Use messages, not images
- Create publicity stunts
- Drive sales through high quality, good distribution, and public relations
- Practice brainstorming
- Be available

Nicolas G. Hayek Milestones

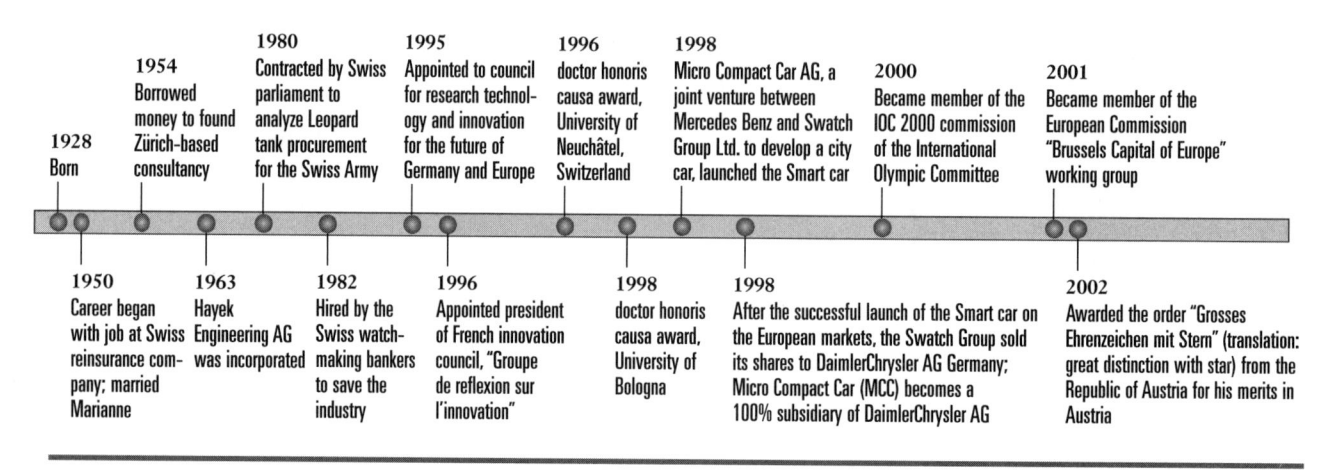

1928 Born

1950 Career began with job at Swiss reinsurance company; married Marianne

1954 Borrowed money to found Zürich-based consultancy

1963 Hayek Engineering AG was incorporated

1980 Contracted by Swiss parliament to analyze Leopard tank procurement for the Swiss Army

1982 Hired by the Swiss watchmaking bankers to save the industry

1995 Appointed to council for research technology and innovation for the future of Germany and Europe

1996 Appointed president of French innovation council, "Groupe de reflexion sur l'innovation"

1996 doctor honoris causa award, University of Neuchâtel, Switzerland

1998 doctor honoris causa award, University of Bologna

1998 Micro Compact Car AG, a joint venture between Mercedes Benz and Swatch Group Ltd. to develop a city car, launched the Smart car

1998 After the successful launch of the Smart car on the European markets, the Swatch Group sold its shares to DaimlerChrysler AG Germany; Micro Compact Car (MCC) becomes a 100% subsidiary of DaimlerChrysler AG

2000 Became member of the IOC 2000 commission of the International Olympic Committee

2001 Became member of the European Commission "Brussels Capital of Europe" working group

2002 Awarded the order "Grosses Ehrenzeichen mit Stern" (translation: great distinction with star) from the Republic of Austria for his merits in Austria

Entrepreneurial Marketing

In the Beginning

Nicolas is the son of an American dentist who was on the faculty at the American University of Beirut. His mother, a Christian Lebanese who brought up Nicolas, bore the vast majority of the responsibility for his upbringing. Nicolas feels he developed his masculinity on his own and points to this as the source of his assertiveness. In his school years, he recalls a strong yearning for acceptance that has not diminished during his lifetime. Nicolas credits his entrepreneurial spirit to his childhood growing up in a special neighborhood. During Nicolas' youth [in a Crusader descendant's environment[4]], his father was rarely around so Nicolas became the de facto "man of the family." As a young boy and "man of the family" Nicolas developed dignity and maturity. The obstinate, entrepreneurial philosophy he developed stems from basic childhood experiences in his special home environment.[5]

As a teen, Nicolas became increasingly brooding. He began challenging any explanation that was not well researched or free from prejudice and bias.[6]

When his family moved to Europe, Nicolas pursued and passed his baccalaureate (a-levels) in French, going on to study math, chemistry, and physics in France at the University of Lyon. Upon graduation, Nicolas moved to Switzerland with his family. Family considerations and financial hardship caused Nicolas to forgo studying nuclear physics in the United States.[7]

An Entrepreneur Is Born

In Switzerland, Nicolas met Marianne, a Swiss woman from an industrial family. Meeting Marianne would forever change Nicolas' career direction by providing him with his first industrial experience. When his father-in-law was incapacitated by poor health, Nicolas took over the family foundry, producing, for example, railroad brake shoes for the Swiss federal railways and engine blocks for the automotive industry. Nicolas was already a father when his father-in-law enlisted his support to run his small company.[8]

Despite the fact that Nicolas had no knowledge of the foundry's practices, he was able to transform the company into a success. Nicolas accomplished this in part because of his entrepreneurial spirit as well as his capacity to motivate people. He earned enough money with the company that in his early 20s he was able to purchase the rented company building for his father-in-law. Nicolas was successful because he was able to compete via innovation. Competing via innovation would become a trademark for Nicolas.

Nicolas knew early in his career the key attributes of an innovator, as indicated in the *Swatch Guide for Students*:

- "creativity, intuition and originality
- a knowledge of the market and a feel for new opportunities
- enthusiasm for anything new

> *My father-in-law owned the company but he didn't own the premises, the equipment, the machines, or the furnaces ... All this was not his. He was paying rent every year. He could have been thrown out anytime. I increased production and made so much profit that I purchased the building and equipment for him.[9]*
>
> — Nicolas G. Hayek

Mentor Insight

Compete via innovation

- interdisciplinary know-how
- intelligence
- mental flexibility, impartiality
- the ability to learn and absorb
- willingness to accept responsibility, initiative
- the ability to function under pressure
- the ability to communicate
- willingness to work as part of a team, tact and sensitiveness
- willingness to take risks
- the ability to accept failure and deal with success . . ."[10]
- motivate people and create a positive atmosphere and mentality[11]
- high degree of moral integrity to become an example for his employees[12]

His ability to earn a large sum of profits for the family enterprise was a seminal moment in Nicolas' life. This is because, from that moment on, he knew he would continue his life as an entrepreneur.[13]

"But when his father-in-law, a draftsman, finally returned to work, he was less than enthused about the way Hayek had revolutionized the business, profits notwithstanding. So Hayek left . . ."[14] However, his father-in-law was very unhappy when Hayek decided to leave and to create his own enterprise.[15]

Early Career

In 1950 following working for his father-in-law, Nicolas' career continued with a job in the math division of a Swiss reinsurance company. From 1951, at the age of 23, he occupied several management positions in the industry. However, Nicolas realized that his entrepreneurial visions were subject to severe limitations since his superiors didn't like his "weird" ideas. In Nicolas' early career, he didn't even consider adjusting his approach to industry and society norms.[16]

In 1954, Nicolas tested fate by borrowing $3,000 and founding an engineering consultancy in Zürich offering strategies for efficient production and marketing of new products. Nicolas used his personal possessions as collateral for his new venture.[17]

Perhaps because of his age or his image as a snotty know-it-all, Nicolas initially had few customers for his engineering consultancy. Clients just overlooked him. He learned the hard way what it takes to attract clientele. Nonetheless, Nicolas believed in his skills and was patient. With two young children and a wife depending on him, Nicolas knew he had to act. Luck must have been on Nicolas' side as he was soon engaged by a German manufacturer who wanted Nicolas to protect his company against bankruptcy.[18]

Nicolas left his office located in Switzerland, traveled to Germany (a huge market at the beginning of a boom phase) and succeeded within one week in putting a foundry in Ennepetal back on its feet. The German entrepreneur who had engaged Nicolas was so fond of the Swiss's qualities that he hired him immediately for a second contract, which paid six times the previous amount. This income enabled Nicolas to expand his Zürich offices.[19]

Nicolas began to develop a reputation as an unconventional problem solver who knew no taboos and whose mind was bursting with ideas. Big companies gradually began to pay attention to him.[20]

Nicolas was living in Zürich only on weekends while working for many companies in Germany during the week. He eventually grew homesick and returned home. Nicolas liked Zürich because of its physical beauty and for economic reasons. He was magically attracted by Zürich's dynamics; for him the city was a modern oasis in Switzerland. Nicolas had previously decided to headquarter his company in Zürich and to locate his home at the Hallwiler See (20 miles outside of Zürich).[21]

In . . . [1963,[22]] Nicolas officially incorporated his own industrial consulting company called Hayek Engineering AG. Hayek Engineering AG featured Nicolas' unique approach of selling for an upscale fee his unconventional entrepreneurial skills as an industrial engineering consultant. Nicolas' company, (a special enterprise for rationalization studies, recapitalization and optimization plans, and the realization of plans, project management, and engineering), soon yielded him both a national and international reputation which provided him with more than 300 customers from over 30 nations. Among these customers was the sultan of Oman, [as well as Mercedes-Benz, BMW, Krupp, Thyssen, VW, and the German government.[23]][24]

Nicolas built a successful consulting practice and engineering company in large part because of his clear vision of reality (developed during his childhood) and pitiless critique of his own flaws and those of other entrepreneurs.[25]

Around 1981, after having restructured the Swiss national television, the Swiss national railroads, and many other governmental industrial organizations, Nicolas was contracted by the Swiss parliament. The Swiss parliament contracted Nicolas to analyze the costs associated with the Swiss Army purchasing the Leopard tank. The tank was produced in Germany, and Switzerland intended to license the production of the Leopard tank. Germany would have sold the complete Leopard tank for 3 million Deutschemarks to Switzerland (it was offered to NATO at the same price). However, the same German tank licensed for assembling in Switzerland would have cost 14 million Deutschemarks (or 12 million Swiss francs).[26]

Certain members of the Military Commission of the Swiss parliament did not accept the conclusions and recommendations of the Swiss Ministry of Defense, which claimed that buying the much more expensive Swiss assembled tank would result in better quality, new industries, and new jobs. Nicolas' analysis and presentation of hard facts showed that members of the Swiss industry had taken advantage of their relationship with officials in the Ministry of Defense by multiplying their costs in a very unacceptable way. Nicolas' report unveiled hundreds of problems and facts that were in blatant opposition to the recommendations of the Ministry of Defense. The report also exposed the complete lack of project management regarding quality control and cost control, and other important factors. About 40 companies, some of them owned by the state, would have been involved in the assembly of the Leopard tank under a general contract.[27]

Nicolas handed his report over to parliament. The effect was that of an exploding bomb. Nicolas proved that the amount of money intended to invest in this project was at least 200 percent too high and that no real industry would be created after the tanks were delivered to the army five years later, because Switzerland does not and cannot export tanks.[28]

The findings of Nicolas' study made the headlines in the Swiss media. And naturally, the industry lobby was enormously unhappy and attacked Nicolas personally, in parliament and in the media. Nevertheless, at the end of that debate he was elected "Troubleshooter of the year" by the Swiss press. The parliament organized project management and improved their control over the procurement system. A few years later the project management of the Leopard tank produced in Switzerland gave him credit, in parliament, for his achievement. Hayek saved Switzerland between 4 billion and 5 billion Swiss francs.[29]

Nicolas entered the financially challenged 1980s with the trust of the Swiss people in the wake of the Leopard affair.[30]

During this period, the Swiss watchmaking industry, rich in tradition and dominating the world market, was facing ruin due to the missed opportunities of the quartz era in the 1970s.[31]

This situation took the Swiss completely by surprise. Nicolas was hired by the banks involved in financing the Swiss watchmaking industry because of his reputation as a creative and strong entrepreneur and his expertise in analysis and project management, as well as for his credibility with the Swiss people. Some of the banks hoped he would propose closing and selling the watchmaking industry's assets.[32]

Nicolas analyzed the problem in the same way he had approached his previous work challenges. He decided to examine merging the two most important, but ailing Swiss watch companies ASUAG and SSIH by doing what he knew best. He clearly analyzed the status quo versus future possibilities and, subsequently, merged them. In doing so, the Swatch Group (at that time called SMH (Société Suisse de Microélectronique et d'Horlogerie) came into being. Within one year, the Swiss watchmaking industry got a new, modern face. Hayek recalls the situation at the beginning of the 1980s:

> I got a phone call from somebody asking me, 'Can we still survive economically in the Swiss watchmaking industry after three restructurings have been conducted within five years?' So the question was, can we still survive after the Japanese are significantly cheaper, better and faster in the photo industry as well as in the other manufacturing processes in . . . [Europe.] Weren't we finished? After all the years where we in Switzerland had been leading in the watchmaking industry it appeared to be like that. Therefore I was asked whether I could save the day or not. I took care regarding the situation and rapidly figured out that we could not only survive but we could recapture the number one spot, and that the problems are not only labor cost problems of the workforce but above all management problems. This is where I began.[33]
>
> – Nicolas G. Hayek

202   Entrepreneurial Marketing

The Swiss Economic Miracle

The months that followed were action-packed for Nicolas, and marked a turnaround, not only in the Swiss watchmaking industry but also in Nicolas' life. He worked obsessively. The restructuring of the Swiss watchmaking industry led to the creation of . . . [the Swatch Group.] Nicolas wrote one of the most exciting chapters in the Swiss and European history by being the savior of the watchmaking industry. Since that time, Nicolas has been known as the father of the Swiss economic miracle.[34]

> **Mentor Insight**
>
> Have a credible, popular spokesperson

The Swiss people embraced Nicolas as a miracle maker and as the most popular person in Switzerland after the president. To this day, grandmothers on the street hug Nicolas when they see him.[35] Nicolas demonstrated the market impact of having a popular, credible spokesperson by his serving as the spokesperson and savior for the Swiss watchmaking industry.

Simultaneously but independent of the industrial crisis, a new product was introduced. This product enabled the newly reformed Swiss watchmaking industry to make a quantum leap.[36]

When the Asuag Company, one of the merged firms, managed with a team of 60 to 70 technicians, designers and engineers to create a new way to produce a watch, Nicolas recognized immediately the production and marketing viability for this product. The new product line was later called Swatch Watch and it had a profound impact on the market; Swatch is a revolutionary yet inexpensive watch.[37]

Nicolas, drawing once again on his reputation as a popular, credible entrepreneur and spokesperson persuaded people that you could have a quality Swiss-made watch that was priced inexpensively. Under Nicolas' management, The Swatch Group united quality and low prices.[38]

The Backdrop on the Birth of Swatch

Swatch was something completely new in terms of technical standards, design, and market strategy and therefore it had the capacity to outrival its competitors. More than 60 specialists worked in the early 1980s to create this product.[39]

Mismanagement and misjudgment were reasons behind the bad condition of the Swiss watchmaking industry.[40]

. . . Another reason behind the bad condition of the Swiss watchmaking industry was the introduction of cheap Japanese watches, which had flooded the European market in the late 1970s. Swiss manufacturers, who focused on precision and value, were incapable of developing a counterstrategy. Their deeply rooted self-image of expensive, high-quality Swiss-made watches restrained them from evolving to meet this challenge. In this difficult time, the Swiss still had a handful of advantages. Not the least of which was their highly specialized and experienced personnel.[41]

In 1983, Nicolas and his team launched Swatch. In two years time it was becoming apparent that the strategy behind launching the Swatch was working. The battle was won in 1988 when the Swatch Group celebrated the sale of 50 million Swatches in five years.

> **Mentor Insights**
>
> Develop emotionally appealing products
>
> Continuously add beauty to every product

Creating an Emotional Attachment to Your Watch

A core part of Nicolas' turnaround strategy for the Swiss watchmaking industry was to develop emotionally appealing products. This Mentor Insight is a key strategy in fostering budget-boosting public relations. Nicolas accomplished this feat by making the Swatch brand synonymous with fun. He retained top artists and creative innovators to craft fashionably exciting watches in which the designers continuously added beauty to a wide selection of Swatch watches. The emotional attachment that consumers were developing for their Swatches led them to change their orientation toward wearing a watch. Before Swatch, people usually owned one watch, but with the introduction of the Swatch, it became fashionable to have a different Swatch to complement every outfit and occasion. People bought multiple Swatches to add style to their fashion attire.

Nicolas' contribution was paramount in getting the Swiss not to give up when their watchmaking industry faced ruin. He was convinced that the Swatch idea was the solution and he wasn't afraid of risking his own reputation. Plastic was introduced into the watchmaking industry when electronic watches were supplemented by mechanical ones.[42] Despite a slow introduction of plastic in the Swiss watchmaking industry, due partly to Swiss manufacturers' rigid sense of honor, with their "backs against the wall," Swiss manufacturers were able to use plastic to make a high-quality watch inexpensively. Again, innovation was implemented to compete and ultimately win against the Japanese and Asian watchmaking industry.

> **Mentor Insight**
>
> Compete via innovation

The Product Pyramid

Nicolas launched an ambitious and drastic overhaul of all Swatch Group watch brands, fueled by the major success of the Swatch brand.[43] Nicolas was able to capture all market segments of the watch-buying consumer by having a product pyramid of brands.

"Hayek modeled the total . . . [the Swatch Group] watchmaking business design on what he calls a 'birthday cake' or product pyramid structure . . . analogous to the product pyramid created by Alfred Sloan at General Motors in the 1920s. In order to appeal to a broad income range, GM constructed a hierarchy of brands, from Chevrolet at the bottom to Cadillac at the top. Hayek built a product pyramid or 'birthday cake' with three layers: the lower market segment with watches up to approximately Sfr. 100; the middle market segment with watches up to approximately Sfr. 1000; and the upper and luxury market segment with watches priced up to one million Swiss francs or more . . ."[44]

For the Swatch Group, the product pyramid consists of the entire scope of Swatch Group brands: Breguet, Blancpain, Jaquet Droz, Glashütte-Original, Léon Hatot, Omega, Longines, and Rado represent the luxury and prestige segment and the upper end of Swatch Group brands; Union, Tissot, Certina, Mido, Pierre Balmain, Hamilton, and Calvin Klein represent the midrange-priced watch brands; Swatch, Flik Flak, and Endura represent the basic segment.[45]

> **Mentor Insight**
>
> Create a story to enhance your brand message

Each brand within the product pyramid had a distinctive marketing message. For example, Nicolas and his team created a story behind each watch brand. Storytelling doesn't happen just in books and movies. Creating a story behind your brand is a tactic utilized by many successful entrepreneurial marketers. In our expanded definition of budget-boosting public relations, creating a memorable story behind your brand message is a very valuable tool toward achieving potentially profitable results. Consumers can relate to products better when they know the history behind the product's creation. Consumers purchase Nike sneakers because they envision that they can "just do it" like the elite athletes in the Nike commercials. In today's competitive markets, you must not only engage a consumer's emotional interest in your product, but also captivate the customer with the story behind the product's brand. In Part II of this module, we will elaborate on some of the Swatch Group's brand stories.

> **Mentor Insight**
>
> Use messages, not images

Nicolas' marketing strategy to entice watch-buying consumers to buy the Swatch Group's pyramid of watches included his heartfelt philosophy to use messages and not images. He believes that consumers, because of their inherent biases, can misinterpret a static image. He feels, however, that a message is clear, dynamic, and more likely to be perceived in the same way by different consumers. Nicolas believes that, if you want to create a product people will have an emotional attachment to, you must have a message people can believe in. This is why Nicolas focused on creating messages to market his brands. Perhaps the most distinctive message that Nicolas and his team crafted was "high quality, low cost, challenging society, and joy of life." This message was communicated in Germany by mounting a 162-meter functioning Swatch on the tallest skyscraper in Frankfurt which was occupied by a conservative German bank. On the watch was the message:

> **Mentor Insight**
>
> Create publicity stunts

Swatch

Swiss

60 DM

(See Part II on p. 217 for a photograph of a 162-meter giant Swatch that was mounted on the Commerzbank building in Frankfurt.)

Within a month everyone in Germany knew the meaning behind the Swatch watch: high quality, low cost, provocativeness and joy of life.[46]

Nicolas didn't have a large marketing budget but he was able to create a significant amount of market awareness through this publicity stunt.

> **Mentor Insight**
>
> Compete via innovation

> *It's time we let young people who think unconventionally—the kind of individuals who are ready to tackle obstacles and surmount them—take over at the helm. We already had them. We gave them a free rein in the watchmaking industry. Anybody who came along with new ideas was immediately introduced to the boss.*[47]
>
> – Nicolas G. Hayek

Creating publicity stunts is an entrepreneurial survival tactic for budget-boosting public relations. A well-crafted publicity stunt can create a large amount of market awareness on a limited marketing budget. Publicity stunts became a cornerstone of Nicolas' marketing strategy.

Nicolas knew how to empower his employees to foster the kind of innovation that was needed to save the Swiss watchmaking industry. He also knew how to hire a wide variety of employees from multiple job disciplines to create the large network of in-house knowledge that would be needed to be innovative.

> *Our engineers and specialists in all kinds of fields—micromechanics, tool making, . . . technology, injection molding, assembly—in short, the entire production technology department, often had to go to the limits of what was considered possible to solve the sort of problems we were faced with. Many of the ideas and breakthroughs that eventually made Swatch a reality came from this team of about 200 people.*[48]
>
> – A man who was one of the pioneering people behind the creation of the Swatch product.

Public Relations Activities to Impact the Bottom Line

Nicolas never lost sight of the bottom line as his career soared. He is an entrepreneur focused on creating new jobs, new wealth, and profitable results. This philosophy carried over to his public relations practices. Every marketing strategy that Nicolas and his team formulated was designed to sell watches at a profit. Nicolas was able to sell watches for less through significant innovation in the watch manufacturing process. Nicolas realized early on that every person wearing one of his watch brands was a walking billboard. He estimated that one person wearing a Swatch could potentially be seen by many people. Nicolas was able to drive sales by having a high quality product that was well distributed and memorably publicized by creating the emotionally appealing, fun, and provocative Swatch product line. His team effectively communicated each of the Swatch Group watch brands through easy-to-understand, attention-getting messages. Nicolas and his watch brands are an outstanding example of how you can use public relations to drive sales. Nicolas' unswerving attention directed at driving sales through public relations activities is what sets apart traditional public relations from budget-boosting public relations.

> **Mentor Insight**
>
> Drive sales through high quality, good distribution, and public relations

Nicolas Today

Nicolas is a creative entrepreneur and troubleshooter who "switches and swatches" across time, places, and "volumes." In doing so, he has become a popular figure for the media, showcasing modern morale, entrepreneurial viewpoints that are profound in nature and sound but simple common sense.[49]

His daughter Nayla, [member of the Swatch Group Board of Directors;[50]] his son George Nicolas, [the latter his father's successor as CEO and President of the Swatch Group Management Board; and his grandson Marc Alexander, Managing Director of Blancpain[51],] are all employed in the company. Nicolas has lived with his wife Marianne in a modern bungalow made of glass and concrete at the Hallwiler See (Lake Hallwil) outside Zürich for 40 years.[52]

It is during his daily drive from Lake Hallwil to Biel/Bienne for the past 20 years that Nicolas brainstorms some of his most creative ideas by writing down his ideas on scraps of paper and affixing these scraps to his car dashboard with magnets.[53]

Additionally, Nicolas still has a set of projects for further consideration in his drawer. Among these is his favorite plan, thus far not realized, for an ecologically innovative car, the Swatchmobil.[54]

The Swatchmobil is supposed to become one of the first hybrid cars manufactured in large quantities.[55]

In 1991, Nicolas convinced Volkswagen to create SMH Volkswagen Automobil AG in Biel, Switzerland. They started with a joint group of engineers from Swatch Group and Volkswagen to develop a hybrid car and a normal low consumption small car with the same message and philosophy as Swatch. The idea became known around the world before the first prototype was made. A change in the top management of VW brought a new CEO with whom Nicolas did not entirely agree. So the Swatch Group purchased VW's 50 percent of shares and convinced DaimlerChrysler, which in 1994 was called Mercedes-Benz, to build the car with the Swatch Group despite the slow economic period of that time. This created the Micro Compact Car (MCC) company, 51 percent owned by Mercedes, 49 percent owned by the Swatch Group. For the first two years, Nicolas was chairman of this new company, switching chairmanship between the two partners every two years. At that time all governments in Europe were courting Nicolas, inviting him to put his new plant in their region. Jacques Chirac, then mayor of Paris and president of the largest political party in France, and Helmut Kohl, then chancellor of Germany, visited Nicolas and his car project in Switzerland.[56]

Nicolas and his engineers helped create every part of the Smart car (small car sold primarily in Europe), its technology, its colors, its marketing, and its distribution system. They also developed and directed the construction of a new car manufacturing plant in France.[57]

After the successful market launch of the Smart car in 1998, Nicolas sold his shares to Mercedes—for a profit for the development of the hybrid car engine developed by the Swatch Group. Since then, MCC has been owned 100 percent by Mercedes.[58]

After expected heavy losses during the first three years of its introduction, the Smart car is now one of the most popular small cars in Europe. In Italy and France it is a legend; in Switzerland and France it is still considered Hayek's car. Many books and TV programs have shown how Nicolas managed the operation. He still has the hybrid car system that Mercedes did not produce.[59]

> **Mentor Insight**
>
> Practice brainstorming

> **Mentor Insight**
>
> Be available

Nicolas is constantly in transit. He constructs nonpolluting cars, he presents his environmental strategies in front of the UN in New York City, he plays tennis [with Martina Hingis[60]] or at Cap d'Antibes [where he owns a house[61]], he conquers new overseas markets, and he advises large firms or even whole state governments around the globe on corporate matters. Few are as sought after as an adviser and idea provider as Nicolas. He doesn't care about his seniority and the fact that his own clock ticks. Nicolas makes himself available. He is still full of dynamic ideas and thirst for action.[62]

Mentorography Part II

As Nicolas G. Hayek switches and swatches through time, he has mastered the art of crafting budget-boosting public relations. As a reminder, the definition of budget-boosting public relations is the ability to utilize public relations practices with a revenue-generating focus to positively impact a company's bottom line in the immediate future.[63] No longer is public relations merely focused on raising the visibility of a company or a brand. In this evolved definition of public relations, the company uses innovative public relations techniques combined with a focus on driving sales to make the profitability of a company soar. The Mentor Insights behind the budget-boosting public relations incorporated by Nicolas G. Hayek and the watchmaking industry are the cornerstones of this evolved discipline.

> **Mentor Insights**
>
> - Continuously add beauty to every product
> - Compete via innovation
> - Develop emotionally appealing products
> - Have a credible, popular spokesperson
> - Be available
> - Create a story to enhance your brand message
> - Practice brainstorming
> - Create publicity stunts
> - Drive sales through high quality, good distribution, and public relations
> - Use messages, not images

Recent History of Swiss Watchmaking

In the 1970s, the Swiss watch industry focused on manufacturing watches that were high-quality precision timepieces. The Swiss watch industry hadn't caught on yet that people were more interested in wearing watches as a fashion statement than as a timepiece. Expensive price points for the high-quality Swiss watches helped create a market for a different type of watch. The introduction of the digital watch in the mid 1970s took the Swiss watch manufacturers by surprise for multiple reasons. One reason was that digital watches were introduced to the market starting at about $200 and quickly flooded the market, forcing prices down to $5 for plastic versions. A $5 watch made consumers re-evaluate the meaning of their watches.

Another reason that digital watches took the Swiss watch manufacturers by surprise is because inexpensive wristwatches became a matter of fashion rather than function. Previously watches were primarily worn to keep track of time. The $5 watch changed people's perceptions toward their watches. No longer could people say they "needed" an expensive timepiece in order to get accurate time.

The expensive nature of wristwatches prior to 1975 had established a consumption pattern of people owning one "good" watch, which they wore on a daily basis. Having different watches for different occasions was not prevalent in larger markets. Swatch, a contraction of "second watch," or "Swiss watch," represented a clear shift in marketing strategy, recognizing that growth could occur by selling more watches rather than selling watches for more. By introducing fashion into watches, the Swatch Group and Nicolas were able to "add beauty to everything," which became the vehicle for systematic beautification of the Swatch Group watch brands. However, the Swatch concept demanded Swiss quality at competitive prices. Nicolas recognized that in order to establish the Swiss-made brand in the prestige market, the Swiss needed to be competitive in the lower price market. Nicolas needed to employ innovation to find a way to bring beauty with Swiss quality to the market at a reasonable price.

> **Mentor Insight**
> Continuously add beauty to every product

> **Mentor Insight**
> Compete via innovation

In the late seventies, the Japanese and Swiss watch industries competed against each other to create the thinnest watch in the world. The Japanese made a watch only 4 mm thick, the Swiss four months later made one 3.5 mm, the Japanese six months later achieved 3 mm, and the Swiss four months later, 2 mm. And then the Swiss lost patience and decided to make a watch that was 0.98 mm thick. It was a very difficult project. André Beiner, at that time vice president of Asuag Fontainemelon/Neuchâtel, and a group of engineers decided to achieve this deed by cutting small holes for each component in the lower part of the watch. By doing so Beiner and his engineers found out that instead of putting the assembled movement with 151 components into the case, they could insert each component alone in the watch. The result was that they needed only 51 pieces, instead of up to 151. This was a complete revolution in watchmaking.[64] See Mentor Method 8.1 "Swatch Schematic" on the next page.

This streamlined manufacturing process that consisted of innovative yet fewer pieces resulted in a higher quality as well as a less expensive way to make a watch. Asuag management decided to use the system not only for thin watches, but for other watches too. The Asuag people wanted to sell the system to another watchmaker because they were worried about the Swiss making such an inexpensive watch. Nicolas immediately recognized a market opportunity. Nicolas started his counterattack on the Japanese not in the upper end of the market but in the lower end of the market segment with the watch named Swatch.[65]

The development of the lower market segment became a top priority. Only by producing in large volume could Nicolas keep the 90 factories (today the Swatch Group owns 160 factories) and the know-how of the Swiss watchmaking company alive for the future.[66]

Mentor Method 8.1

Swatch Schematic[67]

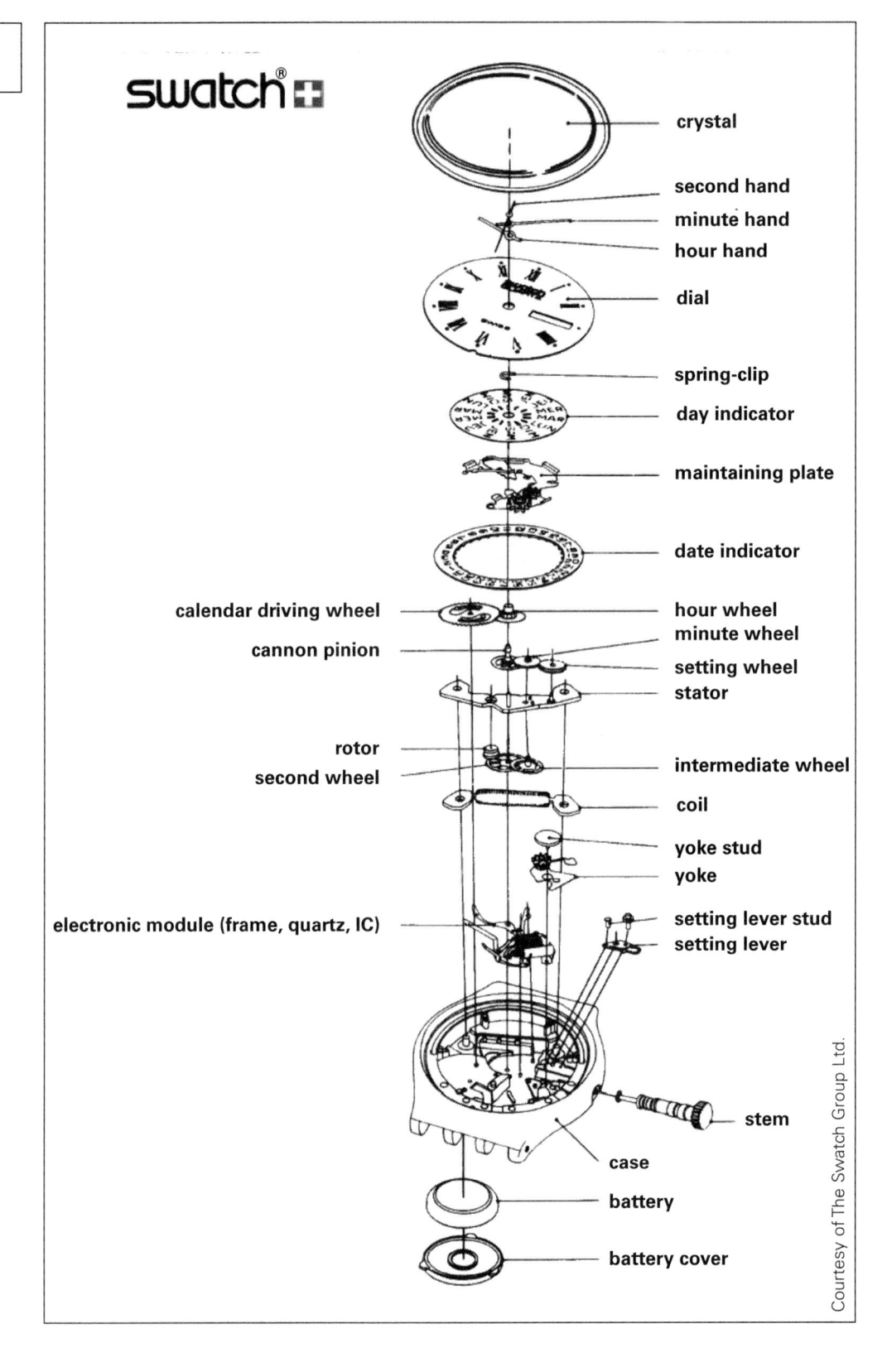

swatch

- crystal
- second hand
- minute hand
- hour hand
- dial
- spring-clip
- day indicator
- maintaining plate
- date indicator
- calendar driving wheel
- hour wheel
- minute wheel
- cannon pinion
- setting wheel
- stator
- rotor
- second wheel
- intermediate wheel
- coil
- yoke stud
- yoke
- electronic module (frame, quartz, IC)
- setting lever stud
- setting lever
- stem
- case
- battery
- battery cover

Courtesy of The Swatch Group Ltd.

210   Entrepreneurial Marketing

> **Mentor Insight**
>
> Continuously add beauty to every product

Nicolas combined high quality Swiss watchmaking with the inexpensive streamlined watch manufacturing processes and then added one additional element to create the Swatch brand. That additional element was the concept of adding beauty to the Swatch watch design. On page 212 is a chronological timeline of highlights of ways Nicolas and his team continuously added beauty to the Swatch product line. This timeline features the Swatch brand as an example. However, it's important to note that beauty is also a hallmark of the other 17 Swatch Group brands that are equally cared for by Nicolas.

Nicolas saw the beautification of the Swatch product line as his entrepreneurial marketing mission.

Hayek's Philosophy on the Artistry of Entrepreneurship

I am not a businessman; I am an entrepreneur making innovation. Meaning that I consider Picasso as an entrepreneur who has created things and who has been able to market them, to communicate them, and to sell them.[68]

– Nicolas G. Hayek

Low-Cost Quality Watch

The very term "lower price" watch is quite misleading, since it predisposes one to believe that the benefit being delivered is a watch at low cost, when in fact consumers were seeking fashion, or fun. "Low price" was important because it allowed the consumer to rationalize the capricious decision to buy a watch for fun.

Do not let the term "quality" be defined by your engineering staff. Your customers must define "quality"!

Producing a quality level higher than that sought by your customers is an engineering narcissism that will misdirect your firm's efforts. Given the long Swiss tradition of time being a serious, functional matter, it was difficult for the Swiss watch industry to comprehend and react to this trivialization of their proud national industry. Meanwhile, Japanese watchmakers targeted established traditional products where mass-produced "quality" could gain mass markets.

A classic case in marketing is that of Harley-Davidson. At one time, its future looked bleak. Quality was low in the consumer's eyes, as well as by any other standard. Honda and a few other Japanese motorcycle manufacturers had introduced trail bikes successfully and were systematically moving into the larger bike market. Harley-Davidson survived by strategic market positioning. Basic marketing techniques were used to position Harley-Davidson as American and other motorcycles as Un-American. The Japanese couldn't replicate this market position. This marketing effort bought Harley-Davidson the time it needed to get its quality in line with consumer expectations and to leverage that improvement into even

Swatch Adding Beauty Timeline

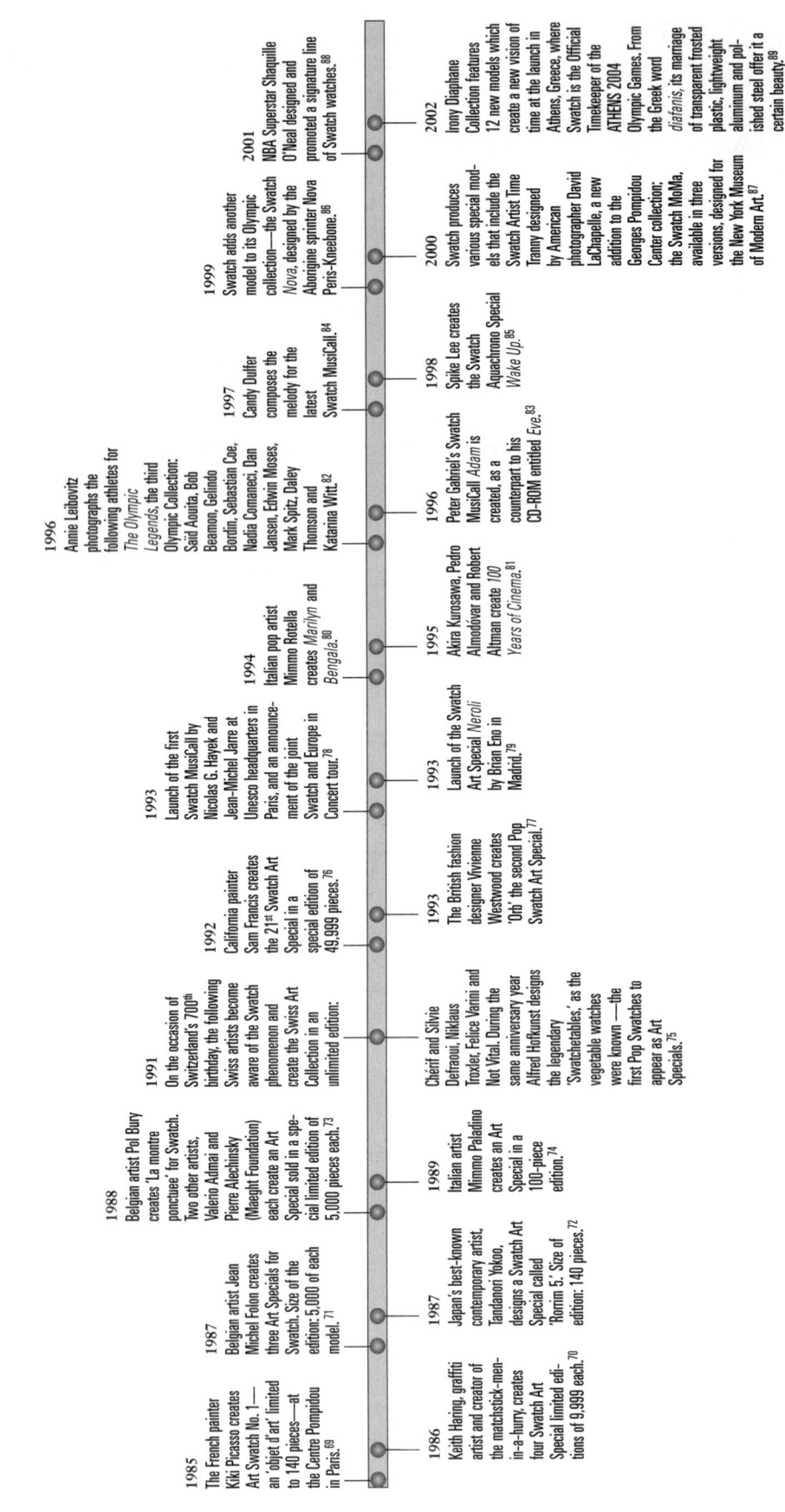

1985
The French painter Kiki Picasso creates Art Swatch No. 1—an 'objet d'art' limited to 140 pieces—at the Centre Pompidou in Paris.[69]

1986
Keith Haring, graffiti artist and creator of the matchstick-men-in-a-hurry, creates four Swatch Art Special limited editions of 9,999 each.[70]

1987
Belgian artist Jean Michel Folon creates three Art Specials for Swatch. Size of the edition: 5,000 of each model.[71]

1987
Japan's best-known contemporary artist, Tandanori Yokoo, designs a Swatch Art Special called 'Rorrim 5.' Size of edition: 140 pieces.[72]

1988
Belgian artist Pol Bury creates 'La montre ponctuée' for Swatch. Two other artists, Valerio Admai and Pierre Alechinsky (Maeght Foundation) each create an Art Special sold in a special limited edition of 5,000 pieces each.[73]

1989
Italian artist Mimmo Paladino creates an Art Special in a 100-piece edition.[74]

1991
On the occasion of Switzerland's 700th birthday, the following Swiss artists become aware of the Swatch phenomenon and create the Swiss Art Collection in an unlimited edition: Cherif and Silvie Defraoui, Niklaus Troxler, Felice Varini and Not Vital. During the same anniversary year Alfred Hofkunst designs the legendary 'Swatchetables,' as the vegetable watches were known —the first Pop Swatches to appear as Art Specials.[75]

1992
California painter Sam Francis creates the 21st Swatch Art Special in a special edition of 49,999 pieces.[76]

1993
The British fashion designer Vivienne Westwood creates 'Orb' the second Pop Swatch Art Special.[77]

1993
Launch of the first Swatch MusiCall by Nicolas G. Hayek and Jean-Michel Jarre at Unesco headquarters in Paris, and an announcement of the joint Swatch and Europe in Concert tour.[78]

1993
Launch of the Swatch Art Special *Neroli* by Brian Eno in Madrid.[79]

1994
Italian pop artist Mimmo Rotella creates *Marilyn and Bengala*.[80]

1995
Akira Kurosawa, Pedro Almodóvar and Robert Altman create *100 Years of Cinema*.[81]

1996
Annie Leibovitz photographs the following athletes for *The Olympic Legends*, the third Olympic Collection: Said Aouita, Bob Beamon, Gelindo Bordin, Sebastian Coe, Nadia Comaneci, Dan Jansen, Erwin Moses, Mark Spitz, Daley Thomson and Katarina Witt.[82]

1996
Peter Gabriel's Swatch MusiCall *Adam* is created, as a counterpart to his CD-ROM entitled *Eve*.[83]

1997
Candy Dulfer composes the melody for the latest Swatch MusiCall.[84]

1998
Spike Lee creates the Swatch Aquachrono Special *Wake Up*.[85]

1999
Swatch adds another model to its Olympic collection—the Swatch *Nova*, designed by the Aborigine sprinter Nova Peris-Kneebone.[86]

2000
Swatch produces various special models that include the Swatch Artist Time Tranny designed by American photographer David LaChapelle, a new addition to the Georges Pompidou Center collection; the Swatch MoMa, available in three versions, designed for the New York Museum of Modern Art.[87]

2001
NBA Superstar Shaquille O'Neal designed and promoted a signature line of Swatch watches.[88]

2002
Irony Diaphane Collection features 12 new models which create a new vision of time at the launch in Athens, Greece, where Swatch is the Official Timekeeper of the ATHENS 2004 Olympic Games. From the Greek word *diafanis*, its marriage of transparent frosted plastic, lightweight aluminum and polished steel offer it a certain beauty.[89]

Entrepreneurial Marketing

greater brand equity. A motorcycle is not about transportation any more than a horse is. The consumer benefit of riding either a motorcycle or a horse is primarily psychological: how you *feel* about the experience.

When creating the Swatch product line, Nicolas incorporated this same emotional appeal.

> **Mentor Insight**
> Develop emotionally appealing products

Emotionalization

Interviewer: "How do you 'emotionalize' a watch? Do you mean to say that Swatch turned something that was mundane and functional into a fashion statement?

[Nicolas G. Hayek:] That's how most people describe what we did. But it's not quite right. Fashion is important. The people at our Swatch Lab in Milan and our many other designers do beautiful work. The artists who make our Swatch special collections design wonderful watches . . . But take a trip to Hong Kong and look at the styles, the designs, the colors. They make pretty watches over there too.

We are not just offering people a style. We are offering them a message. This is an absolutely critical point. Fashion is about image. Emotional products are about message—a strong, exciting, distinct, authentic message that tells people who you are and why you do what you do. There are many elements that make up the Swatch message. High quality. Low cost. Provocative. Joy of life. But the most important element of the Swatch message is the hardest for others to copy. Ultimately, we are not just offering watches. We are offering our personal culture."[90]

Additional Comment from Nicolas Regarding Emotionalization

If you want to be a successful CEO of an emotional consumer product you have to keep the fantasy of your sixth year. My wife says that I am a 74-year-old man with the dreams of a 6-year-old boy.[91]

– Nicolas G. Hayek

> **Mentor Insight**
> Have a credible, popular spokesperson

Celebrity Spokespeople

Traditionally, fashion marketing has relied upon strong promotional efforts. Nicolas understands this concept and relies on the heavy use of spokesmodels for many fashion lines. Cindy Crawford and Anna Kournikova are exemplary of how spokespeople can represent the emotional benefit delivered in an Omega watch. Their images, both literally

The Art of Budget-Boosting Public Relations **Module 8** 213 and figuratively, connect emotionally with the benefits promised by the purchase of an Omega.

Examples of having a credible, popular spokesperson in your marketing campaign can be seen in the following advertisement.

Mentor Method 8.2

Advertisement for Omega Featuring Cindy Crawford[92]

CINDY CRAWFORD'S CHOICE

CONSTELLATION «Quadra»

The Omega Constellation is a rare blend of style and elegance, a superb example of the watchmaker's art. This is no wonder, since Cindy Crawford assisted Omega in its design, creating the only watch she is proud to wear.

OMEGA

www.omegawatches.com

Courtesy of The Swatch Group Ltd.

> **Mentor Method 8.3**
>
> **Omega Ambassadress Anna Kournikova**[93]

> **Mentor Insight**
>
> Be available

Nicolas also sees the need for a firm to have a personality and to stand for a purpose beyond generating wealth for the owner. Nicolas clearly works for a cause other than profit. He loves the Swiss culture and people, and would appear to be as committed an example of a Swiss patriot as can be found in our present world.

24/7/365

Nicolas' zeal for his cause makes him an effective leader. Nicolas makes himself available for a wide range of inquiries. By making himself available, Nicolas gains leverage for his communications' strategies.

Successful entrepreneurial-style leaders like Nicolas G. Hayek make themselves available to anyone, even people who seem outside the scope of current initiatives. This is because these leaders inherently understand the possibilities of an unexpected chance to communicate their message via unproven communication channels. These types of leaders have a willingness to be open and flexible to being available to others. Nicolas is a leader who has an emotionally intelligent philosophy regarding making himself available.

> *I never forget that I'm a very small particle, very, very small, in a very small planet, in a small sun system, in a huge universe, and I'm really relatively not so very important. People love you because you stay very human, very modest, and you're in touch with them. You are always available when somebody calls. You don't put bodyguards around you; you don't have a driver all the time . . .*[94]
>
> – Nicolas G. Hayek

> **Mentor Insight**
> Create a story to enhance your brand message

Storytelling

Further utilizing his zeal and storytelling nature, Nicolas builds a story behind every brand in his line. For example, he enjoys telling the story behind the Jaquet Droz watch line:

"Who was Pierre Jaquet Droz (1721–1790)? One of the greatest names in watchmaking and mechanical engineering in the Neuchâtel Jura. A native of La Chaux-de-Fonds (Switzerland), this talented craftsman, who started his career as mathematician and physicist, succeeded in charming and astonishing the crowned heads of Europe and Asia. He made a name for himself with his automata and clocks. His main customer was King Ferdinand VI of Spain, who in 1758 installed some of Jaquet Droz's creations in the Royal Palace in Madrid. Others were given by Lord MacCartney, British Ambassador to China, to Emperor Ch'ien Lung. These automata still fascinate visitors to international museums and continue to enthrall enthusiasts. In November 1999, for example, a yellow gold, enameled pocket watch set with rubies incorporating a singing bird, made in 1785 and attributed to Jaquet Droz, was sold at an auction in Geneva for a sum of over CHF 800,000 . . ."[95]

> *Jaquet Droz was going to be burned by the Inquisition in Spain, because they considered him as a witch, as someone who is not really human,... and this Jaquet Droz [brand] we sell with this message.*[96]
>
> – Nicolas G. Hayek

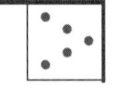

Nicolas is an outstanding spokesperson for the company because of his ability to develop fascinating stories for each of the Swatch Group brands. What corporate spokesperson has more credibility? Nicolas is an able communicator and he can synthesize the needs of every brand in the line in his communications. He is a rare breed: seldom can someone possess sound professional judgment and knowledge, be adept at interpersonal relations and communications, and be truly creative. Nicolas doesn't just support creativity in his operations, he is the creative catalyst.

> **Mentor Insight**
> Have a credible, popular spokesperson

Genesis of Ideas

Ideas come to me from [being] alone. I'm full of ideas. You see, I drive my car everyday 97 kilometers, from my home to my office, for twenty-five years. During this trip I'm alone listening to music, I have lots of paper scattered around my car, with magnets on them, and every time I get a new idea I write it down. Many of these ideas have been realized. Not every one of them certainly, and not 51 percent of them, but many of them have been realized. This becomes possible the minute you can see life as it really is vs. complicating matters.

And don't let society influence you too much, with all the stupid things that we put around us, and the slogans that the press pushes on us everyday. And the beliefs that we have that we are more civilized than anybody else. If you keep realizing where you are on this earth and realize what do I want to do and what do I want to achieve, and with what means, life is easy, it is very simple to find things.[97]

– Nicolas G. Hayek

Mentor Insights

Practice brainstorming

Create publicity stunts

Nicolas describes how the Swatchmobil was an idea on a slip of paper, how it grew into the present Smart car, and how many people wished to work on this new technology. Nicolas provides the spark of inspiration in his corporate brainstorming. His creativity, storytelling, networking skills and credibility led to the success of Swatch in creating top-notch publicity events. Great publicity stunts are not serendipitous: they require planning and hard work.

A Remarkable Publicity Stunt

The purpose of the promotion was to communicate high quality, low cost, having very much fun in life, and provocativeness. The purpose of the publicity stunt was to communicate this message in an inexpensive way. We made [an approximately] 140-meter-big watch running, really working, and I convinced the biggest bank skyscraper owner . . . in Frankfurt to hang it on the building, after we got all the permissions from the city fathers and engineers and everybody necessary. [I convinced them] to let us write:

Swatch
Swiss
60 DM

So, we had all the messages which included that it was a quality watch because it was a Swiss-made watch. The message that it was an inexpensive watch because previously you couldn't purchase a Swiss-made watch of such high quality for 60 DM. That it was a provocative watch because what could be more provocative than placing an inexpensive plastic watch on the richest and most expensive building in Germany. A message of fun in life because it was funny to do this in the middle of Frankfurt. In less than one month's time, even every baby in Germany knew what Swatch was.[98]

– Nicolas G. Hayek

Mentor Method 8.4

162-Meter Swatch Mounted on the Side of Frankfurt Skyscraper[99]

Courtesy of The Swatch Group Ltd.

The Art of Budget-Boosting Public Relations   **Module 8**

Selected Highlights of Additional Swatch Publicity Stunts Timeline

January 1984
Freestyle Skiing World Cup with Swatch.[100]

Summer 1985
Professional Swatch surfing team.[102]

September 1984
First break dance world championship at the Roxy in New York.[101]

September 1985
'Street Art Painting' with Swatch in Paris.[103]

1986
Giant Swatch at the Expo in Vancouver.[104]

June 1986
'International Street Art Painting' with Swatch in Basel.[105]

November 1986
Swatch auction at Sotheby's in Geneva. 'Time and Motion' exhibition with Swatch in London.[106]

1986–88
Swatch is main sponsor of the 'Freestyle Grand Prix.'[107]

July 1987
Swatch kite-flying festival in Holland.[108]

September 1987
Pop Swatch Clock Tower in Tokyo.[109]

March 1988
'Balloon Spectacular' in Australia.[110]

1989
Auction at Sotheby's Milan.[111]

June 1992
'Earth Summit' in Rio.[112]

September 1992
'Swatch the World' in Zermatt, Switzerland.[113]

1993
Swatch is named the Official Timekeeper of the Olympic Summer Games in Atlanta. Nicolas G. Hayek makes the announcement at the Olympic Museum in Lausanne, Switzerland.[114]

1994
The Swatch Centennial Race in Selinunte, Sicily, is the setting for the launch of the Swatch Historical Olympic Games Collection.[115]

1994
An exhibition put together in cooperation with the Atlanta Olympic Committee for the Olympic Games begins its promotional tour around the world.[116]

1995
Nicolas G. Hayek speaks at the United Nations headquarters in New York and presents the Swatch *UNlimited*, commissioned by the UN in commemoration of its 50th anniversary.[117]

July 1996
Nicolas G. Hayek carries the Olympic Flame toward the opening of the 1996 Olympic Games in Atlanta. Swatch acts as Official Timekeeper for the first time; 500,000 people visit the Swatch pavilion in Centennial Olympic Park.[118]

1996
A gigantic Swatch, backed by half a million voices, counts down to the New Year in New York City's Times Square.[119]

1997
For the New Year: jump for Swatch in Vienna, the Swatch Soul City where the world's largest snowboarding ramp soars in the Prater and a gigantic Swatch counts down the minutes to the New Year.[120]

October 1998
In part as a millennium publicity campaign, Swatch Internet Time based on the new Biel Meridian (BMT) launched in Biel by Nicolas G. Hayek, Nick Hayek Jr, and Nicholas Negroponte, co-founder and chairman of the MIT Media Lab. Internet Time divides the 24-hour day into 1,000 units called '.beats'.[121]

April 1999
At the European Space Agency's control center in Darmstadt, Germany the press follows the adventures of the Swatch satellite christened *beatnik* on its space mission and meets the Spanish astronaut Pedro Duque. Fourteen Swatch .Beat *Spacewalk* models are produced to mark the occasion.[122]

April 1999
Over 120,000 fans follow the launch of the Swatch .Beat line live on the net in a disco in Antwerp, Belgium.[123]

September 1999
The new Swatch *Beat Aluminium* line is presented to the press during a spectacular event set against the icy eeriness of the Rhône Glacier at the heart of the Swiss Alps. A nocturnal laser show and an ice grotto are only some of the features of this equally extraterrestrial and unforgettable launch.[124]

2000
Swatch was the Official Timekeeper for the Sydney 2000 Games. For the first time in the history of the Olympics, Swatch posted photo-finish results for a dozen disciplines on the Internet. The launch of an Olympic watch collection commemorated the Games, drawing on the landscape and culture of Australia.[125]

2001
When the gavel fell at the end of the night at Sotheby's in New York, the 25 unique lots of Swatch timepieces and art had raised $800,000 for 'God's Love We Deliver', an organization that delivers meals to homebound AIDS patients.[126]

2002
To commemorate the 20 James Bond movies, Swatch and Eon Pictures created one watch for each film, using themes and elements from the movies for the design.[127]

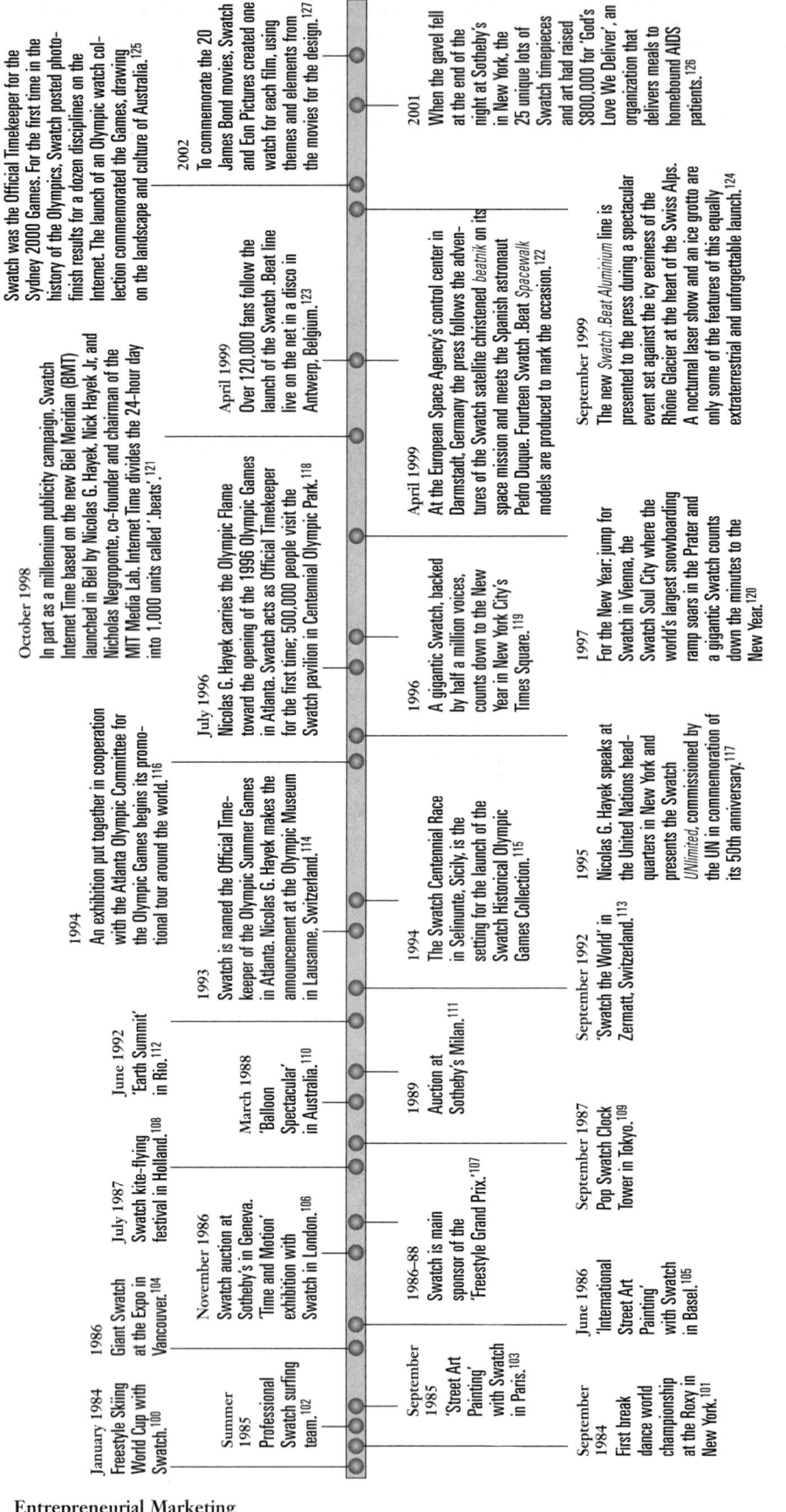

Secrets to Nicolas' Success

How has Nicolas maintained his success in such a competitive and challenging industry as watchmaking? How were he and his team able to sell 100 million Swatch products in the first 10 years and today over 300 million? Quite simply, Nicolas has never taken his eyes off the bottom line. Every public relations activity that Hayek conducts, from the remarkable publicity stunts to the stories behind the brand messages of his watch lines, is artfully crafted to drive a significant profit. Nicolas and the Swatch team have created a stunning product that is showcased on millions of adoring customers. Nicolas knows that those loyal wearers of the Swatch are perhaps the biggest public relations ploy he has in his tool kit.

He understands that the segment of the market (the lower end market) that the Swatch brand occupies is very important to his brand strategy.

> *The lower layer of the market is very important because each emotional product that you have—watches, cars, anything that is an emotional, mass-merchandised product—is seen on the wearer by as many as 5,000 people every year. That is to say, if you wear a watch, wherever you go, 5,000 people a year will see it, consciously or unconsciously. And from these 5,000 at least .1 percent will think it is a very nice watch and want to buy the same. So every customer who wears your watch creates publicity for you. This is why it is very important for you to be in mass production.*[128]
>
> – Nicolas G. Hayek

Mentor Insight

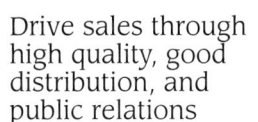

Drive sales through high quality, good distribution, and public relations

Mentor Insights

Continuously add beauty to every product

Develop emotionally appealing products

It boggles the mind to think of the effect human billboards, which are testimonies to conspicuous consumption, might have in generating future Swatch sales. Clearly Nicolas has mastered the art of driving sales by having a high quality product that is well distributed and highly publicized through contemporary public relations practices.

Nicolas understands the principle of the psychological product; that is, the structuring of psychic benefits beyond the functional attributes of the product. It would be hard to sell a new perfume based upon the fact that it smells pleasant, just as it would be difficult to sell a watch based upon the premise that it tells time. Hence, Nicolas' commitment to add beauty to everything thereby fostered emotional attachment to the product.

Nicolas expertly devised strategies to solidify an emotional attachment to the Swatch brand. Under his leadership, the customer became the central focus when he crafted the tactics that would forever change the face and image of time. The tactics Nicolas incorporated featured messages to communicate and capture the watch buying public's admiration. Wearing a Swatch signifies a unique sense of style and courageous spirit. Customers of Swatch watches are known for possessing a certain playfulness and unconventional thinking. A Swatch is not merely a watch to these loyal customers; a Swatch is an essential fashion accessory. High quality, low cost, provocation, and joy of life are the hallmarks of the Swatch brand messages that motivated millions of Swatch purchases from intrigued customers.

> **Mentor Insight**
>
> Use messages, not images

It is interesting that Nicolas prefers to lay out the consumer benefits of his watches in messages, not trusting images to properly position his lines. Traditional marketers typically project images of the end benefits or effects of the end benefits to consumers, and allow viewers themselves to interpret the images. Nicolas says: "I was giving a speech at Harvard a few years ago, explaining that we use messages because they are more dynamic than images. One of the people around the professor asked me, 'What's the difference between a message and an image?'"[129] Nicolas described a situation in which three people of different demographic backgrounds saw the same image, but perceived it differently because of their personal biases. He went on to describe an adjoining message that had a positive and consistent connotation to all three. Nicolas' point is that one should use words, not images, in communication materials because messages can't be misconstrued and are much more dynamic than images.

A review of marketing communications from the Swatch Group reveals the use of messages occasionally accompanied by images or high profile spokespersons. Clearly, the Swatch Group uses a synergy between message and image. The message component is used to prevent any miscommunication the marketplace might have based upon vague imagery. Further, messages allow storytelling, which has been a constant theme in the profiles included in this book. Using messages and not images is worth consideration in any budget-boosting public relations campaign.

What Is a Watch?

This question cuts to the heart of the Swatch Group's future. Many young people today do not wear a watch because they carry a cell phone that displays the time. Hence, cell phones are direct competition. Can a watch be defined as wearable technology? This definition would put the Swatch Group in competition with cell phones, PDAs, wireless Internet, security systems, geo-satellite positioning services, and any personal technology one might care to carry. Recently, a firm started selling children's watches that cannot be removed without a call to emergency response services, and with the capability to self-locate in much the same way LoJack does for automobiles.

Mentorography Conclusion

Having budget-boosting public relations does not just happen. It is the result and culmination of many factors—creativity, innovation, personal availability, beauty, and emotional appeals, combined with the personal attention of a CEO spokesperson of great zeal and charisma. Above all else, budget-boosting public relations is about never losing focus of the bottom line when crafting public relations activities. It's about driving sales through high quality, good distribution, and public relations. Budget-boosting public relations is becoming increasingly important to the enterprise as the effects of advertising wane.

There are many important lessons to be learned from Nicolas and the Swatch Group. We've distilled them for you with the budget-boosting public relations Mentor Insights:

Mentor Insights

- Continuously add beauty to every product
- Compete via innovation
- Develop emotionally appealing products
- Have a credible, popular spokesperson
- Be available
- Create a story to enhance your brand message
- Practice brainstorming
- Create publicity stunts
- Drive sales through high quality, good distribution, and public relations
- Use messages, not images

We encourage you to utilize budget-boosting public relations activities in your start-up practices and entrepreneurial ventures. Implementing these practices may just make you the savior of your start-up in the same way that Nicolas is the savior of the Swiss watchmaking industry.

Mentorography Questions

1. If you were to create a new product line of watches for The Swatch Group Ltd., what would be your brand positioning in the product pyramid? Describe the reasons why you have selected this product positioning.

2. Develop a story for the new product line of watches you have created. How will you publicize the brand story in the marketplace?

3. Develop a publicity stunt to publicize the new product line. How will you go about implementing this publicity stunt? What are your reasons for selecting this particular publicity stunt?

4. What strategies can you develop to ensure that the public relations tactics you are outlining for the new product line of watches will yield a profitable outcome? What strategies did Nicolas G. Hayek develop at The Swatch Group Ltd. to ensure that the public relations activities that were being implemented would result in profitable sales?

5. What additional strategies and tactics that were not mentioned in this module should be considered in the discipline of budget-boosting public relations?

Endnotes

[1] Reprinted and translated with permission of © DIRK LEHRACH VERLAG e.K., Düsseldorf, 1999, Berndt Schulz. SWATCH oder die Erfolgsgeschichte des Nicolas Hayek, Dirk Lehrach Verlag, Düsseldorf: Germany, Chapter 1. Anfänge, p. 25, (English) Translation into English by Christian F. Munz (unpublished).

[2] Budget-Boosting Public Relations Discipline named by Molly Lavik, February 22, 2002.

[3] Definition of Budget-Boosting Public Relations developed by Molly Lavik, February 22, 2002.

[4] Courtesy of Béatrice Howald, Head of Public Relations, Press Office, The Swatch Group Ltd., September 3, 2002.

[5] Reprinted and translated with permission of © DIRK LEHRACH VERLAG e.K., Düsseldorf, 1999, Berndt Schulz. SWATCH oder die Erfolgsgeschichte des Nicolas Hayek, Dirk Lehrach Verlag, Düsseldorf: Germany, (English) Translation into English by Christian F. Munz (unpublished).

[6] Ibid.

[7] Courtesy of Béatrice Howald, Head of Public Relations, Press Office, The Swatch Group Ltd., September 3, 2002.

[8] Ibid.

[9] Adrian J. Slywotzky and David J. Morrison, *The Profit Zone: How Strategic Business Design Will Lead You to Tomorrow's Profits*, (Times Business, a division of Random House, Inc., New York, 1997), p. 112.

[10] *Swatch Guide for Students: A collection of fascinating information and facts about the craziest plastic watch in the world.*, "Fact Sheet on Topic 6: Unconventional thinking—and acting," The Swatch Group Ltd.

[11] Courtesy of Béatrice Howald, Head of Public Relations, Press Office, The Swatch Group Ltd., September 3, 2002.

[12] Ibid.

[13] Reprinted and translated with permission of © DIRK LEHRACH VERLAG e.K., Düsseldorf, 1999, Berndt Schulz. SWATCH oder die Erfolgsgeschichte des Nicolas Hayek, Dirk Lehrach Verlag, Düsseldorf: Germany, (English) Translation into English by Christian F. Munz (unpublished).

[14] Adrian J. Slywotzky and David J. Morrison, *The Profit Zone: How Strategic Business Design Will Lead You to Tomorrow's Profits*, (Times Business, a division of Random House, Inc., New York, 1997), p. 112.

[15] Courtesy of Béatrice Howald, Head of Public Relations, Press Office, The Swatch Group Ltd., September 3, 2002.

[16] Reprinted and translated with permission of © DIRK LEHRACH VERLAG e.K., Düsseldorf, 1999, Berndt Schulz. SWATCH oder die Erfolgsgeschichte des Nicolas Hayek, Dirk Lehrach Verlag, Düsseldorf: Germany, (English) Translation into English by Christian F. Munz (unpublished).

[17] Courtesy of Béatrice Howald, Head of Public Relations, Press Office, The Swatch Group Ltd., September 3, 2002.

[18] Reprinted and translated with permission of © DIRK LEHRACH VERLAG e.K., Düsseldorf, 1999, Berndt Schulz. SWATCH oder die Erfolgsgeschichte des Nicolas Hayek, Dirk Lehrach Verlag, Düsseldorf: Germany, (English) Translation into English by Christian F. Munz (unpublished).

[19] Ibid.

[20] Ibid.

[21] Ibid.

[22] Courtesy of Béatrice Howald, Head of Public Relations, Press Office, The Swatch Group Ltd., September 3, 2002.

[23] Ibid.

[24] Reprinted and translated with permission of © DIRK LEHRACH VERLAG e.K., Düsseldorf, 1999, Berndt Schulz. SWATCH oder die Erfolgsgeschichte des Nicolas Hayek, Dirk Lehrach Verlag, Düsseldorf: Germany, (English) Translation into English by Christian F. Munz (unpublished).

[25] Ibid.

[26] Courtesy of Béatrice Howald, Head of Public Relations, Press Office, The Swatch Group Ltd., September 3, 2002.

[27] Ibid.

[28] Ibid.

[29] Ibid.

[30] Ibid.

[31] Reprinted and translated with permission of © DIRK LEHRACH VERLAG e.K., Düsseldorf, 1999, Berndt Schulz. SWATCH oder die Erfolgsgeschichte des Nicolas Hayek, Dirk Lehrach Verlag, Düsseldorf: Germany, (English) Translation into English by Christian F. Munz (unpublished).

[32] Ibid.

[33] Ibid.

[34] Ibid.

[35] Nicolas G. Hayek phone interview conducted by Molly Lavik and Bruce Buskirk, December 2001.

[36] Reprinted and translated with permission of © DIRK LEHRACH VERLAG e.K., Düsseldorf, 1999, Berndt Schulz. SWATCH oder die Erfolgsgeschichte des Nicolas Hayek, Dirk Lehrach Verlag, Düsseldorf: Germany, (English) Translation into English by Christian F. Munz (unpublished).

[37] Courtesy of Béatrice Howald, Head of Public Relations, Press Office, The Swatch Group Ltd., September 3, 2002.

[38] Reprinted and translated with permission of © DIRK LEHRACH VERLAG e.K., Düsseldorf, 1999, Berndt Schulz. SWATCH oder die Erfolgsgeschichte des Nicolas Hayek, Dirk Lehrach Verlag, Düsseldorf: Germany, (English) Translation into English by Christian F. Munz (unpublished).

[39] Courtesy of Béatrice Howald, Head of Public Relations, Press Office, The Swatch Group Ltd., September 3, 2002.

[40] Ibid.

[41] Reprinted and translated with permission of © DIRK LEHRACH VERLAG e.K., Düsseldorf, 1999, Berndt Schulz, SWATCH oder die Erfolgsgeschichte des Nicolas Hayek, Dirk Lehrach Verlag, Düsseldorf: Germany, (English) Translation into English by Christian F. Munz (unpublished).

[42] Ibid.

[43] Ibid.

[44] Adrian J. Slywotzky and David J. Morrison, *The Profit Zone: How Strategic Business Design Will Lead You to Tomorrow's Profits*, (Times Business, a division of Random House, Inc., New York, 1997), p. 120.

[45] Courtesy of Béatrice Howald, Head of Public Relations, Press Office, The Swatch Group Ltd., September 3, 2002.

[46] Nicolas G. Hayek phone interview conducted by Molly Lavik and Bruce Buskirk, December 2001.

[47] *Swatch Guide for Students: A collection of fascinating information and facts about the craziest plastic watch in the world.*, "Fact Sheet on Topic 6: Unconventional thinking—and acting," The Swatch Group Ltd.

[48] Ibid.

[49] Reprinted and translated with permission of © DIRK LEHRACH VERLAG e.K., Düsseldorf, 1999, Berndt Schulz. SWATCH oder die Erfolgsgeschichte des Nicolas Hayek, Dirk Lehrach Verlag, Düsseldorf: Germany, (English) Translation into English by Christian F. Munz (unpublished).

[50] Courtesy of Béatrice Howald, Head of Public Relations, Press Office, The Swatch Group Ltd., September 3, 2002.

[51] Courtesy of Béatrice Howald, Head of Public Relations, Press Office, The Swatch Group Ltd., February 7, 2003.

[52] Nicolas G. Hayek phone interview conducted by Molly Lavik and Bruce Buskirk, December 2001.

[53] Ibid.

[54] Reprinted and translated with permission of © DIRK LEHRACH VERLAG e.K., Düsseldorf, 1999, Berndt Schulz. SWATCH oder die Erfolgsgeschichte des Nicolas Hayek, Dirk Lehrach Verlag, Düsseldorf: Germany, (English) Translation into English by Christian F. Munz (unpublished).

[55] Courtesy of Béatrice Howald, Head of Public Relations, Press Office, The Swatch Group Ltd., September 3, 2002.

[56] Ibid.

[57] Ibid.

[58] Ibid.

[59] Ibid.

[60] Ibid.

[61] Ibid.

[62] Reprinted and translated with permission of © DIRK LEHRACH VERLAG e.K., Düsseldorf, 1999, Berndt Schulz. SWATCH oder die Erfolgsgeschichte des Nicolas Hayek, Dirk Lehrach Verlag, Düsseldorf: Germany, (English) Translation into English by Christian F. Munz (unpublished).

[63] Definition of Budget-Boosting Public Relations developed by Molly Lavik, February 22, 2002.

[64] Courtesy of Béatrice Howald, Head of Public Relations, Press Office, The Swatch Group Ltd., September 3, 2002.

[65] Ibid.

[66] Ibid.

[67] Reprinted with permission from The Swatch Group Ltd.

[68] Nicolas G. Hayek phone interview conducted by Molly Lavik and Bruce Buskirk, December 2001.

[69] *Swatch Guide for Students: A collection of fascinating information and facts about the craziest plastic watch in the world.*, "Fact Sheet on Topic 7: World-famous artists and designers work for Swatch," The Swatch Group Ltd.

[70] Ibid.

[71] Ibid.

[72] Ibid.

[73] Ibid.

[74] Ibid.

[75] Ibid.

[76] Ibid.

[77] Ibid.

[78] Swatch Chronology, provided by The Swatch Group Ltd.

[79] Ibid.

[80] Ibid.

[81] Ibid.

[82] Ibid.

[83] Ibid.

[84] Ibid.

[85] Ibid.

[86] Ibid.

[87] The Swatch Group Ltd. Annual Report 2000, New Products section, p. 17.

[88] Courtesy of Béatrice Howald, Head of Public Relations, Press Office, The Swatch Group Ltd., November 29, 2002.

[89] Swatch Chronology, provided by The Swatch Group Ltd.

[90] William Taylor, "Message and Muscle: An interview with Swatch Titan Nicolas Hayek," *Harvard Business Review*, March–April, 1993, pp. 102–103.

[91] Courtesy of Béatrice Howald, Head of Public Relations, Press Office, The Swatch Group Ltd., September 3, 2002.

[92] Reprinted with permission of The Swatch Group Ltd.

[93] Reprinted with permission of The Swatch Group Ltd. Image appeared previously in The Swatch Group Ltd. Annual Report 2000, p. 22.

[94] Nicolas G. Hayek phone interview conducted by Molly Lavik and Bruce Buskirk, December 2001.

[95] The Swatch Group Ltd. Annual Report 2000, p. 32.

[96] Nicolas G. Hayek phone interview conducted by Molly Lavik and Bruce Buskirk, December 2001.

[97] Ibid.

[98] Ibid.

[99] Courtesy of The Swatch Group Ltd.

[100] *Swatch Guide for Students: A collection of fascinating information and facts about the craziest plastic watch in the world.*, "Fact Sheet on Topic 8: Swatch goes out on the streets," The Swatch Group Ltd.

[101] Ibid.

[102] Ibid.

[103] Ibid.

[104] Ibid.

[105] Ibid.

[106] Ibid.

[107] Ibid.

[108] Ibid.

[109] Ibid.

[110] Ibid.

[111] Ibid.

[112] Ibid.

[113] Ibid.

[114] Swatch Chronology, provided by The Swatch Group Ltd.

[115] Ibid.

[116] Ibid.

[117] Ibid.

[118] Ibid.

[119] Ibid.

[120] Ibid.

[121] Ibid.

[122] Ibid.

[123] Ibid.

[124] Ibid.

[125] Ibid.

[126] Ibid.

[127] Ibid.

[128] Adrian J. Slywotzky and David J. Morrison, *The Profit Zone: How Strategic Business Design Will Lead You to Tomorrow's Profits*, (Times Business, a division of Random House, Inc., New York, 1997), p. 121.

[129] Nicolas G. Hayek phone interview conducted by Molly Lavik and Bruce Buskirk, December 2001.

CONCLUSION

Soaring to Greater Heights

So What Does It All Mean?

The goal of this book has been to facilitate an understanding of entrepreneurial marketing through the examination of top practitioners. We have chosen role models who have had success and experience to provide the most valuable virtual mentoring experience possible.

There are several common themes that emerged with the Mentor Insights we discussed while exploring the mindset of some of the greatest entrepreneurial marketers of our time. We refer to these key insights as "Overarching Mentor Insights." We summarize the Overarching Mentor Insights, share with you an update on each Mentor's recent activities and make a prediction on the future of entrepreneurial marketing in the conclusion that follows.

Overarching Mentor Insights

Overarching Mentor Insights are written as a one to two word synopsis of the Mentor Insight phrase they signify. The uniting factor between the Overarching Mentor Insight and the Mentor Insight are the words that are shared between the two. We refer back to the Entrepreneurial Marketing Wheel conceptual model that was introduced in the Preface on p. xxii to elaborate on the significance of the Overarching Mentor Insights. As a reminder, the Entrepreneurial Marketing Wheel analogy featured the rim (entrepreneurial marketing business concepts and sales as the connecting factor) the spokes (Mentor Insights) and the hub (customer centric). The axle represents the Overarching Mentor Insights in the completion of our analogy. This is because the addition of an axle enables the Entrepreneurial Marketing Wheel to rotate forward. The axle ultimately functions as the key element needed to propel the new venture forward with enough momentum to obtain a sustainable and profitable enterprise. The analogy of this concept is conceptualized in the Forward Motion of Entrepreneurial Marketing Model.

The Forward Motion of Entrepreneurial Marketing Model

Entrepreneurial Marketing Wheel — Overarching Mentor Insights — Entrepreneurial Marketing Wheel

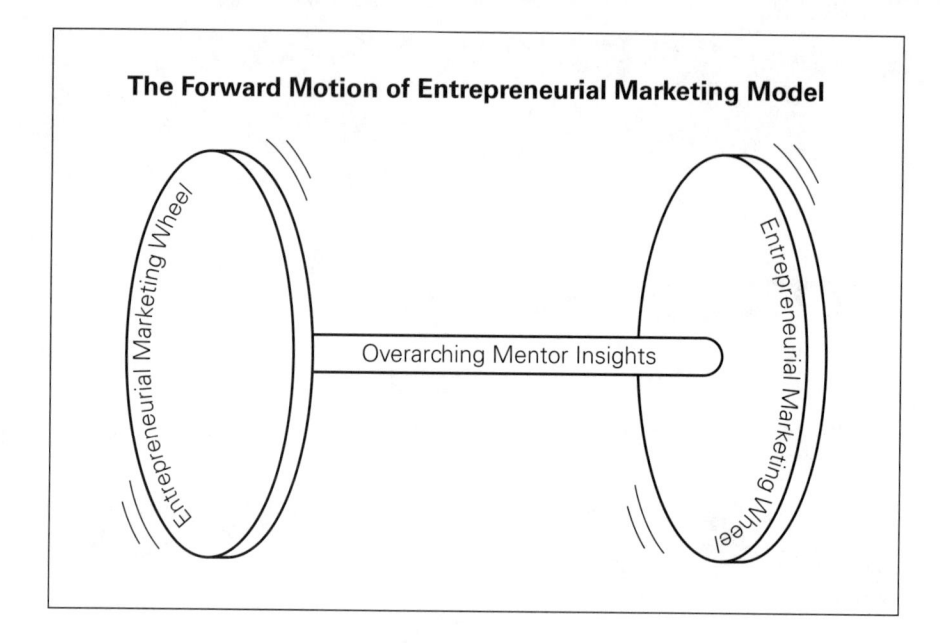

The Overarching Mentor Insights that emerged in this book are:

- Customer focus
- Management team
- Storytelling
- Innovation
- Ethics

A close examination of these Overarching Mentor Insights revealed that the Mentors repeatedly exhibited the characteristics described in the introduction to this book. As a reminder, these common characteristics included having:

- Vision
- Creativity
- Focus
- Passion
- Drive
- Perseverance
- Opportunistic Nature
- Problem-solving Ability
- Self-discipline
- Frugality
- Empathy

- Social Responsibility
- Spirituality
- Good Timing
- Luck

The definitions for the characteristics of the entrepreneurial marketer mindset can be found on p. xxviii–xxx of the Introduction.

Customer Focus

A theme that became apparent with the entrepreneurial marketers we profiled was a razor-sharp focus on the customer's wants and needs. Paul Orfalea of Kinko's perhaps summarized it best:

> *Kinko's has never been about machines; it has always been about people, their wants and needs and how best to serve them. In the beginning, the head of a store was a person who was comfortable with machines. Nowadays we prize co-workers with excellent people skills. We do more than prize them; we <u>train</u> them to have those skills.*
>
> *How serious are we about good customer relations? Serious enough to invest millions in training, testing, and more training. In the future no one is going to touch a customer until he or she has had two weeks in the classroom.*[1]
>
> – Paul Orfalea

A key characteristic that we found in entrepreneurial marketers is their dogged determination to prevail. Entrepreneurial marketers truly persevere where others fail. Especially when it comes to the difficult challenges associated with staying customer focused and incorporating customers' feedback into the entrepreneurial marketing mix. Paul Orfalea persevered with Kinko's because of his keen focus on the customer. He was known as a happy wanderer who could more often be found in a Kinko's store talking to customers than at his desk. Paul has dyslexia but his personal challenges never interfered with his ability to practice empathy for the customer. Today Paul is a major benefactor of childcare facilities that help parents provide daycare for their children while maintaining active careers. Paul is empathetic to the working person's plight and his commitment to the cause has inspired loyal customers, co-workers (internal customers), and colleagues.

Anita Roddick also exhibited a great deal of empathy at The Body Shop. Anita's empathy built a strong bond with her customers when she ran The Body Shop.

Specifically, Anita understood that there were not many if any other companies that could claim the loyal following that The Body Shop is known for cultivating. Customers of The Body Shop were treated from day one as highly regarded and respected family members. The socially responsible philosophy and initiatives of The Body Shop endeared many customers to The Body Shop brand.

Customer focus is also one of Guy Kawasaki's career trademarks. He doesn't just preach these words of wisdom. They are a major guiding principle in how Guy operates his business as well as insights you can derive from the books he has written.

What do these entrepreneurs who employ a strict adherence to customer focus have in common? Success!

Management Team

Another theme that surfaced which is also an Overarching Mentor Insight is the importance of the management team to the entrepreneurial marketer's ultimate success. Dirk Gates was able to leverage the innovativeness of the product he was creating to attract to Xircom veterans in the industry with a high level of expertise in the areas he needed. Dirk wisely noted the importance that passion and drive play launching a new product. He knew firsthand the agony an engineer felt when his designs were built but never sold in the marketplace. Dirk was empathetic to engineers' needs and leveraged this understanding to attract top talent to his management team. How does an entrepreneur who doesn't yet have the resources to bring in the talent he needs to be profitable survive? Someone like Ken Park, who is also currently faced with a tough economy, stays in business with that dogged determination and perseverance we keep mentioning. Guy Kawasaki put together an "all-star" line-up for his management team at Garage using himself as the magnet to attract the talent. Leonard Armato had a similar strategy. He attracted top names in the industry to help run his ventures through the allure of having an opportunity to work with elite athletes' and celebrities' marketing plans. At E*TRADE, the bottom performing 10 percent of associates were helped to find jobs that better suited them inside or outside of E*TRADE. By implementing this program among others, Christos Cotsakos had been able to successfully avoid mass lay offs at E*TRADE during the more challenging times.

What do all these experts in creating a strong management team have in common? They possess an opportunistic nature that allows them to triumph where others fail. They have visionary ideas that attract and retain great management teams. They possess foresight in their approach of cultivating extraordinary management teams.

Storytelling

An unanticipated theme and Overarching Mentor Insight that emerged with the profiled entrepreneurial marketers is that they utilize the art of storytelling as a major component in their marketing strategies. Storytelling consistently bolsters entrepreneurial marketing strategies. Leonard Armato utilizes storytelling by publicizing the fascinating nature and personalities of the elite athletes he represents. Dirk Gates told the story of the success of Xircom with an office wall display of his award-winning advertising campaigns. Ken Park is an engaging storyteller who weaves interesting angles and ideas around his HyperCD technology to engage the customer. Christos Cotsakos employed the art of storytelling in his award-winning and much talked about Super Bowl advertisements. He did this by telling the story of E*TRADE via a chimpanzee. Nicolas G. Hayek developed strong and highly creative brand messages behind each of his watch brands including his watchmaking industry-saving product, Swatch. Anita Roddick is an eminently gifted storyteller. Her brilliantly written accounts of the social injustices faced by humankind are arguably at the forefront of what motivated the fiercely loyal customers of The Body Shop. Anita was one of the first entrepreneurs to use her marketing as a platform for socially responsible messages. Anita led the movement for elevating social responsibility in global corporations.

What do all these storytellers have in common? Fascinated customers. These entrepreneurial marketers are able to author strategies that showcase storytelling tactics that keep their customers riveted.

Innovation

The Mentors profiled in this text each embraced innovation as the methodology for market entry and success, and as the manner in which they continued to compete. Leonard Armato, a person who prays and meditates at the beginning and end of each day, used a strong adherence to self-discipline in his marketing tactics to come up with ideas that incorporate innovation. His self-discipline also sets a positive example for the elite athletes he represents. Leonard Armato crafted a brand marketing strategy for Shaq that employed innovative tactics utilizing the Internet.

Specifically, Leonard had the vision to spearhead a strategy for Shaq to house his Web site in an Internet sports portal back in the mid-1990s, before the practice was commonplace.

Paul Orfalea had the visionary insight to know when it was good timing to take a major infusion of capital to keep Kinko's ahead of the competition. This was illustrated when Paul for the first time gave up a part of Kinko's to take in venture capital dollars so that he could enhance the innovative products at Kinko's with digital copier machines. Paul was arguably frugal with his profits from Kinko's because as an entrepreneurial marketer he had a keen focus on saving money. When the time came to get venture capital financing, his commitment to frugality made it possible for him to easily raise the financing to add the technology necessary to keep Kinko's on the cutting edge.

Creating innovative products was the guiding principle upon which Dirk Gates founded Xircom. To combat 3Com's X-Jack, Xircom developed an innovative new product that provided a method of transmitting data between a phone and laptop computer known as the RealPort™.

Innovation is synonymous with the E*TRADE brand name. Thanks to Christos Cotsakos' prior leadership, innovation developed throughout E*TRADE from its technologically advanced product line to its encouraging staff to take frequent calculated risks. Those who aren't innovators don't last or belong at E*TRADE.

Nicolas G. Hayek became the savior of the Swiss watchmaking industry by recognizing the market opportunity a team of experts created when they employed innovation to get the Swiss watch manufacturing process reduced from 151 components to 51. It required an ample amount of problem solving ability to change the watch manufacturing processes, but the end result was worth the effort.

What do these innovators have in common? They are all exceptional problem-solvers. These entrepreneurial marketers are able to implement complex strategies to innovate their businesses and marketing practices against their competition.

Ethics

Some of the previously most respected corporations are being questioned with regard to their ethical practices. Ethics has emerged as an important area that entrepreneurial marketers can employ to set themselves above the fray. Marketing is an area in traditional business where ethics has been somewhat forgotten. The entrepreneurial marketers we profiled have put an emphasis on ethical behavior in creating their marketing strategies.

As Xircom grew, Dirk Gates saw it as his role to maintain the corporate culture that had originally attracted his team. Leonard Armato operated his businesses with open honesty. Ken Park also shared with his team the ups and downs of an Internet start-up. He stood fast behind a distribution platform that helped the masses that still mostly rely on dial-up Internet access. Guy Kawasaki underscored the importance of spirituality in his message by establishing a karmic code to live by. Anita Roddick elevated the role of ethics in global corporations. Several chapters in her book *Business as Unusual: The Triumph of Anita Roddick* are dedicated to this important subject and to the role that ethics should play in marketing. Anita exposed the tyranny behind the beauty industry that had said that cosmetics could reverse the aging process and that everyone should strive to look like a high-fashion model. Anita created marketing campaigns that were honest and let people know the truth about cosmetics. She openly acknowledged to her customers that cosmetics couldn't reverse aging:

> *We have to tell ourselves: "If you really didn't ever want to get wrinkles, then, you should have stopped smiling years ago!"*[2]
>
> – Anita Roddick

Anita focused her marketing strategies on devising socially responsible tactics instead of using these tactics to sell her products. She is also someone who is adept at utilizing her creativity to come up with innovative solutions to overcoming social injustices. She used delivery vehicles to display large images of missing children. She used her corporate success to inform the world about the importance of becoming a vigilant consumer against the inhumane practices of sweatshops. She went to third-world countries and created direct distribution systems with impoverished women so that they could transform their existence.

Anita Roddick is an ethically driven individual who has become a role model to many.

What do all these ethical entrepreneurial marketers have in common? They share a strong adherence to values-based leadership. They don't just "talk the talk." These ethical entrepreneurial marketers have the courage to tell the truth and do what is right.

Luck

There is one final ingredient you will need to make your new venture a roaring success. Luck! It goes without saying that to be a successful entrepreneurial marketer you need not only good timing, but also a little luck. Luck isn't necessarily something that just happens. We believe the entrepreneurial marketers we profiled made their luck by working hard and developing remarkable entrepreneurial marketing strategies.

Updates on Featured Entrepreneurial Marketers

Christos M. Cotsakos, Ph.D.

In E*TRADE Financial's 2002 year end press release (January 22, 2003), the Company reported a 275 percent growth in earnings per share year over year while revenues grew from $345 million to $349 million. Christos was quoted as saying "E*TRADE Group is pleased to have produced the most profitable year in the history of the company earning $0.45 per share from ongoing operations, while growing revenue in 2002. We are proud to report our tenth consecutive quarter of ongoing profitability in the worst quarter for the financial services industry since the crash of the equity markets in 1987." Christos credits E*TRADE Financial's success to the Company's guiding principles, culture, and values-based leadership.[3]

On January 24, 2003 Christos M. Cotsakos resigned as Chairman, CEO and director of E*TRADE Financial stating, "I am extremely proud of what we have accomplished over the past seven years and it is with great confidence that I hand the success and momentum to Mitch Caplan to further build on the core strengths of E*TRADE. I'd like to thank the Board and our associates for making these past seven years an extraordinary experience. My success is not going to be determined by where E*TRADE's stock is today. It's going to be determined by where it is five years from now."[4]

Christos' future plans include writing business books, teaching underprivileged children, and mentoring young entrepreneurs.[5]

Guy Kawasaki

Guy Kawasaki continues as the CEO of Garage Technology Ventures, Inc., a venture capital investment bank. He is also very active in public speaking and has taken up ice hockey at age 48.[6]

Leonard Armato

During the summer of 2002, Leonard and the AVP completed two very successful NBC telecasts. The television ratings have exceeded NBC's expectations as well as the expectations of the sponsors. The AVP on NBC has far outperformed in the television ratings of sports properties such as Women's National Basketball Association, Indy Racing League, Championship Auto Racing Teams, Arena Football, and Amateur Golf.

Prior to the start of the 2003 Tour, AVP had signed a multi year agreement with about all the companies that "tried out" the AVP Tour last year. This is very big for the AVP to have this long-term stability and the time for these companies to "activate" their sponsorship of AVP; included are Nissan, Bud Light, Gatorade, Wilson and Pepsi.[7]

Anita Roddick OBE

Anita's viral marketing pattern that was successfully created in The Body Shop will be used in the same practice with Anita's new company, which she is currently forming, called Anita Roddick Publications Ltd. Anita will be collaborating with intellectuals, Non-Governmental Organizations, charities and others worldwide to create publications on such issues as activism, spirituality, and empowerment, to name but a few. The first two books, *A Revolution In Kindness* and *Brave Hearts Rebel Spirits*, are due out in the late spring 2003.[8]

Paul Orfalea

Since Paul officially retired from Kinko's, Inc. in April 2000, he claims to be "repurposed." His family's non-profit organization, the Orfalea Family Foundation, focuses on issues such as early care and education, intergenerational programs, learning differences, and work-life corporate benefits. Paul also devotes time to one of his true passions, stock market investments. He continues to be in high demand around the country for public speeches addressing business organizations and colleges with his inspirational history. Paul also loves having time to spend with his family in Santa Barbara.[9]

Ken Park

Since the interview, BBM. HyperCD has entered into negotiations with Sharp Holding to become the focal point of their disc marketing strategies. Ken has also launched a new initiative called InnerSports where the focus is to build serialized collectible trading cards and to focus on leveraging consumer product packaging as the next big media channel opportunity—bringing affinity programming to targeted and passionate audiences. The company's first effort was the Soccer Skilz training series with Spalding Sports Worldwide, Inc. and the Major Indoor Soccer League, soon to be extended into various other sports as well.[10]

Dirk Gates

Dirk has entered a new phase of his career. He has joined the boards of several small high-tech start-up companies. His is enjoying getting back into the entrepreneurial spirit of a start-up with small but growing revenue and advising them on the best growth strategies. He is finding that contributing some of his time and experience can really make a big difference in the direction of a start-up company.[11]

Nicolas G. Hayek

Since the interview, Nicolas was named Advertiser of the Year at the 49th International Advertising Festival in Cannes (June 2002). Moreover, the government of the Republic of Austria is honoring him for his merits for Austria by awarding him the Grosses Ehrenzeichen mit Stern (translation: Great Distinction with Star), the highest distinction of the Republic of Austria for a foreigner. In December 2002 Nicolas was awarded the International Leading Entrepreneur Award at the 5th Monte Carlo Business Angels Forum.[12]

Despite all the honors, Nicolas unwaveringly pursues his goal: to maintain the number one position for the Swatch Group in the worldwide watch industry. During the rather difficult 2002, the Swatch Group not only maintained this position but gained market share.[13]

With effect from January 1, 2003, Mr. Nicolas G. Hayek, the Chairman of the Board of Directors, acting on behalf of the whole Board of Directors and Group Management Board, is handing over responsibility for operational management of the Swatch Group to Mr G. Nick Hayek Jr. As President of the Group Management Board, Mr G. Nick Hayek Jr. will be taking over full operational responsibility within the Group.[14]

As Chairman of the Board of Directors, Mr N. G. Hayek will continue to take decisive action to promote and supervise the development of the Group, in line with the normal tasks and responsibilities of the Board of Directors. In addition to these tasks, Mr Nicolas G. Hayek will continue to hold the following positions in future: Operational Chairman of Breguet SA, Chairman of the Board of Directors of Blancpain SA, Chairman of the Board and Chief Executive Officer of Omega SA, President of SMH Immobilien (Engineering Division), Co-President of the "Luxury Movements" working group, and strategic and operational consultant to the technology and manufacturing companies.[15]

He is happy to observe that the future looks bright—for him and for the Swatch Group.[16]

We encourage you to visit **http://buskirklavik.swlearning.com** for future updates on the entrepreneurial marketers profiled in this book.

Future Predictions for Entrepreneurial Marketing

We predict a day in the not-so-distant future when entrepreneurial marketers will be among the hottest commodities in the marketplace. Entrepreneurial marketers, with their progressive strategies and repertoire of skills, will be highly sought after. Entrepreneurial marketers will emerge as the new leaders of global enterprises, leading these business entities down the path of socially responsible practices that will help our troubled world heal.

Up, Up and Away!

Thank you for joining us on this journey through the Entrepreneurial Marketing Domain. We hope you have gained insights that help your business endeavors soar to greater heights. We also hope you enjoyed the adventure!

Endnotes

[1] Paul Orfalea with Leonard Tourney, "Making Better Best: Achieving Balance in Business and Life," (Unpublished manuscript), p. 71.

[2] Anita Roddick, *Business as Unusual: The Triumph of Anita Roddick*, (Thorsons, An Imprint of HarperCollins Publishers, Hammersmith, London, 2000), p. 99.

[3] Courtesy of Brigitte VanBaelen, Chief Community Development Officer and Corporate Secretary, E*TRADE Financial, January 31, 2003.

[4] Ibid.

[5] Ibid.

[6] Courtesy of Guy Kawasaki, Founder & CEO, Garage Technology Ventures, Inc., March 3, 2003.

[7] Courtesy of Leonard Armato, Commissioner, AVP, November 19, 2002.

[8] Courtesy of Karen Bishop, Anita Roddick Publications, Ltd., November 1, 2002.

[9] Courtesy of Lois Mitchell, Executive Director, Orfalea Family Foundation, November 4, 2002.

[10] Courtesy of Ken Park, Founder & CEO, BBM. HyperCD, October 7, 2002.

[11] Courtesy of Dirk Gates, Founder, Xircom–An Intel Company, February 12, 2003.

[12] Courtesy of Béatrice Howald, Head of Public Relations, Press Office, The Swatch Group Ltd., November 14, 2002.

[13] Courtesy of Béatrice Howald, Head of Public Relations, Press Office, The Swatch Group Ltd., February 7, 2003.

[14] Courtesy of Béatrice Howald, Head of Public Relations, Press Office, The Swatch Group Ltd., November 14, 2002.

[15] Courtesy of Béatrice Howald, Head of Public Relations, Press Office, The Swatch Group Ltd., February 7, 2003.

[16] Courtesy of Béatrice Howald, Head of Public Relations, Press Office, The Swatch Group Ltd., November 14, 2002.

APPENDIX 1:
LET'S TALK BUSINESS NETWORK, INC.

We have discussed ideas for entrepreneurial marketers to obtain resources in this book. We will continue to update you on places entrepreneurial marketers can turn for guidance and mentoring on the *Entrepreneurial Marketing: Real Stories and Survival Strategies* web site: **http://buskirklavik.swlearning.com**.

We encourage you to visit this site often for updates on valuable resources.

Let's Talk Business Network (LTBN) is an example of the type of resources that are available for entrepreneurial marketers. Below is a description of LTBN and its benefits provided by Chairman and CEO Mitchell Schlimer.[1]

"The objective of the Let's Talk Business Network, Inc. (LTBN) is to provide entrepreneurs with an unparalleled support system and unique educational tools to truly help them become more successful and achieve their business and personal goals. LTBN is building the premier entrepreneurial support network and support communities with peer to peer collaboration at the heart of its services. LTBN also provides one on one consulting to members, educational environments to learn from other entrepreneurs, proprietary content from Let's Talk Business radio and other unique resources created to help insure the success of its clients. As a Network, LTBN members leverage their experiences and contacts in order to generate additional sales, especially through the best type of lead possible, which is a referral.

LTBN provides its services to CEO's, Entrepreneurs and Corporations who sell their products through independent business partners and owners. LTBN's corporate clients include Avaya Communication, IBM, Grant Thornton, and many others.

Benefits of membership in LTBN

1. You are not isolated or lonely when building your business.

2. Surrounded by other entrepreneurs who you can not only learn from, but also grow with.

3. Get access to incredible resources, dynamic educational environments and the entrepreneurial founders of LTBN.

4. You experience the value and power of having an entire support network dedicated to helping you become more successful.

5. Build relationships and friendships that can not only last for a lifetime, but also can lead to additional business.

Contact information:
Mitchell Schlimer
Chairman/CEO
Let's Talk Business Network, Inc.
54 West 39th, 12th floor
New York, NY 10018
http://www.LTBN.com"[2]

Endnotes

[1] Courtesy of Mitchell Schlimer, Chairman/CEO, Let's Talk Business Network, Inc., November 14, 2002.

[2] Ibid.

INDEX

A
access to sales revenues, 160
acquisitions, 10
adaptation of socially responsible cultures, 93
adoption of franchising, 101
advantages of branding, 69, 79
advertising. *See* marketing
alliances, creating partnerships, 68, 77
ambassadorships, branding, 83–85
analysis of innovation, 134–36
angels (early investors), 35, 52
Apple Computers, 30
Armato, Leonard, 65–86
availability, 78, 215
AVP Pro Beach Volleyball Tour, 65–86
awards for leadership skills, 13

B
balancing work and personal life, 118, 132–34
banking, historic perspective of, 19–20
BBM. HyperCD, 143–68
Beauty Myth, The, 103
beliefs
    giving permission to believe, 31
    staying true to, 94
    willingness to risk everything for, 5–6, 7, 17
board of directors, selection of, 187
Body Shop, The, 89–111
brainstorming, 207, 217
branding, 10, 11–12, 20, 65–86
    advantages, 69, 79
    ambassadorships, 83–85
    evaluation of, 85–86
    identity guidelines, 85
    marketing new products, 184
    origins of the term, 75–76
    positive mental attitudes, 83
    resilience, 82–83
    storytelling, 205, 216, 219

building brand equity, 81
business models
    direct customer distribution, 154–55
    diversification of, 37–38

C
campaigns, marketing, 41, 80–81. *See also* marketing
capital. *See also* financing; venture capital
    keeping pace with technology, 127
    raising, 27–59
career paths, importance of, 6–9, 15
celebrities as spokespeople, 203, 213–15
change, embracing, 12–13
claims, seeking funding, 48
communications
    integrated marketing, 72, 80–81
    leadership skills, 94, 102
competition via innovation, 199, 204, 209
connected constituencies, 161
continuous obsolescence, practicing, 2–6, 9–10, 22
corporate overview presentations, 55–56
costs, lowering while maintaining quality, 211–15
Cotsakos, Christos M., 1–24
Crawford, Cindy, 213–15
creativity, encouraging, 119
credibility, instilling with customers, 18
crisis, rules of engagement for, 13
criteria for venture capital, 59
cultures
    Customer Relationship Management (CRM), 115–39
    socially responsible corporate, 93
Customer Relationship Management (CRM), 115–39

customers, obtaining, 95–96
customer service
    exceeding needs, 192–93
    feedback, 93, 100–101, 160–61
    focus on, 14, 31
    instilling credibility, 18
    marketing new products, 187
    retaining customers, 119, 135
    striving for satisfaction, 120, 136
    usage profiles, 160–61
    value propositions, 44–45
cycles, brand resilience, 82–83

D

decision-makers, pitching to, 77
demand, customer, 95, 106–108
diffusion of innovations, 110–11
Digital Media Campus, 71–72
dignity, treating people with, 9–10
direct customer distribution, 145, 148–50, 154–55
Distribution-Dominance Solar System model, 156–58
distribution-dominating tactics, 143–68
distribution of marketing campaigns, 80–81
diversification
    of business models, 37–38
    of portfolios, 9–10

E

early investors, 30, 52
economic downturns
    adapting to, 37–38
    persevering through, 35, 36–37
electronic application kits, 157–58
elevator pitches, 45–49
emotional intelligence, 84
emotionally appealing products, development of, 204, 213, 219
engineering new products, 186–87
ensuring long-term profitability, 9–10
equity, branding, 81. *See also* branding
ethics, 84, 103–5
E*TRADE, 1–24
evaluation of branding, 85–86
event marketing, 38–39
events, launching new products, 191–92
executive summaries, 49–54
expansion, planning, 22
experimentation, encouraging, 119

F

failure, willingness to, 2–6, 13, 16. *See also* risks
feedback, customer service, 93, 100–101, 160–61
financial industry, historic perspective of, 19–20
financing, 27–32
    adapting to changing economies, 37–38
    angels (early investors), 35, 52
    corporate overview presentations, 55–56
    elevator pitches, 45–49
    event marketing, 38–39
    marketing campaigns, 41
    persevering through economic downturns, 35, 36–37
    preparing to seek venture capital, 39–41
    seeking, 45–49
    venture capitalists, 32–34
franchising, 101, 129–30

G

Garage Technology Ventures, Inc., 27–59
Gates, Dirk, 169–93
globalization, 98
grassroots activities, 73–75, 78
growth
    controlling, 130–34
    planning, 22

H

Hayek, Nicolas G., 197–220
H.E.R.O. pyramid, 104–5
high risk. *See also* risks
    importance of, 3
history of new product marketing, 181
honesty, 9–10
hooks, seeking funding, 46–48
humor, using in marketing, 11

I

identity guidelines, branding, 85
imagination, utilizing, 4–5, 10, 18
incorporation of proprietary technologies, 33
infectious agents (viral marketing), 89–90, 110–11

242   Entrepreneurial Marketing

innovation
    analyzing, 134–36
    competition via, 199, 204, 209
    diffusion of, 110–11
    encouraging, 119
    utilizing, 4–5, 10, 18, 98
integrated marketing
    communications, 72, 80–81
integration after acquisitions, 10–11
integrity, 84, 117
Intel, 169–93
interest, generating when seeking
    funding, 49
Internet
    embracing capabilities, 146
    impact on distribution, 159–61
investments, brand equity, 69
investors
    angels (early investors), 35
    elevator pitches, 45–49
    selecting, 34, 51

K
karma, rules of, 40–41
Kawasaki, Guy, 27–59
Keep It Simple Stupid (KISS)
    method, 173
Kinko's Inc., 115–39

L
launching new product events, 191–92
leadership skills, 14–15
    awards, 13
    communications, 94, 102
    selecting teams, 5
    viral marketing, 101–2
life-long learning, 119, 139
logos, 76. *See also* branding
long-term profitability, ensuring,
    9–10, 21

M
Macintosh, 30
management
    board of directors, 187
    Customer Relationship
        Management (CRM), 115–39
    empowering, 132
    proactive, 122, 137–38
    teams, 34, 50–51
Management Plus Enterprises, 65–86
mapping, process, 188–90

marketing
    electronic application kits, 158
    event, 38–39
    featuring storytelling, 15–17
    fostering fearlessness of failure,
        16–17
    integrated communications, 72,
        80–81
    new products, 169–93
    preparing presentations, 56–57
    raising capital, 27–59
    using humor in, 11
    viral, 89–111. *See also* viral
        marketing
    virtual (Internet), 153, 163–64
markets
    creating customer traffic, 129
    definitions, 42–45
    recognizing opportunities, 72–75
    research, 136–37, 174, 185–86
    target, 148–50
matrices, strategies, 14
mentors, importance of, 3–4
messages
    in pubic relation campaigns, 205
    viral marketing, 100
Microsoft, 30
mission statements, 14, 99–100
multichannel strategies, 10
multi–touch point strategies, 10
myths
    The Beauty Myth, 103
    dispelling, 94, 95–96

N
new products, marketing, 169–93
new ventures, raising capital, 27–59

O
obsolescence, practicing continuous,
    2–6, 9–10, 22
obtaining venture capital, 57–60
O'Neal, Shaquille, 68–71
online trading, 10. *See also* E*TRADE
operational excellence, inspiring,
    188–90
Orfalea, Paul, 115–39

P
packaging, 77
Park, Ken, 143–68
partnerships, 68, 77, 122, 162–63

Index   243

passion, 31
    encouraging, 101
    evangelizing ventures, 41–57
performance-based corporate cultures, 12
permission to believe
    giving, 31
    seeking funding, 48
perseverance, 67, 76
Personalized Digital Financial Media, 10
personal service, offering, 18
planning
    expansion, 22
    starting point of strategic, 21
    strategies, 23–24
portfolios, diversifying, 9–10
positive mental attitudes, 83
pre-approaches, seeking funding, 48
presentations
    corporate overview, 55–56
    preparing, 56–57
proactive management, 122, 137–38
problems, solving other people's, 94, 106
process mapping, 188–90
products (new), marketing, 169–93
profiles, customers, 160–61
profitability
    ensuring long-term, 9–10, 21
    integrated marketing communications, 80–81
    placing principles above, 91, 96
proprietary technologies, incorporating, 33
publicity stunts, creating, 205, 217
public relations, 197–220

Q

qualifications to seek venture capital, 39–41
quality
    driving sales via, 206, 219
    lowering costs while maintaining, 211–15
    making a priority, 124, 138

R

raising capital, 27–59. *See also* financing
recognizing market opportunities, 72–75, 171, 181–83
regulations, banking, 19–20
relationships
    Customer Relationship Management (CRM), 115–39
    customers. *See* customer service
    Distribution-Dominance Solar System Model, 158
    maintaining, 145
    rules of karma, 40–41
research, markets, 136–37, 174, 185–86
resilience, branding, 74, 82–83
resources
    allocating, 78
    directing brands and technologies, 10, 20
respect, treating people with, 9–10
risks
    importance of, 3, 17
    rewards for, 16–17
    willingness to stand by beliefs, 5–6, 7, 17
Roddick, Anita, 89–111
rules
    of engagement for crisis, 13
    of karma, 40–41

S

sales revenues, access to, 160
satisfaction, customer. *See* customer service
single segment concentration, 21
skills
    leadership, 14–15
        awards, 13
        communications, 94, 102
        selecting teams, 5
        viral marketing, 101–2
    staying focused, 33
small businesses
    direct customer distribution, 154–55
    models, 174–75
specialization, 22
spokespersons, selection of, 203, 213–16
star power, 69, 80
starting point of strategic planning, 21
storytelling
    branding, 205, 216, 219
    featuring, 2–6, 15–17
    utilizing creative, 92, 93–94

strategies
    branding, 65–85
    Customer Relationship Management (CRM), 115–39
    distribution-dominating tactics, 143–68
    ensuring long-term profitability, 9–10
    formulating, 1–24
    implementing, 22
    marketing new products, 169–93
    matrices, 14
    multichannel, 10
    multi–touch point, 10
    planning, 23–24
    public relations, 197–220
    raising finances, 27–60
    viral marketing, 89–111
summaries executive, 49–54
Swatch Group Ltd., The, 197–220

T

target markets, 148–50
teams
    implementing strategies, 22
    leadership skills. *See* leadership skills
    management, 34, 50–51
    selecting best people for, 5, 22–23
technologies
    directing resources toward, 10, 20
    keeping pace with, 127
    proprietary, 33
Traditional Channels Planet, 161–62

U

usage profiles, customers, 160–61

V

value propositions, 44–45
venture capital, 27–59, 32–34
    criteria, 59
    obtaining, 57–60, 175
    preparing to seek, 39–41
viral marketing, 89–111
    adaptation of socially responsible cultures, 93
    The Beauty Myth, 103
    ethics, 103–5
    evolving product offerings, 93
    leadership skills, 101–2
    messages, 100
    obtaining customers, 95–96
    utilizing creative storytelling, 93–94
virtual marketing (Internet), 153, 163–64
vision
    establishing clear-cut, 172–74, 183
    maintaining, 6–7, 21

W

word-of-mouth. *See also* viral marketing
    capitalizing on, 150
    creating, 98, 109–11
    occurrences during distribution, 161
World Wide Web (WWW), 146. *See also* Internet

X

Xircom, 169–93